T0318930

CliffsTestPrep®

TAKS™

CliffsTestPrep®

TAKS™

by

Jerry Bobrow, PhD

Contributing Authors/Consultants

Paul Soifer, PhD

Dale Johnson, MA

Michele Spence, BA

Gary Thorpe, MS

Wiley Publishing, Inc.

About the Author

Dr. Jerry Bobrow, PhD, is a national authority in the field of test preparation. As executive director of Bobrow Test Preparation Services, he has been administering the test preparation programs at over 25 California institutions for the past 29 years. Dr. Bobrow has authored over 30 national best-selling test preparation books, and his books and programs have assisted over two million test-takers. Each year, Dr. Bobrow personally lectures to thousands of students on preparing for graduate, college, and teacher credentialing exams.

Author's Acknowledgments

My loving thanks to my wife, Susan, and my children, Jennifer, 26, Adam, 23, and Jonathon, 19, for their patience and support in this long project. My sincere thanks to Michele Spence, former chief editor of CliffsNotes, for her invaluable assistance. I would also like to thank Marcia Johnson for final editing and careful attention to the production process.

Finally, sincere appreciation is also given to the following authors and companies for allowing me the use of excerpts and visual materials from their outstanding works:

Map of Elections of 1868 from America! America! by L. Joanne Buggey, Gerald A. Danzer, Charles L. Mitsakos, and C. Frederick Risinger, Copyright 1977 by Scott Foresman and Company, Used by permission of Pearson Education, Inc.

"Charles Lindbergh and his wife, half-length portrait, standing," Copyright 1927, Prints and Photographs Division, Library of Congress

Manzanar Photographs by Ansel Adams 1943, Prints and Photographs Division, Library of Congress

"Why I'm Like This" by Cynthia Kaplan, copyright © 2002 by Cynthia Kaplan, Reprinted by permission of Harper Collins Publishers Inc., William Morrow

"Slipping Beauty," by Jerome Weidman, Published in Story Jubilee, Permission by Whitney Burnett

"All My Relations," from Dwellings: A Spiritual History of the Living World by Linda Hogan, Copyright © 1995 by Linda Hogan. Used by permission of W. W. Norton & Company, Inc.

"Mr. President," Reprinted with the permission of Scribner, an imprint of Simon & Schuster Adult Publishing Group, from He Was a Midwestern Boy On His Own by Bob Greene. Copyright © 1991 by John Deadline Enterprises, Inc.

Picture of John Lind's Sod House, Fred Hultstrand History in Pictures Collection, NDIRS – NDSU, Fargo

"Calling Home," from Going After Cacciato by Tim O'Brien, copyright © 1975, 1976, 1977, 1978 by Tim O'Brien. Used by permission of Dell Publishing, a division of Random House, Inc.

Picture of Grave Stones, Permission by GRAF-FITI CREATIONS

Love With No Bounds from IMARA Woman, reprinted by permission of publisher & CEO, Sandy C. Brawley

Picture of farmhouse in dust bowl, Prints and Photographs Division, Library of Congress

Publisher's Acknowledgments

Editorial

Project Editor: Marcia L. Johnson

Senior Acquisition Editor: Greg Tubach

Copy Editor: Helen Chin

Production

Proofreader: Debbye Butler

Wiley Publishing, Inc. Composition Services

CliffsTestPrep® TAKS™

Published by:
Wiley Publishing, Inc.
111 River Street
Hoboken, NJ 07030-5774
www.wiley.com

Copyright © 2004 by Jerry Bobrow, PhD
All Rights Reserved

Published by Wiley, Hoboken, NJ
Published simultaneously in Canada

Library of Congress Cataloging-in-Publication Data
Bobrow, Jerry.
  TAKS™ / by Jerry Bobrow ; contributing authors, Paul Soifer ... [et al.].
    p. cm. — (CliffsTestPrep)
  Includes index.
  ISBN 0-7645-5940-0 (pbk.)
  1. Texas Assessment of Knowledge and Skills—Study guides. 2. Achievement tests—Texas—Study guides. 3. Competency based educational tests—Texas. I. Title. II. Series.
  LB3060.33.T47B63 2004
  373.126'2—dc22
                                        2004009879

ISBN: 0-76455-940-0

10 9 8 7 6 5 4 3 2 1
1B/RW/QX/QU/IN

Note: If you purchased this book without a cover, you should be aware that this book is stolen property. It was reported as "unsold and destroyed" to the publisher, and neither the author nor the publisher has received any payment for this "stripped book."

NO PART OF THIS PUBLICATION MAY BE REPRODUCED, STORED IN A RETRIEVAL SYSTEM, OR TRANSMITTED IN ANY FORM OR BY ANY MEANS, ELECTRONIC, MECHANICAL, PHOTOCOPYING, RECORDING, SCANNING, OR OTHERWISE, EXCEPT AS PERMITTED UNDER SECTIONS 107 OR 108 OF THE 1976 UNITED STATES COPYRIGHT ACT, WITHOUT EITHER THE PRIOR WRITTEN PERMISSION OF THE PUBLISHER, OR AUTHORIZATION THROUGH PAYMENT OF THE APPROPRIATE PER-COPY FEE TO THE COPYRIGHT CLEARANCE CENTER, 222 ROSEWOOD DRIVE, DANVERS, MA 01923, 978-750-8400, FAX 978-646-8600. REQUESTS TO THE PUBLISHER FOR PERMISSION SHOULD BE ADDRESSED TO THE LEGAL DEPARTMENT, WILEY PUBLISHING, INC., 10475 CROSSPOINT BLVD., INDIANAPOLIS, IN 46256, 317-572-3447, OR FAX 317-572-4355.

THE PUBLISHER AND THE AUTHOR MAKE NO REPRESENTATIONS OR WARRANTIES WITH RESPECT TO THE ACCURACY OR COMPLETENESS OF THE CONTENTS OF THIS WORK AND SPECIFICALLY DISCLAIM ALL WARRANTIES, INCLUDING WITHOUT LIMITATION WARRANTIES OF FITNESS FOR A PARTICULAR PURPOSE. NO WARRANTY MAY BE CREATED OR EXTENDED BY SALES OR PROMOTIONAL MATERIALS. THE ADVICE AND STRATEGIES CONTAINED HEREIN MAY NOT BE SUITABLE FOR EVERY SITUATION. THIS WORK IS SOLD WITH THE UNDERSTANDING THAT THE PUBLISHER IS NOT ENGAGED IN RENDERING LEGAL, ACCOUNTING, OR OTHER PROFESSIONAL SERVICES. IF PROFESSIONAL ASSISTANCE IS REQUIRED, THE SERVICES OF A COMPETENT PROFESSIONAL PERSON SHOULD BE SOUGHT. NEITHER THE PUBLISHER NOR THE AUTHOR SHALL BE LIABLE FOR DAMAGES ARISING HEREFROM. THE FACT THAT AN ORGANIZATION OR WEBSITE IS REFERRED TO IN THIS WORK AS A CITATION AND/OR A POTENTIAL SOURCE OF FURTHER INFORMATION DOES NOT MEAN THAT THE AUTHOR OR THE PUBLISHER ENDORSES THE INFORMATION THE ORGANIZATION OR WEBSITE MAY PROVIDE OR RECOMMENDATIONS IT MAY MAKE. FURTHER, READERS SHOULD BE AWARE THAT INTERNET WEBSITES LISTED IN THIS WORK MAY HAVE CHANGED OR DISAPPEARED BETWEEN WHEN THIS WORK WAS WRITTEN AND WHEN IT IS READ.

Trademarks: Wiley, the Wiley Publishing logo, CliffsNotes, the CliffsNotes logo, Cliffs, CliffsAP, CliffsComplete, CliffsQuickReview, CliffsStudySolver, CliffsTestPrep, CliffsNote-a-Day, cliffsnotes.com, and all related trademarks, logos, and trade dress are trademarks or registered trademarks of John Wiley & Sons, Inc. and/or its affiliates. All other trademarks are the property of their respective owners. Wiley Publishing, Inc. is not associated with any product or vendor mentioned in this book.

For general information on our other products and services or to obtain technical support, please contact our Customer Care Department within the U.S. at 800-762-2974, outside the U.S. at 317-572-3993, or fax 317-572-4002.

Wiley also published its books in a variety of electronic formats. Some content that appears in print may not be available in electronic books.

WILEY

Table of Contents

Preface

We know that passing the TAKS examinations are important to you!

And we can help.

As a matter of fact, we have spent the last thirty years helping over a million test takers successfully prepare for important exams. The techniques and strategies that students and adults have found most effective in our preparation programs at 26 universities, county offices of education, and school districts make this book your key to success on the TAKS.

Our easy-to-use TAKS Preparation Guide gives you that *extra edge* by:

- Introducing important test-taking strategies and techniques
- Reviewing the subject area objectives
- Analyzing sample problems
- Providing two simulated practice exams with explanations
- Including analysis charts to help you spot your weaknesses

We give you lots of strategies and techniques with plenty of practice problems.

There is no substitute for working hard in your regular classes, doing all of your homework and assignments, and preparing properly for your classroom exams and finals. But if you want that *extra edge* to do your best on the TAKS, follow our Study Plan and step-by-step approach to success on the TAKS.

Study Guide Checklist

Check off each step after you complete it.

- ❏ 1. Read the TAKS information materials available online at www.taks.tea.org.
- ❏ 2. Look over the Format of the TAKS Examinations (p. 1).
- ❏ 3. Learn How You Can Do Your Best (p. 2–3).
- ❏ 4. Read Questions Commonly Asked About the TAKS (p. 2).
- ❏ 5. Carefully Read Part 1: Working Toward Success and do all the exercises.

    English Language Arts (pp. 7–44)

    Mathematics (pp. 45–76)

    Social Studies (pp. 77–90)

    Science (pp. 91–110)

- ❏ 6. Following the objectives, review any basic skills that you need to review.
- ❏ 7. Take Practice Examination 1 (pp. 113–203). After you take each of the tests in Practice Examination 1, check your answers on that test and analyze your results using the Answer Key (pp. 204–207), the Analysis Chart (pp. 208), the Answers and Explanations (pp. 209–236).

    English Language Arts (pp. 209–213)

      Check answers and analyze results

    Mathematics, (pp. 213–227)

      Check answers and analyze results

    Social Studies (pp. 227–232)

      Check answers and analyze results

    Science (pp. 232–236)

      Check answers and analyze results

❑ 8. Take Practice Examination 2 (pp. 239). After you take each of the tests in Practice Examination 2, check your answers on that test and analyze your results using the Answer Key (pp. 331–334), the Analysis Chart (pp. 335), the Answers and Explanations (pp. 336–366).

> English Language Arts (pp. 239–257)
>
>> Check answers and analyze results
>
> Mathematics, (pp. 258–289)
>
>> Check answers and analyze results
>
> Social Studies (pp. 290–310)
>
>> Check answers and analyze results
>
> Science (pp. 311–330)
>
>> Check answers and analyze results

❑ 9. Review your weak areas and then selectively review the strategies and samples in Part 1: Working Toward Success (pp. 7–110.

Introduction

Format

Each different exam is scheduled on a different day. There are no time limits for any of the tests, but the following table offers some recommendations.

Format of the TAKS Exams		
Exam	**Types of Questions**	**Recommended Time**
English Language Arts Test	48 Multiple-Choice Questions 3 Short-Answer Questions 1 Essay	About 2 hours (see district and campus coordinator manual online)
Mathematics Test	60 Questions (almost all Multiple Choice)	About 2 hours
Social Studies Test	55 Multiple-Choice Questions	About 2 hours
Science Test	55 Questions (almost all Multiple Choice)	About 2 hours

Because this is a new test, times and number of questions may be adjusted slightly in later tests.

Questions Commonly Asked about the TAKS Exams

Q: How much time do I have to complete each test?

A: There is no time limit for each exam. You may take as much time as you need. The estimated or recommended time is about 2 hours for each exam.

Q: How often are the exit level tests given?

A: The exit level tests are tentatively scheduled to be given 4 times each year (see calendar online).

Q: What is a passing score?

A: Raw scores (actual number right) will be converted to scaled scores and a passing (met standard level) will be set. Check with your school district or the Texas Education Agency for established passing scores.

Q: What grade level are the tests?

A: The exit tests are standardized to assess the knowledge and ability that students have gained through 11th grade.

Q: Should I guess on the tests?

A: Yes! Since there is no penalty for guessing, guess if you have to. If possible, try to eliminate some of the choices to increase your chances of choosing the right answer.

Q: **How should I prepare?**

A: Keep up with your class work and homework in you regular classes. There is no substitute for a sound education. As you get closer to your exit level tests, using an organized test preparation approach is very important. Carefully follow the Study Plan in this book to give you that organized approach. It will show you how to apply techniques and strategies and help focus your review. Carefully reviewing the Information Booklet for each exit level available from the Texas Education Agency will also give you an edge in doing your best.

Q: **How can I get more information?**

A: The Texas Education Agency has prepared some outstanding information booklets. These booklets are available online at http://www.tea.state.tx.us/teks/

How You Can Do Your Best

A Positive Approach

To do your best, use this positive approach:

- First, look for the questions that you can answer and should get right.
- Next, skip the ones that give you a lot of trouble. (But take a guess.)
- Remember, don't get stuck on any one of the questions.
- Finally, go back and try to work the ones that gave you a lot of trouble.

Here's a closer look at this system:

1. Answer the easy questions as soon as you see them.
2. When you come to a question that gives you trouble, don't get stuck.
3. Before you go to the next question, see if you can eliminate some of the incorrect choices to that question. Then take a guess from the choices left!
4. If you can't eliminate some choices, take a guess anyway. Never leave a question unanswered.
5. Put a check mark in your question booklet next to the number of a problem for which you did not know the answer and simply guessed.
6. After you answer all of the questions, go back and work on the ones that you checked (the ones that you guessed on the first time through).

Don't ever leave a question without taking a guess. There is no penalty for guessing.

The Elimination Strategy

Sometimes the best way to get the right answer is by eliminating the wrong answers. As you read your answer choices, keep the following in mind:

- Eliminate poor answer choices right away.
- On most sections, if you feel you know the right answer, quickly look at the other answers to make sure your selection is best.
- Try to narrow your choices down to two so that you can take a better guess.

Remember, getting rid of the wrong choices can leave you with the right choice. Look for the right answer choice and eliminate wrong answer choices.

Here's a closer look at the elimination strategy. Take advantage of being allowed to mark in your testing booklet. As you eliminate an answer choice from consideration, make sure to mark it out in your question booklet as follows:

A̶

?B

C̶

?D

Notice that some choices are marked with question marks, signifying that they may be possible answers. This technique will help you avoid reconsidering those marked-out choices you have already eliminated and will help you narrow down your possible answers. These marks in your testing booklet do not need to be erased.

Avoiding the "Misread"

One of the most common errors is the "misread," that is, when you simply misread the question.

A question could ask,

> *If* $3x + x = 20$, *what is the value of* $x + 2$?

Notice that this question doesn't ask for the value of x, but rather the value of $x + 2$.

A question could ask,

> *Which of these classifications is most general?*

Notice that you are looking for the most general.

A question could be phrased as follows:

> *All of the following statements are true except—*

>> or

> *Which of the following organs is not part of the digestive system?*

Notice that the words "except" and "not" change the above questions significantly.

To avoid "misreading" a question (and therefore answering it incorrectly), simply circle or underline what you must answer in the question. For example, do you have to find x or $x + 2$? Are you looking for what is true or the exception to what is true? To help you avoid misreads, circle or underline the questions in your test booklet in this way:

> *If* $3x + x = 20$, *what is the value of* <u>x + 2</u>?

> *Which of these classifications is* <u>most general</u>?

> *All of the following statements are true* <u>except</u> —

> *Which of the following organs is* <u>not part of the digestive system</u>?

And, once again, these circles or underlines in your question booklet do not have to be erased.

PART I

WORKING TOWARD SUCCESS

This section presents a variety of sample problems within the objective categories and introduces important test-taking strategies and techniques and how to apply them.

Read this section very carefully. Underline or circle key techniques. Make notes in the margins to help you understand the strategies and question types. Mark the objective categories where you need additional review.

Introduction to the English Language Arts Test

The English Language Arts Grade 11 Exit Level Examination consists of forty-eight (48) multiple-choice questions, three (3) short-answer questions, and one essay. The multiple-choice answer choices are alternately labeled **A, B, C, D,** or **F, G, H, J.** The test is divided into two sections, Reading and Written Composition, and Revising and Editing. The content of these sections is based on six (6) objectives that will be discussed in this chapter.

Reading and Written Composition

The Reading and Written Composition section of the TAKS English Language Arts Test includes two (2) passages and one (1) visual representation. These are followed by four (4) groups of multiple-choice questions and one (1) group of short-answer (open-ended) questions. The first group of questions refers to the first passage only; the second group refers to the second passage only; the third group refers to both passages (not the visual representation); the fourth group refers to the visual representation only; and the open-ended questions refer to both passages (not the visual representation). The open-ended questions are followed by a topic on which you are to base an essay. The essay topic is related to the theme of the passages and visual representation.

You will have approximately twenty-eight (28) multiple-choice questions, approximately three (3) open-ended questions, and the essay.

Reading

This section of the exam tests your abilities under Objectives 1, 2, and 3. An objective is simply a statement about the skill you are to demonstrate. All three objectives concern your ability to understand "culturally diverse texts," which are passages written from a variety of points of view and cultural backgrounds. You will be expected to show your

1. "Basic understanding of the passages."
2. "Understanding of the effects of literary elements and techniques" used in the passages.
3. "Ability to analyze and critically evaluate both the passages and the visual representation."

The multiple-choice questions based on the two passages test objectives **1, 2,** and **3.** The multiple-choice questions based on the visual representation test objective **3** only. The open-ended questions test objectives **2** and **3.**

This section of the exam tests reading skills you've developed during your school years in understanding and analyzing texts and graphic representations. Following are the areas tested and types of understanding and analysis you will be asked to demonstrate.

Objective 1: A Basic Understanding of the Passage

To understand the passage you should focus on the

- **Vocabulary:** the meaning of the words used in the passage

  Even if you don't immediately know the meaning, you're expected to determine it from context (the surrounding words and sentences), from your understanding of prefixes, suffixes, and roots, from your knowledge of a word that may be similar, or from the connotation of the word (things suggested by it, apart from its dictionary meaning).
- **Main Idea:** the central idea, the gist

  You may be asked to identify the overall, main idea of a passage as a whole or of a portion (paragraph) of the passage.
- **Supporting Details:** items directly related to the main idea and supporting it

  Supporting details add additional information concerning the main idea. This information may be in the form of examples, facts, or further description.

- **Summary:** a recap of the main points

  You may be asked to identify a correct summary of the passage or a portion of the passage. A summary would include both the main idea and the most important supporting details.

Objective 2: An Understanding of the Effects of Literary Elements

Objective 2 has two major parts: literary elements and literary techniques. To understand the effects of literary elements you should focus on the

- **Characters:** the person or people depicted in the passage or visual representation

  Characters may be presented through direct comments by the author, the characters' actions (including speech), or the characters' thoughts.

- **Setting:** the physical environment of the characters, the occupation and manner of daily living of the characters, and the time period of the passage

  Watch for words that refer to time, place, conditions, and surrounding elements.

- **Plot:** the action of a passage, the order of events

  Plot usually involves conflict resulting in a crisis, or turning point.

- **Theme:** the central idea, the general concept

  Themes are often expressed as a sentence. For example, "The saying 'measure twice and cut once' applies to more than woodworking."

Objective 2: An Understanding of the Effects of Literary Techniques

To understand the effects of literary techniques you should note the

- **Literary Language:** imaginative language

  Literary language includes, among others, similes (comparisons using *as*—"the boy moved as quickly as a jackrabbit"), metaphors (direct comparisons that don't use *as*—"the boy was a jackrabbit leaping through the field"), and personification (giving human characteristics to an animal or thing).

- **Literary Terms:** words used to describe elements and techniques of literature

  You are expected to understand the meanings of literary terms. While you won't be specifically asked to define the terms, they are used in questions, and in order to answer the questions, you need to know exactly what's being asked. Literary terms include *flashback, mood, symbolism, imagery, analogy, climax, satire, irony, foreshadowing,* and many others.

- **Point of View:** the vantage point from which a story is told

  The point of view (also a literary term) in a passage may be *first person* ("I"—in which a character in the story is the narrator), or *third person* ("he," "she," "it"—in which the author tells the story). In the *third person* point of view, the author may be *omniscient* (knowing everything about characters, their thoughts and actions, and events and free to comment on them) or *limited* (seemingly knowing only certain specific things about characters or events).

- **History:** the time, culture, and state of the world in which the story is set

  The time period, the social, geographic, and cultural environment, and historical events at the time can have a great deal to do with the actions and attitudes of the characters involved.

Objective 3: The Ability to Analyze and Critically Evaluate the Passages and the Visual Representation

You may be asked to understand the passages and visual representation beyond the concrete details presented there. You may be asked—based not only on what the text specifically says, but also the logical extension of an idea present, the emotional content of the language, and other elements—to make inferences or predictions or draw conclusions about the information presented. When looking beyond the concrete details you should be aware of

- **Inferences:** conclusions reached based on hints, or suggestions, in a passage

  Inferences are not directly stated.

- **Predictions:** suggesting what might logically happen next based on what has been specifically shown in a passage

  Valid predictions always follow logically from information in the passage.

- **Conclusions:** determining what is likely to be correct based on evidence in the passage

  Conclusions must be reasonable base on the information you've been given.

- **Tone:** the author's implied attitude toward a subject

  Words describing tone are *playful, serious, ironic, angry, nostalgic, remorseful,* and many others.

- **Purpose:** the author's intended effect on the reader

  Words describing purpose are *to persuade, to entertain, to amuse, to inflame, to share personal feeling, to inform,* and many others.

- **Word Choice:** the vocabulary chosen by the author

  The words chosen by the author are usually not accidental. Word choice can help you make inferences and predictions, draw conclusions, and identify the author's tone and purpose.

- **Media Techniques and Purposes:** methods used to inform, mislead or have an impact on the viewer, reader or listener

  Understanding all of the above is particularly helpful in analyzing and making critical judgments about media presentations (those in newspapers, magazines, advertisements, radio and television programs, and so forth). Such judgments may include deciding on the believability of what's being said, the intent to inform or mislead the reader or listener, the intent to have a particular emotional impact on the reader, and the writer's or speaker's purpose in making the presentation. Questions on the visual representation may directly involve understanding media techniques and purposes.

Directions

There are four basic types of directions for the Reading section of the exam.

- **General Directions:** "Read the two selections and the viewing and representing piece. Then answer the questions that follow."

- **Directions for the First, Second, and Third Group of Multiple-Choice Questions:** "Use (name of the passage or passages) (pp. __) to answer questions __."

- **Directions for the Fourth Group of Multiple-Choice Questions:** "Use the visual representation on page __ to answer questions __."

- **Directions for the Open-Ended Questions:** "Answer the following questions in the space provided on the answer document."

Analysis

Now let's take a closer look.

Things you should know about the multiple-choice Reading section

You should know the following:

- The two passages and the visual representation upon which the multiple-choice questions are based are called a *triplet* because they are related in that they all deal with the same *theme*. As mentioned, a theme is the central idea, or general concept, and it is sometimes expressed as a sentence. Even if a question doesn't directly ask you to state the theme, generally understanding it is helpful in answering other questions. Here are some examples of possible themes:
  - Feeling compelled to do something can lead to mixed results.
  - Fear can be overcome in a variety of ways.

- A small event can change one's life in a big way.
- One of the passages is fiction, a "literary selection," either a short story or part of a longer work. The other passage is nonfiction, called an "expository" or "informational" piece, such as an essay or article.
- There may be a short paragraph before a passage to explain some elements of the historical context of the passage to you.
- The number of words in the passages and the visual representation total approximately 3,000 to 3,500.
- Each paragraph of a passage is numbered, but the sentences in the paragraph are not numbered. Questions often include a reference to the paragraph number so you can find it quickly.
- The visual representation is primarily graphic, rather than text. It may be a photograph, a poster, an advertisement, an Internet Web page, a chart, or any other visual presentation that is on the same theme as the passages. There may be some text with the visual representation, but it won't be the main focus. Even so, the text can be important and there may be questions concerning it.
- Multiple-choice questions based on the passages, either singly or together, test objectives 1, 2, and 3, concerning basic understanding of the passage as a whole, understanding of literary elements and techniques, and critical analysis and evaluation.
- Multiple-choice questions based on the visual representation test only objective 3, concerning critical analysis and evaluation. In these questions you may be asked, among other things, to identify the persuasive method used by the media.
- The number of questions on each passage and the visual representation may vary, but in general, you'll find about twelve or thirteen questions on each of the passages, about two or three on the passages considered together, and about two or three on the visual representation.
- You *may* use a dictionary while answering these questions.

Strategies for answering the multiple-choice Reading questions

Use the following strategies:

- After you read the passages and look at the visual representation, quickly identify the theme for yourself.
- Take advantage of the fact that you can write in your test booklet. Circle or underline the key words in the questions to be sure you understand what is being asked.
- Be an active reader. Take advantage of the fact that the test leaves room for you to write next to the passages. Make quick notes about important points and your understanding of them as you read.
- For questions concerning vocabulary, there are "clues" in the text that allow you to choose the right definition. For these questions, circle or underline the word in the passage and then consider the surrounding material to arrive at your answer.
- The sample questions that follow and the practice tests will give you a good idea of the types of questions you'll find on the exam. And the explanations will give you further strategies for dealing with each type.
- Be sure to check as you work that your answers are in the correct space on the answer sheet. The fact that the answer choice letters alternate between A, B, C, D and F, G, H, J helps you to keep track of where you are.
- Don't forget to use the positive approach. Look for questions you can get right. Don't get stuck. Come back to the difficult questions. But never leave a question without at least taking a guess.

Things you should know about the open-ended Reading questions

As you prepare for the open-ended reading questions you should note the following:

- A short-answer (open-ended) question refers to one passage or the other or to both passages. It won't refer to the visual representation.
- If the question refers to one passage alone, you'll have five lines for your answer. If the question refers to both passages, you'll have eight lines for your answer.
- Each open-ended question is scored on a scale from 0 to 3. The meaning of these scores is as follows: 0, answer is insufficient; 1, answer is partly sufficient; 2, answer is sufficient; 3, answer is exemplary (excellent).

■ The open-ended questions never test objective 1; that is, they don't ask about the main idea. They don't test your "basic understanding" of the passage. They do test objectives 2 and 3, concerning your understanding of literary elements and techniques, as well as critical analysis and evaluation.

Strategies for answering the open-ended Reading questions

Use the following strategies:

■ Since you don't have much room to write the answers to these questions (only a few sentences), it's important to *plan ahead*. Write quick notes for yourself on the points you want to make in your answer. Your notes can be as simple as a list of key words.

■ No one will grade you on your penmanship, but your answer must be readable in order to be scored. Planning ahead helps here, too, because you won't have to go back and cross out or try to fit in another point.

■ Support your answer with evidence from the passage. You can use a direct quotation, or a paraphrase, or a short summary. You can also refer to a paragraph number, but if you refer to an entire paragraph, rather than a specific part of it, make sure that the whole paragraph is support for your answer, not just a sentence or two.

■ Be sure you answer only the question asked. Don't add information that has nothing to do with the question.

■ Your answers to these questions are scored on *content*. That is, they are scored on appropriateness and clarity of your answer, on how well and completely it answers the question asked. The only time errors in spelling, grammar, or usage affect your score is when there are so many that they cause problems in the sense and clearness of the answer.

Suggested Approach with Sample Passages, Visual Representation, and Questions

Review the sample passages and visual representation and answer the questions. Pay special attention to the suggested approaches as you read the answer explanations.

Directions: Read the two selections and the viewing and representing piece. Then answer the questions that follow.

Sample Passage 1

Slipping Beauty

By Jerome Weidman

1   He was a little man with an untidy beard and a prominent paunch that seemed startlingly out of place because of his emaciated appearance. Winter and summer he wore a battered cap, a leather vest, and a look of indifferent resignation, well seasoned with disgust, that gave no hint of the almost violent loquacity he could attain without even a moment of preparation. In a world of trucks and automobiles he drove a flat, open wagon behind a huge, drooping horse. And although his seltzer bottles came in neatly cased boxes of ten, he preferred to carry them by their spouts, five in each hand, like clusters of grapes, and take his chances on opening doors with shoulder shoves and kicks. His service was erratic, but adequate, and when, by his strange method of rotation, your name came up again to the top of his list, you could no more prevent him from making his delivery than you could convince him that his prices were exorbitant. He has come on Sundays and holidays, during parties and illness, and once, when a severe snowstorm had tied the city's traffic into a knot, he rang the bell after midnight and carried in his ten bottles of seltzer without a word of apology or explanation.

2   "Look here, Mr. Yavner," I said irritably, "you can't make deliveries as late as this. You can't come ringing bells at this—"

3   "I can't?" he asked and his eyes widened in a look of surprise that should have warned me.

My notes about what I am reading

11

My notes about what I am reading

4   I knew from experience that it wouldn't do any good. But when you're aroused after midnight from a sleep that you have attained with difficulty and need very much to admit a middle-aged man with his hands full of seltzer bottles that, considering the temperature and the season, you don't need at all, you are apt to forget the things that experience has taught you.

5   "I mean," I said stubbornly, "you'll just have to learn, Mr. Yavner, that when—"

6   "Learn?" he said, and the surprise was now in his voice. "I gotta learn?"

7   I could tell by the glint in his eye that, from the standpoint of my much-needed sleep, I could have chosen a far more opportune time to bring order into Mr. Yavner's chaotic delivery system. I made a hasty, desperate attempt to head him off.

8   "Not that I *mean* anything, Mr. Yavner," I began, conciliatingly. But I was too late.

9   "In America," Mr. Yavner was saying, shaking his head like a tolerant master with a slow pupil, "in America there's no such thing as learn. In America *nobody* learns. In America they only *teach.*"

10   He set down his clusters of empty seltzer bottles and faced me squarely.

11   "A minute you could listen," he said bluntly. "In the old country, my father, he should rest in peace, he told me I shouldn't play with the knife, I'll cut myself; so if I didn't listen to him, and I played with the knife, so what happened, so I cut myself! He told me, maybe, I shouldn't go in street without the coat, I'll catch a cold; so I went in the street without a coat, so like he said, I caught a cold! But in America?"

12   He shrugged for emphasis and the habitual look of disgust on his face deepened a shade or two.

13   "Go try teach children something in America, go," he said. "Listen what I got. I got two daughters, the Above One should take care of them, they're beauties. Sucha two girls like I got, it could be—I don't care—even a governor, he would *still* be happy to have sucha two daughters, the way mine look. The oldest, my Yettie, is already ten years she's bringing money in the house, steady, every week. She went to business school, she studied hard, she got a good job, she makes steady wages, she puts in the bank, she brings home; is good, no? Comes at night, she comes home, she eats, she helps maybe the mother a little, she reads a book, she listens a little the radio, she goes to sleep like a regular person. Is bad, maybe? In Europe, a girl like that, a girl like my Yettie, she knows to cook, to sew, to bake, to clean, she knows what a dollar is; a girl like that in Europe she could find a dozen—a dozen? A hundred!—she could find a hundred fellahs they should kiss their fingers to the *sky* seven days a week if she would only *look* on them a little the right way! But in America? Go be smart in America!

14   "Then my other daughter, my Jennie, the baby. To look at?—a doll! But lazy?—the Above One should save us from sucha lazy ones. Came in the middle high school, all of a sudden she got tired! By her, it's no more school. By me, she says no school, so all right, is no school. But instead she should get a job like her older sister, like Yettie, instead that, so a whole day she lays in bed with the magazines and the tsigarettes, and the whole night she's running around with the boys, those little *rutzers,* they'n got even a *job,* not one of them in the whole bunch! A whole night long you don't see her, and comes by day, the whole day it's magazines and the tsigarettes. A whole day long it's smook, smook, smook, smook, smook, smook, smook, smook! No job, no work, no nothing! Only like a king's daughter she lays in bed the whole day, and you gotta bring her eat, yet, too, and the whole night she's running around the Above One alone knows where!

15   "But I'm a father; by me is the same thing my Yettie, she works and brings money in house, or my Jennie, she lays in bed there a whole day. So I talk to her. I tell her she should make something from herself; she should get a job and go sleep early like a regular person and get up early and put money in bank and stop so much with the tsigarettes and the boys! Like her sister Yettie, I tell her she should be. She should learn

to cook and sew and keep a house clean and put a little money in bank, so'll come a nice fellah some day, with a good steady job, he'll see what a nice girl she is, she knows what's in a house to do, so he'll marry her, like some day'll happen with her sister Yettie, I tell her, and she'll make for him a good wife. So you think she listens to me? Like I should talk to the wall!

My notes about what I am reading

16   "In Europe, a father talks to a child, so it happens she should know the father was right. But in America?"

17   He leaned toward me and tapped my shoulder with his finger as he spoke.

18   "In America is different," he said. "One day, she's laying there in the bed with the magazines and the tsigarettes and the smook; all of a sudden the blankets they catch on fire, in a minute more it's the whole bed, then the curtains, and in a one, two, three is there the fire engines and the policemen and the firemen and there's excitement!— Above One in heaven, don't ask! And from the firemen there comes running in one, a nice young fellah, and he picks her up and carries her down from house, and before you can turn yourself around he falls in love with her and two weeks later, they're in a big hurry, they run get married! And he's got yet such a steady job by the city, there, a whole year regular he gets wages."

19   Mr. Yavner paused, and the disgust in his face gave way to a look of meditative resignation.

20   "How you think it makes a father feel, he sees his oldest daughter sitting and sitting and the youngest, she gets married? Is nice, maybe? So my Yettie, she's older, she went to business school, she's got a job, she knows to cook, to sew, and to everything, so she's still sitting, waiting! And my Jennie, she's younger, from schools she got right away tired, a job she never had, a whole day she layed in bed smoking tsi-garettes, and a whole night she ran around; so my Jennie, *she's* the one she's got now a fine husband with a steady job!"

21   He reached down for his clusters of bottles, swung the door open with his foot, and held it wide for a moment with his shoulder as he looked in at me.

22   "That's your America," he said with the faintest hint of derision in his voice. "That's where you want I should learn things," he said, as he stepped away from the door, and it shut behind him with a crash that echoed throughout the midnight still-ness of the house.

Sample Passage 2

Mr. President

By Bob Greene

1   "We're going to have spaghetti tonight," said Thomas Lucas on his seventeenth birthday. "My mom makes excellent spaghetti. Especially the sauce. She uses sausage, chicken, mushrooms, peppers—I've only made spaghetti sauce once, but it can't come close to Mom's."

My notes about what I am reading

2   Thomas Lucas was sitting in the wood-paneled living room of his family's home in Salt Rock, West Virginia. He is a big, handsome kid—five feet eleven, 185 pounds— and on top of the television set in the living room was a photograph of him in his red-and-white Barboursville High School football uniform. Last year Thomas was a starting defensive tackle on the team.

3   But things have changed for Thomas Lucas since last summer. His life will never be the same—and, in at least a minor way, the lives of American high school students will never be the same, either.

4   Because Thomas Lucas won an election last summer. And he is now the first male to be the national president of Future Homemakers of America.

5   Thomas Lucas's family lives in the West Virginia hollows. This is Chuck Yeager country, where the men are supposed to be tough, laconic, rugged, and all of the other adjectives that have always added up to a definition of maleness. So it is all the more surprising that the first male president of Future Homemakers of America should come from here.

6   "In junior high school," Thomas said, "the boys are all required to take home economics as well as shop, and the girls are all required to take shop as well as home economics. In high school you don't have to do that, but when I was a freshman I decided that I'd keep taking home economics. And when the teacher announced that there would be a Future Homemakers of America meeting, I went to it.

7   "I didn't do it for any particular reason. I just did it to meet some kids. I was the only boy there. But it turned out that I liked it."

8   Approximately 11 percent of the 315,000 members of Future Homemakers of America nationwide are males. But, until very recently, it was unthinkable for a boy to become president of the forty-one-year-old organization.

9   "A lot of people define homemaking as just sewing and cooking," Thomas said. "But my definition of a homemaker is someone who contributes to the well-being of the family. That should be a male as well as a female. You have to understand, there was never a time when I thought that men and women weren't equal. I was born in 1969, and that was at the beginning of the women's movement."

10   As might be expected, Thomas has taken some teasing from his schoolmates about this whole thing. "Yeah, there have been some remarks," he said. "The macho image of a lot of high school guys is the same that it has always been. You know, 'I'm tough.' Always getting in fights to prove their masculinity. All this boastfulness about themselves, and putting down other people. They're so locked into that image that they can't associate outside that.

11   "People couldn't understand that I was a football player and that I was also in FHA. But football and FHA are just two different things that I did. I'm not playing football this year, because of my FHA duties. That's okay with me.

12   "You hear so much about football being a character builder. If you ask me, football creates animosity between people. I know that it's supposed to develop sportsmanship and develop physical well-being and make you feel good about yourself. But all football was for me was going out there and knocking heads with someone every day. Future Homemakers of America is a hundred times more of a character builder than football, and Future Homemakers of America has offered me a hundred times more good things than football ever could."

13   Thomas is aware that for many boys, the quintessential modern hero is the movie character Rambo. "Look, I saw *Rambo* three times," he said. "I liked the story of it. It was an exciting movie, and very suspenseful. But it's fantasy. What I'm doing is real."

14   Thomas's stepfather, Larry Brown, came into the living room. Brown is forty-one years old and a dealer account manager with Ford Motor Credit Company. He is a burly, bearded man, and he listened to his son talking about Future Homemakers of America.

15   "When I was in high school, something like this would never be done," Brown said. "The boys just didn't take home economics. My conception, when I was growing up, was that the wife was the homemaker and the husband was the provider. And there are still a lot of men who would rather have their son be the football captain than the president of FHA.

16   "But I'm very proud of Thomas, and the more I learn about what he's doing, the more proud I am. Frankly, if anything, we felt at first that he was a little too dedicated to it. We saw Future Homemakers becoming his whole life. But what can we say? He set his sights on becoming national president, and now he is.

17   "In this day and age, I think it's wrong to want to bring your son up to be macho. I think that what Thomas was just saying about the macho image you get from movies is right. Basically, the macho image is ignorant. The macho guys you see in the movies seem to be playing with about half a deck upstairs."

18   "What Thomas is doing represents a change for everybody. With more and more women in the work force, men are going to have to adapt, and accept learning skills around the house. They're not going to have any choice."

19   Thomas cut in. "The real prejudice against what I'm doing doesn't come from kids my own age," he said. "Oh, there's some of that, but I can handle it. But the bad stereotype comes from adults. Not to put down you adults or anything, but teenagers are a little more liberal in their thinking than adults.

20   "Like at the national convention in Orlando, where I was elected. I had my delegate name tag on, and there was this woman in the lobby of the hotel who was just staying there as a guest—she wasn't a part of the FHA convention. And she looked at me and she looked at my tag, and she said, 'Oh, you're a homemaker, are you?' She kind of snickered. I knew she was making fun."

21   Thomas's mother, Sue Brown, thirty-eight, walked into the living room for a moment from the kitchen, where she had been preparing dinner.

22   "I've never believed that a woman should have all the homemaker's chores," she said. "Oh, women do help keep the social aspects of the family going. They send out the greeting cards and buy the presents for Christmas and call people to invite them to things. On things like that, men have to be sort of dragged along. It shouldn't be that way. It's unfair.

23   "But Thomas—Thomas has done household chores since he was small."

24   "I mow the yard," Thomas said. "I take out the garbage. I dust. I do the dishes. I make the bed. Mom still does most of the cooking."

25   "You can be a man and still be like Thomas," his mother said. "Thomas is no sissy. I don't think he's going to be a househusband and just stay home when he gets older. But he's been taught to do his share. And I think his being elected national president proves that it doesn't matter if you're from a hollow in West Virginia. Your mind can go anywhere."

26   There was a knock at the front door, and Thomas's mother went to answer it. In a few moments a lanky young man walked into the living room. He was Anthony Thompson, a high school buddy of Thomas's, and he had been invited to come over for the birthday dinner.

27   "Thomas was always a go-getter," Anthony said. "I think it's great that he made it to president."

28   It didn't seem to occur to Anthony that there was anything particularly unusual about the fact that the group that Thomas had "made it to president" of was the Future Homemakers of America. He seemed simply to admire the accomplishment.

29   "In junior high school, Thomas and I both ran for student body president, and I won," Anthony said. "But now Thomas has established himself in a far more prestigious position than president of Salt Rock Junior High School."

30   Anthony said that he had no desire to join FHA. "I guess that I just don't have the interest that Thomas has," he said. "I'm not saying that I think it was a weird thing for him to do. There are a lot of people who would think it would be a feminine move, but I don't think so. I'm sure that there will be some feeling against him in school this year now that he's national president, and that some people will stereotype him. But he can handle it. I know he can.

31   "People are just brought up in different ways. Take my grandparents. My grandmother waits on my grandfather hand and foot. He wouldn't be able to exist without

her. I think all Thomas is saying is that it's about time for boys to learn stuff that has always been thought of as women's stuff."

My notes about what I am reading

32   Anthony said that although he respects what Thomas is doing, he has other goals for himself. "I want to join the Navy," he said.

33   Thomas said that he had some specific areas on which he wanted to concentrate as national president of FHA. "I want to help develop and expand drug-abuse programs, programs about drinking and driving, programs about teen pregnancies. When people hear about Future Homemakers of America, they tend to think in terms of the cooking and sewing, and think that's it. But cooking and sewing is really only a small part of FHA. Those things are necessary, because everyone should know how to keep their own home going. FHA is really a lot more than that, though.

34   "I hope to get married and have two or three kids. That's one of the nice things about being one of the few boys in FHA—you really get to meet a lot of girls."

Sample Visual Representation

During World War II, the character in this poster, known as Rosie the Riveter, came to symbolize American working women, and was used to recruit them. Because so many men were in the military, women were needed in the workforce, in positions they had not traditionally filled. It became common, for example, to see women engineers, heavy machinery operators, freight haulers, and lumber and steel workers. Women came to be employed during the war in all sectors of American industry.

Multiple-Choice Questions on Passage 1

Use "Slipping Beauty" (pp. 11-13)
to answer questions 1-11

---

1 In paragraph 1, the word *prominent* means—

   A well known

   B growing

   C projecting

   D distinguished

This question tests **basic understanding—vocabulary**. The sentence (the first sentence of the paragraph) gives you enough information to choose the correct answer. The word *prominent* can mean well known (**A**) or distinguished (**D**) (as in "she is a prominent person in city government"), but in this sentence, the meaning of the word is *projecting* (**C**). That meaning is clear because the sentence says that the man's paunch (stomach) is *out of place* because he seems otherwise *emaciated* (extremely thin). The paunch, therefore, must contrast with the thinness, suggesting it is large, or projecting from his otherwise thin body. The correct answer is **C**.

---

2 Based on paragraph 1, the reader can assume that the man described is being characterized as a person who—

    F makes a good living

    G is well organized

    H is likely to be sensitive to the feelings of others

    J would be uninterested in modern devices

This question covers **analysis and evaluation—inference**. The man delivering the seltzer bottles drives a "flat, open wagon behind a huge, drooping horse," while the rest of the world uses "trucks and automobiles." To answer this question, you need to move beyond what the passage says and determine what is *likely* to be true, based on the information given, but isn't directly stated. In this case, it's logical to assume that a man who uses a horse-pulled wagon in the midst of cars and trucks is apparently not interested in modern, mechanical devices. Choice **F** is incorrect because the man is emaciated and wears a battered cap, which doesn't in any way suggest he makes a good living. Nor does he seem particularly well organized, since he seems to make his deliveries at random times. The fact that he rings the bell after midnight suggests that he is *not* sensitive to the feelings of others (**H**). The correct answer is **J**.

---

3 Which line from the selection best shows Mr. Yavner's attitude toward his younger daughter?

    A *. . . she could find a hundred fellahs they should kiss their fingers to the* sky *seven days a week if she would only* look *on them . . .*

    B *She should learn to cook and sew and keep a house clean and put a little money in the bank . . .*

    C *Go try teach children something in America, go . . .*

    D *In Europe, a father talks to a child, so it happens she should know the father was right.*

This question covers **literary elements—characters**. The attitudes of characters can be shown by their actions or their words or, in some cases, by the words of the author. In this passage, we know of Mr. Yavner's attitudes through what he says. All of the answer choices are direct quotations from him. Choices **C** and **D** reflect his attitude toward teaching children in general, so neither is the best answer to a question concerning his attitude toward his daughter. Choice **A** is his comment about his older daughter, Yettie. Only choice **B** concerns what he thinks about his younger daughter, Jennie. The correct answer is **B**.

---

4 It is clear from paragraphs 2 through 4 that the narrator's interaction with Mr. Yavner —

    F is a new experience for him

    G is made more difficult because of the physical conditions

    H is unavoidable

    J causes Mr. Yavner to regret his intrusion

This question tests **basic understanding—supporting details**. The details of these paragraphs lead to answer **G**. The narrator has been "aroused after midnight" after having difficulty getting to sleep in the first place, so he is tired, and not fully himself. In addition, the temperature and the season are mentioned as making the author "forget the things that experience has taught" him. It's clear from this detail also that this is *not* a new experience for the narrator (**F**), and there are no details that suggest Mr. Yavner regrets anything (**J**). Choice **H** might at first be a tempting answer, because you might think that once the narrator has opened the door, what follows is unavoidable. But you should be careful not to choose an answer for which there is no evidence in the passage. There is nothing in the passage to suggest, for example, that the narrator couldn't have simply refused to answer the door or shut it as soon as he saw Mr. Yavner. The correct answer is **G**.

---

5 In what way is Mr. Yavner's story ironic?

   A Mr. Yavner doesn't understand the ways of America.

   B Yettie remains unmarried, but Jennie is married.

   C Raising children, whether in Europe or America, can be difficult.

   D The narrator is unable to convince Mr. Yavner that he shouldn't make deliveries after midnight.

This question covers **literary techniques—literary terms—irony.** For this exam, you are expected to know the meaning of literary terms such as *irony.* You won't be asked to define them, but you must know their meanings in order to answer the questions concerning them. The term *irony* describes a situation in which an outcome is the opposite of what would reasonably be expected. For Mr. Yavner, the idea that his younger daughter, Jennie (who Mr. Yavner thinks is lazy and irresponsible and not much of a marriage catch), is married, while his older daughter, Yettie (who Mr. Yavner thinks is responsible and industrious and wonderful with housekeeping chores), remains single and without a suitor is an ironic situation. The correct answer is **B.**

---

6 The point of view of this passage results in the fact that the reader—

   F is aware of what the author thinks

   G cannot know what any character thinks

   H knows what Mr. Yavner thinks only through his dialogue

   J doesn't know what the narrator thinks

This question covers **literary techniques—point of view.** The point of view of this passage is called "first person"; that is, the story is told in an "I" form by a character in the story (the man who answers the door, the narrator, whose name we never are told). In this point of view, the reader can know the thoughts of only the "I" character, so everything is colored by that character's perceptions. The only way the reader knows what Mr. Yavner might think is through his dialogue (what he says) (**H**). For this question, you need to be careful not to confuse the *author* with the *character who tells the story.* They are not the same (so **F** is incorrect). The correct answer is **H.**

---

7 Paragraph 11 is mainly about—

   A Mr. Yavner's need to have the narrator listen to him

   B Mr. Yavner's example of how he was once badly hurt

   C Mr. Yavner's difficulty in dealing with his younger daughter

   D Mr. Yavner's belief that children should listen to their parents

---

This question tests **basic understanding—main idea.** Some questions may ask you about the main idea of an entire passage, but this one asks only about the main idea of a single paragraph. The paragraph is all in Mr. Yavner's own words in which he explains what happened to him when he didn't listen to his father's advice. His main concern here is about how children should listen to their parents (**D**), not how the narrator should listen to him (**A**) or his specific difficulties with his younger daughter (**C**). He does mention cutting himself with a knife (**B**) (although how *badly* he cut himself we don't know), but that isn't the main point of the paragraph. The correct answer is **D.**

---

8 The author's purpose for using the terms *disgust* and *resignation* in both paragraph 1 and paragraph 19 to describe Mr. Yavner is probably to—

   F reinforce the idea that the character is thoroughly unlikable

   G emphasize the differences between the narrator and Mr. Yavner

   H suggest the character's inability to change his thinking

   J introduce the possibility that Mr. Yavner will one day return to Europe

---

This question covers **analysis and evaluation—tone and word choice.** In the use of these two terms, at the beginning and close to the end of the story, the author emphasizes Mr. Yavner's inability to change his thinking, as well as his inability to accept the ways of his new country. Yavner is disgusted by the ways of America in the raising of daughters and expectations concerning them. At the same time, he has become somewhat resigned to the situation, although resignation does not indicate acceptance or change in his thinking. He simply seems to feel that he can do nothing about it. The character is not made to seem thoroughly unlikable (**F**); he is, after all, devoted to his daughters and concerned about them, even though he seems eccentric. We don't know how the narrator feels about raising children, so the differences between him and Mr. Yavner (**G**) are not the point here. Choice **J** is irrelevant and is not suggested in any way in the story. The correct answer is **H**.

---

9 In this story, Jennie's *magazines, tsigarettes,* and *smook* symbolize—

    A European standards of behavior
    B the failure of American educational systems
    C parental guidelines
    D the daughter's refusal to learn

This question covers **literary techniques—literary terms—symbolism.** Jennie apparently refuses to listen to her father's advice on how a young woman should behave. Instead, she spends her time reading magazines and smoking cigarettes (*tsigarettes* and *smook* as Mr. Yavner pronounces them). So the magazines, cigarettes, and smoke symbolize—to Mr. Yavner—his daughter's refusal to learn from his experience and meet his expectations. Her behavior is the opposite of European standards, which Mr. Yavner mentions (**A**), and certainly does not follow his guidelines (**C**). The American educational system (**B**) is mentioned only in passing and isn't central to the story. The correct answer is **D**.

---

10 At the end of the story, as compared to the beginning of the story, Mr. Yavner—

    F has realized his mistake in expecting too much from his daughters
    G has remained the same in his opinion about the appropriate behavior of daughters
    H has realized his mistake in delivering his seltzer at night
    J has begun to think that Jennie might actually be the smarter daughter

---

This question covers **literary elements—plot.** In many stories, a main character undergoes some sort of change, often because events in the story cause a change in that character's thinking. In this story, however, Mr. Yavner is basically the same at the end as he is at the beginning. The correct answer is **G**.

---

11 In paragraph 13, Mr. Yavner uses exaggeration—

    A so that the narrator will not expect him to learn anything
    B to improve the narrator's opinion of him
    C to compare the qualities of two people
    D to make sure that no one thinks badly of his daughters

This question covers **literary language—exaggeration.** Mr. Yavner wildly exaggerates the attributes of his older daughter, Yettie, to emphasize their excellence in comparison with the attributes of his younger daughter, Jennie. The correct answer is **C**.

Multiple-Choice Questions on Passage 2

Use "Mr. President" (pp. 13-16)
to answer questions 12-23.

---

12 Paragraph 12 is mainly about—

    F the positive effect of sports
    G the importance of a good self-image to a teenager
    H the comparative value of football to an individual
    J the superiority of FHA as a model for teens

This question tests **basic understanding—main idea**. Paragraph 12 is a direct quotation from Thomas Lucas in which he states his opinion of the value of football versus the value of FHA *to him*. Notice the phrases *for me* and *has offered me*. Thomas isn't speaking of the value of sports in general or for anyone other than himself. So just the fact that choices **F, G,** and **J** all speak of sports or teenagers in general makes them incorrect answers. The correct answer is **H.**

---

13 The author's purpose in including paragraphs 14 through 18 is probably to—

    A indicate Thomas's family's support for his decisions

    B emphasize the values of Larry Brown's generation

    C avoid overloading the article with only Thomas's comments

    D suggest that males often think alike

This question covers **analysis and evaluation—author's purpose.** The author probably includes the comments of Thomas's stepfather to show that Thomas's family supports his somewhat unusual decision to be involved in FHA. Larry Brown does mention the values of his generation, but his emphasis is on his thoughts on the matter *now,* not the older points of view (**B**). The correct answer is **A.**

---

14 Read the following dictionary entry.

minor \minər\ adj. **1.** of lesser importance **2.** under legal age **3.** inferior **4.** pertaining to a minority

Which definition best matches the use of the word *minor* in paragraph 3?

    F Definition 1

    G Definition 2

    H Definition 3

    J Definition 4

This question tests **basic understanding—vocabulary.** By using the phrase *at least in a minor way,* the author is softening the effect of the statement that *the lives of American high school students will never be the same.* That is, their lives will be affected, but in a way of *lesser importance* when compared to Thomas's life. The correct answer is **F.**

---

15 In paragraph 5, the *Chuck Yeager* mentioned is most likely to be—

    A another male member of the Future Homemakers of America

    B a sports figure in Salt Rock, West Virginia

    C someone admired by the local population

    D a male who would refuse to be an FHA member

This question covers **literary techniques—history.** You don't need to know who Chuck Yeager is in order to answer this question correctly. The clause *This is Chuck Yeager country* alone tells you that whoever this person is, he is undoubtedly looked up to here and perhaps comes from this area. In addition, the remainder of the sentence makes it clear that Yeager must in some way be a model for the tough, laconic (using few words), rugged male. At the same time, however, there is no suggestion that Yeager would necessarily *refuse* to be an FHA member (**D**). That's something that simply can't be determined from the context. In fact, Chuck Yeager is an American test pilot who was a fighter pilot in World War II and was the first to break the sound barrier, in 1953. The correct answer is **C.**

16 Which of these is the best summary of the selection?

    F   Thomas Lucas, a football player from Salt Rock, West Virginia, joined the Future Homemakers of America, which he found that he liked very much. He used to play football but gave that up. His stepfather thought that macho guys are playing with a half a deck. He was made fun of by the townspeople but didn't allow that to keep him from enjoying the group.

    G   Thomas Lucas, a high school student in Salt Rock, West Virginia, became interested in the Future Homemakers of America and not only joined the group but became its first male national president. He says that the club isn't just about cooking and sewing and cleaning but also about such programs as those dealing with drug abuse. Despite his unusual decision and the fact that some students and parents didn't understand why he made it, he was supported by his mother, stepfather, and friend.

    H   Thomas Lucas's stepfather, mother, and friend supported him in his decision to be a member of the FHA, although other students in his school didn't understand why he did it. When he went to a national convention in Orlando for the FHA, a woman made fun of him because of his membership. He decided that football wasn't for him but the Future Homemakers of America was.

    J   As president of the Future Homemakers of America, Thomas Lucas wants to focus on drug-abuse and drinking and driving programs, as well as programs concerning teen pregnancy. He does many chores around the house and learned a great deal from the FHA programs about taking care of a house. He discovered that he liked FHA better than football and stayed with his decision.

This question tests **basic understanding—summary.** In answering a summary question, you should choose the answer that includes all the important points of a passage, doesn't exclude important points, and doesn't include minor points. All of the choices except **G** do one or both of the last two. The important points of the selection are Thomas's name, the area in which he lives and the attitudes there concerning appropriate male behavior, his interest in FHA, his becoming the first male president of the group, the support he's given by family and friends, and his major ideas about the group. The correct answer is **G.**

17 The area in which Thomas Lucas lives may have an impact on his decision because—

    A   there are few opportunities in the area for home economics study

    B   the attitudes there may favor stereotypical pursuits for males and females

    C   football is the only sport offered at the high school

    D   Thomas's parents are different from other parents in their support of their son

This question covers **literary elements—setting.** Thomas's decision to run for president of FHA is likely to have been more difficult because of the attitudes of those in the area, which seem to promote, according to Thomas and his family and the author, the more stereotypical pursuits of football for boys and home economics for girls. A stereotype is a standardized idea about a person or group, which is generally simplified and often, therefore, untrue. It's a term you should be familiar with. The correct answer is **B.**

18 Thomas's decision to run for president of FHA is a serious one for him, but the tone of the selection is—

    F   frivolous

    G   agitated

    H   objective

    J   jubilant

This question covers **analysis and evaluation—tone.** The tone of a piece of writing is set by the author by means of his or her word choice. Tone is usually described by a word indicating a particular emotion or lack of it. In this case, while the author does not in any way dismiss the seriousness of Thomas's decision, his manner of presentation is not emotional, but rather reportorial, that is, objective, as is a news writer's copy. The essay is made up almost entirely by the straightforward reporting of what various individuals have to say. The few comments made directly by the author are also generally objective, reporting what the author sees and hears during his interview. The only extended comments that might be thought of as the author's opinions occur in paragraph 5, where he suggests what the local attitudes might be, but even these comments could not be described as frivolous, agitated, or jubilant (**F, G,** and **J**). The correct answer is **H.**

---

19 In paragraph 17, Thomas's stepfather uses an analogy to—

    A   refer to a misconception in Thomas's thinking

    B   describe the perceptions of local citizens

    C   show that he is personally just "one of the guys"

    D   indicate his opinion of some movie characters

This question covers **literary language—imaginative language—analogy.** An analogy is a comparison of two things in order to make clearer some attribute of one of them. But an analogy doesn't have to use the word *like* or *as,* as does the comparison in a simile. Nor does it have to directly compare, as a metaphor does, by saying something *is* something else (as in, say, *the girl is a rocket, racing down the path*). The analogy here is a little harder to see than are those in these examples. By saying that *macho* people in the movies are *playing with about half a deck upstairs,* Larry Brown is comparing their brains to an incomplete deck of playing cards, suggesting that they certainly aren't fully equipped to function well. The correct answer is **D.**

---

20 One reason Thomas thinks that some people are not supportive of his decision to be involved with FHA is that—

    F   the author has come to interview him and his family

    G   his parents did not originally think his decision was a good one

    H   his friend Anthony prefers football to FHA

    J   a woman in Orlando laughed at him

This question tests **basic understanding—supporting details.** The author has probably come to interview Thomas and his family (**F**) because this is an unusual and interesting story, but there is no evidence that the author wouldn't support Thomas or that Thomas thinks that he wouldn't. And although there is some suggestion that Thomas's parents may have thought Thomas was perhaps a little too involved in FHA, to the exclusion of everything else, that doesn't necessarily mean that they thought his decision wasn't a good one (**G**). It's clear that Anthony *does* support him (**H**), whether he prefers football for himself or not. But Thomas specifically mentions the woman in Orlando who *snickered* (laughed) at him as someone who was obviously not supportive. The correct answer is **J.**

---

21 The theme of this passage primarily involves—

    A   gender expectations

    B   football versus home economics

    C   methods of child rearing

    D   rural attitudes as opposed to urban attitudes

This question covers **literary elements—theme.** What Thomas has done is very unusual—both being involved with FHA and becoming the group's national president. The reason it's unusual is that boys don't generally do things like this—that is, people's expectations for them have to do with their *gender,* whether they are male or female. The correct answer is **A.**

---

22 Given what we know of Thomas from this passage, it is most likely that in the future he will—

    F   remain in FHA after he graduates from high school

    G   continue to be interested in doing things to keep his home going

    H   try to convince his classmates that they should join FHA

    J   run for a state elective office

This question covers **analysis and evaluation—prediction.** The question asks what is *most* likely, given what we know *from the passage.* We don't know from the passage whether FHA is an organization only for those in high school or whether adults are members too, so that fact alone makes **F** somewhat questionable. Thomas does not in any way indicate that he wants to bring his classmates around to his way of thinking or get them involved in FHA, so **H** isn't a good answer. He might run for a state elective office one day (**J**), as anyone might who exhibits the capacity to be involved with something as much as he does, but here he doesn't express any interest in doing so. He does, however, specifically state that *everyone should know how to keep their own home going,* so it's most logical to think he won't change his mind about that. The correct answer is **G.**

---

23 When Thomas says in paragraph 34 *you really get to meet a lot of girls,* his intent probably is—

    A   to show he is as macho as anyone else

    B   to indicate that he's not so different from other boys

    C   to remind the author that the author may have misjudged him

    D   to reassure his parents

This question covers **analysis and evaluation—conclusion.** This question, similar to a "prediction" question, asks you to reach a conclusion based on the evidence in the passage. In this type of question, you have to be careful not to conclude something without sufficient evidence. In this case, the easiest way to approach the question is to eliminate answers that are most likely wrong. You can eliminate **A** because the passage makes it clear that Thomas and his parents don't think that being "macho" is a good thing. You can eliminate **C** because there is no judgment made by the author, as far as we (or Thomas) would know. You can eliminate **D** because as far as we can see from the passage, his parents are thoroughly supportive and don't seem to need reassuring about anything concerning Thomas's decisions. That leaves **B,** which is a reasonable answer. Teenage boys are generally interested in teenage girls. Thomas indicates that he is, too, making him not really so different from his classmates. The correct answer is **B.**

Multiple-Choice Questions on Passages 1 and 2

Use "Slipping Beauty" and "Mr. President" (pp. 11-16)
to answer questions 24 and 25.

---

24 Both Mr. Yavner in "Slipping Beauty" and Thomas in "Mr. President" are concerned to some degree with—

    F   the role of parents in raising their children

    G   the role of children in meeting their parents' expectations

    H   the differing cultures in two countries

    J   contributing to the betterment of the family

This question covers **literary elements—characters.** Mr. Yavner is interested in the role of parents (**F**). He thinks that parents should teach their children how to behave. Thomas *may* be interested in that also, but he doesn't comment on it at all, so we don't know. The same is true of choice **G:** Mr. Yavner definitely thinks children should do what their parents expect them to, but again, Thomas doesn't talk about this. Only Mr. Yavner comments on *two countries,* or rather a country (America) and a continent (Europe). But both Thomas and Mr. Yavner express concern with the betterment of the family. Mr. Yavner works hard, it seems, to provide for his family and thinks his daughters ought to take care of things at home and work to bring in some money. Thomas expresses a specific interest in keeping the *home going* and is also interested in programs that would benefit a family (such as drug-abuse programs). The correct answer is **J.**

---

25 "Slipping Beauty" differs from "Mr. President" in that conflict in "Slipping Beauty"—

    A   is only between the narrator and Mr. Yavner, while more than two characters are in conflict in "Mr. President"

    B   is evident in male and female behavior, while that in "Mr. President" involves only females

    C   is a major element of the story, while that in "Mr. President" is not

    D   involves a struggle against nature, but that in "Mr. President" involves a struggle within an individual

---

This question covers **literary elements—plot—conflict.** Conflict in literature is a struggle of some kind. It can be between characters, between a character and the natural world, between a character and society, or within a single character. Conflict is a major element in "Slipping Beauty." The story is primarily about Mr. Yavner and his daughters and the conflict between them. In addition, the passage involves Mr. Yavner's conflict with American culture and his inability to adapt to it. But conflict in "Mr. President" is a very minor element in the story, if, indeed, it could be said to be present at all. The only conflict there might be is between Thomas and society, which might be said to have other expectations for him. But Thomas is quite comfortable with himself, and the conflict, if present at all, is minimal. This is a difficult question, and the easiest way to approach it may be to eliminate wrong answers. You can eliminate **A** because the primary conflict in "Slipping Beauty" is between a father and his daughters (even though they aren't physically present in the story). You can eliminate **B** because, while it is true that conflict in "Slipping Beauty" involves both males and females, most of "Mr. President" has to do with males. And you can eliminate **D** because Mr. Yavner's conflict is not against nature, and there is no internal conflict in "Mr. President." The correct answer is **C.**

Multiple-Choice Questions on the Visual Representation

Use the visual representation on page 16 to answer questions 26-28.

---

26 What attribute in the picture of Rosie the Riveter best reflects the purpose of the poster?

   F   Determination
   G   Devotion
   H   Strength
   J   Passion

This question covers **media techniques—purpose.** The purpose of the poster is to recruit women into nontraditional, and seemingly nonfeminine, working roles. The emphasis in the poster is on strength, suggesting that women are, indeed, strong enough to take on all these working roles. Rosie is flexing her bicep, showing the world just how strong she is. The correct answer is **H.**

---

27 What element in the poster suggests that working women are patriotic?

   A   The direct eye contact
   B   The clenched fist
   C   The word *We*
   D   The words *Can Do*

This question covers **media techniques—emotional appeal.** The information given above the poster tells you that this poster was used to recruit women during the war. The word *We* would suggest to the viewer that such work was a cooperative effort of the whole country, not just the individual, and would support the war effort, a patriotic endeavor. The word appeals to emotion in that it implies that such work is not simply work but a bigger, more important team effort. The correct answer is **C.**

---

28 What element in the poster would suggest to the viewer that looks should be of low priority?

   F   The scarf covering Rosie's hair
   G   The rolled up sleeve
   H   The exclamation mark after *It*
   J   The insignia on Rosie's collar

This question covers **media techniques—suggestion.** The poster presents a woman who is both strong and pleasant looking. But the emphasis is on strength, the ability to do a job well. The fact that Rosie's hair is covered by a scarf suggests to the viewer that while a woman might sometimes want to make her hair attractive, in this case, concern with looks (hair) is beside the point, given the great importance to the country in getting the job done. There is another message here also (not mentioned in this question) in that many industrial jobs require that nothing on a person (not hair, clothes, or jewelry) should be hanging loose because they might be caught in machinery and be a safety hazard. The correct answer is **F.**

Open-Ended Questions on Passages 1 and 2

Directions: Answer the following questions in the space provided on the answer document.

---

29 In "Slipping Beauty," what tells the reader that Mr. Yavner is an immigrant to America from another country? Support your answer with evidence from the story.

Possible Answers for Question 29: Literary Elements—Characters

Example Short Answer with a Score of 3

There are two reasons the reader knows that Mr. Yavner is an immigrant. First, his speech shows that English is not his native language—he mispronounces words like "smook," "tsigarettes," and "sucha." Second, he talks about being with his father in the "old country" and mentions what people would think of his daughter in Europe.

This answer clearly identifies how the reader knows Mr. Yavner is an immigrant and both reasons cite direct evidence from the story.

Example Short Answer with a Score of 1

Mr. Yavner doesn't speak right. He also doesn't like the way America is. And he thinks his daughter doesn't behave the way she should.

This student does see that Mr. Yavner's speech is a primary reason for thinking he is an immigrant, but only vaguely connects the American culture and the daughter's behavior to Yavner's immigrant status. This writer also gives no evidence from the story to support the statements.

---

30 What is the most likely reason that the author of "Mr. President" included Anthony's comments? Support your answer with evidence from the selection.

Possible Answers for Question 30: Analysis and Evaluation—Author's Purpose

Example Short Answer with a Score of 3

When the author quotes Anthony, he is showing the support Thomas has from his classmate, not only the support from his parents. Knowing what Anthony thinks makes the interview more rounded. It is clear from Anthony's comments that he thinks Thomas made a good choice (paragraphs 28–29) although other students may stereotype Thomas ("But he can handle it. I know he can").

This student has given a plausible reason that Anthony's comments have been included by the author. The reader gets to hear from Thomas himself, Thomas's parents, and Thomas's friend, making the interview seem more complete. And the writer cites specific evidence from the passage concerning Anthony's point of view.

Example Short Answer with a Score of 1

Anthony came to the door, so it wouldn't have been right for the author not to speak to him. And then Anthony can tell all about how he feels and how the rest of the high school kids feel. Anthony admires the accomplishment.

It seems more logical to assume that the author arranged for Anthony to join them rather than that he just turned up. But apart from that, this student doesn't understand that the author could have simply left Anthony's comments out of the selection. This writer does indicate an understanding of what Anthony's comments add to the selection but is too general to make this a higher scoring short answer.

---

31 How are expectations an important theme in both "Slipping Beauty" and "Mr. President"? Support your answer with evidence from **both** selections.

Possible Answers for Question 31: Literary Elements—Theme

Example Short Answer with a Score of 3

Mr. Yavner expects his daughters to follow his advice, and Yettie does (most of paragraph 13), but Jennie doesn't ("Like her sister Yettie, I tell her she should be"). Also, he expects his daughters to be married, but only Jennie is, even though she isn't the "good" daughter. Thomas doesn't do what's usually expected of a teenage boy—"he is now the first male to be the national president of Future Homemakers of America." In "Slipping Beauty," a child doesn't meet expectations and is disapproved of. In "Mr. President," a child doesn't meet expectations and is admired.

This student has produced a concise and direct discussion of the theme of expectations in the two passages and has used excellent direct quotations and a reference to "most" of a paragraph to support the statements.

Example Short Answer with a Score of 1

The narrator expects Mr. Yavner to deliver the seltzer when he's supposed to and not in the middle of the night. Mr. Yavner expects his younger daughter to go to work and not hang around the house all day smoking. Thomas expected to be made president of FHA, and he was. His parents didn't expect him to do that but are happy he did. Thomas's stepfather says "I'm very proud of Thomas." The other kids probably didn't expect him to do what he did and probably aren't very happy about it.

This student did directly approach the question of expectations but ended up giving only a list of them from the selections without any analysis. And the fact that the narrator may have some expectations that are related to the theme is questionable. There is one attempt to use evidence, with the quotation from the stepfather, but that isn't enough to raise the score of this answer, which is probably a little better than a 1 answer, but not quite a 2.

Scoring Your Own Practice Open-Ended Answers

Have an English teacher, tutor, or someone else with good writing skills evaluate your practice open-ended answers using the following checklist. This evaluation will give you a general idea of your approximate score and will help you identify areas that you need to focus on to improve your writing. Remember, though, that while each of these points is important in your essay score, the essay is scored as a whole, on its overall effectiveness.

Checklist for the Open-Ended Answers

Assign each area a 0 (insufficient), 1 (partly sufficient), 2 (sufficient), or 3 (exemplary).

Does the writer

_____ Directly answer the question asked?

_____ Reasonably and clearly answer the question asked?

_____ Provide evidence from the passage to support the answer?

_____ Avoid irrelevant information?

Approximate score for the overall effectiveness of the answer _____

Written Composition

This section of the exam tests your abilities under Objectives 4 and 5. You will be expected to write an essay, "in a given context," that shows your ability to complete these objectives.

Objective 4: Produce an effective composition for a specific purpose

The essay section of the exam tests your writing skills. You will be asked to write an essay for a specific purpose. You are expected to produce a clear, logical, and complete response to a "prompt," that is, a topic given in the exam.

Objective 5: Produce a piece of writing that demonstrates the conventions of spelling, capitalization, punctuation, grammar, usage, and sentence structure

Your essay will need to observe the rules of standard written English. Your score will depend both on content and on your ability to write in standard English, following the mechanical and grammatical rules you've been taught during your school years.

Directions

The directions for Written Composition will be given on a single page titled WRITTEN COMPOSITION. You will be given a prompt in a box, followed by information to help you write, that is placed in a second box. Note the format of the page and the information given.

WRITTEN COMPOSITION

> Write an essay . . .

The information in the box below will help you remember what you should think about when you write your composition.

REMEMBER TO

- ❏ write on the topic given
- ❏ make your writing thoughtful and interesting
- ❏ check that each sentence you write adds to your composition as a whole
- ❏ make sure that your ideas are clear and easy for the reader to follow
- ❏ write about your ideas in detail so that the reader can better understand what you are trying to say
- ❏ proofread to correct errors in spelling, capitalization, punctuation, grammar, and sentence structure

---

USE THIS PREWRITING PAGE TO PLAN YOUR COMPOSITION

Analysis

Now let's take a close look at the Written Composition section.

Things You Should Know About the Written Composition Section

You should know that

- The "prompt" is a topic provided for you. The topic will relate to the theme of the passages and visual representation in the Reading section. The prompt for an essay on the theme of "Slipping Beauty" and "Mr. President" might be phrased

  "Write an essay explaining how you or someone else acted in a way that would not be generally expected of him or her as a male or as a female and the result of the person's actions."

- You *may* refer in your writing to either of the passages or to the visual representation, but you are *not required* to do so.

- You will be provided paper on which to make notes, write your draft, revise your essay, and copy your edited essay in its final form. You'll be given approximately a page for prewriting, two pages for your draft, and two pages for your final composition.

- The content of your essay does not have to be "true." That is, it doesn't have to deal with an actual occurrence in your or someone else's life. The incident and result could be entirely "created" by you, or the essay could combine real and created happenings. No one will check on the essay's factual accuracy. However, if you do make up events, be sure they are believable and on topic.

- The items you are told to "remember," given in the directions, are important. They are the basis on which your essay will be graded.

- Although you must respond directly and completely to the topic given, you are free to approach it in any way you like, as long as the essay is written in standard English prose (poetry is not acceptable). For example, you could respond by writing a persuasive essay in which you argue a point, trying to get a reader to agree with a particular point of view; you might write in the form of a short story if you chose to do that; or you could write in the more common personal essay (*I*) form, relating a personal experience.

- You may use a dictionary in this section of the exam.

- The essay is scored 1 (ineffective), 2 (somewhat effective), 3 (generally effective), or 4 (highly effective).

Strategies for Writing the Essay

You should carefully review the following key strategies for writing a good essay.

- **Organize your thoughts before you begin to write.**

  Jot down an outline of the points you might make. An outline on the male/female expectations topic could look like this:

  My Sister Connie

  Grandpa's gift of tools
      Christmas when she was 5
          Play tools
          Tomboy—running, swimming, fighting
          Curious—taking things apart
      Her birthday when she was 10
          Real tools
          Try at building a birdhouse
  Time with Grandpa
      Watching him make new cabinet doors
      Him watching her try
      Teaching her patience
      Her first solo project—a bookcase
  She becomes carpenter's apprentice
      Difficulty getting hired
      Determination
  Connie becomes a contractor
      Own business
      Successful
      Hires many others

  Or use a cluster diagram to organize your points. A cluster diagram on the same topic might look like this:

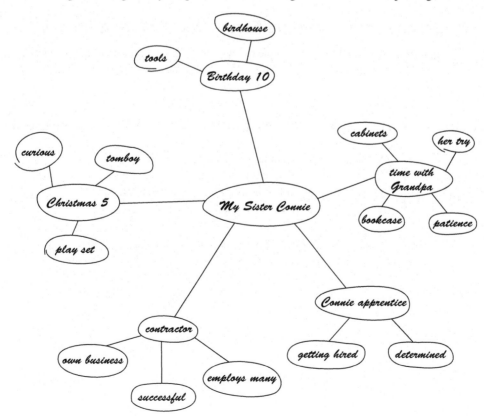

- **Respond directly, clearly, and completely to the topic.**

  Make sure you are addressing the topic given.

  Don't include ideas that have no understandable connection to the topic.

  Do include a clear opening and conclusion to tie the essay together.

  Organize the essay so that a reader can easily follow your ideas.

  Connect your points logically. Use appropriate transitions.

  Write in a way that makes one idea flow understandably into the next.

  Don't unnecessarily repeat ideas.

- **Be sure you include enough information on each idea.**

  Include supporting information with each main idea.

  Use specifics, when you can, rather than generalities.

- **As you write, think of your connection to the reader.**

  Write "believably." The readers should feel they are hearing the voice of a "real" person, with something of interest to say from his or her individual background and point of view.

- **Pay careful attention to mechanics, grammar, and usage in your writing.**

  They *are* considered when readers score your composition.

- **Revise your paper.**

  As you write, you are creating a "draft," not the final composition.

  Review your essay for each of the points given above.

  Now is the time to—if it improves the essay—add information, delete information, move sentences or paragraphs, and check for and correct any error in grammar, usage, spelling, punctuation, or capitalization.

- **After making corrections, do a read-though to be sure the writing is clear and correct and is the best work you can do.**

- **Carefully copy the final version of the composition onto the space provided for that purpose.**

  Write as clearly as you can. If the reader can't read what you write, he or she can't appropriately score it.

Suggested Approach with a Sample Essay Question and Essays

Read the sample essay question. Then read the two sample essays. Pay special attention to the boxes containing comments and suggestions about the writing. Next, write your own practice essay and follow the checklist and procedure to get a general score of your essay.

Essay Question on the Theme of Passages 1 and 2 and the Visual Representation

> Write an essay explaining how you or someone else acted in a way that would not be generally expected of him or her as a male or as a female and the result of the person's actions.

> MAKE SURE THAT YOU WRITE YOUR COMPOSITION ON THE TWO LINED PAGES IN THE ANSWER DOCUMENT

Sample Essays for the Essay Question

Essay with a Score of 3 to 4

> One Christmas when my sister Connie was five she was excited to find a set of toy plastic tools under the tree. There they were— a bright red hammer, screwdriver, pliers, and saw, along with a real, but oversized, tape measure. It was our Grandpa's doing. Girls, he said, ought to know how to make a picture frame and take apart a carburator and put a watch back together and build a fence.

Good introduction, right on topic, about a specific person

> He had a willing pupil in my sister (or so I've heard, since she's nine years older than I am and I wasn't around yet then). Connie was never one for dolls and tea parties. You'd be more likly to see her hanging upside down from a tree branch, racing with the kids down the block, mixing it up in a free-for-all wrestling match with the neighborhood boys, or investigating the interesting things that held her tricycle together. I'm sure our mother sometimes despaired of it all, but Connie always was, well, Connie.

Excellent, interesting details

You will be judged on spelling and mechanics, but a few errors won't greatly affect your score

> Grandpa and Connie began spending their late afternoons together. Ten minutes after she was home from school, she could always be found in Grandpa's workshop, banging along with her red hammer while Grandpa carefully sanded down a cabinet door or fitted the roof onto a bird house. By the time Connie was eight, she had graduated to metal tools and real nails and wood. By the time she was ten, she soloed, always under Grandpa's patient but watchful eye, on her first grown-up project, a bookcase. I still have that bookcase in my bedroom.

Effective repetition helps hold essay together

> While Connie was in high school, she needed a part time job to help pay expenses. No babysitting for her. No McDonald's or Burger King or Wendy's for her. Oh, no. She applied at the local union to become a carpenter's apprentice. I'm sure the guys there smirked more than a little when my five foot two sister told them what she wanted. I'm sure someone must have suggested to her that maybe she should send her brother to apply instead. I'm also sure that she didn't give up—because carpenter's apprentice she finally became—after months of badgering those doubters. I think they must have just thrown up their hands and given up in the face of her persistence.

Friendly, conversational tone engages reader

Nice emphasis on Connie's character and others' reactions

> Connie's all grown up now. After high school, she completed business courses at the community college. After that, she worked for a local contractor—one of those doubting guys at the union—as a finishing carpenter in the houses he was building. After that, she started her own contracting business, in-home remodeling. Ten people work for her now (and her plumber is a woman). No one expected my sister to end up where she has, but those ten people whose income now depends on her are very glad she did.

Effective closing— essay takes Connie from 5 at beginning to grown up now

Directly on topic, result of person's actions

Essay with a Score of 1 to 2

OK to mention passages or visual representation but not necessary. But this is only vaguely connected to topic—what one person did and result

Thomas in "Mr. President" didn't do what people expect boys to do. He became president of the Future Homemakers of America. The daughter in "Slipping Beauty" didn't either because she just hung around the house all day smoking and reading magazines but she got married anyway. Women in the war didn't do what women are supposed to do either they did rough jobs instead because they had to because the men were all fighting the war.

A few mechanical errors won't hurt, but this essay has many errors and the grade would suffer because of that

Students may write in persuasive style, but these personal opinions aren't on specified topic—just on male/female behavior in general

It's OK not to do just boy things or girl things. Some guys thing they should be just macho and play football and not cook or anything. They think it's girly to do that. But guys can cook, like chefs in big fancy restaurants. But I think it goes to far to make boys do things they don't like to do, like sewing and things like that. And then they will be teased by other boys and be miserable in high school. Its teasing like that that makes kids do bad things and not study and then not graduate. I think its pushing too much to try to get boys to do girls things and girls to do boys things. I don't know why people want to do this all the time.

I know a girl one time that went out for the football team. She wanted to be a pass receiver I think. Anyway, she showed up one day at practice and boy was the coach surprised. The team thought she was kind of stupid for doing that. But she really wanted to do it. And she was pretty big and strong too. The school board wouldn't let her though and her parents sued everybody about it and it was a real mess for awhile. I guess it was OK that she wanted to play but she could have got together a team that wasn't at school, that she could just play on you know. She didn't have to make such a big deal out of it.

Student attempts to address topic here but wanders again into personal opinion rather than telling the story

That's what I mean. Lets not get silly about it all. Its important that kids can do what they want to do, but theres limits people should pay attention to. There really are some things that girls should do and boys should do and sometimes they shouldn't cross over.

Weak ending—once again opinion and not on topic

Scoring Your Own Practice Essays

Have an English teacher, tutor, or someone else with good writing skills evaluate your practice essays using the following checklist. This evaluation will give you a *general idea* of your approximate score and will help you identify areas that you need to focus on to improve your writing. Remember, though, that while each of these points is important in your essay score, the essay is scored as a whole, on its overall effectiveness.

Checklist for the Essay

Assign each area a 1 (ineffective), 2 (somewhat effective), 3 (generally effective), or 4 (highly effective)

Does the writer

_____ Focus on the topic, clearly showing ideas that directly address the topic?

_____ Provide an essay that seems to be complete and includes an appropriate and effective beginning and conclusion?

_____ Avoid including information irrelevant to the topic as a whole?

_____ Use paragraphs that logically follow one another and have appropriate transitions between them?

_____ Organize the essay in a way that is reasonable and clear?

_____ Avoid unnecessary repetition and wordiness?

_____ Appropriately develop each of the ideas presented?

_____ Include thoughtful, interesting ideas?

_____ Use language and tone that involve and interest the reader?

_____ Effectively reflect his or her individual voice and personality?

_____ Employ correct spelling, punctuation, grammar, and usage?

_____ Use well-chosen sentence structures, phrases, and words to successfully communicate with the reader?

Approximate score for the overall effectiveness of the essay _____

Revising and Editing

The Revising and Editing section of the TAKS English Language Arts Test consists of two (2) reports, similar to those a student might write for a class, each followed by approximately ten (10) multiple-choice questions. In addition, a short sample report and three (3) sample questions appear as a Revising and Editing Sample after the essay question in the Reading and Written Composition section.

Objective 6: Tests Skills in Improving Writing

You will be asked to identify problems in the student reports in organization, sentence structure, grammar and standard English usage, and mechanics, and choose the best revision, if one is needed, from the multiple-choice answers. There is a single overall objective (objective 6) for this section. You are expected to "demonstrate the ability to revise and proofread to improve the clarity and effectiveness of a piece of writing."

Following are the areas tested and types of problems you will be asked to identify and correct in each area.

Mechanics

- **Punctuation:** commas, colons, semicolons, quotation marks, apostrophes, and end of sentence punctuation
- **Capitalization**
- **Spelling**

Grammar and Usage

- **Word Choice:** correct word in the context of similar sounding words (such as *accept, except*), appropriate homonym (words that sound alike but have different spellings, such as *it's, its* or *led, lead*), appropriate tone (level of formality or informality)
- **Parts of Speech:** adjectives versus adverbs, nouns versus verbs

- **Pronouns:** unnecessary use, clarity of reference, pronoun/antecedent agreement, case (subjective/objective)
- **Verb Forms:** subject/verb agreement (singular/plural), indication of appropriate time in context (shift of tense), tense form (such as *fought* rather than *fighted*).

Sentence Structure

- **Parallelism:** words and phrases that should be in the same grammatical form
- **Redundancy:** unnecessary repetition of information
- **Sentence Combining:** avoiding wordiness (for example, in two or more short sentences that would be better as one), appropriately using a variety of parts of speech (gerunds, participles, and so forth), improving clarity of meaning, improving style, correcting other errors
- **Misplaced (Unclear) and Dangling Modifiers**
- **Awkwardness:** unclear meaning
- **Run-on Sentences:** incorrect punctuation joining complete sentences
- **Sentence Fragments:** lack of subject and main verb

Organization

- **Transitions:** words and phrases that logically connect ideas
- **Sequence:** logical progression of ideas
- **Unconnected Information:** sentences that don't have a logical connection to the topic being written about

Directions

At the end of the Reading and Written Composition section there are three short sample questions with Short Sample Directions. When you actually start the Revising and Editing section, you will be given the Longer Passage Directions.

Short Sample Directions

Following are the directions for the short sample questions.

> "Read the introduction and the passage that follows. Then read each question and fill in the correct answer on page – of your answer document."

Notice that the short sample report and the approximately three sample questions appear on the exam just after the essay section and are separately numbered (**S-1, S-2, S-3**). The three sample questions are meant to familiarize you with the form of the report, and questions and are not scored. Following the sample questions are these additional directions: "Stop. Revising and Editing. Do not go on to the Revising and Editing section. When you finish the Reading and Written Composition section, raise your hand and wait for a test administrator to assist you."

Longer Passages Directions

Following are the directions for the longer passages in the actual Revising and Editing section.

> "Read the following passages and mark your answers on page – of your answer document. Remember that you are NOT permitted to use dictionaries or other reference materials on this section of the test."

The main Revising and Editing section is separate from the Reading and Written Composition section. You will be asked to raise your hand when you have completed the Reading and Written Composition section. After a test administrator assists you, you will be allowed to begin the Revising and Editing section. In this section, you will have to read the reports and answer the approximately twenty (20) questions about them. Notice that you may *not* use a dictionary or any other reference material for this section.

Analysis

Let's take a close look at the Revising and Editing section.

Things You Should Know About the Revising and Editing Section

You should know that

- Each report is preceded by a short paragraph about the purpose of the report, who wrote it, and your task in revising and editing it.
- Each sentence in the report is numbered in parentheses immediately before the sentence, allowing you to quickly find it.
- Paragraphs are indented, so when a question refers, say, to the fourth paragraph, you can easily count down to it.
- Questions are asked in sentence and paragraph order. For example, a question about sentence 2 will come before a question about sentence 3; a question about the first paragraph will come before a question about the third paragraph.
- There will be no questions about some sentences.
- Some questions have as their last answer "Make no change." In these questions, the question stem reads "What change, if any . . ." Some questions have four answers. In these questions, you have no "Make no change" option and must choose one of the revisions.
- Not every skill will be tested in every exam.

Strategies for Answering Revising and Editing Questions

As you approach the questions, keep the following strategies in mind:

- You are allowed to mark the passages in your test booklet. As you read a student report, always circle or underline any error or problem you see. When a question refers to that sentence, you'll save a great deal of time if you already know what should be corrected. Incorrect answers are usually (although not always) about different things in the sentence. So, for example, if you've marked a word as being incorrectly spelled, you can quickly pick out the correct answer.
- Don't assume that if there is a question about a sentence, it necessarily has an error that must be corrected. If the question has a "Make no change" option, that *may* be the correct answer.
- Incorrect answers will be clearly wrong. They do not involve a subjective assessment of slight variations in style, for example. If you've identified something in the sentence that you're absolutely sure is incorrect, the answer that addresses that problem is the one you want.
- Never choose an answer that introduces an error, changes the meaning of the sentence, or leaves out necessary information. It is sometimes difficult to notice these new errors, especially in questions involving sentence combining and sentence revising.
- Be sure you are familiar with the meaning of the terms used in this section, such as *change, insert, delete, move, combine, clarified, organization, rewrite,* and *transition.* Your practice with this book will make you comfortable with them.
- The questions that follow, and those in the practice tests will give you an idea of the types of questions on this section of the exam, and the answers will offer more strategies for dealing with each type.
- Be sure to check as you work that your answers are in the correct space on the answer sheet. The fact that the answer choice letters alternate between A, B, C, D and F, G, H, J helps you to keep track of where you are.
- Don't forget to use the positive approach. Look for questions you can get right. Don't get stuck. Come back to the difficult questions. But never leave a question without at least taking a guess.

Suggested Approach with Sample Passages and Questions

Review the sample passages and answer the questions. Pay special attention to the suggested approaches and things to watch for as you read the answer explanations.

Short Sample Passage

Sean has written this report for his physical education class. As part of a peer conference, you have been asked to read the report and think about what suggestions you would make. When you finish reading the report, answer the questions that follow.

Lifelong Exercise

(1) Exercise isn't just for the young. (2) It should be part of you're life from toddlerhood to old age. (3) Whether you are young, middle aged, or elderly, exercise builds the muscle and stamina you need to engage in many physical activities. (4) Exercise helps to keep weight in a healthy range. (5) Exercise also helps the lungs and heart function at their best. (6) Lack of exercise, on the other hand, leads to inability to do the things you want to do and possibly bad health—such as respiratory problems, heart disese, diabetes, and bone loss. (7) It might feel good for the moment to be a couch potato or to spend hours playing video games, but in the long run, you'll regret it.

Multiple-Choice Questions on the Short Sample Passage

> **S-1** What change, if any, should be made in sentence 2?
>
> **A** Change *should be* to **should have been**
> **B** Change *you're* to **your**
> **C** Insert a comma after **toddlerhood**
> **D** Make no change

(2) It should be part of **you're** life from toddlerhood to old age.

This question covers **grammar and word choice—homonyms.** It tests your knowledge of the difference between the contraction *you're* (meaning *you are*) and the possessive form *your* (meaning *belonging to you*). In this sentence, *your* is correct—the *life* belongs to you. The correct answer is **B.**

> **S-2** What is the most effective way to combine sentences 4 and 5?
>
> **F** Exercise helps to keep weight in a healthy range and to allow the lungs and heart to function at their best.
> **G** It helps weight and heart and lungs healthy.
> **H** Exercise helps to keep weight in a healthy range, it also helps the lungs and heart function at their best.
> **J** Exercise keeps weight in a healthy range and keeps the lungs and heart functioning.

(4) **Exercise helps** to keep weight in a healthy range. (5) **Exercise** also **helps** the lungs and heart function at their best.

This question covers **sentence combining—wordiness.** The word *Exercise* begins both sentences 4 and 5 (which means that *helps* is also repeated), and the second one could effectively be eliminated by the change given in choice **F.** Choice **G** is incorrect because there is no clear reference for the *It* and because a word such as *keep* is missing—It helps *keep* weight. . . . Choice **H** is wrong because it connects two sentences with a comma rather than a semicolon. Choice

J is grammatically correct, although it unnecessarily repeats the word *keeps,* but it changes the meaning of the original sentence, saying exercise definitely does these things rather than *helps* to do them. The correct answer is **F.**

S-3	What change, if any, should be made in sentence 6?
A	Change *inability* to **unability**
B	Change *possibly* to **posibly**
C	Change *disese* to **disease**
D	Make no change

---

(6) Lack of exercise, on the other hand, leads to inability to do the things you want to do and possibly bad health—such as respiratory problems, heart disese, diabetes, and bone loss.

This question tests **mechanics—spelling.** *Disease* is correct. Notice that choices **A** and **B** also test spelling here. Often, though, the other answer choices will suggest different sorts of problems that might be present in the sentence. The correct answer is **C.**

Sample Passage 1

Carla's social studies teacher has asked her students to write a report about a crime that involves modern technology. Carla has chosen to write about identity theft. As part of a peer-editing conference, you have been asked to read Carla's draft and to think about the corrections and improvements she should make. When you finish reading the report, answer the questions that follow.

Identity Theft

(1) Technological advances have made it easier for criminals to commit fraud, vandalize, and steal. (2) Copying technology allows counterfeiters to much more quickly reproduce currancy than they did when they had to painstakingly make highly detailed metal plates. (3) Computer vandalism is rampant. (4) Hackers worm their way into business and government computers causing havoc and set loose viruses that fly around the world at digital speed and invade everyone's computers, destroying important data. (5) Computer scams that get people to send their personal information are everywhere. (6) And theft is now possible and easy through computer scams.

(7) At the least, criminals used the information and buy an item or two with someone else's credit card or make a week's worth of phone calls with someone else's cell phone information. (8) At worst, they steal a person's very identity.

(9) What is identity theft. (10) It is the taking of someone's identifying information for the fraudulent purposes of obtaining service, credit, or merchandise. (11) The identity thief really needs only your date of birth your complete name, and your Social Security number. (12) With these pieces of information, the thief can often apply for credit, take money out of your bank accounts, or apply for a new bank account using your name and transfer money out of your real account into the bogus new one. (13) Thieves, if they can, will go even farther if they can get hold of your credit card numbers, your bank, investment, and on-line account passwords. (14) They may also get copies of your birth certificate and set up whole lives for themselves, using your name.

(15) Too little attention has been paid to this by law enforcement authorities and too few stiff penalties have been given to those who are caught at it. (16) Consequently, it is a relatively risk free crime and if you are a victim, you can find yourself spending thousands of dollars and months and sometimes years of your time digging yourself out of the chaos the thief has caused and repairing your credit standing. (17) So its important to be aware of the threat and to take precautions. (18) Never give personal information over the Internet if you can avoid it. (19) Shred your personal documents, including credit card receipts and bank statements, before throwing them in the trash, and check your credit reports with the major Credit Reporting companies at least once a year to be sure no one is tampering with your name, information, and reputation.

Multiple-Choice Questions on Passage 1

32 What change, if any, should be made in sentence 1?
F Change *have made it* to **have made those**
G Change *have made it* to **have made advances**
H Change *have made it* to **had been making it**
J Make no change

(1) Technological advances have made it easier for criminals to commit fraud, vandalize, and steal.

The sentence as given is correct and clear. Sometimes the option *Make no change* is the best one. In a sentence like this, one that has a series of three items (*commit . . . vandalize . . . steal*), you should pay attention to whether the series is parallel, but in this case, it is. The correct answer is **J.**

33 What change, if any, should be made in sentence 2?
A Change *allows* to **allow**
B Change *currancy* to **currency**
C Change *than* to **then**
D Make no change

(2) Copying technology allows counterfeiters to much more quickly reproduce currancy than they did when they had to painstakingly make highly detailed metal plates.

Sentence 2 tests **mechanics—spelling.** *Currency* (paper money) is correct. Choices **A** and **C** introduce new errors. Both *allows* (which agrees with the singular *technology*) and *than* are correct. The correct answer is **B.**

34 What is the most effective way to improve the organization of the first paragraph (sentences 1–6)?
F Delete sentence 3
G Move sentence 4 so that it follows sentence 1
H Move sentence 6 so that it begins the first paragraph
J Move sentence 5 so that it begins the second paragraph

(1) Technological advances have made it easier for criminals to commit fraud, vandalize, and steal. (2) Copying technology allows counterfeiters to much more quickly reproduce currancy than they did when they had to painstakingly make highly detailed metal plates. (3) Computer vandalism is rampant. (4) Hackers worm their way into business and government computers causing havoc and set loose viruses that fly around the world at digital speed and invade everyone's computers, destroying important data. **(5) Computer scams that get people**

to send their personal information are everywhere. (6) And theft is now possible and easy through computer scams.

(7) At the least, criminals used **the information** and buy an item or two using someone else's credit card or make a week's worth of phone calls using someone else's cell phone information. (8) At worst, they steal a person's very identity.

This question tests **organization—sequence.** Sentence 5 speaks of getting people to send personal *information,* the topic of the second paragraph. So sentence 5 would most sensibly begin that paragraph. Sentence 3 introduces a shift in topic to *vandalism,* so it shouldn't be deleted (**F**). Sentence 4 appropriately follows sentence 3 because it goes on to discuss a type of vandalism, so it shouldn't be moved (**G**). Sentence 6, beginning with *And,* would make no sense at the beginning of the paragraph (**H**). The correct answer is **J.**

---

35 What change, if any, should be made to sentence 7?

    A Change *used* to **use**
    B Change *else's* to **elses**
    C Change *cell* to **sell**
    D Make no change

---

(7) At the least, criminals **used** the information and **buy** an item or two with someone else's credit card or **make** a week's worth of phone calls with someone else's cell phone information.

This question tests **verb forms—shifts of tense.** The present tense verb *use* is correct here, rather than the past tense *used.* The other verbs in the sentence are in the present tense (*buy, make*), and this one should agree with them. The correct answer is **A.**

---

36 What is the most effective way to rewrite the ideas in sentences 9 and 10?

    F What is identity theft; it is the taking of someone's identifying information for the fraudulent purposes of obtaining service, credit, or merchandise.
    G Identity theft is the taking of someone's identifying information for the fraudulent purposes of obtaining service, credit, or merchandise.
    H Identity theft, the taking of someone's identifying information for the fraudulent purposes of obtaining service, credit, or merchandise.
    J Identity theft is the taking of someone's identifying information for the fraudulent purpose of obtaining service, or to obtain credit, or obtaining merchandise.

---

(9) What is identity **theft.** (10) It is the taking of someone's identifying information for the fraudulent purposes of obtaining service, credit, or merchandise.

This question covers **sentence structure—improving style and mechanics—punctuation—end of sentence.** Sentence 9 is a rhetorical question—that is, it asks a question only so the writer can answer it. In addition to the fact that asking a rhetorical question often isn't an effective writing technique, this question lacks a needed question mark. Choice **G** deletes the question and substitutes *Identity theft* for *It,* making the sentence clear. There are errors in all of the other choices. Choice **F** has no question mark and instead uses an incorrect semicolon. Choice **H** is a sentence fragment; it has no main verb. Choice **J** is wordy and is not parallel in the use of *obtaining, to obtain,* and *obtaining.* The correct answer is **G.**

---

37 What change, if any, should be made in sentence 11?

    A Change *thief* to **theft**
    B Change *needs* to **need**
    C Insert a comma after *birth*
    D Change *Social* to **social**

---

(11) The identity thief really needs only your date of **birth your** complete name, and your Social Security number.

This question covers **mechanics—punctuation**—the **comma**. A comma is needed after *birth* in the series of three things—*birth, . . . name, . . . number.* Both *Social* and *Security* should be capitalized (making choice **D** incorrect). The correct answer is **C**.

---

38 What change, if any, should be made in sentence 15?

    F   Change *Too* to **To**

    G   Change *attention* to **attenshun**

    H   Change *this by* to **this crime by**

    J   Make no change

---

(15) Too little attention has been paid to **this** by law enforcement authorities and too few stiff penalties have been given to those who are caught at **it.**

This question covers **pronouns—clarity of reference.** The word *this* in sentence 15 is not clear because there is no word that *this* refers to, so the reader would ask *this what?* You need to add a word to which *this* refers, and *crime* (or another word with a similar meaning) is what is meant here. Also, in this sentence, the word *it* is a problem because it also has nothing to refer to. Adding *crime* clears up that problem as well. The correct answer is **H.**

---

39 What change, if any, should be made in sentence 16?

    A   Delete the comma after *Consequently*

    B   Insert a comma after *crime*

    C   Change *thousands* to **thousand's**

    D   Make no change

---

(16) Consequently, it is a relatively risk free **crime and** if you are a victim, you can find yourself spending thousands of dollars and months and sometimes years of your time digging yourself out of the chaos the thief has caused and repairing your credit standing.

This question tests **sentence structure—run-on sentences and mechanics—punctuation—comma.** Sentence 16 is a compound sentence, and the two independent clauses need to be separated by a comma before the *and* that joins them (*risk free crime, and if you are*). The correct answer is **B.**

---

40 What change, if any, should be made in sentence 17?

    F   Change *So* to **And so**

    G   Change *its* to **it's**

    H   Change *precautions* to **percautions**

    J   Make no change

---

(17) So **its** important to be aware of the threat and to take precautions.

This question covers **grammar and usage—word choice—homonyms.** The contraction *it's* (meaning *it is*) is correct here, not the possessive *its* (meaning *belonging to it*). There's no reason to add the *And* at the beginning of the sentence, which is clear as originally written. The correct answer is **G.**

---

41 What change, if any, should be made in sentence 19?

    A   Change *Shred* to **Shredding**

    B   Delete the comma after *documents*

    C   Change *Credit Reporting* to **credit reporting**

    D   Change *no one is* to **they are**

---

(19) Shred your personal documents, including credit card receipts and bank statements, before throwing them in the trash, and check your credit reports with the major **Credit Reporting** companies at least once a year to be sure no one is tampering with your name, information, and reputation.

This question tests your understanding of **mechanics–capitalization**. *Credit Reporting* is not the name of a company; that is, it isn't a proper noun or proper adjective. So it should not be capitalized. Choice **A** would make the first sentence of the compound sentence a fragment. The comma is necessary after documents (choice **B**) to set off the phrase *including credit card receipts and bank statements*. The correct answer is **C**.

Sample Passage 2

Brandon's English teacher asked her students to write a report on the life of a twentieth-century author whose books they enjoy reading but whose works they haven't studied in class. Brandon decided to write his report on author Stephen King.

Scary Stuff

(1) Stephen King is a prolific writer of novels, screen plays, short stories, and nonfiction. (2) He was born in Portland, Maine, in 1947. (3) Although he has spent most of his life and lived mostly in Maine, in childhood he lived briefly in Indiana and Connecticut. (4) He attended the University of Maine and graduated with a bachelor's degree in English in 1970.

(5) He met his future wife, Tabitha Spruce, at college, and they were married in 1971. (6) King taught English at Hampden Academy in Hampden, Maine, for several years. (7) During this time he sold stories to men's magazines. (8) His novel *Carrie* was accepted and published by Doubleday in 1973. (9) The success hugely of *Carrie* allowed King to pursue his writing full time.

(10) Since then King has published over forty best-selling books. (11) Some were written under the pseudonym of Richard Bachman. (12) Some of his popular novels include *'Salem's Lot, The Shining, Cujo, The Dead Zone, Fire Starter,* and *Misery.* (13) Many of his books will be made into movies, including the Oscar-winning *Green Mile.* (14) This book was originaly published in six parts, and King was often compared with Dickens, who also wrote novels serialized in magazines. (15) King has also produced a series of novels titled *The Dark Tower.* (16) The final book or books in this series have not yet been written. (17) In addition, King has written materials directly for the screen, including the acclaimed *Shawshank Redemption.*

(18) King is known as a "horror" novelist, he doesn't usually write about the standard "ghosts and goblins and nasty creatures" that we often associate with "horror." (19) He often finds what's frightening in everyday things. (20) This output has slowed somewhat since he was involved in a terrible car accident in 1999, when a van hit him as he walked along the road near his house. (21) But their is a happy note in that he does continue to write, a fact that pleases his fans. (22) He has been recognized as an important and talented author, Joyce Carol Oates introduced him, when he spoke at

Princeton University, as a "literary/cultural phenomenon" and "the best-selling writer on earth." (23) She went on to say, "Like all great writers of Gothic horror, Stephen King is both a storyteller and an inventor of startling images and metaphors, which linger long in the memory and would seem to spring from a collective, unconscious, and thoroughly domestic-American soil."

Multiple-Choice Questions on Passage 2

---

42 What is the most effective way to combine the ideas in sentences 1 and 2?

   F Stephen King, a prolific writer of novels, screen plays, short stories, and nonfiction, was born in Portland, Maine, in 1947.

   G Stephen King is a prolific writer of novels, screenplays, short stories, and nonfiction, he was born in Portland, Maine, in 1947.

   H Stephen King became a prolific writer of novels, screenplays, short stories, and nonfiction when he was born in Portland, Maine, in 1947.

   J Stephen King is a prolific writer; he wrote novels, screen plays and short stories and also nonfiction; Stephen King was born in Portland, Maine, in 1947.

---

(1) Stephen King is a prolific writer of novels, screen plays, short stories, and nonfiction. (2) He was born in Portland, Maine, in 1947.

This question tests your understanding of **sentence structure—sentence combining—improving style.** Choice **F** smoothly combines the sentences and correctly separates the information *a prolific writer . . . nonfiction* from the main sentence with commas. Choice **G** incorrectly separates two sentences (where there is no conjunction) with a comma. **H** changes the meaning of the sentences, suggesting that King became a writer at the time he was born. **J** is wordier than the original and doesn't effectively combine the ideas. The correct answer is **F.**

---

43 What change should be made in sentence 3?

   A Change *briefly* to **breifly**

   B Delete the comma after *Maine*

   C Change *has spent* to **will spend**

   D Delete *and lived mostly*

---

(3) Although he **has spent most of his life** and **lived mostly** in Maine, in childhood he lived briefly in Indiana and Connecticut.

This question covers **sentence structure—redundancy.** The phrase *and lived mostly* is redundant; it repeats information already given by the phrase *has spent most of his life.* The spelling *briefly* is correct, as is the comma after *Maine* and the verb tense of *has spent,* rather than the future *will spend,* which changes the meaning of the sentence. The correct answer is **D.**

---

44 What change, if any, should be made in sentence 9?

   F Insert a comma after *Carrie*

   G Change *allowed* to **had allowed**

   H Change *success hugely* to **huge success**

   J Make no change

---

(9) The success **hugely** of *Carrie* allowed King to pursue his writing full time.

This question covers **grammar and usage—parts of speech— adjectives versus adverbs.** The adjective *huge,* not the adverb *hugely,* is needed here to modify the noun *success.* The other two changes introduce an error. The correct answer is **H.**

---

45 What change, if any, should be made in sentence 13?

    A   Change *his* to **their**

    B   Change *will be* to **have been**

    C   Change the comma after *movies* to a semicolon

    D   Make no change

---

(13) Many of his books **will be** made into movies, including the Oscar-winning *Green Mile.*

This question covers **grammar and usage—verb forms—appropriate time in context.** The future tense of *will be* makes no sense in this sentence. If *Green Mile* has won an Oscar, it has already been made into a movie. The possessive pronoun *his* is correct, referring to King's books, and changing the comma after *movies* to a semicolon would create a sentence fragment. The correct answer is **B.**

---

46 Brandon wants to add this sentence to the third paragraph (sentences 10–17):

That may be because he wrote so quickly he feared his readers would think he wasn't taking enough time to write carefully.

Where should this sentence be inserted?

    F   After sentence 11

    G   After sentence 12

    H   After sentence 14

    J   At the end of the paragraph

---

(10) Since then King has published over thirty best-selling books (11) Some were written under the **pseudonym** of Richard **Bachman.** (12) Some of his popular novels include *'Salem's Lot, The Shining, Cujo, The Dead Zone, Fire Starter,* and *Misery.* (13) Many of his books will be made into movies, including the Oscar-winning *Green Mile.* (14) This book was originally published in six parts, and King was often compared with Dickens, who also wrote novels serialized in magazines. (15) King has also produced a series of novels titled *The Dark Tower.* (16) The final book or books in this series have not yet been written. (17) In addition, King has written materials directly for the screen, including the acclaimed *Shawshank Redemption.*

This question tests your understanding of **organization—sequence.** The added sentence gives a reason that an author might use a pseudonym, an alias, rather than his or her own name, on some books. So it logically goes after sentence 11, which talks about the pseudonym Richard Bachman. The correct answer is **F.**

---

47 What change, if any, should be made in sentence 14?

    A   Change *originaly* to **originally**

    B   Change *King* to **it**

    C   Change *magazines* to **magazine's**

    D   Make no change

---

(14) This book was **originaly** published in six parts, and King was often compared with Dickens, who also wrote novels serialized in magazines.

This question tests your understanding of **mechanics—spelling.** The correct spelling is *originally.* If *King* were changed to *it,* the sentence would say that the book (a thing) was compared to Dickens (a person), which would not be correct. The correct answer is **A.**

---

48 What word should be added at the beginning of sentence 18?

    F If

    G However

    H Because

    J Although

---

(18) King is known as a "horror" **novelist, he** doesn't usually write about the standard "ghosts and goblins and nasty creatures" that we often associate with "horror."

This question covers **sentence structure—run-on sentences and organization—transitions.** As it stands, sentence 18 is two sentences incorrectly connected by a comma. Adding *Although* makes a subordinate clause, which is correctly followed by the comma. Also, *Although* makes sense here—although King is known as a horror writer, he doesn't use the standard ghosts and so forth. *If, However,* and *Because* don't make sense in this context. The correct answer is **J.**

---

49 How can the meaning of sentence 20 be clarified?

    A Change *This* to **The writer's**

    B Change *has slowed* to **has deteriorated**

    C Change *him* to **it**

    D Delete *as he walked*

---

(20) **This output** has slowed somewhat since he was involved in a terrible car accident in 1999, when a van hit him as he walked along the road near his house.

This question covers **grammar and usage—pronouns—clarity of reference and sentence structure—awkwardness—unclear meaning.** It is impossible to be sure what the vague *This output* refers to—it could be just the ghosts and goblins referred to in sentence 18 or the everyday things mentioned in sentence 19 or something else. Adding *writer's* makes it clear that the total of the writer's output has slowed, which makes sense given the car accident. The correct answer is **A.**

---

50 What change, if any, should be made in sentence 21?

    F Change *But* to **And**

    G Change *their* to **there**

    H Change *fans* to **fans'**

    J Make no change

---

(21) But **their** is a happy note in that he does continue to write, a fact that pleases his fans.

This question covers **grammar and usage—word choice—homonyms.** The possessive *their* is the wrong word for the sense of this sentence. *There* is correct. The correct answer is **G.**

---

51 What change, if any, should be made in sentence 22?

    A Delete *been*

    B Change the comma after *author* to a semicolon

    C Change *University* to **university**

    D Make no change

---

(22) He has been recognized as an important and talented **author, Joyce** Carol Oates introduced him, when he spoke at Princeton University, as a "literary/cultural phenomenon" and "the best-selling writer on earth."

This question tests your understanding of **mechanics—semicolons and sentence structure—run-on sentences.** The two independent sentences are incorrectly joined by a comma. It should be a semicolon. Deleting *been* changes the meaning of the sentence. *University* should be capitalized as part of the proper name *Princeton University.* The correct answer is **B.**

Introduction to the Mathematics Test

The Mathematics Grade 11 Exit Examination consists of sixty (60) questions, most of which will be four-part (4) multiple-choice questions. The multiple-choice answer choices are alternatively labeled **A, B, C, D,** or **F, G, H, J.** "Not Here" may be used as a fourth answer choice in some multiple-choice questions. A few questions will be open-ended griddable questions. For this question type, you will be given an eight-column grid to record and bubble in your answer.

Although you do not have a time limit on this test, the suggested time is two (2) hours.

Mathematics Chart

The Mathematics Chart will have a measurement conversion chart on the front and a chart of formulas on the back. Make sure you understand the conversions and are familiar with the formulas.

The front of the Mathematics Chart will have two rulers. The ruler on the left side of the page will be in metric form and the ruler on the right side of the page will be in customary form. Be careful to use the proper ruler in answering a question.

Two pages (actually two sides of a page) that are similar to this will appear on your Mathematics Test:

Mathematics Chart

LENGTH

Metric	Customary
1 kilometer = 1000 meters	1 mile = 1760 yards
1 meter = 100 centimeters	1 mile = 5280 feet
1 centimeters = 10 millimeters	1 yard = 3 feet
	1 foot = 12 inches

CAPACITY AND VOLUME

Metric	Customary
1 liter = 1000 milliliters	1 gallon = 4 quarts
	1 gallon = 128 ounces
	1 quart = 2 pints
	1 pint = 2 cups
	1 cup = 8 ounces

MASS AND WEIGHT

Metric	Customary
1 kilogram = 1000 grams	1 ton = 2000 pounds
1 gram = 1000 milligrams	1 pound = 16 ounces

TIME

1 year = 365 days

1 year = 12 months

1 year = 52 weeks

1 week = 7 days

1 day = 24 hours

1 hour = 60 minutes

1 minute = 60 seconds

Centimeters

Inches

Mathematics Chart

Perimeter	rectangle	$P = 2l + 2w$ or $P = 2(l + w)$
Circumference	circle	$C = 2\pi r$ or $C = \pi d$
Area	rectangle	$A = lw$ or $A = bh$
	triangle	$A = \frac{1}{2} bh$ or $A = \frac{bh}{2}$
	trapezoid	$A = \frac{1}{2} (b_1 + b_2)h$ or $A = \frac{(b_1 + b_2)h}{2}$
	circle	$A = \pi r^2$
Surface Area	cube	$S = 6s^2$
	cylinder (lateral)	$S = 2\pi rh$
	cylinder (total)	$S = 2\pi rh + 2\pi r^2$ or $S = 2\pi r(h + r)$
	cone (lateral)	$S = \pi rl$
	cone (total)	$S = \pi rl + \pi r^2$ or $S = \pi r(l + r)$
	sphere	$S = 4\pi r^2$
Volume	prism or cylinder	$V = Bh*$
	pyramid or cone	$V = \frac{1}{3} Bh*$
	sphere	$V = \frac{4}{3} \pi r^3$

B represents the area of the Base of a solid figure.

Pi	π	$\pi \approx 3.14$ or $\pi \approx \frac{22}{7}$
Pythagorean Theorem		$a^2 + b^2 = c^2$
Distance Formula		$d = \sqrt{(x_2 - x_1)^2 + (y_2 - y_1)^2}$
Slope of a Line		$m = \frac{y_2 - y_1}{x_2 - x_1}$
Midpoint Formula		$M = \left(\frac{x_2 + x_1}{2}, \frac{y_2 + y_1}{2} \right)$
Quadratic Formula		$x = \frac{-b \pm \sqrt{b^2 - 4ac}}{2a}$
Slope-Intercept Form of an Equation		$y = mx + b$
Point-Slope Form of an Equation		$y - y_1 = m(x - x_1)$
Standard Form of an Equation		$Ax + By = C$
Simple Interest Formula		$I = prt$

Strategies for the Mathematics Test

Before you take a careful look at the objectives with sample problems, let's review some specific test-taking strategies for the Mathematics Test. These strategies can be very helpful in solving a problem.

Circle or Underline. Take advantage of being allowed to mark on the test booklet by always underlining or circling what you are looking for. This will ensure that you are answering the right question.

Pull Out Information. "Pulling" information out of the word problem structure can often give you a better look at what you are working with; therefore, you gain additional insight into the problem.

Work Forward. If you quickly see the method to solve the problem, then do the work. Work forward.

Work Backward. In some instances, it will be easier to work from the answers. Do not disregard this method because it will at least eliminate some of the choices and could give you the correct answer.

Eliminate. From initial information, or using common sense, you may be able to eliminate some of the answers. If you can eliminate an answer, mark it out immediately in the question booklet.

Use Your Calculator. Some questions will need to be completely worked out. If you don't see a fast method but do know that you could compute the answer, use your calculator. You should be provided a graphing calculator at the exam site.

Substitute Simple Numbers. Substituting numbers for variables can often be an aid to understanding a problem. Remember to substitute simple numbers, since you have to do the work.

Use 10 or 100. Some problems may deal with percent or percent change. If you don't see a simple method for working the problem, try using the values of 10 or 100 and see what you get.

Be Reasonable. Sometimes you will immediately recognize a simple method to solve a problem. If this is not the case, try a reasonable approach and then check the answers to see which one is most reasonable.

Sketch a Diagram. Sketching diagrams or simple pictures can also be very helpful in problem solving because the diagram may tip off either a simple solution or a method for solving the problem.

Mark in Diagrams. Marking in or labeling diagrams as you read the questions can save you valuable time. Marking can also give you insight into how to solve a problem because you will have the complete picture clearly in front of you.

Approximate. If it appears that extensive calculations are going to be necessary to solve a problem, check to see how far apart the choices are and then approximate. The reason for checking the answers first is to give you a guide to how freely you can approximate.

Glance at the Choices. Some problems may not ask you to solve for a numerical answer or even an answer including variables. Rather, you may be asked to set up the equation or expression without doing any solving. A quick glance at the answer choices will help you know what is expected.

Graphing Calculators

The TAKS Mathematics Test allows the use of graphing calculators, and you should be provided one at the test site. Even though no question will require the use of a calculator—that is, each question can be answered without a calculator—in some instances, using a calculator will save you valuable time.

You should

- Check for a shortcut to any problem that seems to involve much computation. But use your calculator if it will be time effective. If there appears to be too much computation or the problem seems impossible without the calculator, you're probably doing something wrong.

- Before doing an operation, check the number that you keyed in on the display to make sure that you keyed in the right number. You may wish to check each number as you key it in.

- Make sure that you clear the calculator after each problem. You may need to clear your calculator as you work a problem to go on to the next part; if this is the case, be sure to write down your answer before you go on to the next step.

Take advantage of using a calculator on the test. Learn to use a calculator efficiently by practicing. As you approach a problem, first focus on how to solve that problem and then decide if the calculator will be helpful. Remember, a calculator can save you time on some problems, but also remember that each problem can be solved without a calculator. A calculator will not solve a problem for you by itself. You must understand the problem first.

Sample Problems and Strategies

The content of the examination is based on ten (10) objectives. These objectives are summarized in the following sections and include three (3) or four (4) sample questions with explanations and strategies for each one.

Objective 1: Functional Relationships

The topics included are:

- Linear and quadratic functions
- Equations, inequalities
- Linear equation forms
- Representations of functional relationships
- Dependent and independent quantities

The foundations of Objective 1 are formed from the concepts of patterns, relationships, and algebraic thinking.

---

1 Ms. Green invests a total of $8,000 in two certificates of deposit (CD's). One CD has an annual rate of 5% and the other CD has annual rate of 6%. If x is the amount invested at 5% and y is the total amount of interest earned during the first year from both investments, which of the following is an equation that represents this total interest y?

    A $y = 0.05(8,000) + 0.06(8,000)x$
    B $y = 0.05(x) + 0.06(8,000 - x)$
    C $y = 0.06(8,000 + x) - 0.05(8,000)$
    D $y = 0.06(8,000) + 0.05(x - 8,000)$

First, make sure that you underline what you are looking for. In this case "an equation that represents this total interest y?" Next, pull out important information, in this case:

    $8,000 invested

    x is invested at 5%, the rest at 6%

    y is the total amount of interest from both

A total of $8,000 is invested. Since x is invested at 5% and the rest is invested at 6%, then $(8,000 - x)$ is invested at 6%. So the equation that represents this total interest y is

    $y = 0.05(x) + 0.06(8,000 - x)$

The correct answer is **B**.

2 The inequality $x + y < 4$ is best represented by which of the following graphs?

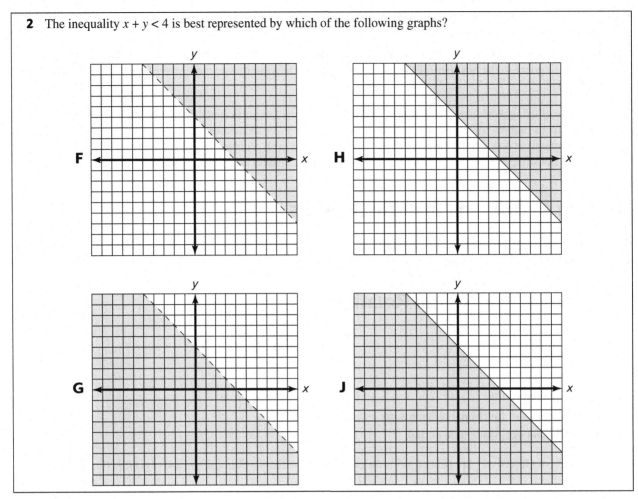

A careful look at the inequality $x + y < 4$ lets you know that the line must be dotted; otherwise, it would be "≤" (equal to or less than). So you can immediately eliminate choices H and J. Mark out choices **F** and **G** in your test booklet. The only difference between choices F and G is which side of the line is shaded. If you simply test the point (0,0), you see that it is a possible solution to the inequality, so it must be included in the shaded area. Since the sign is <, you may have realized that the area below should be shaded. The correct answer is **G.**

If you had been asked to actually plot this inequality from the beginning, you would first find the line by starting with $x + y = 4$ and plugging in numbers.

$$x + y = 4$$

x	y
0	4
2	2
4	0

You would plot this line (remember it is dotted), then test a point on one side of the line to see if it is a possible solution to the inequality $x + y < 4$. Shade the side that includes the possible solution. Fortunately, on this particular problem, all of this work was not necessary.

---

3 A taxi cab driver charges \$3.00 for the initial pickup and \$.50 for each mile traveled. The relationship can be expressed as the function $f(x) = 3 + .50x$ where $f(x)$ is the total amount collected by the driver. Which of the following is an independent quantity in this functional relationship?

    A   The total collected by the driver

    B   The amount charged for miles traveled

    C   The charge for the initial pickup

    D   The number of people in the cab

First, circle or underline the words "independent quantity." This is what you are looking for. Keep in mind that in this case "independent" means *does not rely on*—as opposed to "dependent," which means *relies on something else*. The charge for the initial pickup is the same each time. It is not dependent (does not rely on) on any other factors. Choices **A** and **B,** the total collected and the amount charged, are dependent on the miles traveled. Choice **D,** the number of people in the cab, is not a part of this functional relationship. The correct answer is **C.**

Objective 2: Properties and Attributes of Functions

The topics included are:

- Linear and quadratic functions
- Expressions or equations describing patterns
- Linear equation forms
- Simplify polynomial expressions
- Solve equations and inequalities

The foundations of Objective 2 are formed from the concepts of patterns, relationships, and algebraic thinking.

---

1 Which expression is equivalent to $2m(3m - 1) + (m + 1)(3m - 1)$?

    A $9m^2 - 1$

    B $9m^2 + 1$

    C $6m^2 + 3m - 1$

    D $9m^2 - 9m - 1$

This question asks you to simplify an expression. You could have worked it out completely, or you could have noticed that the distributive property would be helpful.

$$2m(3m - 1) + (m + 1)(3m - 1) = [2m + (m + 1)][(3m - 1)]$$

Using the distributive property

$$= (3m + 1)(3m - 1)$$

Next notice that this is the difference of two squares

$$= 9m^2 - 1$$

The correct answer is **A.**

You could have worked this problem as follows without using the distributive property:

$$2m(3m - 1) + (m + 1)(3m - 1) = 6m^2 - 2m + [(m + 1)(3m - 1)]$$
$$= 6m^2 - 2m + [3m^2 + 3m - m - 1]$$
$$= 6m^2 - 2m + [3m^2 + 2m - 1]$$
$$= 9m^2 - 1$$

This method of simplifying would also give you the correct answer, but requires more work.

2 Which of the following best describes the range represented in the graph below?

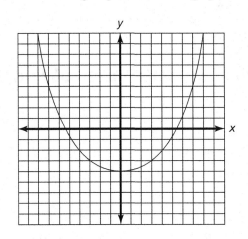

 F $x \geq 4$
 G $y \geq 4$
 H $2 \geq x \geq -2$
 J $2 \geq y \geq -2$

Focus on the range (the limit on y axis). If the question were about the domain, you would focus on the limit on the x-axis. Notice that the limit of the curve on the y-axis is –4. Nothing goes below –4, so the correct answer is **G.**

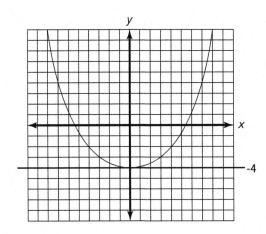

3 What is the area of the shaded region of the square that surrounds the rectangle?

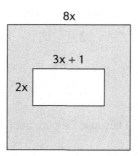

8x

3x + 1

2x

A $64x^2 - 8x$
B $58x^2 + 2x$
C $58x^2 - 2x$
D $64x^2 + 8x$

Note that you're looking for "area of shaded region." So you want to find the area of the large square and subtract the area of the small rectangle. Now find the area of the square by multiplying $8x$ times $8x$, since each side of a square is the same length. This gives $64x^2$. Next multiply $2x$ times $3x + 1$ to find the area of the rectangle. This gives $6x^2 + 2x$. Finally subtract the area of the rectangle from the area of the square as follows:

$$64x^2 - (6x^2 + 2x)$$
$$64x^2 - 6x^2 - 2x$$
$$58x^2 - 2x$$

So the correct answer is **C.** The most common mistake is choice **B,** since many people forget to take the negative sign through each term.

4 The number pattern shown below can continue infinitely.

   0, 1, 3, 7, 15, . . .

Which of the following expressions defines the sequence?

F $2n - 1$
G $2n + 1$
H $3n - 1$
J $3n + 1$

You could answer this question by working from the answer choices. That is, take each answer choice and plug in $n = 0$, $n = 1$, $n = 2$, and so on, to see if you get the same pattern.

$$2n - 1 = 2^0 - 1 = 1 - 1 = 0$$
$$2n - 1 = 2^1 - 1 = 2 - 1 = 1$$
$$2n - 1 = 2^2 - 1 = 4 - 1 = 3 \text{ and so on.}$$

This gives the proper pattern, so the correct answer is **F.**

You could have also approached the problem by first marking the pattern as follows:

$$\begin{array}{ccccc} 1 & 2 & 4 & 8 \\ \frown & \frown & \frown & \frown \\ 0, & 1, & 3, & 7, & 15,\ldots \end{array}$$

So the pattern is that each number is increasing by a power of 2.

$$2^0, 2^1, 2^2, \ldots$$

At this point you could eliminate choices **H** and **J** because they are not based on powers of 2. Then you would need to again plug in $n = 0$, $n = 1$, $n = 2$, and so on.

Objective 3: Linear Functions

The topics included are:

- Linear relationships in various forms
- Slope intercept form $y = mx + b$
- x- and y-intercepts
- Linear function and proportional change problems
- Direct variation

The foundations of Objective 3 are formed from the concepts of patterns, relationships, and algebraic thinking.

---

1 Two equations are each represented by lines on the grid. One line passes through the points (1,2) and (−2, −4). The other line passes through the points (−3, −2) and (0,0).

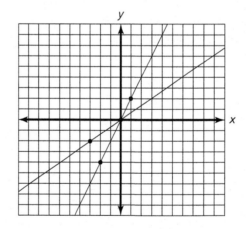

Which of the following pair of equations identifies the two lines?

A $y = -2x$ and $y = \left(-\dfrac{2}{3}\right)x + 1$

B $y = -2x$ and $y = \left(\dfrac{2}{3}\right)x$

C $y = 2x$ and $y = \left(\dfrac{2}{3}\right)x + 1$

D $y = 2x$ and $y = \left(\dfrac{2}{3}\right)x$

Do only as much work as necessary and eliminate answers whenever possible. Some insight into slope and y intercept would be very helpful. Remember that a positive slope goes up to the right and a negative slope goes down to the right. Keep in mind that the y intercept is where the line crosses the y-axis.

Now notice that each line above goes up to the right, so the slope of each line is positive. You could eliminate choices **A** and **B** since those equations have negative slopes (notice they're in slope intercept form $y = mx + b$ where m is the slope and b is the y intercept, so the slope is easy to spot). Next, eliminate choice **C** because the second equation has a y intercept of +1. The correct answer is **D.**

You could have gone through the steps of actually working out the equations of each line from the information given, but eliminating answer choices was much faster and easier.

---

2 If the amount of money varies directly with the number of investors, and if 40 people invest a total of $10,000, then approximately how many people will be necessary to have a total investment of $250,000?

   F   100 people
   G   625 people
   H   1,000 people
   J   4,000 people

Probably the easiest way to solve this problem is to set up a proportion as follows:

$$\frac{40}{10,000} = \frac{x}{250,000} \qquad \frac{[\text{number of people}]}{[\text{investment}]}$$

Solve by cross multiplying

$$40\,(250,000) = 10,000x$$
$$10,000,000 = 10,000x$$

Then divide by 10,000

$$\frac{10,000,000}{10,000} = \frac{10,000x}{10,000}$$

So $1,000 = x$. The correct answer is **H.**

Notice that this question says "approximately," so if you didn't remember that a proportion would work, you could use a reasonable approach to at least eliminate some choices. Your approach would be to check how much room you have between answers and then try to be reasonable in approximating from those answers. For example, if "40 people invest a total of $10,000" then choice **F,** 100 people would invest $250,000 is not reasonable. Eliminate choice **F.** Choice **J** is not reasonable since 4,000 is 100 times 40, and 100 times $10,000 is $1,000,000. Eliminate choice **J.** This could have helped you narrow down the answer choices to **G** and **H.**

---

3 What is the slope of the line identified by $3y = 4(x + 3)$?

   A   4
   B   3
   C $\frac{4}{3}$
   D $\frac{3}{4}$

To answer this "mechanical" question, simply change the equation into slope intercept form $y = mx + b$:

$$3y = 4(x + 3)$$
$$3y = 4x + 12$$

Next divide by 3, which leaves

$$y = \left(\frac{4}{3}\right)x + 12$$

So the slope is $\frac{4}{3}$. The correct answer is **C.**

Objective 4: Linear Equations and Inequalities

The topics included are:

- Linear relationships in various forms
- Equation of inequality necessary
- Solutions as a number or a range
- Reasonable solutions

The foundations of Objective 4 are formed from the concepts of patterns, relationships, and algebraic thinking.

---

1 Given the two equations below

$x + y = 6$ and $2x - y = 3$

Which of the following ordered pairs is the solution?

A (2,4)
B (5,1)
C (3,3)
D No solution

In this question you could either solve the system of equations or plug in the answer choices. Let's solve the system of equations.

First, combine the equations to eliminate a variable,

$$x + y = 6$$
$$\underline{2x - y = 3}$$
$$3x \quad\;\; = 9$$

Now dividing by 3 leaves $x = 3$.

Since $x = 3$, simply plug x into either equation and solve

$$x + y = 6$$
$$(3) + y = 6$$

So $y = 3$. The correct answer is **C**, (3,3).

The other method of plugging in the answers would go like this.

Since choices **A**, **B** and **C** each total 6, you would only need plug into the second equation to find the right answer.

Choice **A,** (2,4):

$$2(2) - (4) = 3$$
$$4 - 4 \neq 3$$

Eliminate choice **A.**

Choice **B,** (5,1):

$$2(5) - (1) = 3$$
$$10 - 1 \neq 3$$

Eliminate choice **B.**

Choice **C,** (3,3):

$$2(3) - (3) = 3$$
$$6 - 3 = 3$$

Choice **C** is correct.

Note that some questions could have the answer choice of "No solution," "No intersection" or "Not here," as a possible answer, although "No solution" is not the correct answer here.

---

2 Matt spent less than 20 minutes reading the newspaper. During that time Matt read x number of comic strips at 2 minutes each and y number of articles at 6 minutes each. Graph the inequality $2x + 6y < 20$ on the grid below.

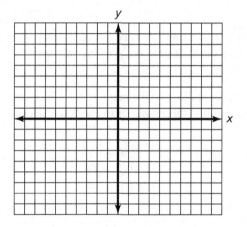

Which point represents a possible number of comic strips and articles that Matt could have read?

   F   (4, 2)
   G   (1, 3)
   H   (3, 2)
   J   (2, 3)

The graph of the inequality $2x + 6y < 20$ would look like this:

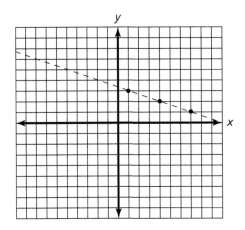

Remember to actually graph the inequality, use the equality $2x + 6y = 20$ and then find the possible values with the help of a simple chart. In this case you could actually divide the equation by 2, simplifying it to $x + 3y = 10$, then plug in values.

$$x + 3y = 10$$

x	y
1	3
4	2
7	1

Since the original inequality is $2x + 6y < 20$, the line would be dotted. You would shade below the line. Check this by testing the point (0,0) to see which part to shade. If (0,0) are possible values of the inequality, then you should shade the side that includes that point.

Now simply plot the points from the answer choices on the graph to see which one is in the shaded area. You could have actually plugged into the inequality to find the answer or to check the answer. The correct answer is **H,** (3,2).

Check as follows:

$$2(3) + 6(2) < 20$$
$$6 + 12 < 20$$
$$18 < 20$$

3 Tickets for the local high school football game were $3.50 for students with a student body card and $6.00 for all others. If 1,800 people attended the game and $7,800 was taken in at the gate, how many students with a student body card attended the game?

Record your answer and fill in the corresponding bubbles on the answer sheet. Be sure to use the correct place value.

				.			
⓪	⓪	⓪	⓪		⓪	⓪	⓪
①	①	①	①		①	①	①
②	②	②	②		②	②	②
③	③	③	③		③	③	③
④	④	④	④		④	④	④
⑤	⑤	⑤	⑤		⑤	⑤	⑤
⑥	⑥	⑥	⑥		⑥	⑥	⑥
⑦	⑦	⑦	⑦		⑦	⑦	⑦
⑧	⑧	⑧	⑧		⑧	⑧	⑧
⑨	⑨	⑨	⑨		⑨	⑨	⑨

Notice that this type of question requires you to bubble in the actual value. Also notice that you are looking for "how many students with student body cards attended the game."

Let's set up the two equations.

If x stands for the number of students with student body cards attending the game and y stands for all others, then the first equation would be

$$x + y = 1,800$$

The total number attending is 1,800.

Now considering the price for each, since x is $3.50 per ticket and y is $6.00 per ticket you would get the following equation

$$3.50x + 6y = 7,800$$

Solve this system of equations as follows. Your calculator can be helpful here.

$$x + y = 1,800$$
$$3.50x + 6y = 7,800$$

Multiplying the top equation by 6 gives

$$6x + 6y = 10,800$$
$$3.50x + 6y = 7,800$$

Now subtract the second equation from the first and you get

$$
\begin{aligned}
6.00x + 6y &= 10,800 \\
(-)\ 3.50x + 6y &= \ \ 7,800 \\
\hline
2.50x \qquad &= \ \ 3,000
\end{aligned}
$$

Next dividing by 2.50 gives

$$x = 120$$

So 120 students with student body cards attended the game.

Now carefully grid this answer as follows:

	1	2	0	.			
⓪	⓪	⓪	●		⓪	⓪	⓪
①	●	①	①		①	①	①
②	②	●	②		②	②	②
③	③	③	③		③	③	③
④	④	④	④		④	④	④
⑤	⑤	⑤	⑤		⑤	⑤	⑤
⑥	⑥	⑥	⑥		⑥	⑥	⑥
⑦	⑦	⑦	⑦		⑦	⑦	⑦
⑧	⑧	⑧	⑧		⑧	⑧	⑧
⑨	⑨	⑨	⑨		⑨	⑨	⑨

Objective 5: Quadratic and Other Nonlinear Functions

The topics included are:

- Laws of exponents
- Effects of changes on graphs of quadratic equations
- Conclusions from graphs of quadratic functions
- Solutions for quadratic equations

The foundations of Objective 5 are formed from the concepts of patterns, relationships, and algebraic thinking.

---

1 What is the y intercept of the graph of the equation $y = x^2 + 4x + 3$?

    A -3

    B -1

    C   3

    D   4

To find the y intercept, simply plug in 0 for x and solve.

$$y = x^2 + 4x + 3$$
$$y = (0)^2 + 4(0) + 3$$
$$y = 3$$

The correct answer is **C**.

---

2 For all nonnegative values of x, how is the graph of the equation $y = 3x^3$ affected when the equation is changed to $y = -3x^3$?

    F   The curve is now in quadrant IV instead of quadrant I.

    G   The x value doubles as the y value increases.

    H   The x value is always less than the y value.

    J   The graph is rotated 90° about the origin.

To answer this question you need to plug in values for x and find the value for y in each equation. Make a simple chart for each equation and plug in 0 for x, then 1 for x, then 2 for x, and so on.

$$y = 3x^3 \qquad\qquad y = -3x^3$$

x	y
0	0
1	3
2	24

x	y
0	0
1	-3
2	-24

If you plotted the points (0,0), (1,3), (2,24) for the first equation, you would see that the curve would be graphed in quadrant I (the upper right quadrant) where both coordinates are positive.

If you were to plot the points (0,0), (1,–3), (2,–24) for the second equation, you would see that the curve is graphed in quadrant IV (the lower right quadrant) where the x value is positive and the y value is negative. The correct answer is **F.**

---

3 What is the solution set for the equation $16(4x - 2)^2 = 64$?

   A {0,2}
   B {0,1}
   C {1,2}
   D {1,3}

You could work from the answers by simply plugging in each choice. Using this method you would see that 2 is not a solution, so you could eliminate choices **A** and **C.** If you plug in 3 you will see that it is also not a solution, so you could eliminate choice **D,** leaving choice **B** as the only possibility.

Or you could actually solve the quadratic equation.

$$16(4x - 2)^2 = 64$$

To solve the quadratic, first, divide each side of the equation by 16. This gives you

$$(4x - 2)^2 = 4$$

Next, take the square root of each side:

$$4x - 2 = 2 \ \text{ or } \ 4x - 2 = -2$$

Adding –2 to each side gives:

$$4x = 4 \ \text{ or } \ 4x = 0$$

So $x = 1$ or $x = 0$.

The correct answer is **B.**

You could have also solved as follows:

$$16(4x - 2)^2 = 64$$
$$(4x - 2)^2 = 4$$
$$16x^2 - 16x + 4 = 4$$
$$16x^2 - 16x = 0$$
$$16(x^2 - x) = 0$$
$$x^2 - x = 0$$
$$x(x - 1) = 0$$

So $x = 0$ or $x - 1 = 0$.

Objective 6: Geometric Relationships and Spatial Reasoning

The topics included are:

- Formal geometric terms
- Geometric concepts
- Geometric theorems and properties
- Similar figures
- Solving geometry problems

The foundations of Objective 6 are formed from the basic concepts of lower level geometry and special reasoning.

---

1 Taylor bought a 500-piece puzzle that is in the shape of a rectangle when all the pieces are correctly put together. If all the pieces of the puzzle are the same shape, which shape can the pieces NOT be?

   A   Rectangle

   B   Triangle

   C   Square

   D   Hexagon

Triangles can be put together to create rectangles, as can squares, and rectangles. There is no arrangement of hexagons that could make a rectangle. A closer look at the actual figures will make this evident.

      A   B   C   D

The correct answer is **D.**

---

2 Scott is cutting a square sandwich in half. The dimensions of the sandwich are 2 units × 2 units. If Scott cuts the sandwich diagonally from corner to corner, how long is the longest side of one half of the sandwich?

   F $\sqrt{3}$

   G   2

   H $2\sqrt{2}$

   J   4

Cutting a square in half diagonally creates two congruent, 45-45-90 triangles. The ratio of the sides of a 45-45-90 triangle is $1:1:\sqrt{2}$. When x represents the length of a leg of the triangle, $x\sqrt{2}$ equals the hypotenuse.

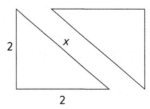

Since each side of the sandwich is 2 units, the longest side (hypotenuse) of the half sandwich is $2\sqrt{2}$. The correct answer is **H.**

3 Rectangle ABCD is graphed on the coordinate grid below

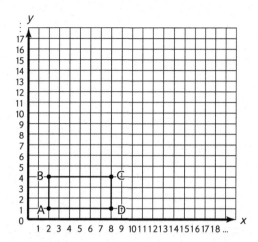

Which set of coordinates represents the vertices of a rectangle congruent to rectangle ABCD?

A (5,8), (5,11), (11,11), (11,8)

B (9,2), (9,7), (13,3), (13,8)

C (4,5), (4,7), (8,7), (8,5)

D (14,6), 14,9), (16,4), (16,11)

Quickly plot each set of coordinates.

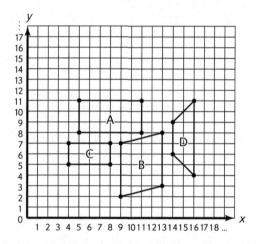

First notice that choices **B** and **D** are not rectangles, so you can eliminate them. You can probably spot that choice **A** creates a rectangle that looks exactly like rectangle ABCD, with the 4 corresponding sides equal in length to those in rectangle ABCD.

If the right answer isn't easy for you to spot from the coordinate grid, then find the length and width of the rectangle (which is 6 × 3). Now you can check the length and width of the two choices that are also rectangles, choices **A** and **C**. The correct answer is **A**; only choice **A** has the same dimensions as rectangle ABCD.

4 In the triangle below, CD is an angle bisector, angle ACD is 30°, and angle ABC is a right angle.

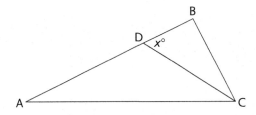

What is the measurement of angle *x* in degrees?

F 30°

G 45°

H 60°

J 75°

When you are given a diagram to work with, marking in that diagram as you read the question can save you valuable time. It can also give you insight into how to solve the problem because you will have the complete picture clearly in front of you.

Here, you should read the problem and mark as follows:

In the triangle above, CD is an angle bisector (*Stop and mark in the drawing*); angle ACD is 30° (*Stop and mark the drawing*); and angle ABC is a right angle (*Stop and mark the drawing*). What is the measurement of angle *x* in degrees? (*Stop and mark in or circle what you are looking for in the drawing.*)

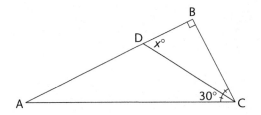

Now, with the drawing marked in, it is evident that, since angle ACD is 30°, angle BCD is also 30° because they are formed by an angle bisector (divides an angle into two equal parts). Since angle ABC is 90° (right angle) and angle BCD is 30°, then angle *x* is 60° because there are 180° in a triangle.

The correct answer is **H.**

Always mark in diagrams as you read descriptions and information about them. You should also circle, mark, or identify with a letter, the angle or line segment you are trying to find. This will give you a visual representation of what the question is asking you to look for.

Objective 7: Two- and Three-Dimensional Representations of Geometric Relationships and Shapes

The topics included are:

- Formal geometric terms
- Geometric concepts, properties, theorems, and definitions
- Solving geometric problems
- Representations of three-dimensional objects
- Representations on coordinate planes

The foundations of Objective 7 are formed from the basic concepts of lower level geometry and special reasoning.

1 Which of the following could be folded along the dotted lines to form a rectangular solid?

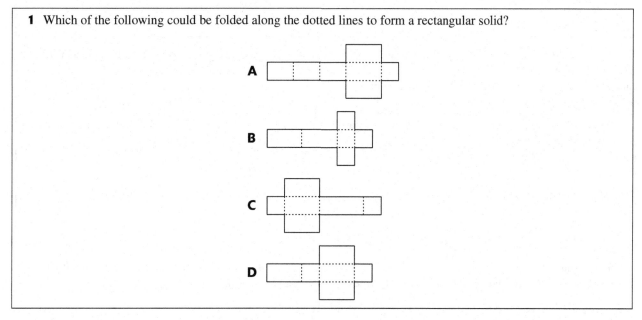

You should focus (or put an X) on the piece of each diagram that has the most parts connected to it. Then mentally fold the rest of the sides around the piece you marked, making it easier for you to spot the answer that will form a rectangular solid.

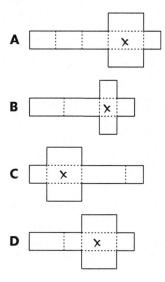

Notice that choice **D** folds perfectly into a rectangular solid.

---

2 Three different views of an object constructed with cubes are shown below. Each cube is the same size and has a volume of one cubic inch.

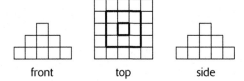

| front | top | side |

How many cubes are needed to construct the solid?

F 9
G 25
H 26
J 35

First you should carefully review each view of the solid to get a better understanding of how it is put together. You'll see that the bottom layer is made up of 25 cubes (5×5). The next layer is made up of 9 cubes (3×3). And the top is one cube. So the total number of cubes needed to build the solid is $25 + 9 + 1 = 35$. The correct answer is **J.**

---

3 The following pair of equations represents two parallel lines: $x = 3y + 2$ and $x = 3(2 + y)$. What is the value of their slopes?

A $-\dfrac{1}{2}$

B $\dfrac{1}{3}$

C 3

D 6

When an equation is in slope intercept form, $y = mx + b$, m is the slope of the line. Since the lines are parallel their slopes are the same. You should convert one of the lines to slope intercept form.

$$x = 3y + 2$$
$$\underline{-2 \qquad -2}$$
$$x - 2 = 3y$$

Now divide both sides by 3.

$$y = \frac{x}{3} - \frac{2}{3} \text{ or } y = \left(\frac{1}{3}\right)x - \frac{2}{3}$$

In this form it is clear that m (the slope value) $= \frac{1}{3}$. The correct answer is **B.**

---

4 Circle A has a center point at $(0,1)$ and a point B on the circumference at $(2,3)$. What is the circumference of the circle?

F $\pi\sqrt{2}$
G $2\sqrt{\pi}$
H $2\pi\sqrt{2}$
J $4\pi\sqrt{2}$

First sketch the circle and note the coordinates $(0,1)$ and $(2,3)$. You could use the graph paper provided in the back of the exam.

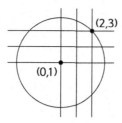

Next, find the distance from point A to point B. Using the information given, draw a triangle with segment AB as a hypotenuse. Once you find the length of AB, you will have the radius of circle A, and can then find the circumference. To find the length of the legs do the following:

$$(x_2 - x_1) = (2 - 0) = 2$$

$$(y_2 - y_1) = (3 - 1) = 2$$

You now have two legs measuring 2 units each.

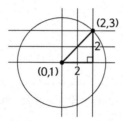

Using the Pythagorean theorem you can find that the hypotenuse, segment AB, equals $2\sqrt{2}$.

$$a^2 + b^2 = c^2$$

$$2^2 + 2^2 = c^2$$

$$4 + 4 = c^2$$

$$8 = c^2$$

$$\sqrt{8} = c$$

So $c = \sqrt{8}$, which can be simplified to $2\sqrt{2}$.

You may have spotted that since two of these sides are the same, and that you have a right angle, this is a 45-45-90 triangle. The ratio of the sides is $1:1:\sqrt{2}$. So you could have found the hypotenuse without using the Pythagorean theorem.

Remember that a line segment from the center of a circle to any point on the circumference is the radius (r). To find a circle's circumference you use the following formula

circumference = $2\pi r$

Now substitute $r = 2\sqrt{2}$ into the formula $c = 2\pi r$:

$$c = 2\pi \left(2\sqrt{2}\right)$$

Multiplying gives you $c = 4\pi\sqrt{2}$, which is the circumference.

The correct answer is **J.**

Objective 8: Concepts and Uses of Measurement and Similarity

The topics included are:

- Formal geometric terms
- Perimeter, area, volume
- Measurement
- Pythagorean Theorem
- Proportional reasoning and ratios
- Prisms, pyramids, spheres, cones and cylinders
- Geometric concepts, properties, theorems, formulas and definitions

The foundations of Objective 8 are formed from the basic concept of lower level measurement.

---

1 An extra-large pizza has a diameter of 2 ft. If the circular pizza is cut into 8 equal slices, what is the approximate area of two slices?

    A   0.78 ft.^{2}

    B   2ft.^{2}

    C   4 ft.^{2}

    D   6.28 ft.^{2}

You are looking for the "approximate area of two slices." Remember, sketching the figure can be helpful in giving you insight into the problem.

Let's sketch the figure first.

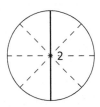

To find the area of the whole pizza, you use the formula $a = \pi r^2$, where a is the area and r is the radius. This formula is given on the Mathematics Chart at the front of the test.

Since r = half of the diameter and the diameter is 2 ft., you know that $r = 1$ ft. When you plug in the r value you find that the area of the whole pizza is approximately 3.14 ft.^{2} $(a = \pi r^2 = \pi (1)^2 = \pi)$.

Since you are only looking for the area of two slices, and you know there are 8 slices, you must divide the area of the whole pizza by 4. When you divide 3.14 ft.^{2} by 4 you will come out with approximately 0.78 ft.^{2}. You could have used your calculator here, but notice that only one answer choice is reasonable. The correct answer is **A**.

2 Use the ruler on the Mathematics Chart to measure the dimensions of the composite figure to the nearest tenth of a centimeter.

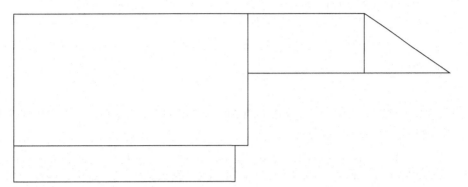

Which best represents the approximate perimeter of this composite figure?

F 20 cm

G 32 cm

H 40 cm

J 48 cm

In this case, since you are asked to find the perimeter in centimeters, you really need to only measure the distance around the outside of the composite figure.

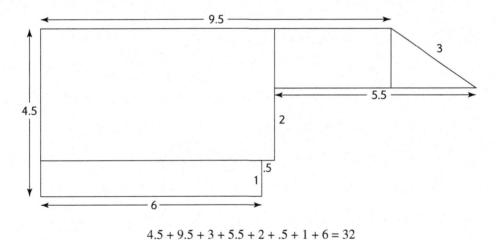

$$4.5 + 9.5 + 3 + 5.5 + 2 + .5 + 1 + 6 = 32$$

The correct answer is **G.**

If the question would have asked for the total area, you would have needed to measure the dimensions of each individual figure that make up the composite figure. You would have found the area of each and then found a total area. This would have been done in parts. But, the question asked for the perimeter, so *only* the outside measurement was necessary.

3 The radius of a small sphere was multiplied by a factor of 3 to create a larger sphere.

How does the volume of the larger sphere compare to the volume of the smaller sphere?

A It is $\frac{1}{3}$ the size.

B It is 3 times the size.

C It is 9 times the size.

D It is 27 times the size.

Since you are finding the volume of two spheres, you should use the equation $v = \frac{4}{3}\pi r^3$, where v is the volume and r is the radius. This formula is provided on the Mathematics Chart at the front of the test.

You should have recognized the scale factor and simply noticed that since r is cubed in the formula, 3 times the radius would be cubed for the volume, giving 27 times the volume of the smaller sphere. The correct answer is **D.**

Or, you could have solved each volume equation using $r = 1$ for the smaller sphere and then $r = 3$ for the larger sphere.

If you try $r = 1$, you get $v = \frac{4}{3}\pi(1)^3 = \frac{4}{3}\pi(1)$.

If you try $r = 3$, you get $v = \frac{4}{3}\pi(3)^3 = \frac{4}{3}\pi(27)$.

Before simplifying you can see that the second volume is 27 times the first.

4 On the map below, A Street and B Street are parallel. Also, 2nd St. and 3rd St. are parallel. Third Street is perpendicular to A Street. Ryan Blvd. intersects each of the streets as shown. All of the streets are straight line segments.

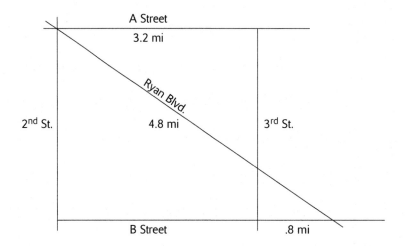

While traveling down Ryan Blvd., what is the distance between 3rd St. and B Street?

F .6 mi

G 1.2 mi

H 2.4 mi

J 2.8 mi

First, mark the distance you are looking for. Then make any marks on the map that will be helpful.

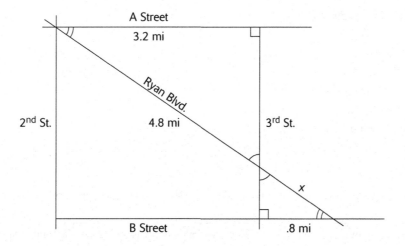

Notice the ratio of the corresponding sides of the two triangles formed so that you can set up the following proportion:

$$\frac{.8}{3.2} = \frac{x}{4.8}$$

The left side reduces:

$$\frac{1}{4} = \frac{x}{4.8}$$

Cross multiplying gives

$$4.8 = 4x$$

Next divide by 4:

$$1.2 = x$$

The correct answer is **G**.

You may have noticed originally from the dimensions given that the smaller triangle was $\frac{1}{4}$ the size of the larger one. From this you could have matched the corresponding parts and calculated $\frac{1}{4}$ or $4.8 = 1.2$.

Objective 9: Percents, Proportional Relationships, Probability and Statistics

The topics included are:

- Proportion
- Mean, mode, median, and range
- Match data on graphs
- Evaluate, predict, conclude using graphs
- Circle graph, bar graph, histogram
- Theoretical probability and experimental results

The foundations of Objective 9 are formed from the basic concepts of lower level probability and statistics.

---

1 Jamie bought a water gun marked at $12.56. When the sales tax was added on, the total cost of the water gun was $15.70. What was the sales tax rate to the nearest percent?

    A   20%

    B   23%

    C   25%

    D   30%

First you must subtract $12.56 from $15.70 to find the amount of sales tax that was added on. You now have the sales tax of $3.14 and you need to find what percentage of the marked price the tax is. You divide 3.14 by 12.56 and you now have 0.25 or 25%. The correct answer is **C.**

---

2 The chart below shows the amount of money collected during a school's magazine sale.

Magazine Sale Income				
Cost of magazine	$10	$12	$15	$19
Number Sold	18	19	5	5

Which of the following is the mode of the cost of the magazines sold during the magazine sale?

    F $5

    G $10

    H $12

    J $15

The mode is the cost that appears the most. Nineteen $12 magazines were sold. The correct answer is **H.**

---

3 Eight out of ten dentists surveyed recommended Popsodent toothpaste. Which of the following is a valid conclusion based on the information given?

    A   Two out of ten dentists recommend another brand of toothpaste.

    B   Popsodent is the best tasting toothpaste.

    C   More patients use Popsodent toothpaste than any other brand.

    D   At least one dentist surveyed could have recommended another brand.

The fact that "eight out of ten dentists surveyed recommended Popsodent toothpaste" does not tell us anything about the other dentists. They may not recommend any toothpaste; eliminate choice **A**. Choice **B**, taste is never addressed. For choice **C** to be a valid conclusion you would have to assume that patients follow the recommendations of their dentists. Also, what about patients who go to dentists other than those surveyed? Since two dentists didn't recommend Popsodent, they could have recommended another brand. The correct answer is **D**.

---

4 Union High School is planning to order yearbooks for the student body. The following chart shows the percentages of students in each class that usually order yearbooks.

Class	Percent
Freshman	40%
Sophomore	60%
Junior	85%
Senior	95%

Based on the information above, if there are 400 freshman and 500 sophomores, how many more sophomores than freshman will probably order yearbooks?

F 160
G 240
H 300
J Not here.

Since there are 500 sophomores and 60% of them usually order yearbooks, then 300 sophomores should order yearbooks (60% of 500). Since there are 400 freshman and 40% of them usually order yearbooks, then 160 freshman should order yearbooks (40% of 400). "How many more . . ." lets you know that you need the difference, so subtract $300 - 160 = 140$. This answer is not listed here, so **J** is the correct answer.

Objective 10: Underlying Processes and Mathematical Tools

The topics included are:

- Identify needed information
- Supply steps in problem solving
- Support for conclusions
- Match informal language to mathematical language and/or symbols
- Conclusions, examples, counterexamples

The foundations of Objective 10 are formed from the basic concepts of underlying processes and mathematical tools found in lower grade levels.

1 Hills Canyon is a small community that has 700 people living in it. In Hills Canyon 300 people have DSL Internet connections and 200 people have cable television. If 100 people have both DSL Internet connections and cable television, which of the following is the best representation of how many people have only DSL Internet connections, only cable television, both DSL Internet connections and cable television, and neither DSL internet connections nor cable television?

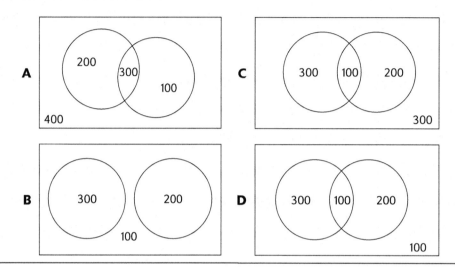

You have a total of 700 people. Of those, 300 have DSL Internet connections. Since you know that 100 of those people also have cable television, to find how many have only DSL Internet connections, you must subtract 100 from 300. You now know that 200 people have only DSL. You also know that 200 people have cable television and that 100 of those people also have DSL Internet connections.

To find how many have only cable television, you subtract 100 from 200. You now know that 100 people have only cable television.

To find how many people have neither, you find the sum of the number of people who have only DSL internet connections (200) and the number of people who only have cable television (100) and the number of people who have both DSL internet connections and cable television (100).

$$200 + 100 + 100 = 400$$

The sum is 400 people. If you subtract 400 from the total number of people (700), the remaining people are the people who have neither DSL internet connections nor cable television.

$$700 - 400 = 300$$

Therefore, the correct answer is **C.**

2 A recent survey of radio station listeners showed the following results: 10% of the listeners were Asian-American; 25% of the listeners were Caucasian; 25% of the listeners were African-American; and 40% of the listeners were Hispanic. Which of the following graphs most accurately shows the comparison of radio station listeners?

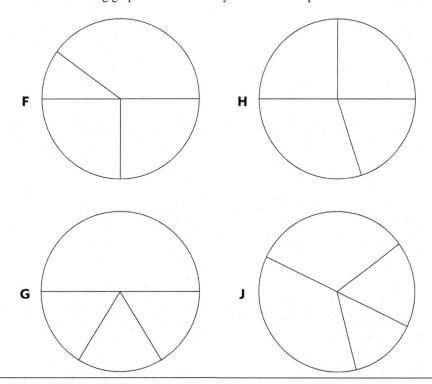

First notice that you are looking for the graph that "most accurately shows the comparison." Next, pull out the important information. The percentages were 10%, 25%, 25%, and 40%. Now, you should focus on the two 25% parts and what they would look like on a graph. Since these parts would be one quarter of the circle, you could eliminate choices G and J since they have no parts indicating one quarter or 25% of the circle. Remember, the pie graph can be split into two halves each containing 50% by drawing a diameter of the circle. If the bottom half is split equally, then each part would be one quarter of the circle or 25%. The top half would have to be split into two parts, one showing about one-tenth of the circle or 10% (a fairly small part), while the remaining part would be about 40% (four times as large). The best representation of this would be as follows:

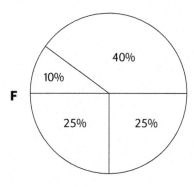

The correct answer is **F.**

3 A color television set is marked down 20% to $320. Which of the following equations could be used to determine the original price, P?

    A $\$320 - 0.20 = P$

    B $0.20P = \$320$

    C $P = \$320 + 0.20$

    D $0.80P = \$320$

Notice that this is a procedure problem. A procedure problem does not ask for an answer, but rather a procedure—in this case, what equation could you use to find the answer?

If the color television is marked down 20%, then its current price is 80% of the original price, or $0.80P = \$320$. Therefore, the correct answer is **D.**

Introduction to the Social Studies Test

The Social Studies Grade 11 Exit Level Examination consists of fifty-five (55), four-part (4) multiple-choice questions. A typical question is either a question or a sentence stem where one of four possible answers correctly completes the statement. The answer choices are alternatively labeled **A, B, C, D** or **F, G, H, J.** There are questions on the examination that ask you to interpret a map or a photograph, explain the data shown in a chart, graph, or table, draw conclusions from a diagram, and analyze brief excerpts from historical sources. The sources may include speeches or writings of famous Americans, critical documents such as the Declaration of Independence or the Constitution, and Supreme Court decisions. For all these types of questions, you are very clearly told to use the map, photograph, chart, diagram, or excerpt **"and your knowledge of social studies"** to answer the question. You may find some questions more difficult than others, and it will take you more time to handle a question based on a visual.

Sample Problems and Strategies

The content of the examination is based on five (5) objectives. These objectives are summarized below, and are followed by five (5) sample questions with explanations of the correct answer.

Objective 1: Understanding of the Issues and Events of American History

Objective 1 covers U.S. history from the American Revolution, but with focus on the late 19th and 20th centuries. Because it treats such a long period, you can expect as many as thirteen (13) questions on this objective. The topics include major people, events, and dates, for example:

- Significance of key dates in American history
    - 1776 (Declaration of Independence)
    - 1787 (U.S. Constitution)
    - 1861–1865 (Civil War)
    - 1898 (Spanish-American War)
    - 1914–1918 (World War I)
    - 1929 (Stock Market Crash)
    - 1941–1945 (World War II)
- Causes of the American Revolution, development of the Constitution, and the important individuals involved in these events, for example, Thomas Jefferson and George Washington
- Emergence of the U.S. as a world power between 1898 and 1920
    - The Spanish-American War
    - The causes of American involvement in World War I
    - The Fourteen Points
    - The Treaty of Versailles
- Significant issues and personalities of America in the 1920s
    - Prohibition
    - The Red Scare and immigration policy
    - The changing role of women
    - William Jennings Bryan and Clarence Darrow (the Scopes Trial)
    - Charles Lindberg (first solo flight across the Atlantic Ocean)

- Military and foreign policy developments during World War II and the Cold War

  The Holocaust

  The Normandy Invasion

  The decision to use the atomic bomb

  The Truman Doctrine

  The Marshall Plan

  NATO

  The Korean War

  The Vietnam War

- Domestic issues that arose in the context of World War II and the Cold War

  The internment of Japanese and Japanese-Americans

  The GI Bill of Rights

  McCarthyism

  The anti-war movement

Here are some examples of questions based on Objective 1:

---

1 A factor in President Truman's decision to drop the atomic bomb on Japan was—

    A   to limit American and Japanese casualties

    B   to force Germany to surrender unconditionally

    C   to encourage Russia to declare war on Japan

    D   to prevent Japan from invading China

Even if you don't know that Truman was concerned about the high number of combat deaths predicted for both sides if the United States had to invade Japan, you should be able to get the answer by the process of elimination. Germany had already surrendered to the allies when the atomic bomb decision was made and Russia agreed to declare war on Japan after Germany was defeated; Japan invaded China in 1931 and again in 1937. The correct answer is **A.**

---

2 Thomas Jefferson played a major role in writing the—

    F   Constitution of the United States

    G   Federalist Papers

    H   Bill of Rights

    J   Declaration of Independence

You are expected to know the roles that key figures in the American Revolution and the early national period played. Although a committee was created by the Second Continental Congress to prepare the Declaration of Independence, Jefferson was the principal author. He was not a delegate to the Federal Convention (May–September 1787) that developed the Constitution. The Federalist Papers, a series of articles defending the Constitution, was written by Alexander Hamilton, John Jay, and James Madison. The correct answer is **J.**

Use the information in the box and your knowledge of social studies to answer the following question.

> ### KEY EVENTS
>
> - Nineteenth Amendment
> - Stock Market Crash
> - Trial of Sacco and Vanzetti
> - Red Scare

3 These important historical events took place during—

    A   the Progressive Era
    B   the Great Depression
    C   the 1920s
    D   the Gilded Age

The exam emphasizes the major periods of American history following Reconstruction at the end of the Civil War, and the important events associated with them. All the events listed occurred in the 1920s—the Nineteenth Amendment in 1920 gave women the right to vote; the trial of Sacco and Vanzetti was an outgrowth of the anti-radical sentiment during the decade associated with the Red Scare. The Stock Market Crash is often seen as the start of the Great Depression but it occurred in the Fall of 1929. You should know that the Gilded Age refers to the period from the end of Reconstruction to the turn of the century while the Progressive Era covers the years 1900–1920. The correct answer is **C**.

4 When World War I broke out in August 1914, the United States—

    F   immediately entered the war against Germany
    G   declared its neutrality
    H   made an alliance with Russia
    J   stopped all trade with Europe

The basic fact you need to know is that the U.S. did not declare war on Germany until April 1917. The United States was officially neutral for the first three years of the fighting in Europe. Indeed, President Woodrow Wilson called on Americans to "be neutral in fact as well as in name." Despite our neutrality, American trade with Britain and France grew dramatically between 1914 and 1917 while trade with Germany declined just as dramatically during the same time period. The correct answer is **G**.

Use the excerpt and your knowledge of social studies to answer the following question.

> Chronic wrongdoing, or an impotence which results in a general loosening of the ties of civilized society may, in America, as elsewhere, ultimately require intervention by some civilized nation...
>
>   —*President Theodore Roosevelt, 1904*

5 This statement was used to justify American intervention in which country?

    A   Japan
    B   Spain
    C   China
    D   Nicaragua

The statement is taken from the Roosevelt Corollary to the Monroe Doctrine, which broadly applied to the Western Hemisphere and more specifically to Central America and the Caribbean. Nicaragua is the only country in the region listed. Be careful about jumping to conclusions here. President Roosevelt won the Nobel Peace Prize for negotiating an end to the war between Russia and Japan, and his administration supported free trade with China through the Open Door Policy. The correct answer is **D**.

Objective 2: Understanding How Geography Influences Historical Issues and Events

Objective 2 deals with the impact of geography on American and world history. It does not cover a large number of topics, and you can expect nine (9) questions on the exam from this objective. The topics include:

- Use of the tools of geography, such as maps, charts, and graphs, to analyze information
- Impact of geography on events in American history, e.g., the building of the Panama Canal, as well as the effects of migration within and immigration to the United States on American society
- Physical landscape and other environmental factors influence population movements
- Patterns of the spread of ideas, goods, and disease from one region of the world to another
- Impact of physical and human geography on societies in different regions of the world
- Role of technological advances and scientific discoveries in shaping human society over the course of history

Here are examples of questions from Objective 2:

Use the table and your knowledge of social studies to answer the following question.

Immigrants to the United States, 1821–1940, Select Decades (in thousands)					
Year	*Total Immigrants*	*Europe*	*Western Hemisphere*	*Asia*	*Other*
1821–1830	144	99	12	—	32
1851–1860	2,598	2,453	75	42	29
1881–1890	5,247	4,738	425	68	16
1901–1910	8,795	8,136	361	246	53
1911–1920	5,736	4,376	1,141	195	23
1921–1930	4,107	2,477	1,516	99	16
1931–1940	528	348	160	15	5

> **1** The decline in immigration during the decade 1911–1920 is explained by—
>
> **A** the serious economic depression in the United States
> **B** legislation that restricted the number of foreigners allowed in the United States
> **C** good employment opportunities in Europe and Asia
> **D** the outbreak of World War I

The First World War (1914–1918) severely restricted the flow of immigrants from Europe, which was obviously the most important source. The fighting itself, the military draft, and the danger from submarines for ships crossing the Atlantic were factors. Significant legislation to limit immigration was not passed by Congress until 1924 in the National Origins Act. Its impact is shown in the data for 1921–1930 and 1931–1940. Historically, immigration did vary depending on economic conditions in the United States and a potential immigrant's homeland, but neither was significant in 1911–1920. The correct answer is **D**.

Use the map and your knowledge of social studies to answer the following question.

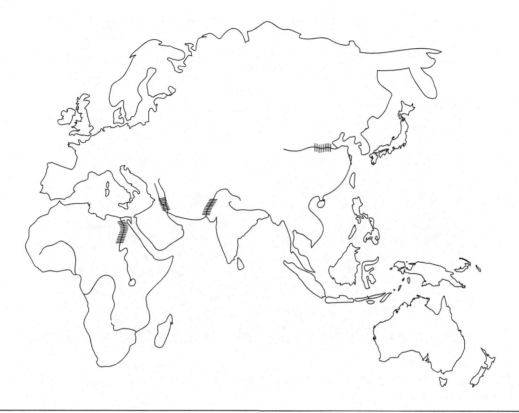

> **2** The ancient civilizations highlighted on the map all had what in common?
>
> **F** They were established at the same time.
> **G** They were part of the same trading network.
> **H** They developed along rivers.
> **J** They became part of the Roman Empire.

All were riverine civilizations. Mesopotamia means "the land between the two rivers," i.e., the Tigres and Euphrates Rivers; Egypt is the gift of the Nile River; the roots of Indian civilization go back to the banks of the Indus River; the early Chinese urban communities in the Huang He (Yellow River) valley. Mesopotamian civilization dates from 3500 BCE, while settlements by the Indus River appear about a thousand years later, and China is younger still. The correct answer is **H.**

> **3** Which of the following was introduced into the Western Hemisphere by the Europeans and dramatically changed the lives of Native Americans on the Great Plains?
>
> **A** horses
> **B** corn
> **C** cattle
> **D** potatoes

This question tests your knowledge of the Columbian or Great Biological Exchange. You should be able to eliminate two answers immediately—corn and potatoes were foodstuffs introduced into Europe and then the rest of the world from the Western Hemisphere. Cattle, which the Europeans did bring with them, had little impact on the nomadic Native American tribes on the Great Plains. The introduction of the horse, on the other hand, made the Plains Indians more mobile and more efficient buffalo hunters. The correct answer is **A.**

Use the photograph and your knowledge of social studies to answer the following question.

> **4** The best caption for this photograph, which shows a housing development in Levittown, Long Island, built after World War II is—
>
> **F** The Fruits of the GI Bill of Rights
> **G** Moving to Suburbia
> **H** Farm Land Lost
> **J** Construction Means Jobs

The GI Bill did provide many veterans the money they needed to buy a home, and the high postwar birth rate, the so-called Baby Boom, created a demand for housing. Housing construction was important to improving economy after the war. But the photograph clearly portrays the suburbanization of the country after the war, and the best caption is the one that includes this concept. The correct answer is **G.**

> **5** In addition to flood control and water for both irrigation and domestic use, Hoover Dam on the Colorado River provides—
>
> **A** employment
> **B** recreation
> **C** water purification
> **D** hydroelectric power

Hoover Dam is a multi-purpose reclamation project. While the jobs created in the construction of the dam were important during the Great Depression and an important recreation area—Lake Mead—was established, the generation of hydroelectric power was always essential to the project. Money from the sale of electricity paid for the dam's construction, and Hoover continues to provide relatively cheap power to Arizona, Nevada, and many communities in Southern California. The correct answer is **D.**

Objective 3: Understanding How Economic and Social Factors Influence Historical Issues and Events

Objective 3 covers economic and social developments primarily in the United States from the late 19th century through the 20th century, and includes a significant number of topics to test you over. You can expect around thirteen (13) questions from this objective on the exam. Here are the topics:

- Economic and social developments in the U.S. from 1877 to 1898, including industrialization and the rise of big business, growth of the railroads and organized labor, problems of the farmers, urbanization, child labor, and the status of minorities and immigrants

- Reform, third party, and civil rights movements in the 19th and 20th centuries, and the role of such leaders as Susan B. Anthony, W. E. B. Du Bois, and Martin Luther King, Jr.

- Economic developments in the U.S. from the end of World War I to the contemporary period, i.e., prosperity of the 1920s, the causes of the Depression and response of the New Deal programs, economic impact of World War II, international economic relations in the postwar world

- Contributions of minority groups—gender, racial, ethnic, and religious—to American society and their struggle for economic and political equality

- Impact of science and technology on both the economic development of the U.S. and on the daily lives of Americans; technological advances in electric power, communications, transportation, and medicine are relevant

- Analyze data to determine standard of living or level of development around and compare different methods by which goods and services are produced, e.g., subsistence agriculture, cottage industry, market economy

Here are examples of questions based on Objective 3:

---

1 The Grange was concerned with issues affecting—

   A   Native Americans
   B   skilled workers
   C   immigrants
   D   farmers

This question basically asks you for a definition of an important late 19th-century institution. The Grange or Patrons of Husbandry was created after the Civil War to address the poor economic conditions in American agriculture. It succeeded in getting laws passed in several Midwest states regulating the railroads, which the farmers saw as the main cause of many of their problems. The correct answer is **D.**

Use the excerpt and your knowledge of social studies to answer the following question.

Throughout the state of Alabama all types of conniving methods are used to prevent Negroes from becoming registered voters and there are some counties without a single Negro registered to vote despite the fact that the Negro constitutes a majority of the population.

—Martin Luther King, Jr., 1963

---

2 An example of the "conniving methods" mentioned by Martin Luther King, Jr. is the—

   F   voting age requirement
   G   poll tax requirement
   H   residency requirement
   J   registration requirement

The poll tax was one of several ways by which African Americans were denied the right to vote beginning in the late 19th century. Other methods included literacy tests and the all-white primary. By the time Martin Luther King, Jr. made this statement, Congress had approved a constitutional amendment outlawing the poll tax in federal elections. The states ratified the amendment (Twenty-fourth Amendment) in 1964. The correct answer is **G.**

---

3 In subsistence agriculture, farmers—

    A produce crops to sell in the local market
    B sell whatever they produce to the government
    C use all they grow to feed themselves
    D exchange crops for manufactured goods

The key element in subsistence farming is that there is effectively no surplus. All the food produced is consumed by the farmer and his/her family. The ability to sell or even exchange (or barter) indicates the existence of a market-based system. The correct answer is **C.**

Use the photograph and your knowledge of social studies to answer the following picture.

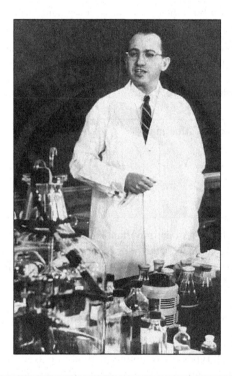

---

4 Dr. Jonas Salk, shown in the photograph above, developed a vaccine in 1954 against which crippling disease that often struck children?

    F measles
    G whooping cough
    H smallpox
    J polio

If you cannot identify Jonas Salk as the scientist associated with the polio vaccine, you can get the correct answer through the process of elimination—none of the other choices is a "crippling disease." You might also be aware that vaccines for smallpox were available long before 1954 and, for measles and whooping cough, some time after. The correct answer is **J.**

> **5** Confidence in the banking system was restored during the Depression by—
>
> **A** taking the U.S. off the gold standard
> **B** establishing the Securities and Exchange Commission
> **C** abolishing the Federal Reserve Board
> **D** creating the Federal Deposit Insurance Corporation

The Federal Reserve System was created in 1913 and remains important to the financial and economic health of the country. While President Franklin Roosevelt did take the country off the gold standard and the SEC was an important New Deal agency, neither had an impact on the people's confidence in the banks. The Federal Deposit Insurance Corporation (FDIC) was intended to prevent runs on banks by persuading people their money was safe. The FDIC originally insured bank deposits up to $2,500; today, the limit is $100,000. The correct answer is **D.**

Objective 4: Understanding of the Political Influences on Historical Issues and Events

Objective 4 basically tests your knowledge of the principles and structure of the American government. You can expect approximately nine (9) questions from this objective on the exam. The topics covered include:

- Development of representative government in the U.S. during the colonial period and political ideas in the Constitution, as well as the influence of other significant historical documents on the American system of government

    The Magna Carta

    The English Bill of Rights

    The Declaration of Independence

    The Federalist Papers

- Basic principles included in the Constitution

    Limited government

    Republicanism

    Checks and balances

    Separation of powers

    Popular sovereignty

    Individual rights

- The amendment process in the Constitution and the relationship between the national and state governments under federalism

    The amendments adopted after the Civil War (the 13th, 14th, and 15th amendments)

    The states' rights issues involved in the Civil War, e.g., the nullification crisis

    Rights and responsibilities of American citizens and the protection of these rights, including freedom of expression, through the Bill of Rights

- The expansion of civil and political rights through American history

    Amendments relating to the right to vote (19th, 24th, and 26th amendments)

    Key Supreme Court decisions (*Brown v. Board of Education*)

    Important legislation (Civil Rights Act of 1964)

Here are some examples of questions based on Objective 4:

---

1 The purpose of the system of checks and balances in the Constitution is to make sure that—

   A   the president can control Congress

   B   one branch of government does not dominate the others

   C   the armed forces are under civilian control

   D   Congress has a role in foreign policy

Under the Constitution, the federal government is divided into three coequal branches—the legislative branch (Congress) that makes the laws, the executive branch (President) that executes the laws, and the judicial branch (federal courts) that interprets the laws, and each branch has power that can limit the other branches. For example, the president can make treaties, but treaties must be approved by the Senate before they go into effect; Congress passes laws, but the Supreme Court can declare a law unconstitutional. The correct answer is **B.**

Use the excerpt and your knowledge of social studies to answer the following question.

The ordinance is founded . . . on the strange position that any one State may not only declare an act of Congress void, but prohibit its execution; that they may do this consistently with the Constitution . . .

—President Andrew Jackson, 1832

---

2 President Jackson issued this statement in response to—

   F   the removal of the Cherokees from Georgia

   G   Congress' action of the Second Bank of the United States

   H   South Carolina's Ordinance of Nullification

   J   the Supreme Court's decision in the Charles River Bridge case

---

The key phrase in the excerpt is "declare an act of Congress void," which is the essential concept behind nullification. Under the Ordinance, South Carolina declared the tariffs of 1828 and 1832 passed by the Congress null and void and not binding on the state. This question is a little tricky because all of the other actions or policies mentioned did take place during the Jackson administration. Note that Jackson was an advocate of Indian removal, and would not have issued a statement against it. It should also be clear from the excerpt that Jackson was referring to something that a state did. The correct answer is **H.**

---

3 Supreme Court's decision in *Brown v. Board of Education* (1954)—

   A   led immediately to the end of segregation in public schools throughout the country

   B   only applied to the public schools in Topeka, Kansas

   C   was not enforced by President Eisenhower

   D   gradually resulted in the integration of public education in the South

---

While the Supreme Court struck down the "separate but equal" doctrine that was the basis for segregated schools throughout the South, the decision had little immediate results. Indeed, the Supreme Court called for the implementation of the decision "with all deliberate speed." You should be aware that President Eisenhower, although he did not support the Supreme Court's ruling, sent federal troops to Little Rock, Arkansas, in 1957 to make sure a court order integrating Central High School was followed. The correct answer is **D.**

Use the diagram and your knowledge of social studies to answer the following question.

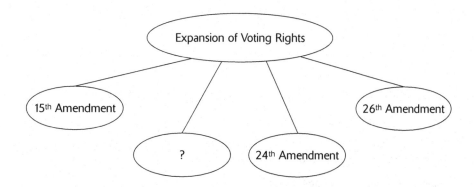

4 Which of the following best completes the diagram?

    F   18th Amendment
    G   21st Amendment
    H   19th Amendment
    J   17th Amendment

The 19th Amendment gave women to vote. None of the other amendments listed as answers deals with the expansion of voting rights. You should be aware that a possible answer is the 23rd Amendment (1961) that gave the right to vote in presidential elections to residents of the District of Columbia. The 15th Amendment (1870) gave African Americans and any person of color who is a citizen the right to vote; the 24th Amendment (1964) eliminated the poll tax, extending the right to vote to many African Americans in the South, and the 26th Amendment (1971) lowered the voting age to 18. The correct answer is **H**.

5 The Supreme Court ruled that burning an American flag is protected under the Constitution as—

    A   freedom of speech
    B   the right to assembly
    C   the right to petition the government
    D   the right against self-incrimination

The Supreme Court in *Texas v. Johnson* (1989) stated that burning the flag as part of a political demonstration was symbolic speech, and protected under the First Amendment. You should know that answers **B** and **C** are also taken from the First Amendment. Clearly, burning the flag has nothing to do with the protection against self-incrimination provided for in the Fifth Amendment. The correct answer is **A.**

Objective 5: Use of Critical Thinking Skills to Analyze Social Studies Information

Objective 5 covers the skills needed to properly analyze and interpret information in the social studies. There will likely be about eleven (11) questions on the exam from this objective on these skills. Here are the topics:

- Use of primary and secondary sources in the study of American history
- Use of various techniques to analyze information
  - Sequencing
  - Categorizing
  - Cause-and-effect relationships

> Compare and contrast
>
> Finding the main idea
>
> Summarizing
>
> Making generalizations
>
> Drawing inferences and conclusions

- Interpret information in the form of graphs, charts, time lines, and maps
- Identify different points of view about historical events and recognize bias in historical sources

Here are some examples of questions based on Objective 5:

---

1 Which of the following is a secondary account on the American Revolution?

    A a diary of a soldier in the Continental Army

    B a letter from George Washington to the Continental Congress

    C the debate in the British Parliament over the cost of fighting in the colonies

    D a book giving a historian's interpretation of the Declaration of Independence

---

The diary, letter, and the debate in Parliament are all primary sources because they are contemporary with the events that they describe; the book by a historian, while likely to rely on primary sources, is a secondary source. It is written long after the events. The only time the book would be considered a primary source is for a study on how historians have interpreted the Declaration of Independence. The correct answer is **D.**

Use the table and your knowledge of social studies to answer the following question.

Number of Armed Services Personnel, in Thousands				
Year	*Army*	*Navy*	*Marine Corps*	*Air Force*
1950	593	381	74	411
1955	1,109	661	205	960
1960	873	617	171	815
1965	969	670	190	825
1970	1,323	691	260	791
1975	784	535	196	613
1980	777	527	188	558
1985	781	571	198	602
1990	732	579	197	535
1995	509	435	175	400

---

2 Which of the following conclusions is supported by the information presented?

    F More women serve in the Air Force than in the Marine Corps.

    G The Navy is the largest branch of the armed services.

    H The increase in military personnel between 1950 and 1955 was likely due to the Korean War.

    J The Marine Corps consistently needed more people than any other branch of the service.

The table does not divide personnel by gender so there is no way for you to know whether more women serve in the Air Force than in the Marines; it is obvious by a quick glance at the numbers that the Army is the largest branch. The question of need is not addressed by the table, and you should know that the Marines are considered a more elite force than the other branches of the military. The correct answer is **H.**

Use the map and your knowledge of social studies to answer the following question.

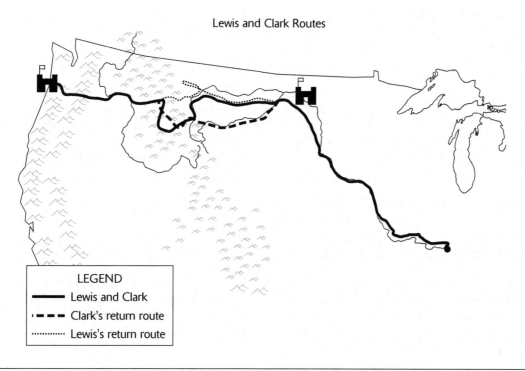

Lewis and Clark Routes

LEGEND
——— Lewis and Clark
∎ ∎ ∎ Clark's return route
········· Lewis's return route

---

3 According to the map of Lewis and Clark's exploration of the lands of the Louisiana Purchase, which group states were formed out of the new territory?

  A Missouri, Nebraska, Montana
  B Illinois, Missouri, Arkansas
  C Indiana, Michigan, Wisconsin
  D South Dakota, North Dakota, California

The Lewis and Clark expedition jumped off from St. Louis, and followed the Missouri River northwest through territory that became the states of Missouri, Nebraska, South and North Dakota, and Montana. They reached the Pacific Ocean from the Columbia River that serves as the boundary between Oregon and Washington. Although Arkansas was part of the Louisiana Purchase, Indiana, Michigan, and Wisconsin are part of the old Northwest Territory. The correct answer is **A.**

Use the chart and your knowledge of social studies to answer the following question.

SEQUENCE OF EVENTS—THE COMING OF THE CIVIL WAR				
Election of 1860; Lincoln elected president	South Carolina secedes from the union	Deep south secedes; Confederate States of America formed	Attack on Fort Sumter	?

4 Which completes this sequence of events?

F Lincoln declares war on the Confederate States of America.

G Virginia, North Carolina, Tennessee, and Arkansas join the Confederacy.

H The remaining slave states secede from the Union.

J Lincoln takes the oath of office as president.

There were two secessions—the Deep South states seceded before the attack on Fort Sumter, and the Upper South states seceded after. All slave states did not join the Confederacy; the border states—Delaware, Maryland, Kentucky, and Missouri—remained in the Union. Lincoln's inauguration took place before Fort Sumter, and there was never a formal declaration of war against the Confederacy. The correct answer is **G.**

5 Which of the following was an immediate cause of the involvement of the U.S. in World War II?

A Great Britain was fighting alone against Germany.

B Germany attacked the Soviet Union in June 1941.

C U.S. imposed an embargo on essential materials to Japan.

D Japanese forces attacked the American naval base at Pearl Harbor.

By the time of the attack on Pearl Harbor (December 7, 1941), the U.S. was heavily involved in providing as much assistance to Great Britain as possible. Further, the U.S. did impose a very restrictive embargo in July 1941 in response to the Japanese move into French Indochina. Tensions were certainly building in both Europe and Asia, but it was Pearl Harbor that led directly to the declaration of war against Japan. The correct answer is **D.**

Introduction to the Science Test

The Science Grade 11 Exit Examination consists of fifty-five (55) questions, most of which will be four-part (4) multiple-choice questions. The multiple-choice answer choices are alternately labeled A, B, C, D, and F, G, H, J. "Not Here" may be used as a fourth answer choice in some multiple-choice questions. A few questions will be open-ended griddable questions. For this question type you will be given an eight-column grid to record and bubble in your answer.

Although the Science Test has no time limit, the suggested time is 2 hours.

Science Chart

You will have a Science Chart for assistance on this exam. The Science Chart will have a chart of formulas on one side and a periodic table on the other side. Make sure that you are familiar with the formulas and understand the constants/conversions table at the bottom of the page. The formulas page will also have a metric ruler marked in centimeters.

Two pages (actually two sides of a page) that are similar to the following will appear on your Science Test. You will find the Science Chart at the front of the actual science test, as well as at the front of the practice tests in this book.

FORMULA CHART
for Grade 11 Science Assessment

Density = $\dfrac{\text{mass}}{\text{volume}}$

$D = \dfrac{m}{v}$

$\left(\begin{array}{c}\text{heat gained or}\\ \text{lost by water}\end{array}\right) = \left(\begin{array}{c}\text{mass in}\\ \text{grams}\end{array}\right)\left(\begin{array}{c}\text{change in}\\ \text{temperature}\end{array}\right)\left(\begin{array}{c}\text{specific}\\ \text{heat}\end{array}\right)$

$Q = (m)(\Delta T)(C_p)$

Speed = $\dfrac{\text{distance}}{\text{time}}$

$s = \dfrac{d}{t}$

Acceleration = $\dfrac{\text{final velocity} - \text{initial velocity}}{\text{change in time}}$

$a = \dfrac{V_f - V_i}{\Delta t}$

Momentum = mass × velocity

$p = mv$

Force = mass × acceleration

$F = ma$

Work = force × distance

$W = Fd$

Power = $\dfrac{\text{work}}{\text{time}}$

$P = \dfrac{W}{t}$

% efficiency = $\dfrac{\text{work output}}{\text{work input}} \times 100$

$\% = \dfrac{W_O}{W_I} \times 100$

Kinetic energy = $\dfrac{1}{2}$ (mass × velocity²)

$KE = \dfrac{mv^2}{2}$

Gravitational potential energy = mass × acceleration due to gravity × height

$GPE = mgh$

Energy = mass × (speed of light)²

$E = mc^2$

Velocity of a wave = frequency × wavelength

$v = f\lambda$

Current = $\dfrac{\text{voltage}}{\text{resistance}}$

$I = \dfrac{V}{R}$

Electrical power = voltage × current

$P = VI$

Electrical energy = power × time

$E = Pt$

Constants/Conversions
g = acceleration due to gravity = 9.8 m/s²
c = speed of light = 3×10^8 m/s
speed of sound = 343 m/s at 20°C
1 cm³ = 1 mL
1 wave/second = 1 hertz (Hz)
1 calorie (cal) = 4.18 joules
1000 calories (cal) = 1 Calorie (Cal) = 1 kilocalorie (kcal)
newton (N) = kgm/s²
joule (J) = Nm
watt (W) = J/s = Nm/s
volt (V)   ampere (A)   ohm (Ω)

Centimeters 0 1 2 3 4 5 6 7 8 9 10 11 12 13 14 15 16 17 18 19 20

Periodic Table of the Elements

Key:

Atomic Number	14
Symbol	Si
Atomic Mass	28.086
Name	Silicon

Mass numbers in parentheses are those of the most stable or most common isotope.

Group	1 IA	2 IIA	3 IIIB	4 IVB	5 VB	6 VIB	7 VIIB	8 VIII	9 VIII	10 VIII	11 IB	12 IIB	13 IIIA	14 IVA	15 VA	16 VIA	17 VIIA	18 VIIIA
1	1 H 1.008 Hydrogen																	2 He 4.0026 Helium
2	3 Li 6.941 Lithium	4 Be 9.012 Beryllium											5 B 10.81 Boron	6 C 12.011 Carbon	7 N 14.007 Nitrogen	8 O 15.999 Oxygen	9 F 18.998 Flourine	10 Ne 20.179 Neon
3	11 Na 22.990 Sodium	12 Mg 24.305 Magnesium											13 Al 26.982 Aluminum	14 Si 28.086 Silicon	15 P 30.974 Phosphorus	16 S 32.066 Sulfur	17 Cl 35.453 Chlorine	18 Ar 39.948 Argon
4	19 K 39.098 Potassium	20 Ca 40.08 Calcium	21 Sc 44.956 Scandium	22 Ti 47.88 Titanium	23 V 50.942 Vanadium	24 Cr 51.996 Chromium	25 Mn 54.938 Manganese	26 Fe 55.847 Iron	27 Co 58.933 Cobalt	28 Ni 58.69 Nickel	29 Cu 63.546 Copper	30 Zn 65.39 Zinc	31 Ga 69.72 Gallium	32 Ge 72.61 Germanium	33 As 74.922 Arsenic	34 Se 78.96 Selenium	35 Br 79.904 Bromine	36 Kr 83.80 Krypton
5	37 Rb 85.468 Rubidium	38 Sr 87.62 Strontium	39 Y 88.906 Yttrium	40 Zr 91.224 Zirconium	41 Nb 92.906 Niobium	42 Mo 95.94 Molybdenum	43 Tc (98) Technetium	44 Ru 101.07 Ruthenium	45 Rh 102.906 Rhodium	46 Pd 106.42 Palladium	47 Ag 107.868 Silver	48 Cd 112.41 Cadmium	49 In 114.82 Indium	50 Sn 118.71 Tin	51 Sb 121.763 Antimony	52 Te 127.60 Tellurium	53 I 126.904 Iodine	54 Xe 131.29 Xenon
6	55 Cs 132.905 Cesium	56 Ba 137.33 Barium	57 La 138.906 Lanthanum	72 Hf 178.49 Hafnium	73 Ta 180.948 Tantalum	74 W 183.84 Tungsten	75 Re 186.207 Rhenium	76 Os 190.23 Osmium	77 Ir 192.22 Iridium	78 Pt 195.08 Platinum	79 Au 196.967 Gold	80 Hg 200.59 Mercury	81 Tl 204.383 Thallium	82 Pb 207.2 Lead	83 Bi 208.980 Bismuth	84 Po (209) Polonium	85 At (210) Astatine	86 Rn (222) Radon
7	87 Fr (223) Francium	88 Ra 226.025 Radium	89 Ac 227.028 Actinium	104 Rf (261) Rutherfordium	105 Db (262) Dubnium	106 Sg (263) Seaborgium	107 Bh (262) Bohrium	108 Hs (265) Hassium	109 Mt (266) Meitnerium	110 (269)								

Lanthanide Series

58 Ce 140.12 Cerium	59 Pr 140.908 Praseodymium	60 Nd 144.24 Neodymium	61 Pm (145) Promethium	62 Sm 150.36 Samarium	63 Eu 151.97 Europium	64 Gd 157.25 Gadolinium	65 Tb 158.925 Terbium	66 Dy 162.50 Dysprosium	67 Ho 164.930 Holmium	68 Er 167.26 Erbium	69 Tm 168.934 Thulium	70 Yb 173.04 Ytterbium	71 Lu 174.967 Lutetium

Actinide Series

90 Th 232.038 Thorium	91 Pa 231.036 Protactinium	92 U 238.029 Uranium	93 Np 237.048 Neptunium	94 Pu (244) Plutonium	95 Am (243) Americium	96 Cm (247) Curium	97 Bk (247) Berkelium	98 Cf (251) Californium	99 Es (252) Einsteinium	100 Fm (257) Fermium	101 Md (258) Mendelevium	102 No (259) Nobelium	103 Lr (262) Lawrencium

Calculators

The TAKS Science Test allows the use of calculators, and you should be provided one at the test site. Some problems may involve multiple steps and calculations from data given. Even though no question will require the use of a calculator—that is, each question can be answered without a calculator—using a calculator on some problems may save you valuable time.

- Before doing an operation, check the number that you keyed in on the display to make sure that you keyed in the right number. You may wish to check each number as you key it in.
- Make sure that you clear the calculator after each problem. You may need to clear your calculator as you work a problem to go on to the next part. If this is the case, be sure to write down your answer before you go on to the next step.

Take advantage of using a calculator on the test. Learn to use a calculator efficiently by practicing. As you approach a problem, first focus on how to solve that problem and then decide if the calculator will be helpful. Remember, a calculator can save you time on some problems, but also remember that each problem can be solved without a calculator. Also remember that a calculator will not solve a problem for you by itself. You must understand the problem first.

Sample Problems and Strategies

The content of the examinations is based on five (5) objectives. These objectives are summarized below, and are followed by five (5) to seven (7) sample questions with explanations and strategies.

Objective 1: Understanding the Nature of Science

The topics included are based on concepts of biology and integrated physics and chemistry.

- Classroom, laboratory, and field safety practices
- Inferences drawn from various sources, including advertisements, product labels, Web pages, etc.
- Graphs, charts, and maps - interpret, evaluate, and make predictions
- Measurements and precision
- Knowledge of tools, equipment and materials in science

---

1 Knowing the safety procedures is vital when performing experiments. During a recent science experiment, ammonia gas was released into the laboratory. Several students became dizzy and began having difficulty in breathing. Which of the following is a safety procedure that should be implemented first?

    A Call the principal
    B Find a substance to counteract the ammonia gas
    C Open a few windows
    D Evacuate the laboratory

This question involves safety practices. Focus on what has occurred to cause the unsafe situation—*ammonia gas released into the room.* What would ensure the safety of the students? Evacuating the area makes the most sense. Choices **A, B,** and **C** require students to stay in the room. In any situation where dangerous fumes are present, the first step is to seek fresh air immediately. The correct answer is **D.**

---

2 Water-reactive chemicals should be stored—

    F above eye level
    G on the floor
    H where they will remain dry
    J next to flammables

This safety related question involves the storing of chemicals. Read the question carefully, focusing on the information given. In this case, the chemicals are *water reactive*. This should be the tip-off that you must find the best way to keep them dry during storage. Remember, water-reactive chemicals must be stored where they will not get wet; otherwise, they will react. Note that chemicals should never be stored above eye level or on the floor. Also, you should store chemicals in compatible families—flammables next to flammables, for example. The correct answer is **H.**

Use the information below and your knowledge of science to answer questions 3 and 4.

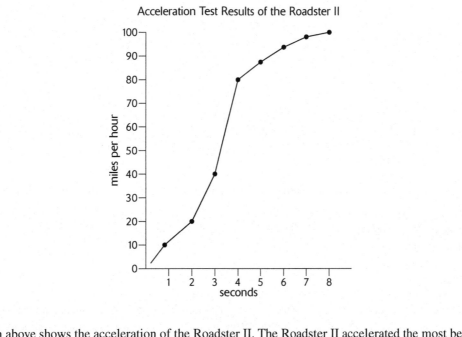

3 The graph above shows the acceleration of the Roadster II. The Roadster II accelerated the most between—

    A   1 and 2 seconds
    B   2 and 3 seconds
    C   3 and 4 seconds
    D   4 and 5 seconds

To answer this question, you must understand how the information is presented. The number on the left side of the graph shows the speed in miles per hour (mph). The information at the bottom of the graph shows the number of seconds. The movement of the line can give important information and show trends. The *more the line slopes upward*, the *greater the acceleration*. The greatest slope upward is between 3 and 4 seconds. The Roadster II accelerates from about 40 to about 80 mph in that time. The correct answer is **C.**

4 The graph above shows the acceleration of the Roadster II. From the graph it can be reasonably predicted that the Roadster II—

    F   will not accelerate as rapidly between 8 and 9 seconds as it did between 5 and 6 seconds
    G   will decelerate slowly between 8 and 9 seconds
    H   will accelerate more rapidly between 8 and 9 seconds than it did between 1 and 2 seconds
    J   will not accelerate to more than 100 miles per hour

This question involves making a prediction from data given in a graph. You should notice that the curve is sloping less and less upward from 4 seconds to 8 seconds. If this trend continues, as it appears it will, then the Roadster II will not accelerate as rapidly between 8 and 9 seconds as it did between 4 and 5. Between 4 and 5 seconds the acceleration was about 10 mph. Between 8 and 9 seconds it should be about 1 to 2 miles per hour. The correct answer is **F.**

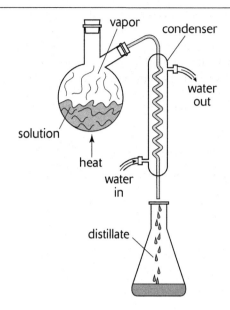

5 An experiment starts with a solution of alcohol dissolved in water in the flask to be heated. This experiment was set up to—

    A   separate alcohol and water
    B   condense water
    C   combine alcohol and water
    D   vaporize water

Here you are being asked to analyze an experiment and draw a conclusion. First, notice the apparatus being used. Next, follow the flow of the actual process that is taking place. Finally, identify what product is left after the process is completed. This figure shows a method of separation called distillation. Distillation occurs when the solution is heated, because the alcohol is driven off as a vapor—separating the alcohol and the water. Distillation is usually carried out in an apparatus called a still, which requires a boiler, a condenser, and a receiver. The correct answer is **A.**

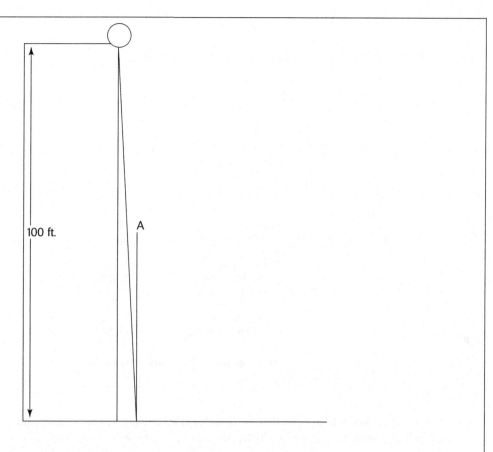

100 ft.

A

6 A hard rubber ball is dropped from a building 100 feet tall as shown above. The ball takes 4 seconds to hit the ground. Using a ruler and some calculations, determine approximately how long it will take the ball to hit the ground from point A, the peak of its bounce.

   F   5 seconds

   G   1.0 seconds

   H   1.5 seconds

   J   longer than 2 seconds

Use the ruler given on the formula chart and measure carefully. Since the building that is 100 feet tall measures 10 centimeters, and the peak of the ball when it bounces measures 5 centimeters, then the ball's bounce is half the height of the building—50 feet. The ball fell 100 feet in 4 seconds, so it should fall 50 feet in approximately half the time. But since it keeps falling faster and faster, depending on the height, then it will be falling more slowly from 50 feet. So the time will be longer than 2 seconds. The correct answer is **J.**

Super Vito

Get the extra energy you need from
one vitamin a day!

Supplement Facts

Serving Size: 1 Tablet

Amount Per Tablet	% Daily Value*
Vitamin C 150 mg	250%
Thiamin 50 mg	3,336%
Riboflavin 10 mg	640%
Niacin 25 mg	125%
Vitamin B6 2 mg	100%
Folic Acid 400 mcg	100%
Vitamin B12 15 mcg	250%
Biotin 5 mcg	2%
Pantothenic Acid 5.5 mg	55%

*100% Daily value is the recommended amount.

7 If a doctor is correct in suggesting that the recommended amount of niacin, folic acid, and biotin 5 is needed to result in hair growth, then according to the label above, one tablet per day would—

A not supply the needed amount of niacin for hair growth
B not supply the needed amount of folic acid for hair growth
C supply the needed amount of pantothenic acid for hair growth
D not supply the needed amount of biotin 5 for hair growth

Here you are given a product advertisement and asked to draw an inference based on the information given. Focus on the specific items being asked about—niacin, folic acid, and biotin 5. Since one tablet supplies only 2% of the recommended amount of Biotin 5, then the correct answer is **D,** not enough biotin will be supplied for hair growth.

Objective 2: Understanding the Organization of Living Systems

The topics included are based on concepts of biology.

- Cellular processes and cell parts
- Structures of nucleic acids (DNA, RNA)
- Genetic principles
- Causes and effects of mutations in living organisms
- Genetic engineering
- Ecology and evolution
- Characteristics of kingdoms
- Functions of biological systems
- Interrelationships of organ systems

MITOSIS

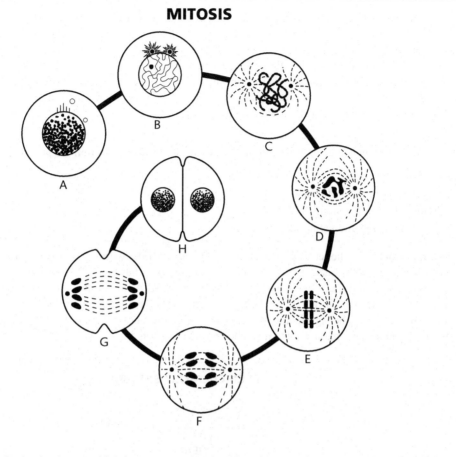

1 In the diagram of mitosis above, which letter correctly identifies the metaphase process in cell division?

A A
B C
C E
D H

This question is asking about the process of cell division and refers to the diagram given. First, follow the flow of the diagram to understand what happens at each stage of the process. Now, carefully focus on finding which stage shows the *metaphase*. You will need to apply your knowledge of mitosis to answer this question. Remember, mitosis is the process of cell division in which the nuclear material of the original cell is divided equally between newer cells. Such multiplication of cells permits the growth of an organism. Letter A represents the resting cell. Mitosis begins as the chromosomes thicken and the centrosome (a part of the cytoplasm) divides during the prophase process, letters B, C, and D. The nuclear membrane disappears and a spindle develops between the two parts of the centrosome. Letter E represents the metaphase when the chromosomes line up in the middle of a cell and gather on the spindle. F is the anaphase, where the chromosomes split. Finally, in the telophase (G and H) the nuclear membrane forms and two new cells result. The correct answer is **C.**

2 Deoxyribonucleic acid is most closely associated with—

F acid rain
G greenhouse gases
H genetic engineering
J cross-pollination experiments

You should have focused on the words "deoxyribonucleic acid." Once you realize that this is the well-known DNA, you should look for an answer involving genetics. In this case, genetic engineering is the choice most closely associated with DNA and genetics. Genetic science can isolate main genes that control crucial chemical activity in cells. A gene can be spliced into bacterial cells that then can be cultured and reproduced. Examples of genetic engineering are the synthesizing of such products as human insulin and interferons and the production of genetically engineered, frost-resistant strawberry plants. DNA, found only in the chromosomes of the cell nuclei and duplicated during cell reproduction, records genetic messages as a coded sequences of bases. The genetic information provides detailed signals that control the development and activity of cells. The correct answer is **H.**

---

3 When a mutation in a gene occurs in an individual, it will not have an effect on the group unless the—

   A environment changes
   B threat of predators is reduced
   C individual lives long enough to breed
   D mutation increases the variability of the group

In analyzing the question, mark the terms *mutation, gene,* and *effect*. If the wording of a question is confusing, restate it—in this case, perhaps as "What factors would cause a mutation *not* to have an effect on a group?" For a mutation to be passed on, the genetic material must be passed on through breeding. A mutation is the result of a change in the makeup of the chromosomes, which contain the genes that determine the characteristics of an organism. When changes occur in sex cells, the result can be significant. Mutations can be both successful and unsuccessful, with beneficial changes being preserved through natural selection. The correct answer is **C.**

THE CIRCULATORY SYSTEM

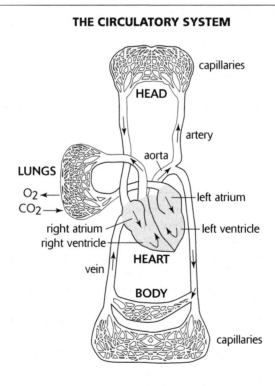

4 Which of the following sequences within the human circulatory system shown above describes the circulation of blood specifically to the body?

   F lungs-body-heart-lungs
   G lungs-heart-body-lungs
   H lungs-body- heart-body-lungs
   J lungs-heart-body-heart-lungs

This question involves the interdependence of organ systems. Take advantage of the information in the diagram. First, notice that each answer choice starts with the lungs, so follow the diagram starting from the lungs. Notice that the circulatory system is a double loop, and any blood must travel both loops before returning to its starting point. If you start at the lungs, where the blood picks up fresh oxygen, you'll see that the blood goes to the left side of the heart, which pumps it out the arteries to the body tissues. The blood returns by the veins to the right side of the heart, which pumps the blood to the lungs, the original starting point. The correct answer is **J**.

---

5 Which of these classifications is most general?

   A Order
   B Family
   C Species
   D Genus

This question involves your knowledge of the classification of organisms—taxonomy. Since you are looking for the "most general," if you don't immediately know the answer, see if you can eliminate any answer that you know is more general than another answer. For example, if you know that genus is more general than species, then you can eliminate species. For your information, the levels of classification from general to specific are kingdom, phylum, class, order, family, genus, species. The correct answer is **A**.

---

6 Which of the following is not included as a kingdom in the six-kingdom system?

   F Animals
   G Plants
   H Fungi
   J Ferns

Notice that this question asks which is "not included." Since ferns are a type of plant, ferns could not be a kingdom. The six-kingdom system includes Archaebacteria, Eubacteria, Protista, Fungi, Plantae, and Animalia. The correct answer is **J**.

---

7 Although most bacteria will be killed by constant exposure to a certain antibiotic, those that survive will become immune. Scientists believe that this immunity is hereditary and eventually natural selection will cause a rise in antibiotic-resistant strains of bacteria because—

   A the bacteria will have been overexposed to some antibiotics
   B those bacteria that survive the antibiotic will not reproduce
   C the majority of antibiotic-resistant strains will live only a few days
   D bacterial resistance to some antibiotics is based on environment

---

Read the information given, carefully looking for clues. Notice the words, "constant exposure," "immunity," and "hereditary." This should help give you some direction in reviewing the choices. Bacterial resistance to some antibiotics is hereditary; that is, it is passed on from generation to generation. The belief is that bacteria that survive this constant exposure to the antibiotic will become immune to its effects and will pass that immunity along to future generations. This is because the bacteria will have been overexposed to the antibiotics. The correct answer is **A**.

Objective 3: Understanding the Interdependence of Organisms and the Environment

The topics included are based on concepts of biology.

- Viruses
- Bacteria
- Evolution
- Natural selection
- Flow of matter and energy
- Biomass
- Predation, parasitism, commensalisms, mutualism
- Food chains and ecosystems
- Adaptations of plants

---

1 In the past, viruses had sometimes been classified as living organisms and sometimes as chemical compounds. Which of the following properties is the best evidence for considering viruses a life form?

    A   They have a crystalline structure.
    B   They are found inside animals, plants, and one-celled organisms.
    C   They produce nucleic acids to reproduce themselves.
    D   They possess the ability to become larger.

Notice that you are looking for the *best evidence*. So look for key characteristics of living things in the answer choices. Some of the key characteristics suggesting classification as a life form are metabolism, growth, respiration, excretion, motion, and, most important, reproduction. The fact that a virus can produce nucleic acids would argue for including it as a life form. Many nonliving substances can increase in size; for example, metals and gases can expand, and rocks can accumulate as conglomerates. Eliminate choice **D.** The correct answer is **C.**

---

2 Digestion is aided by the action of—

    F   viruses
    G   fungi
    H   mold
    J   bacteria

Your focus here should be on *aiding digestion*. Keep in mind that bacteria are often beneficial to organisms and the environment. In this case, bacteria are indispensable for food digestion. Food is degraded in the stomach by acids, then the bile destroys fats, and bacteria in the intestines degrade large biomolecules further into smaller ones that can pass the intestinal surface. Bacteria produce certain enzymes that higher organisms don't produce, which can degrade biomolecules. The correct answer is **J.** You probably could have quickly eliminated some of the other choices.

---

3 Which one of the following pairs is an example of commensalism?

    A   ants and beetles
    B   mistletoe and trees
    C   foxes and chickens
    D   whales and barnacles

Your focus here should be on the meaning of "commensalism." But even if you don't know the meaning of commensalism, you could eliminate some of the choices. Choice **B** can be quickly eliminated because mistletoe, which grows on the branches of trees, is a parasite. Parasitism is when two organisms live in close association with each other, the one, a parasite, depending on the other, the host, for some essential food or nutrition. Choice **C** can be quickly eliminated because this is an example of a predator/prey relationship - predation. So you have narrowed the choices to **A** or **D.** Commensalism is a situation where two organisms live in close association, but only one benefits (usually the smaller one, the commensal). The relationship between whales and barnacles is an example of commensalism. The barnacle attaches itself to the whale, getting both transportation and protection. The whale gets no benefit. The correct answer is **D.**

Use the illustration below and your knowledge of science to answer questions 4 and 5.

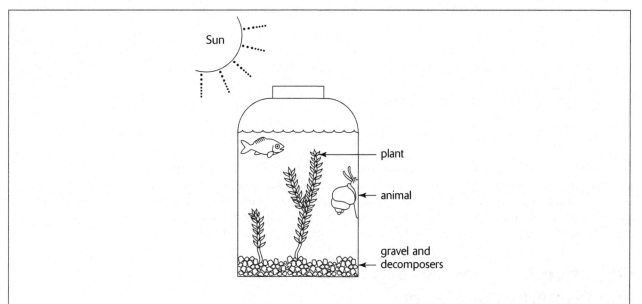

4 A complete world can be created in a sealed jar as shown above. The organisms supply the needs of each other, and the system can go on for months. Every system of plants and animals needs an input of energy to continue life. What is the major energy input in this system?

    F   The growth of the plants continues to supply the needed energy to sustain life in the system.

    G   The heat and motion of the animals provide the needed energy.

    H   The gravel on the floor of the container radiates energy.

    J   Sunlight provides energy to the system through the glass walls of the container.

Sunlight is the source of the continuing energy needed by this system to survive. Sunlight plays the same role in the larger closed system, the Earth. Without this energy input, the plants and then animals would die. Choices **F** and **G** do provide small, fairly unimportant energy sources. The correct answer is **J.**

5 Which of the following best shows the flow of energy through the system?

    A   animal to plant to sun to decomposers

    B   sun to plant to animal to decomposers

    C   decomposers to sun to animal to plant

    D   sun to animal to plant to decomposers

The flow of energy starts with the sun, the source of energy needed for this system to survive (as it is for the closed system of the earth to survive). Eliminate choices **A** and **C** because they do not start with the sun. This energy is converted to food and oxygen through photosynthesis. Animals take this food energy and use it to live and reproduce, in turn giving off carbon dioxide and minerals (through decomposition), which are used by the plants. The correct answer is **B.**

6 Over many generations, each organic species has tended to become better adapted to its place in the environment. Which of the following features is least likely to be explained as adaptation?

    F   the bright color of flowers

    G   the eyes of a mole

    H   a flying squirrel

    J   the sting of a scorpion

Notice that you are looking for *least* likely. The adaptations described in choices **F, H,** and **J** show the development of a feature that helps a plant or animal to perform better in its environment. Flowers need to be seen by bees for pollination. Some squirrels use flight to escape enemies. Scorpions defend themselves by stinging. However, a mole lives underground, and its eyes are almost useless. The eyes are explained as being inherited from some ancestor that lived on the surface. The correct answer is **G.**

7 What is the chronological order of the evolutionary appearance of the following plants?

    A   fern, moss, rose, pine

    B   fern, rose, moss, pine

    C   moss, fern, pine, rose

    D   pine, fern, moss, rose

Using an elimination strategy can be very helpful. The moss and the fern are the two most primitive plants given. Neither reproduces by seeds, so can assume that the chronological order had to begin with one of the two. Eliminate choice **D.** You could also eliminate choice **B** because the rose could not appear before moss. Of the two plants with seeds (the pine and the rose), the plant with flowers is the most advanced. Eliminate choice **A.** By knowing only the simplest and most advanced of the plants listed, you could eliminate all choices but **C.** The correct answer is **C.**

Objective 4: Understanding the Structures and Properties of Matter

The topics included are based on concepts of integrated physics and chemistry.

- Density, viscosity, buoyancy
- Bonding, periodic table placement
- Physical and chemical changes in matter
- Earth science, rock cycle
- Law of conservation of mass
- Balancing of chemical equations
- Structure of water
- pH and electrolytic activity
- Solubility

1 A car is abandoned on a cliff overlooking the ocean; over a period of time, the car begins to rust. Which of the following most closely explains why the car is subject to the rusting process?

    A   Water molecules at the beach combine with the iron in the car to form sulfur dioxide.

    B   The oxygen in the air combines with sulfur dioxide on the moist car to form iron oxide.

    C   The oxygen in the air combines with sulfur dioxide to form acid rain.

    D   The paint on the car inhibits oxidation.

The formation of rust is the result of a chemical reaction. Rust, by definition, is iron oxide. When atoms of oxygen in the air come into contact with moist iron, a new compound results. Anything made of iron will eventually rust if left outside long enough. Salt water would accelerate the process. Choice **D** is a true statement, but the paint inhibits, rather than causes, rusting. The correct answer is **B**.

---

2 According to the periodic table, which element most readily donates electrons?

 F Na
 G Ne
 H Cl
 J He

From your knowledge of science and the periodic table given, you should note that metals in the first column each have one electron in their outer shell. They readily loose this electron. Since Na is in the first column, it would readily donate an electron. You could have eliminated choices **G** and **J**, since Ne and He are both inert gases—their outer shell is filled. You could have eliminated choice **H**, since Cl has 7 electrons in its outer shell and readily accepts an electron. The correct answer is **F**.

$$H_2O + CO_2 \rightarrow O_2 + C_6H_{12}O_6$$

3 What is the coefficient for CO_2 when the above equation is balanced?

 A 1
 B 2
 C 3
 D 6

According to the Law of Conservation of Mass, the number of atoms of each element must be equal on both sides of a chemical equation. A coefficient is the large number in front of a compound. In this case, there should be a total of 12 hydrogen atoms on both sides; 6 carbon atoms on both sides; and 18 oxygen atoms on both sides. The coefficient in front of CO_2 is 6.

$$6H_2O + 6CO_2 \rightarrow 6O_2 + C_6H_{12}O_6$$

The correct answer is **D**.

Numbers of Subatomic Particles in Four Different Atoms			
Atoms	*Electrons (Charge of -1)*	*Neutrons (No Charge)*	*Protons (Charge of +1)*
A	19	21	19
B	18	22	18
C	18	20	17
D	18	18	16

4 Using the chart above, which shows the number of subatomic particles in four different atoms, which of the four atoms shown is argon?

 F A
 G B
 H C
 J D

By looking at the periodic table given at the front of the test, you can see that argon is the 18th element. Each element is defined by the number of protons in the atomic nucleus, so argon has 18 protons in each atom. The last column of the chart above reveals the number of protons in each atom of an element. Argon is atom B in the chart —18 protons. The correct answer is **G.**

---

5 The correct formula for nitrous oxide is—

   A N_2O
   B NO_2
   C N_2O_3
   D N_3O_2

You may be asked to determine the formula and name for a basic compound. The correct formula for nitrous oxide is N_2O. The correct answer is **A.**

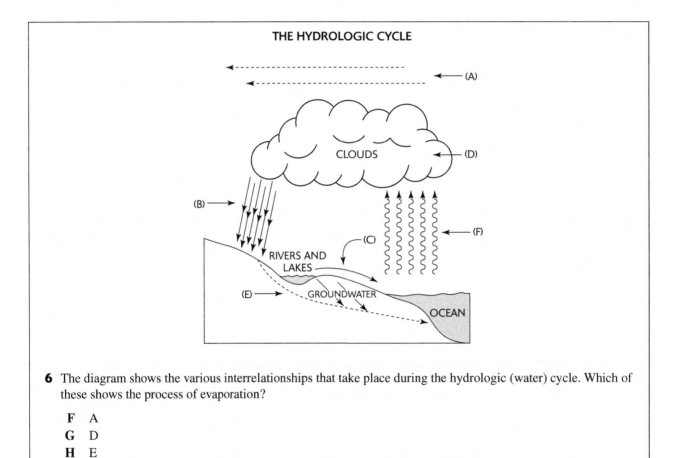

THE HYDROLOGIC CYCLE

6 The diagram shows the various interrelationships that take place during the hydrologic (water) cycle. Which of these shows the process of evaporation?

   F A
   G D
   H E
   J F

Always carefully review the diagram given. Make sure that you understand the various interrelationships in the cycle. The sun's rays warm the oceans changing water into water vapor through the process of evaporation. That point is labeled **F,** choice **J.** Evaporation allows water from rivers, lakes, streams, etc., to escape into the atmosphere. The rest of the cycle is as follows: The moisture-carrying warm air rises to altitudes of lower pressure in the troposphere. The air expands and cools; the cooling results in the condensation of the water vapor, which forms into clouds. The clouds may be blown inland and cool further. As the clouds become saturated, moisture is returned to the earth as precipitation. As the water is returned to the surface, runoff and percolation occur, and the process begins again in a continuous cycle. The correct answer is choice **J.**

7 The acid or alkaline strength of a solution is measured on the pH scale that goes from 0 to 14. Which of the following best describes a chemical solution that has a pH equal to 8.5?

   A   slightly acidic
   B   neutral
   C   slightly alkaline
   D   very alkaline

The acid or alkaline strength of a solution is measured on the pH scale, where 7 is neutral. A pH less than 7 is acidic, whereas a pH greater than 7 is alkaline. The scale looks like this:

pH Scale

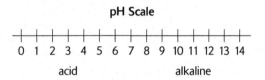

A measure of 8.5 would be slightly alkaline. The correct answer is **C.**

From a test-taking standpoint, even if you didn't know the answer you could have eliminated some choices from the information given. Since you are told that the scale is from 0 to 14, 7 must be the middle or neutral. But you are looking for a pH of 8.5, so you can eliminate choice **B,** neutral. Since 8.5 is close to 7, you know that the solution would be toward the middle, not be at an extreme end. Eliminate choice **D,** very alkaline. Now you are left with choices **A** and **C.** So you could make an educated guess if you didn't immediately spot the answer.

Objective 5: Understanding of Motion, Forces, and Energy

The topics included are based on concepts of integrated physics and chemistry.

- Motion, force, energy (speed, acceleration, work, power, and so on)
- Newton's laws, inertia
- Efficiency of simple machines (levers, motors, wheels and axles, pulleys, and ramps)
- Wave interactions (interference, reflection, refraction, etc.)
- Heat and heat transfer (convection, conduction, radiation)
- Law of conservation of energy
- Wavelength, frequency, amplitude
- Economic and environmental impact

1 A car's velocity changes from 0 m/s to 60 m/s in 10 seconds. What is the car's average acceleration?

   A   1 m/s^2
   B   3 m/s^2
   C   6 m/s^2
   D   60 m/s^2

In this question you are being asked to calculate the *average velocity*. Remember that the formula chart at the beginning of the test gives you the formula in case you don't remember it.

Acceleration is the rate of change of velocity. Because velocity includes both speed and direction, if either value changes, velocity will change. So, acceleration is both the rate of change in velocity and the direction of that change. To calculate average acceleration, divide the change in velocity by the time interval. To find the change in velocity, subtract the initial velocity (starting velocity) from the final velocity:

$$a = \frac{\text{final velocity}}{\text{change in time}} = \frac{v_f - v_i}{\Delta t} = \frac{\Delta v}{\Delta t}$$

The symbol Δ is the Greek letter delta and stands for "change in." When calculating acceleration, be sure to include all proper units and algebraic signs. The unit for velocity is meters per second (m/s) and the unit for time is seconds (s); therefore, the unit for acceleration is m/s^2 or meters per second squared or "meters per second per second."

To solve this problem, substitute into the equation:

$$a = \frac{v_f - v_i}{\Delta t} = \frac{\Delta v}{\Delta t} = \frac{60\,m/s - 0\,m/s}{10\,s} = 6\,m/s^2$$

The correct answer is **C.**

Take advantage of the formula chart. You should review the formula chart at the beginning of this chapter before you take the test to make sure that you are familiar with the formulas and how to use them.

> **2** A ball moving at 10 m/s has a momentum of 25 g m/s. What is the mass of the ball in grams? Record and bubble in your answer to the nearest tenth on the answer document.

In this question you are being asked to find the *mass* of the ball given the momentum and the velocity. A formula involving momentum, mass, and velocity is given in the chart at the front of the exam.

Momentum (p) is defined as a measure of the motion of a body equal to the product of its mass (m) and velocity (v), the formula is $p = m \times v$.

Since you are being asked for the mass of the ball, the formula $p = m \times v$ must be rearranged to $m = p/v$. This was done by dividing by v. Now simply plug in to this rearranged formula to find the mass.

$$\frac{25g\,m/s}{10\,m/s} = 2.5g$$

Finally, record and bubble in your answer as follows:

3 Which of these does not require the presence of particles of matter?

   A radiation
   B conduction
   C convection
   D combustion

Notice that you are looking for the answer that does *not* require the presence of particles of matter. That means that three of the choices *do* require the presence of particles of matter. If you do not know the answer, you could scan the choices and see which one appears to be different from the others.

This could help you get the right answer or at least make an educated guess.

Radiation does not require the presence of particles of matter because radiation is the transfer of energy in the form of waves. An example of radiation is radiant energy, or energy from the sun. Once radiant energy from the sun reaches Earth, some of it is reflected, or bounced back, toward space, and some is absorbed. Only radiant energy that is absorbed changes to thermal energy. The correct answer is **A.**

4 Which optical process produces an image when you look at a mirror?

   F absorption
   G emission
   H refraction
   J reflection

When you look at any object in a mirror, the light rays from the object have been reflected off the mirror toward your eyes. This is called reflection. Choice **F,** absorption, is when light of certain colors is captured by atoms within a substance. Choice **G,** emission, is when the atoms of a substance are forced to radiate, or give off, light of certain colors. Choice **H,** refraction, occurs when light changes direction when it passes through the boundary between two substances. The correct answer is **J.**

5 Which of the following least involves inertia?

   A Passengers in a car move forward when a car stops suddenly.
   B A hockey puck decelerates as it slides in a straight line.
   C The great Egyptian pyramids have not moved for thousands of years.
   D Light rays can form diffraction patterns.

Focus on the words "least involves inertia." This tells you that inertia will probably be a major factor in three of the choices. Remember, you are looking for the *least*.

Inertia is the tendency of an object to remain stationary or to be in motion. Objects resist any change in their motion. An object at rest will continue at rest, while an object in motion will continue moving in the same direction and at the same speed unless acted upon by some outside force, such as gravity or friction. Choice **D** results from light rays interacting. The correct answer is **D.**

6 A serious environmental problem facing the United States today is how to dispose of garbage. Which of the following items would take the longest to decompose?

   F a plastic bag
   G a nonfiltered cigarette butt
   H a glass bottle
   J a tin can

Some questions in this exam may ask you about environmental impacts. In this question you are being asked to determine which will take the *longest* to decompose.

To answer this question you could use an elimination strategy by comparing any two items that you know about. For example, if you know that a cigarette butt (choice **G**) will decompose more quickly than a tin can (choice **J**), you could quickly eliminate choice **G.** Or you might understand that a tin can will rust and decompose more quickly than a glass bottle, which eliminates choice **J.** Now you are only comparing a plastic bag (choice **F**) and a glass bottle (choice **H**). A glass bottle decomposes after about one thousand years; a tin can, fifty years; a plastic bag, ten years; and a cigarette butt, less than five years. The correct answer is **H.** A common-sense approach might have led you to select the item that is most substantial and therefore might take longer to decompose.

PART II

PRACTICE TESTS

Remember there is no time limit on any of the TAKS Exit Level Exams. But you should use the following suggested time limits as you take these simulated tests:

- English Language Arts: Suggested time 2 hours
- Mathematics: Suggested time 2 hours
- Social Studies: Suggested time 2 hours
- Science: Suggested time 2 hours

The problems in these simulated practice exams are similar in style and difficulty to the problems on the actual exam. The TAKS examination is copyrighted and may not be duplicated. These questions are not taken from the actual tests.

Answer Document for Practice Test 1

English Language Arts

1 Ⓐ Ⓑ Ⓒ Ⓓ	6 Ⓕ Ⓖ Ⓗ Ⓙ	11 Ⓐ Ⓑ Ⓒ Ⓓ	16 Ⓕ Ⓖ Ⓗ Ⓙ	21 Ⓐ Ⓑ Ⓒ Ⓓ	26 Ⓕ Ⓖ Ⓗ Ⓙ
2 Ⓕ Ⓖ Ⓗ Ⓙ	7 Ⓐ Ⓑ Ⓒ Ⓓ	12 Ⓕ Ⓖ Ⓗ Ⓙ	17 Ⓐ Ⓑ Ⓒ Ⓓ	22 Ⓕ Ⓖ Ⓗ Ⓙ	27 Ⓐ Ⓑ Ⓒ Ⓓ
3 Ⓐ Ⓑ Ⓒ Ⓓ	8 Ⓕ Ⓖ Ⓗ Ⓙ	13 Ⓐ Ⓑ Ⓒ Ⓓ	18 Ⓕ Ⓖ Ⓗ Ⓙ	23 Ⓐ Ⓑ Ⓒ Ⓓ	28 Ⓕ Ⓖ Ⓗ Ⓙ
4 Ⓕ Ⓖ Ⓗ Ⓙ	9 Ⓐ Ⓑ Ⓒ Ⓓ	14 Ⓕ Ⓖ Ⓗ Ⓙ	19 Ⓐ Ⓑ Ⓒ Ⓓ	24 Ⓕ Ⓖ Ⓗ Ⓙ	
5 Ⓐ Ⓑ Ⓒ Ⓓ	10 Ⓕ Ⓖ Ⓗ Ⓙ	15 Ⓐ Ⓑ Ⓒ Ⓓ	20 Ⓕ Ⓖ Ⓗ Ⓙ	25 Ⓐ Ⓑ Ⓒ Ⓓ	

29 _____
_____
_____
_____
_____

30 _____
_____
_____
_____
_____
_____

31 _____
_____
_____
_____
_____

32 Ⓕ Ⓖ Ⓗ Ⓙ	36 Ⓕ Ⓖ Ⓗ Ⓙ	41 Ⓐ Ⓑ Ⓒ Ⓓ	46 Ⓕ Ⓖ Ⓗ Ⓙ	51 Ⓐ Ⓑ Ⓒ Ⓓ
33 Ⓐ Ⓑ Ⓒ Ⓓ	37 Ⓐ Ⓑ Ⓒ Ⓓ	42 Ⓕ Ⓖ Ⓗ Ⓙ	47 Ⓐ Ⓑ Ⓒ Ⓓ	
34 Ⓕ Ⓖ Ⓗ Ⓙ	38 Ⓕ Ⓖ Ⓗ Ⓙ	43 Ⓐ Ⓑ Ⓒ Ⓓ	48 Ⓕ Ⓖ Ⓗ Ⓙ	
35 Ⓐ Ⓑ Ⓒ Ⓓ	39 Ⓐ Ⓑ Ⓒ Ⓓ	44 Ⓕ Ⓖ Ⓗ Ⓙ	49 Ⓐ Ⓑ Ⓒ Ⓓ	
	40 Ⓕ Ⓖ Ⓗ Ⓙ	45 Ⓐ Ⓑ Ⓒ Ⓓ	50 Ⓕ Ⓖ Ⓗ Ⓙ	

Use a lined 8½ × 11 sheet of paper to write your essay.

CUT HERE

Answer Document for Practice Test 1

Mathematics

1 Ⓐ Ⓑ Ⓒ Ⓓ
2 Ⓕ Ⓖ Ⓗ Ⓙ
3 Ⓐ Ⓑ Ⓒ Ⓓ
4 Ⓕ Ⓖ Ⓗ Ⓙ
5 Ⓐ Ⓑ Ⓒ Ⓓ
6 Ⓕ Ⓖ Ⓗ Ⓙ
7 Ⓐ Ⓑ Ⓒ Ⓓ
8 Ⓕ Ⓖ Ⓗ Ⓙ
9 Ⓐ Ⓑ Ⓒ Ⓓ
10 Ⓕ Ⓖ Ⓗ Ⓙ
11 Ⓐ Ⓑ Ⓒ Ⓓ
12 Ⓕ Ⓖ Ⓗ Ⓙ
13 Ⓐ Ⓑ Ⓒ Ⓓ
14 Ⓕ Ⓖ Ⓗ Ⓙ
15 Ⓐ Ⓑ Ⓒ Ⓓ
16 Ⓕ Ⓖ Ⓗ Ⓙ
17 Ⓐ Ⓑ Ⓒ Ⓓ
18 Ⓕ Ⓖ Ⓗ Ⓙ
19 Ⓐ Ⓑ Ⓒ Ⓓ
20 Ⓕ Ⓖ Ⓗ Ⓙ

21 (grid-in: digits 0–9)

22 Ⓕ Ⓖ Ⓗ Ⓙ
23 Ⓐ Ⓑ Ⓒ Ⓓ
24 Ⓕ Ⓖ Ⓗ Ⓙ
25 Ⓐ Ⓑ Ⓒ Ⓓ
26 Ⓕ Ⓖ Ⓗ Ⓙ
27 Ⓐ Ⓑ Ⓒ Ⓓ
28 Ⓕ Ⓖ Ⓗ Ⓙ
29 Ⓐ Ⓑ Ⓒ Ⓓ
30 Ⓕ Ⓖ Ⓗ Ⓙ
31 Ⓐ Ⓑ Ⓒ Ⓓ
32 Ⓕ Ⓖ Ⓗ Ⓙ
33 Ⓐ Ⓑ Ⓒ Ⓓ
34 Ⓕ Ⓖ Ⓗ Ⓙ
35 Ⓐ Ⓑ Ⓒ Ⓓ
36 Ⓕ Ⓖ Ⓗ Ⓙ
37 Ⓐ Ⓑ Ⓒ Ⓓ
38 Ⓕ Ⓖ Ⓗ Ⓙ
39 Ⓐ Ⓑ Ⓒ Ⓓ
40 Ⓕ Ⓖ Ⓗ Ⓙ

41 Ⓐ Ⓑ Ⓒ Ⓓ
42 Ⓕ Ⓖ Ⓗ Ⓙ
43 Ⓐ Ⓑ Ⓒ Ⓓ
44 Ⓕ Ⓖ Ⓗ Ⓙ
45 Ⓐ Ⓑ Ⓒ Ⓓ
46 Ⓕ Ⓖ Ⓗ Ⓙ
47 Ⓐ Ⓑ Ⓒ Ⓓ
48 Ⓕ Ⓖ Ⓗ Ⓙ
49 Ⓐ Ⓑ Ⓒ Ⓓ
50 Ⓕ Ⓖ Ⓗ Ⓙ
51 Ⓐ Ⓑ Ⓒ Ⓓ
52 Ⓕ Ⓖ Ⓗ Ⓙ
53 Ⓐ Ⓑ Ⓒ Ⓓ
54 Ⓕ Ⓖ Ⓗ Ⓙ
55 Ⓐ Ⓑ Ⓒ Ⓓ
56 Ⓕ Ⓖ Ⓗ Ⓙ
57 Ⓐ Ⓑ Ⓒ Ⓓ
58 Ⓕ Ⓖ Ⓗ Ⓙ
59 Ⓐ Ⓑ Ⓒ Ⓓ
60 Ⓕ Ⓖ Ⓗ Ⓙ

Social Studies

1 Ⓐ Ⓑ Ⓒ Ⓓ
2 Ⓕ Ⓖ Ⓗ Ⓙ
3 Ⓐ Ⓑ Ⓒ Ⓓ
4 Ⓕ Ⓖ Ⓗ Ⓙ
5 Ⓐ Ⓑ Ⓒ Ⓓ
6 Ⓕ Ⓖ Ⓗ Ⓙ
7 Ⓐ Ⓑ Ⓒ Ⓓ
8 Ⓕ Ⓖ Ⓗ Ⓙ
9 Ⓐ Ⓑ Ⓒ Ⓓ
10 Ⓕ Ⓖ Ⓗ Ⓙ

11 Ⓐ Ⓑ Ⓒ Ⓓ
12 Ⓕ Ⓖ Ⓗ Ⓙ
13 Ⓐ Ⓑ Ⓒ Ⓓ
14 Ⓕ Ⓖ Ⓗ Ⓙ
15 Ⓐ Ⓑ Ⓒ Ⓓ
16 Ⓕ Ⓖ Ⓗ Ⓙ
17 Ⓐ Ⓑ Ⓒ Ⓓ
18 Ⓕ Ⓖ Ⓗ Ⓙ
19 Ⓐ Ⓑ Ⓒ Ⓓ
20 Ⓕ Ⓖ Ⓗ Ⓙ

21 Ⓐ Ⓑ Ⓒ Ⓓ
22 Ⓕ Ⓖ Ⓗ Ⓙ
23 Ⓐ Ⓑ Ⓒ Ⓓ
24 Ⓕ Ⓖ Ⓗ Ⓙ
25 Ⓐ Ⓑ Ⓒ Ⓓ
26 Ⓕ Ⓖ Ⓗ Ⓙ
27 Ⓐ Ⓑ Ⓒ Ⓓ
28 Ⓕ Ⓖ Ⓗ Ⓙ
29 Ⓐ Ⓑ Ⓒ Ⓓ
30 Ⓕ Ⓖ Ⓗ Ⓙ

31 Ⓐ Ⓑ Ⓒ Ⓓ
32 Ⓕ Ⓖ Ⓗ Ⓙ
33 Ⓐ Ⓑ Ⓒ Ⓓ
34 Ⓕ Ⓖ Ⓗ Ⓙ
35 Ⓐ Ⓑ Ⓒ Ⓓ
36 Ⓕ Ⓖ Ⓗ Ⓙ
37 Ⓐ Ⓑ Ⓒ Ⓓ
38 Ⓕ Ⓖ Ⓗ Ⓙ
39 Ⓐ Ⓑ Ⓒ Ⓓ
40 Ⓕ Ⓖ Ⓗ Ⓙ

41 Ⓐ Ⓑ Ⓒ Ⓓ
42 Ⓕ Ⓖ Ⓗ Ⓙ
43 Ⓐ Ⓑ Ⓒ Ⓓ
44 Ⓕ Ⓖ Ⓗ Ⓙ
45 Ⓐ Ⓑ Ⓒ Ⓓ
46 Ⓕ Ⓖ Ⓗ Ⓙ
47 Ⓐ Ⓑ Ⓒ Ⓓ
48 Ⓕ Ⓖ Ⓗ Ⓙ
49 Ⓐ Ⓑ Ⓒ Ⓓ
50 Ⓕ Ⓖ Ⓗ Ⓙ

51 Ⓐ Ⓑ Ⓒ Ⓓ
52 Ⓕ Ⓖ Ⓗ Ⓙ
53 Ⓐ Ⓑ Ⓒ Ⓓ
54 Ⓕ Ⓖ Ⓗ Ⓙ
55 Ⓐ Ⓑ Ⓒ Ⓓ

Science

1 Ⓐ Ⓑ Ⓒ Ⓓ
2 Ⓕ Ⓖ Ⓗ Ⓙ
3 Ⓐ Ⓑ Ⓒ Ⓓ
4 Ⓕ Ⓖ Ⓗ Ⓙ
5 Ⓐ Ⓑ Ⓒ Ⓓ
6 Ⓕ Ⓖ Ⓗ Ⓙ
7 Ⓐ Ⓑ Ⓒ Ⓓ
8 Ⓕ Ⓖ Ⓗ Ⓙ
9 Ⓐ Ⓑ Ⓒ Ⓓ
10 Ⓕ Ⓖ Ⓗ Ⓙ
11 Ⓐ Ⓑ Ⓒ Ⓓ
12 Ⓕ Ⓖ Ⓗ Ⓙ
13 Ⓐ Ⓑ Ⓒ Ⓓ
14 Ⓕ Ⓖ Ⓗ Ⓙ
15 Ⓐ Ⓑ Ⓒ Ⓓ
16 Ⓕ Ⓖ Ⓗ Ⓙ
17 Ⓐ Ⓑ Ⓒ Ⓓ
18 Ⓕ Ⓖ Ⓗ Ⓙ
19 Ⓐ Ⓑ Ⓒ Ⓓ

20 (grid-in: digits 0–9)

21 Ⓐ Ⓑ Ⓒ Ⓓ
22 Ⓕ Ⓖ Ⓗ Ⓙ
23 Ⓐ Ⓑ Ⓒ Ⓓ
24 Ⓕ Ⓖ Ⓗ Ⓙ
25 Ⓐ Ⓑ Ⓒ Ⓓ
26 Ⓕ Ⓖ Ⓗ Ⓙ
27 Ⓐ Ⓑ Ⓒ Ⓓ
28 Ⓕ Ⓖ Ⓗ Ⓙ
29 Ⓐ Ⓑ Ⓒ Ⓓ
30 Ⓕ Ⓖ Ⓗ Ⓙ
31 Ⓐ Ⓑ Ⓒ Ⓓ
32 Ⓕ Ⓖ Ⓗ Ⓙ
33 Ⓐ Ⓑ Ⓒ Ⓓ
34 Ⓕ Ⓖ Ⓗ Ⓙ
35 Ⓐ Ⓑ Ⓒ Ⓓ
36 Ⓕ Ⓖ Ⓗ Ⓙ
37 Ⓐ Ⓑ Ⓒ Ⓓ
38 Ⓕ Ⓖ Ⓗ Ⓙ
39 Ⓐ Ⓑ Ⓒ Ⓓ
40 Ⓕ Ⓖ Ⓗ Ⓙ

41 Ⓐ Ⓑ Ⓒ Ⓓ
42 Ⓕ Ⓖ Ⓗ Ⓙ
43 Ⓐ Ⓑ Ⓒ Ⓓ
44 Ⓕ Ⓖ Ⓗ Ⓙ
45 Ⓐ Ⓑ Ⓒ Ⓓ
46 Ⓕ Ⓖ Ⓗ Ⓙ
47 Ⓐ Ⓑ Ⓒ Ⓓ
48 Ⓕ Ⓖ Ⓗ Ⓙ
49 Ⓐ Ⓑ Ⓒ Ⓓ
50 Ⓕ Ⓖ Ⓗ Ⓙ
51 Ⓐ Ⓑ Ⓒ Ⓓ
52 Ⓕ Ⓖ Ⓗ Ⓙ
53 Ⓐ Ⓑ Ⓒ Ⓓ
54 Ⓕ Ⓖ Ⓗ Ⓙ
55 Ⓐ Ⓑ Ⓒ Ⓓ

CUT HERE

Practice Test 1

English Language Arts

Reading and Written Composition

Reading

Directions: Read the two selections and the viewing and representing piece. Then answer the questions that follow.

All My Relations

By Linda Hogan

My notes about what I am reading

1   It is a sunny, clear day outside, almost hot, and a slight breeze comes through the room from the front door. We sit at the table and talk. As is usual in an Indian household, food preparation had begun as soon as we arrived and now there is the snap of potatoes frying in the black skillet, the sweet smell of white bread overwhelming even the grease, and the welcome black coffee. A ringer washer stands against the wall of the kitchen, and the counter space is taken up with dishes, pans, and boxes of food.

2   I am asked if I still read books and I admit that I do. Reading is not "traditional," and education has long been suspect in communities that were broken, in part, by that system, but we laugh at my confession because a television set plays in the next room.

3   In the living room there are two single beds. People from reservations, travelers needing help, are frequent guests here. The man who will put together the ceremony I have come to request sits on one, dozing. A girl takes him a plate of food. He eats. He is a man I have respected for many years, for his commitment to the people, for his intelligence, for his spiritual and political involvement in concerns vital to Indian people and nations. Next to him sits a girl eating potato chips, and from this room we hear the sounds of the freeway.

4   After eating and sitting, it is time for me to talk to him, to tell him why we have come here. I have brought him tobacco and he nods and listens as I tell him about the help we need.

5   I know this telling is the first part of the ceremony, my part in it. It is story, really, that finds its way into language, and story is at the very crux of healing, at the heart of every ceremony and ritual in the older America.

6   The ceremony itself includes not just our own prayers and stories of what brought us to it, but also includes the unspoken records of history, the mythic past, and all the other lives connected to ours, our families, nations, and all other creatures.

7   I am sent home to prepare. I tie fifty tobacco ties, green. This I do with Bull Durham tobacco, squares of cotton that are tied with twine and left strung together. These are called prayer ties. I spend the time preparing alone and in silence. Each tie has a prayer in it. I will also need wood for the fire, meat and bread for food.

8   On the day of the ceremony, we meet in the next town and leave my car in public parking. My daughters and I climb into the backseat. The man who will help us is drumming and singing in front of us. His wife drives and chats. He doesn't speak. He is

GO ON TO THE NEXT PAGE

My notes about what I am reading

moving between the worlds, beginning already to step over the boundaries of what we think, in daily and ordinary terms, is real and present. He is already feeling, hearing, knowing what else is there, that which is around us daily but too often unacknowledged, a larger life than our own. We pass billboards and little towns and gas stations. An eagle flies overhead. It is "a good sign," we all agree. We stop to watch it.

9   We stop again, later, at a convenience store to fill the gas tank and to buy soda. The leader still drums and is silent. He is going into the drum, going into the center, even as we drive west on the highway, even with our conversations about other people, family, work.

10   It is a hot, balmy day, and by the time we reach the site where the ceremony is to take place, we are slow and sleepy with the brightness and warmth of the sun. Others are already there. The children are cooling off in the creek. A woman stirs the fire that lives inside a circle of black rocks, pots beside her, a jar of oil, a kettle, a can of coffee. The leaves of the trees are thick and green.

11   In the background, the sweat lodge structure stands. Birds are on it. It is still skeletal. A woman and man are beginning to place old rugs and blankets over the bent cottonwood frame. A great fire is already burning, and the lava stones that will be the source of heat for the sweat are being fired in it.

12   A few people sit outside on lawn chairs and cast-off couches that have the stuffing coming out. We sip coffee and talk about the food, about recent events. A man tells us that a friend gave him money for a new car. The creek sounds restful. Another man falls asleep. My young daughter splashes in the water. Heat waves rise up behind us from the fire that is preparing the stones. My tobacco ties are placed inside, on the framework of the lodge.

13   By late afternoon we are ready, one at a time, to enter the enclosure. The hot lava stones are placed inside. They remind us of earth's red and fiery core, and of the spark inside all life. After the flap, which serves as a door, is closed, water is poured over the stones and the hot steam rises around us. In a sweat lodge ceremony, the entire world is brought inside the enclosure. The soft odor of smoking cedar accompanies this arrival. It is all called in. The animals come from the warm and sunny distances. Water from the dark lakes is there. Wind. Young, lithe willow branches bent overhead remember their lives rooted in ground, the sun their leaves took in. They remember that minerals and water rose up their trunks, and birds nested in their leaves, and that planets turned above their brief, slender lives. The thunderclouds travel in from far regions of earth. Wind arrives from the four directions. It has moved through caves and breathed through our bodies. It is the same air elk have inhaled, air that passed through the lungs of a grizzly bear. The sky is there, with all the stars whose lights we see long after the stars themselves have gone back to nothing. It is a place grown intense and holy. It is a place of immense community and of humbled solitude; we sit together in our aloneness and speak, one at a time, our deepest language of need, hope, loss, and survival. We remember that all things are connected.

14   Remembering this is the purpose of the ceremony. It is part of a healing and restoration. It is the mending of a broken connection between us and the rest. The participants in a ceremony say the words "All my relations" before and after we pray; those words create a relationship with other people, with animals, with the land. To have health it is necessary to keep all these relations in mind. The intention of a ceremony is to put a person back together by restructuring the human mind. This reorganization is accomplished by a kind of inner map, a geography of the human spirit and the rest of the world. We make whole our broken-off pieces of self and world. Within ourselves, we bring together the fragments of our lives in a sacred act of renewal, and we reestablish our connections with others. The ceremony is a point of return. It takes us toward the place of balance, our place in the community of all things. It is an event that sets us

GO ON TO THE NEXT PAGE

back upright. But it is not a finished thing. The real ceremony begins where the formal one ends, when we take up a new way, our minds and hearts filled with the vision of earth that holds us within it, in compassionate relationship to and with our world.

15   We speak. We sing. We swallow water and breathe smoke. By the end of the ceremony, it is as if skin contains land and birds. The places within us have become filled. As inside the enclosure of the lodge, the animals and ancestors move into the human body, into skin and blood. The land merges with us. The stones come to dwell inside the person. Gold rolling hills take up residence, their tall grasses blowing. The red light of canyons is there. The black skies of night that wheel above our heads come to live inside the skull. We who easily grow apart from the world are returned to the great store of life all around us, and there is the deepest sense of being at home here in this intimate kinship. There is no real aloneness. There is solitude and the nurturing silence that is relationship with ourselves, but even then we are part of something larger.

16   After a sweat lodge ceremony, the enclosure is abandoned. Quieter now, we prepare to drive home. We pack up the kettles, the coffeepot. The prayer ties are placed in nearby trees. Some of the other people prepare to go to work, go home, or cook a dinner. We drive. Everything returns to ordinary use. A spider weaves a web from one of the cottonwood poles to another. Crows sit inside the framework. It's evening. The crickets are singing. All my relations.

The following story, "Calling Home," describes an incident in the lives of American soldiers during the Vietnam War, which ended in 1975.

Calling Home

By Tim O'Brien

1   In August, after two months in the bush, the platoon returned to Chu Lai for a week's standdown.

2   They swam, played mini-golf in the sand, and wrote letters and slept late in the mornings. At night there were floor shows. There was singing and dancing, and afterward there was homesickness. It was neither a good time nor a bad time. The war was all around them.

3   On the final day, Oscar and Eddie and Doc and Paul Berlin hiked down to the 42nd Commo Detachment. Recently the outfit had installed a radio-telephone hookup with the States.

4   "It's called MARS," said a young Pfc at the reception desk. "Stands for Military Air Radio System." He was a friendly, deeply tanned redhead without freckles. On each wrist was a gold watch, and the boy kept glancing at them as if to correlate time. He seemed a little nervous.

5   While they waited to place their calls, the Pfc explained how the system worked. A series of radio relays fed the signal across the Pacific to a telephone exchange in downtown Honolulu, where it was sent by regular undersea cable to San Francisco and from there to any telephone in America. "Real wizardry," the boy said. "Depends a lot on the weather, but, wow, sometimes it's like talkin' to the guy next door. You'd swear you was there in the same room."

6   They waited nearly an hour. Relay problems, the Pfc explained. He grinned and gestured at Oscar's boots. "You guys are legs, I guess. Grunts."

7   "I guess so," Oscar said.

8   The boy nodded solemnly. He started to say something but then shook his head. "Legs," he murmured.

GO ON TO THE NEXT PAGE

9   Eddie's call went through first.

10   The Pfc led him into a small, sound-proofed booth and had him sit behind a console equipped with speakers and a microphone and two pairs of headsets. Eddie began rocking in his chair. He held the microphone with one hand, squeezing it, leaning slightly forward. It was hard to see his eyes.

11   He was in the booth a long time. When he came out his face was bright red. He sat beside Oscar. He yawned, then immediately covered his eyes, rubbed them, then stretched and blinked.

12   "Geez," he said softly.

13   Then he laughed. It was a strange, scratchy laugh. He cleared his throat and smiled and kept blinking.

14   "Geez," he said.

15   "What—"

16   Eddie giggled. "It was . . . You shoulda heard her. 'Who?' she goes. Like that— 'Who?' Just like that."

17   He took out a handkerchief, blew his nose, shook his head. His eyes were shiny.

18   "Just like that—'Why?' 'Eddie,' I say, and Ma says, 'Eddie who?' and I say, "Who do you think Eddie?" She almost passes out. Almost falls down or something. She gets this call from Nam and thinks maybe I been shot. 'Where you at?' she says, like maybe I'm calling from Graves Registration, or something, and—"

19   "That's great," Doc said. "That's really great, man."

20   "Yeah. It's—"

21   "Really great."

22   Eddie shook his head violently as though trying to clear stopped-up ears. He was quiet a time. Then he laughed.

23   "Honest, you had to hear it. 'Who?' she keeps saying. 'Who?' Real clear. Like in the next . . . And Petie! He's in high school now—you believe that? My brother. Can't even call him Petie no more. 'Pete,' he says. Real deep voice, just like that guy on Lawrence Welk—'Pete, not Petie,' he goes. You believe that?"

24   "Hey, it's terrific," Doc said. "It really is."

25   "And clear? Man! Just like—I could hear Ma's cuckoo clock, that clear."

26   "Technology."

27   "Yeah," Eddie grinned. "Real technology. It's . . . I say, 'Hey, Ma,' and what's she say? 'Who's this?' Real scared-soundin', you know? Man, I coulda just—"

28   "It's great, Eddie."

29   Doc was next, and then Oscar. Both of them came out looking a little funny, not quite choked up but trying hard not to be. Very quiet at first, then laughing, then talking fast, then turning quiet again. It made Paul Berlin feel warm to watch them. Even Oscar seemed happy.

30   "Technology," Doc said. "You can't beat technology."

31   "My old man, all he could say was 'Over.' Nothin' else. 'Weather's fine,' he'd say, 'over.'" Oscar wagged his head. His father had been an R.T.O. in Italy. "You believe that? All he says is 'Over,' and 'Roger that.' Crazy."

32   They would turn pensive. Then one of them would chuckle or grin.

33   "Pirates are out of it this year. Not a prayer, Petie says."

34   "I bleed."

My notes about what I am reading

GO ON TO THE NEXT PAGE

35   "Yeah, but Petie—he goes nuts over the Pirates. It's all he knows. Thinks we're over here fightin' the Russians. The Pirates, that's all he knows."

My notes about what I am reading

36   "Crazy," Oscar said. He kept wagging his head. "Over 'n' out."

37   It made Paul Berlin feel good. Like buddies; he felt close to all of them. When they laughed, he laughed.

38   Then the Pfc tapped him on the shoulder.

39   He felt giddy. Everything inside the booth was painted white. Sitting down, he grinned and squeezed his fingers together. He saw Doc wave at him through the plastic window.

40   "Ease up," the Pfc said. "Pretend it's a local call."

41   The boy helped him with the headset. There was a crisp clicking sound, then a long electric hum like a vacuum cleaner running in another room. He remembered . . . his mother always used the old Hoover on Saturdays. The smell of carpets, a fine, powdery dust rising in the yellow window light. An uncluttered house. Things in their places.

42   He felt himself smiling. He pressed the headset tight. What day was it? Sunday, he hoped. His father like to putz on Sunday. Putzing, he called it, which meant tinkering and dreaming and touching things with his hands, fixing them or building them or tearing them down, studying things. Putzing . . . He hoped it was Sunday. What would they be doing? What month was it? He pictured the telephone. It was there in the kitchen, to the left of the sink. It was black. Black because his father hated pastels on his telephones. . . . He imagined the ring. He remembered it clearly, how it sounded both in the kitchen and in the basement, where his father had rigged up an extra bell, much louder-sounding in the cement. He pictured the basement. He pictured the living room and den and kitchen. Pink formica on the counters and speckled pink-and-white walls. His father . . .

43   The Pfc touched his arm. "Speak real clear," he said. "And after each time you talk you got to say, 'Over,' it's in the regs, and the same for your loved ones. Got it?"

44   Paul Berlin nodded. Immediately the headphones buzzed with a different sort of sound.

45   He tried to think of something meaningful and cheerful to say. Nothing forced: easy and natural, but still loving. Maybe start by saying he was getting along. Tell them things weren't really so bad. Then ask how his father's business was. Don't let on about being afraid. Don't make them worry—that was Doc Peret's advice. Make it sound like a vacation, talk about the swell beaches, tell them how you're getting this spectacular tan. Tell them—tell them you're getting skin cancer from all the sun, a Miami holiday. That was Doc's advice. Tell them . . . The Pfc swiveled the microphone so that it faced him. The boy checked his two wristwatches, smiled, whispered something. The kitchen, Paul Berlin thought. He could see it now. The old walnut dining table that his mother had inherited from an aunt in Minnesota. And the big white stove, the refrigerator, stainless steel cabinets over the sink, the black telephone, the windows looking out on Mrs. Stone's immaculate back yard. She was something, that Mrs. Stone. Yes, that was something to ask his father about: Was the old lady still out there in winter, using her broom to sweep away the snow, even in blizzards, sweeping and sweeping, and in the autumn was she still sweeping leaves from her yard, and in summer was she sweeping away the dandelion fuzz? Sure! He'd get his father to talk about her. Something fun and cheerful. The time old Mrs. Stone was out there in the rain, sweeping the water off her lawn as fast as it fell, all day long, sweeping it out to the gutter and then sweeping it up the street, but how the street was at a slight angle so that the rain water kept flowing back down on her, and, Lord, how Mrs. Stone was out

GO ON TO THE NEXT PAGE

there until midnight, ankle-deep, trying to beat gravity with her broom. Lord, his father always said, shaking his head. Neighbors. That was one thing to talk about. And . . . and he'd ask his mother if she'd stopped smoking. There was a joke about that. She'd say, "Sure, I've stopped four times this week," which was a line she'd picked up on TV or someplace. Or she'd say, "No, but at least I'm not smoking tulips anymore, just Luckies." They'd laugh. He wouldn't let on how afraid he was; he wouldn't mention Billy Boy Watkins or Frenchie Tucker or what happened to Bernie Lynn and the others who were gone.

46   Yes, they'd laugh, and afterward, near the end of the conversation, maybe then he'd tell them he loved them. He couldn't remember ever telling them that, except at the bottom of letters, but this time maybe . . . The line buzzed again, then clicked, then there was the digital pause that always comes as a connection is completed, and then he heard the first ring. He recognized it. Hollow, washed out by distance, but it was still the old ring. He'd heard it ten thousand times. He listened to the ring as he would listen to family voices, his father's voice and his mother's voice, older now and changed by what time does to voices, but still the same voices. He stopped thinking of things to say. He concentrated on the ringing. He saw the black phone, heard it ringing and ringing. The Pfc held up a thumb but Paul Berlin barely noticed; he was smiling at the sound of the ringing.

47   "Tough luck," Doc said afterward.

48   Oscar and Eddie clapped him on the back, and the Pfc shrugged and said it happened sometimes.

49   "What can you do?" Oscar said. "The world, it don't stop turning."

50   "Yeah."

51   "Who knows? Maybe they was out takin' a drive, or something. Buying groceries. The world don't stop."

**Use "All My Relations" (pp. 115–117)
to answer questions 1–12.**

---

1 How does the information in this sentence contribute to the reader's understanding of the selection?

Next to him sits a girl eating potato chips, and from this room we hear the sounds of the freeway.

- **A** It shows that children will be involved in what is to come.
- **B** It establishes the historical era in which the passage takes place.
- **C** It creates a mood of calm and introspection.
- **D** It allows the reader to understand the feelings of the participants in the ceremony.

2 The author's purpose in using this point of view is most probably to—

- **F** emphasize her thoughts on the meaning of this ritual
- **G** remind readers that they too are part of *the mythic past*
- **H** show the importance of the ceremony to everyone involved
- **J** contrast the ceremony as it is now with those celebrated in older times

3 A literary technique that is noticeably absent from this selection is—

- **A** a description of the physical environment
- **B** the use of the present tense
- **C** the use of dialogue
- **D** the inclusion of everyday behavior

4 Read the following dictionary entry.

fire \fīər\ *v* **1.** to shoot **2.** to apply fuel to **3.** to inspire **4.** to dismiss from a job

Which definition best matches the use of the word *fired* in paragraph 11?

- **F** Definition 1
- **G** Definition 2
- **H** Definition 3
- **J** Definition 4

5 Paragraphs 4 through 7 are primarily about—

- **A** the author's preparations for the ceremony
- **B** the leader's requirements
- **C** the participants in the ceremony
- **D** the meaning of the sweat lodge ceremony

6 Which of the following adjectives best describes the author?

- **F** Haunted
- **G** Excited
- **H** Weary
- **J** Composed

GO ON TO THE NEXT PAGE

7 The reader can infer that the ceremony of the sweat lodge—

   A changes every time it is performed

   B must be held at the location at which this one is held

   C is intended to foster a oneness between the participants and the world around them

   D has as its purpose the physical healing of the participants

8 The living arrangements where the author meets the man who will lead the ceremony could best be described as—

   F natural

   G primitive

   H chaotic

   J modest

9 The author's description of the willows in paragraph 13 is—

   A a metaphor, which emphasizes the life within them

   B personification, which reinforces the concept of community

   C a simile, which serves to show the difference between plants and animals

   D satirical, using humor to make its point

10 There is laughter at the author's *confession* in paragraph 2 because—

   F she has come for help, but her confession suggests she may not need it

   G she is nervous about what is to come

   H it would seem inconsistent to distrust book learning but not television

   J the leader suggests they can find enlightenment in nontraditional things

11 The author intends the words *all my relations* to refer to—

   A her kinship with something larger than herself

   B the family of all American Indians

   C those who give her the help she needs in arranging the ceremony

   D all other people

12 Which of the following sentences from the selection best sums up its major theme?

   F *It is part of a healing and restoration.*

   G *There is no real aloneness.*

   H *It is a place grown intense and holy.*

   J *The stones come to dwell inside a person.*

GO ON TO THE NEXT PAGE

**Use "Calling Home" (pp. 117–120)
to answer questions 13–23.**

13 In paragraph 3, to what does *the final day* refer?

   A The day before the soldiers will return to the fighting

   B The last day they will be allowed to call home

   C The day before the week's standdown

   D The last day of the war

14 Why does Oscar repeat the word *legs* in paragraph 8?

   F Because he doesn't understand what the Pfc is saying

   G In order to make it clear to the Pfc that the Pfc is in error

   H So that his friends will realize he has heard the term before

   J Because he is reacting negatively to the name given to the soldiers

15 In paragraph 32, the word *pensive* means—

   A amused

   B judgmental

   C thoughtful

   D humble

16 The writing technique used by the author in paragraphs 12 through 36 that most suggests a true-to-life event is—

   F the inclusion of many similes

   G the use of partial sentences

   H the images of chaos and destruction in the soldiers' language

   J the descriptions of the thoughts of the four soldiers

17 What does the sentence *It was neither a good time nor a bad time* suggest about the four soldiers?

   A They have had enough standdowns before that this isn't an interesting occurrence for them.

   B A standdown is better than the fighting, but it is difficult to enjoy it when they soon must return to the war.

   C They are bored with the inactivity and don't like the singing and dancing.

   D Only the chance to call home will make this a good time for the soldiers.

18 Which of these sentences from the selection best indicates the emotional impact of the calls home?

   F *The war was all around them.*

   G *His eyes were shiny.*

   H *The boy checked his two wristwatches, smiled, whispered something.*

   J *Oscar and Eddie clapped him on the back, and the Pfc shrugged and said it happened sometimes.*

GO ON TO THE NEXT PAGE

19 It is clear from Eddie's comments after he makes his call that—

    A he thinks the call should have gone on longer

    B he doesn't want his brother Petie to become a soldier

    C he was able to speak with everyone in his family

    D he feels that his mother cares about him

20 In this story, the kitchen symbolizes—

    F family

    G the United States

    H tranquility

    J shelter

21 A major theme of "Calling Home" is—

    A yearning

    B abandonment

    C habit

    D confusion

22 By making paragraphs 42, 45, and 46 quite long in contrast to the much of the rest of the selection, the author—

    F emphasizes the horror of war

    G provides an effective summary of what has gone before

    H makes Paul the main character of the story

    J allows the reader to more fully empathize with families left behind when soldiers go to war

23 Which sentence from the selection identifies the climax of the story?

    A *Immediately the headphones buzzed with a different sort of sound.*

    B *Paul Berlin barely noticed.*

    C *"Tough luck," Doc said afterward.*

    D *Yes, they'd laugh, and afterward, near the end of the conversation, maybe then he'd tell them he loved them.*

GO ON TO THE NEXT PAGE

**Use "All My Relations" and "Calling Home" (pp. 115–120)
to answer questions 24 and 25.**

24 The main character of "Calling Home" differs
from the main character of "All My Relations"
in that he—

  F probably considers his family as only his
relatives at home

  G needs help in order to feel better

  H has other people around him who understand
what he is going through

  J uses modern mechanical devices

25 Which of the following words taken from the two
selections best relates to a similarity of their
themes?

  A World

  B Aloneness

  C Technology

  D Vision

**Use the visual representation on page 120
to answer questions 26–28.**

26 Which of the following is the most likely creator
of this advertisement?

  F A political action committee

  G The Department of Social Services

  H The U.S. Department of Education

  J A group promoting less strict rules for
adoption

28 Which of the following is most likely the desired
reaction in the viewer of the visual representation?

  F Indignation because the children in the
picture have no homes

  G Understanding of the hard work involved in
being a foster parent

  H Pleasure at the sight of so many happy
children

  J A consideration of becoming a foster parent

27 What in the visual representation most strongly
suggests that families can be more than blood
relatives?

  A The fact that the adults are playing with the
children

  B The number of children in the picture

  C The words *No Bounds*

  D The fact that the children are all African
American

GO ON TO THE NEXT PAGE

Directions: Answer the following questions in the space provided on the answer document.

29 In "All My Relations," what suggests that this is not the author's first experience with a sweat lodge ceremony? Support your answer with evidence from the selection.

31 Could the titles of these passages, "All My Relations" and "Calling Home," effectively be switched? Support your answer with evidence from **both** selections.

30 Why does the author of "Calling Home" include Oscar's comment "The world, it don't stop turning"? Support your answer with evidence from the selection.

BE SURE YOU HAVE WRITTEN YOUR ANSWERS
ON THE ANSWER DOCUMENT.

GO ON TO THE NEXT PAGE

Written Composition

Write an essay explaining what the idea of "family"
means to you or to another specific person.

The information in the box below will help you remember what you should think about when you write your composition.

REMEMBER TO

- write on the topic given
- make your writing thoughtful and interesting
- check that each sentence you write adds to your composition as a whole
- make sure that your ideas are clear and easy for the reader to follow
- write about your ideas in detail so that the reader can better understand what you are trying to say
- proofread your writing to correct errors in spelling, capitalization, punctuation, grammar, and sentence structure

GO ON TO THE NEXT PAGE

USE THIS PREWRITING PAGE TO
PLAN YOUR COMPOSITION.

MAKE SURE THAT YOU WRITE YOUR COMPOSITION ON
THE LINED PORTION OF THE ANSWER DOCUMENT.

GO ON TO THE NEXT PAGE

At this point during an actual exam, you would be given 3 sample revising and editing questions. After completing these 3 samples, you would be directed to stop, raise your hand, and wait for the test administrator to assist you before continuing to the next section.

Revising and Editing

Directions: Read the following passages and mark your answers on your answer sheet. Remember that you are NOT permitted to use dictionaries or other reference materials on this section of the test.

Carl has written this report for a psychology assignment. He has asked you to read the report and think about the corrections and improvements he needs to make. When you finish reading the report, answer the multiple-choice questions that follow.

Jargon in Language and Communication

(1) Jargon may be defined in several ways. (2) It can be simply the language of any particular group or profession; it can be any unintelligible talk—that is, gibberish; it can be language that uses words that are uncommon, unlikely to be understood, or a meaning that is vague. (3) So in one way, whether something is or is not jargon depends on whether you, the listener, understands it.

(4) All language is a system of symbols through which we communicate with one another. (5) In order for effective communication to happen, both the speaker and the listener must agree on the meaning of the symbols (words) being used. (6) Helen Keller, born both blind and deaf, was cut off from the rest of the world because she could not communicate with it. (7) But one day, her teacher finally was able to communicate with her and Keller suddenly realized that certain symbols, in her case sign language, meant certain specific things. (8) She described this experience later. (9) "I knew then that 'w-a-t-e-r' meant the wonderful cool something that was flowing over my hand.

(10) But messing around with jargon can have the opposite effect, hindering communication, whether intended or not. (11) Jargon can occur in the language that's come to be called "bureaucratese," used by both corporate and government bureaucrats. (12) Examples of this can be found, for example, in the terms "downsizing," and "economic adjustment" when what's really meant is "firing" and "recession." (13) The purpose of the jargon in this case is to intentionally make something sound better than it is. (14) Much technology involves jargon as well. (15) The computer and electronics industries are full of it. (16) Many find themselves lost in their world of special meanings and acronyms. (17) "CD-ROM," "gigabyte," "interface," "bus," "CPU," and "fatal exception error" are only a few examples.

GO ON TO THE NEXT PAGE

(18) Cultural groups also make use of jargon. (19) The term for "good" illustrates this point. (20) Teenagers, for example, in each generation seem to take great pleasure in constructing their own language and terms. (21) Over generations "good" has evolved to "neato" to "cool" to "rad" to "phat" to "extreme" . . . and on and on.

(22) Some jargon is necessary, when we need new words to symbolize new processes or concepts. (23) But jargon must be used carefully or it will have the effect of producing the opposite of what language is for, communication. (24) It will, perhaps on purpose, isolate the speaker and make him or her, or his or her group, seem "different" from others.

32 What change, if any, should be made in sentence 2?

- **F** Change the semicolon after *profession* to a comma
- **G** Change *unintelligible* to **unintelligable**
- **H** Change a *meaning that is vague* to **vague**
- **J** Make no change

33 What change, if any, should be made in sentence 3?

- **A** Change both the first and second *whether* to **weather**
- **B** Change *depends* to **depend**
- **C** Change *understands* to **understand**
- **D** Make no change

34 Carl wants to add this sentence to the second paragraph (sentences 4–9).

She had no way to understand what language is.

Where should this sentence be inserted?

- **F** After sentence 5
- **G** After sentence 6
- **H** After sentence 7
- **J** At the end of the paragraph

35 What change should be made in sentence 7?

- **A** Change *was able* to **is able**
- **B** Insert a comma after *with her*
- **C** Change *certain* to **certainly**
- **D** Change *communicate* to **comunnicate**

36 What change, if any, should be made in sentence 9?

- **F** Change *I* to **she**
- **G** Change *meant* to **will mean**
- **H** Insert quotation marks after *hand*
- **J** Make no change

37 What change, if any, should be made in sentence 10?

- **A** Change *messing around with* to **using**
- **B** Change *effect* to **affect**
- **C** Change *intended* to **intend**
- **D** Make no change

GO ON TO THE NEXT PAGE

38 The meaning of sentence 12 can be clarified by changing *this* to—

   F bureaucratese

   G language

   H effects

   J terms

39 What is the most effective way to rewrite the ideas in sentences 14 and 15?

   A Computers and electronics are full of jargon.

   B Technology is full of jargon, electronics and computers involve jargon also.

   C The computer and electronics industries are full of jargon; as is much technology.

   D Much technology, such as that in the computer and electronics industries, involves jargon as well.

40 What is the most effective way to improve the organization of the fourth paragraph (sentences 18–21)?

   F Move sentence 18 to the end of the paragraph

   G Delete sentence 18

   H Move sentence 19 to the end of the paragraph

   J Move sentence 19 to follow sentence 20

41 What change, if any, should be made in sentence 24?

   A Delete the comma after *will*

   B Change *make* to **making**

   C Change *his or her* to **their**

   D Make no change

GO ON TO THE NEXT PAGE

Luis's English teacher has asked his students to interview an older family member or friend about his or her hobby and to write a report based on the interview. As part of a peer-editing conference, you have been asked to read Luis's draft and to think about the corrections and improvements he should make. When you finish reading the report, answer the questions that follow.

Consuela's Garden

(1) My aunt Consuela would like to spend as much time tending to her flower garden as she does tending to clients at her Catering business. (2) As it is, she manages to work in her yard at least twenty hours a week she says, unless it's raining or snowing. (3) And even then, if she can't get outside, she's likely to be curled up on the sofa paging through garden catalogues and dreaming of spring planting.

(4) She had this to say. (5) "Because it's life, and it gives you surprises all the time, just like life does. (6) I walk around the garden early in the morning and say hello to all my plants. (7) Some are just beginning to rise from the ground, just born, with their bright green leaves. (8) Some have buds just straining to burst into bright flowers. (9) But even when the flowers die, the plant is still healthy, and it will be born again next year. (10) Surprises and beautiful gifts, that's what the flowers give me."

(11) "But its such a lot of work," I said. (12) "What do you have to do to keep all the flowers blooming." (13) I found out from her that she has to feed the dirt. (14) She has to add peat and compost and fertilizer. (15) She has to dig it up and turn it over. (16) She has to keep bugs and squirrels and deer from eating them. (17) She has to sometimes dig up the plant and divide it and replant the sections separately.

(18) She likes to see other gardens also. (19) Her blisters and broken fingernails are just part of it, and they don't seem to bother her much. (20) "It's just a little price to pay for so much pleasure." (21) She's never bored or doesn't know what to do to keep her occupied. (22) She visits gardens that are open to the public to discover new plants, such as the St. Louis Botanical Garden she saw on a trip last spring.

42 What change, if any, should be made in sentence 1?

    F Change *would like* to **would have liked**
    G Delete *flower*
    H Change *Catering* to **catering**
    J Make no change

43 What transition should be added to the beginning of sentence 4?

    A Afterward,
    B When I asked her why she loves gardening,
    C In answer to my question,
    D Immediately,

GO ON TO THE NEXT PAGE

44 Luis wants to add the following sentence, which quotes more of Consuela's words, in the second paragraph (sentences 4–10).

Some flowers are past their best time and are waiting for my sharp scissors to snip them off.

Where should this sentence be inserted?

F At the beginning of the paragraph
G After sentence 5
H After sentence 8
J At the end of the paragraph

45 What change, if any, should be made in sentence 11?

A Change *its* to **it's**
B Change *a lot* to **alot**
C Delete the comma after *work*
D Make no change

46 What change, if any, should be made in sentence 12?

F Delete *to do*
G Change the period at the end of the sentence to a question mark
H Delete the quotation marks at the beginning and end of the sentence
J Make no change

47 What is the most effective way to rewrite the ideas in sentences 13 and 14?

A She has to add peat and compost and fertilizer. To feed the dirt.
B Feeding the dirt with peat, compost, and fertilizer I found out from her.
C She told me that she has to feed the dirt by adding peat, compost, and fertilizer.
D She told me she has to feed the dirt, she adds peat and compost and fertilizer.

48 What change, if any, should be made in sentence 16?

F Change *keep* to **is keeping**
G Change *deer* to **animals**
H Change *them* to **the plants**
J Make no change

49 What is the most effective way to improve the organization of the last paragraph (sentences 18–22)?

A Move sentence 18 to the end of the paragraph
B Move sentence 18 to follow sentence 21
C Switch sentences 19 and 20
D Delete sentence 20

GO ON TO THE NEXT PAGE

50 What change, if any, should be made in sentence 21?

    F Change *She's* to **shes**

    G Change *her* to **herself**

    H Change *occupied* to **ocupied**

    J Make no change

51 What is the most effective way to rewrite sentence 22?

    A Visiting gardens that are open to the public, she discovers new plants, such as the St. Louis Botanical Garden she saw on a trip last spring.

    B Last spring, discovering new plants at the St. Louis Botanical Gardens, which is open to the public.

    C To discover new plants, she visits gardens that are open to the public, such as the St. Louis Botanical Garden she saw on a trip last spring.

    D New plants, such as at the St. Louis Botanical Garden, open to the public, are discovered on a trip last spring.

BE SURE YOU HAVE RECORDED ALL OF YOUR ANSWERS
ON THE ANSWER DOCUMENT.

Mathematics

Directions: Read each question and then carefully fill in the correct answer on your answer document. If a correct answer is <u>not here</u>, then mark the letter of the choice for "Not Here."

GO ON TO THE NEXT PAGE

Mathematics Chart

LENGTH

Metric	Customary
1 kilometer = 1000 meters	1 mile = 1760 yards
1 meter = 100 centimeters	1 mile = 5280 feet
1 centimeter = 10 millimeters	1 yard = 3 feet
	1 foot = 12 inches

CAPACITY AND VOLUME

Metric	Customary
1 liter = 1000 milliliters	1 gallon = 4 quarts
	1 gallon = 128 ounces
	1 quart = 2 pints
	1 pint = 2 cups
	1 cup = 8 ounces

MASS AND WEIGHT

Metric	Customary
1 kilogram = 1000 grams	1 ton = 2000 pounds
1 gram = 1000 milligrams	1 pound = 16 ounces

TIME

1 year = 365 days

1 year = 12 months

1 year = 52 weeks

1 week = 7 days

1 day = 24 hours

1 hour = 60 minutes

1 minute = 60 seconds

Inches

Centimeters

GO ON TO THE NEXT PAGE

Mathematics Chart

Perimeter	rectangle	$P = 2l + 2w$ or $P = 2(l + w)$
Circumference	circle	$C = 2\pi r$ or $C = \pi d$
Area	rectangle	$A = lw$ or $A = bh$
	triangle	$A = \frac{1}{2}bh$ or $A = \frac{bh}{2}$
	trapezoid	$A = \frac{1}{2}(b_1 + b_2)h$ or $A = \frac{(b_1 + b_2)h}{2}$
	circle	$A = \pi r^2$
Surface Area	cube	$S = 6s^2$
	cylinder (lateral)	$S = 2\pi rh$
	cylinder (total)	$S = 2\pi rh + 2\pi r^2$ or $S = 2\pi r(h + r)$
	cone (lateral)	$S = \pi rl$
	cone (total)	$S = \pi rl + \pi r^2$ or $S = \pi r(l + r)$
	sphere	$S = 4\pi r^2$
Volume	prism or cylinder	$V = Bh^*$
	pyramid or cone	$V = \frac{1}{3}Bh^*$
	sphere	$V = \frac{4}{3}\pi r^3$

*B represents the area of the Base of a solid figure.

Pi	π	$\pi \approx 3.14$ or $\pi \approx \frac{22}{7}$
Pythagorean Theorem		$a^2 + b^2 = c^2$
Distance Formula		$d = \sqrt{(x_2 - x_1)^2 + (y_2 - y_1)^2}$
Slope of a Line		$m = \frac{y_2 - y_1}{x_2 - x_1}$
Midpoint Formula		$M = \left(\frac{x_2 + x_1}{2}, \frac{y_2 + y_1}{2}\right)$
Quadratic Formula		$x = \frac{-b \pm \sqrt{b^2 - 4ac}}{2a}$
Slope-Intercept Form of an Equation		$y = mx + b$
Point-Slope Form of an Equation		$y - y_1 = m(x - x_1)$
Standard Form of an Equation		$Ax + By = C$
Simple Interest Formula		$I = prt$

GO ON TO THE NEXT PAGE

1 The unfolded surface of a 3-dimensional figure is shown below.

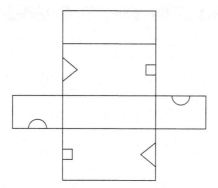

Which of the following 3-dimensional figures does this represent?

A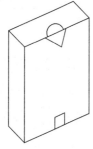

C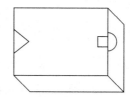

B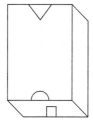

D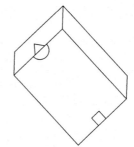

GO ON TO THE NEXT PAGE

2 Mr. Hernandez is repairing portions of a stained glass window for a local church. He needs to cut a piece of glass to replace the shaded piece in the diagram below. What are the three angles of the piece of glass?

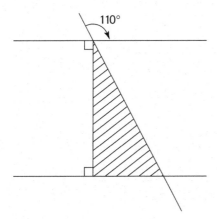

F 90°, 55°, 35°

G 90°, 60°, 30°

H 90°, 70°, 20°

J 110°, 50°, 20°

3 The cost for 2 CDs and 3 DVDs is $19.00. The cost for 3 CDs and 1 DVD is $14.50. To determine c, the cost of 1 CD, and d, the cost of 1 DVD, which pair of equations can be used?

A $2c + d = 19.00$
    $3c + 3d = 14.50$

B $2c + 3d = 19.00$
    $c + 3d = 14.50$

C $3c + 2d = 19.00$
    $3c + d = 14.50$

D $2c + 3d = 19.00$
    $3c + d = 14.50$

4 What effect will there be on the graph of $y = x^2 - 3$ when it is changed to $y = x^2 + 6$?

F The graph widens

G The graph is congruent and its vertex moves up the y-axis

H The graph narrows

J The graph is congruent and its vertex moves down the y-axis

5 The temperature outside drops 37° from its reading at time t. The temperature then rises 15°, giving a reading of −12°. Find the temperature at time t.

A −34°

B 10°

C 34°

D 40°

GO ON TO THE NEXT PAGE

6 Which of the graphs below shows a line parallel to the graph of the equation $y = 2x + 3$?

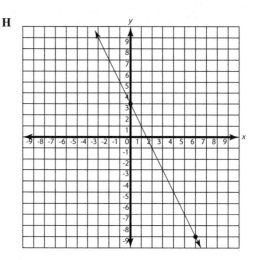

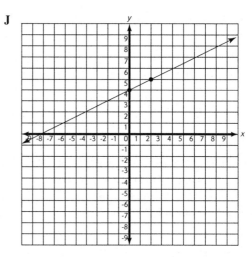

7 The data for vehicles sold in May is shown in the table below. The owner of an automotive dealership plans to construct a pie chart displaying the different vehicles sold in May.

Vehicles Sold in May	
2-Door Coupe	75
4-Door Sedan	15
Station Wagon	30
Pickup Truck	45
SUV	60

The section representing the pickup trucks sold should be marked with what central angle in the pie chart?

A 24°

B 36°

C 48°

D 72°

GO ON TO THE NEXT PAGE

8 A real estate agent has prepared a list of all the houses she has sold during the last year. What statistical measure of data would describe the average cost of homes sold by the agent in the last year?

F   Mean
G   Mode
H   Median
J   Range

9 Use the ruler on the mathematics chart to measure appropriate dimensions of the figure to the nearest tenth of a centimeter.

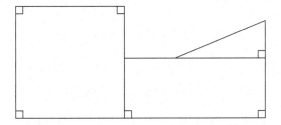

Which of the following gives the approximate area of the figure above?

A   16.3 cm^2
B   17.5 cm^2
C   21.6 cm^2
D   43.8 cm^2

10 Rosario's sells 5 pounds of potatoes for $0.79. Which of the following steps should be used to find the total cost, T, of buying p pounds of potatoes?

F   Divide p by T
G   Multiply T by p
H   Divide T by the cost of 1 pound of potatoes
J   Multiply p by the cost of 1 pound of potatoes

11 The Orange Taxi Company charges $3.70 to get into one of its taxis and $4.25 for each mile the cab is driven. Which equation best shows how the cost, c, and the number of miles, m, ridden by the taxi customer are related?

A $c = 3.70 + 4.25m$
B $c = 3.70m + 4.25m$
C $c = 3.70m + 4.25$
D $c = 3.70 + 4.25$

12 A candy maker buys her chocolate as cubes with dimensions as shown in the diagram below.

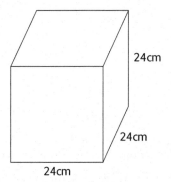

She melts the chocolate cubes and pours them into spherical molds having a radius of 2 cm. About how many spheres can she make from each cube?

F   275
G   354
H   412
J   1,100

GO ON TO THE NEXT PAGE

13 Which of the following choices includes a pair of similar polygons?

A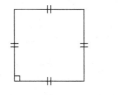

C

B

D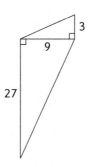

14 A triangular pyramid has how many faces, edges, and vertices?

   F   5 faces, 9 edges, 6 vertices
   G   4 faces, 6 edges, 4 vertices
   H   4 faces, 3 edges, 4 vertices
   J   3 faces, 4 edges, 3 vertices

15 In the graph of the equation $y = x^2 - x - 20$, what are the x-intercepts?

   A $x = 4, x = -5$
   B $x = -4, x = 5$
   C $x = -4, x = -5$
   D $x = 4, x = 5$

GO ON TO THE NEXT PAGE

16 A linear function which relates the number of yards, *y*, to the number of feet, *f*, is $y = (\frac{1}{3})f$. Which of the following choices illustrates the same linear function?

F

f	*Y*
1	3
3	9
7	21

G For every 30 feet run on a football field, the player runs 10 yards

H For every 3 yards a school child jumps, she jumps 6 feet

J For every 60 feet a ball is thrown, it travels 25 yards

17 Ramon is paid $7 per hour (after taxes are deducted) and puts 20% of his earnings in a savings account. How many hours will he have to work in order to have enough money in his savings account to purchase a coat that sells for $77?

A 9
B 11
C 55
D 305

18 Erin is shopping for blank floppy disks for her computer. A package of 20 brand E disks costs $4.25 while a package of 20 brand Q disks costs $5.75. By purchasing a container of brand E disks, what percent of the cost of brand Q disks will Erin save?

F 6.5%
G 26%
H 35%
J 150%

GO ON TO THE NEXT PAGE

19 Coordinate grids are often placed over maps to help identify specific locations. With a coordinate grid placed over a map, three cities are located at points $P(5,7)$, $Q(-6,3)$, and $R(2,-3)$. A fourth city, M, is located at a point midway between cities P and R. Which of the following is the best approximation, in coordinate units, of the distance between cities Q and M?

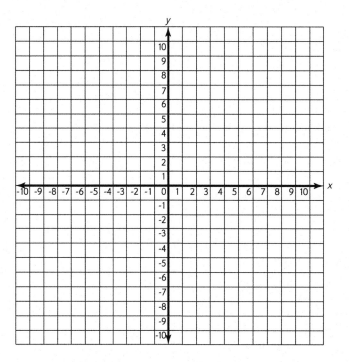

A 9.22

B 9.55

C 85.00

D 91.25

GO ON TO THE NEXT PAGE

20 A square patio, with perimeter 32 ft. is inscribed within a circular lawn as shown in the diagram below. Approximate the length of the radius of the circular lawn to the nearest foot.

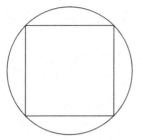

    F 6 ft
    G 7 ft
    H 11 ft
    J 23 ft

21 Solve for m in this equation: $2m + 14 = 3m - 7 + 6m$.

Record your answer and fill in the bubbles on your answer document. Be sure to use correct place value.

22 In which of the following equations does y increase when x increases?

    F $y = -2x$
    G $y = |x|$
    H $y = x^2$
    J $y = x^3$

GO ON TO THE NEXT PAGE

Practice Test 1

23 Rashid had $18. At the automotive store he bought *x* cans of motor oil, at $3 per can, and *y* spark plugs, at $2 each. Excluding tax, Rashid spent less than $18.

Graph the inequality $3x + 2y < 18$ on the grid below.

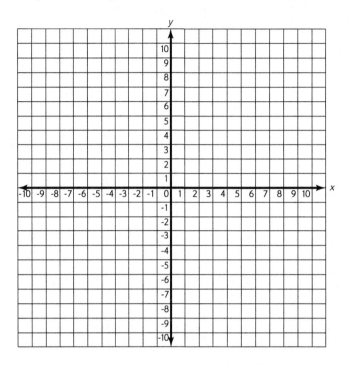

Which point represents a possible number of cans of oil and spark plugs purchased by Rashid?

A (5,3)

B (3,6)

C (2,5)

D (4,4)

24 ∠C and ∠D are supplementary angles. If m∠C is *c*, which equation can be used to find *d*, m∠D?

F $d = 90 - c$

G $d = 90 + c$

H $d = 180 - c$

J $d = 180 + c$

25 The expression $(3x - 4)2x - (4x - 3)(x - 1)$ is equivalent to which of the following?

A $-12x^2 + 3x + 3$

B $-8x^2 + 7x + 1$

C $2x^2 - 15x + 3$

D $2x^2 - x - 3$

GO ON TO THE NEXT PAGE

Practice Test 1

26 A survey was taken by making random phone calls to people in a city. They were asked to choose the political party with which they most agree. The results are shown below.

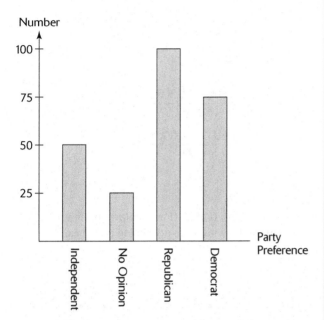

Number

Party Preference

Based on the data displayed above, how many of the city's 10,000 residents are likely to agree with the Democratic Party?

F 750

G 300

H 3,000

J 7,500

27 Figure *TRY* is shown on the coordinate plane.

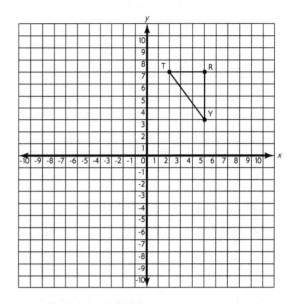

Which transformation creates an image with vertex *R* at the origin?

A Reflect figure *TRY* across the line $x = 2$, then translate this image right 1 and down 6

B Rotate figure *TRY* 90° around *Y*, then translate the image to the left 1 and 3 down

C Reflect figure *TRY* across the *x*-axis, then reflect the image about the *y*-axis

D Translate figure *TRY* down 7 and 6 left

GO ON TO THE NEXT PAGE

28 Using the table below, find the equation that describes *y*, the total cost of buying wallpaper, as a function of *x*, the number of square feet of wallpaper purchased.

Square Feet of Wallpaper (x)	Total Cost (y)
1,100	$2,585
1,760	$4,136
2,340	$5,499

   F $x = 2.35y$
   G $y = .43x$
   H $y = 2.35x$
   J $x = .34y$

29 Which statement best describes the effect on the graph of the function $y = 7.2x + 3.7$ if its *y*-intercept is decreased by 2.9?

   A The *x*-intercept decreases.
   B The *y*-intercept increases.
   C Graph of the new function is parallel to the graph of original function.
   D Slope of new line is greater than slope of original line.

30 A rectangular solid has a volume of 144 in^3. If the length is multiplied by $\frac{1}{2}$, the width by $\frac{1}{3}$, and the height by $\frac{1}{4}$, what will be the volume of this new rectangular solid?

   F 6 in^3
   G 24 in^3
   H 48 in^3
   J 72 in^3

31 For the first year of her new job, Sharon was paid $24,300. After receiving a pay raise, her second year salary rose to $28,800. Which expression represents her percent increase in pay?

   A $\left(\dfrac{24,300}{28,800}\right) \times 100$

   B $\left(\dfrac{28,800}{24,300}\right) \times 100$

   C $\dfrac{(28,800 - 24,300)}{28,800} \times 100$

   D $\dfrac{(28,800 - 24,300)}{24,300} \times 100$

32 The pattern of dots shown below continues infinitely, with more dots being added each step.

Step 1   Step 2   Step 3

What expression below can be used to determine the number of dots in the nth step?

   F $2(n - 1)$
   G $2^n + 1$
   H $2^n - 1$
   J $2(n + 1)$

33 Jorge owns a mobile car-detailing business. He has fixed costs of $600 per week and additional costs for cleaning materials of $5 per car he details. If he charges $55 to detail each car, how many cars must he detail each week before he can make a profit?

   A 10
   B 11
   C 12
   D 120

GO ON TO THE NEXT PAGE

34 From a boat at sea, the angle of elevation to the top of a 150-ft cliff is 30°.

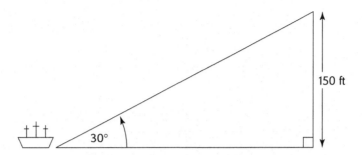

What is the approximate horizontal distance from the boat to the foot of the vertical cliff?

F 106 ft
G 130 ft
H 212 ft
J 260 ft

35 At a movie theater, 327 people attended the 7:00 p.m. showing. If students were charged $4 and adults were charged $7, how many students attended if the total ticket receipts for the showing were $1,683?

A 109
B 125
C 202
D 218

36 Which of the following correctly lists the functions in order from the narrowest to widest graphs?

F $y = 6x^2$, $y = -3x^2$, $y = (\frac{5}{2})x^2$, $y = -(\frac{1}{4})x^2$

G $y = -(\frac{5}{2})x^2$, $y = -(\frac{1}{3})x^2$, $y = 3x^2$, $y = -7x^2$

H $y = (\frac{1}{2})x^2$, $y = -(\frac{7}{4})x^2$, $y = 3x^2$, $y = -5x^2$

J $y = (\frac{1}{2})x^2$, $y = (\frac{3}{2})x^2$, $y = -4x^2$, $y = (\frac{8}{3})x^2$

GO ON TO THE NEXT PAGE

37 A rectangle with vertices (5,5), (5,7), (8,7), (8,5) is shown below.

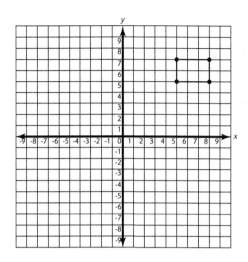

Which rectangle below is similar to the figure above?

A

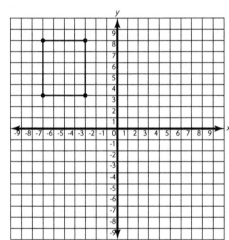

C

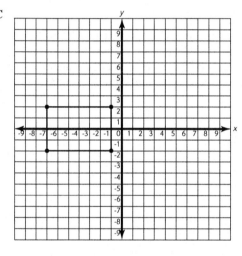

B

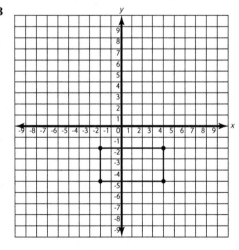

D

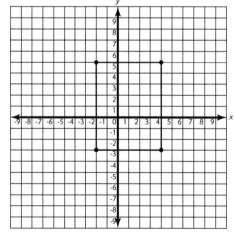

GO ON TO THE NEXT PAGE ▷

38 Which represents the graph of the line containing the point (0, –2) and parallel to $y = (\frac{2}{3})x$?

F

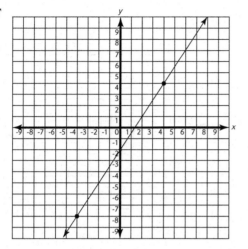

H

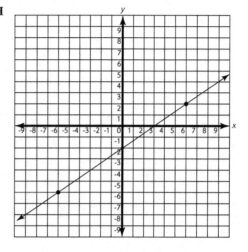

G

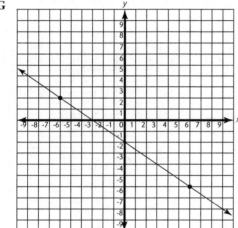

J

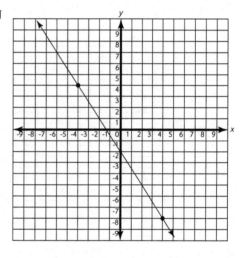

GO ON TO THE NEXT PAGE

39 An investor is locked into 2 short-term investments for 3 months. One investment is currently worth $250, but is losing money at the rate of $2 per day; the second is worth $25 and is earning money at the rate of $5 per day. Which graph shows when the 2 investments will have the same value?

A

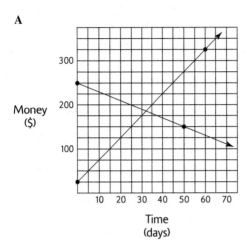

C

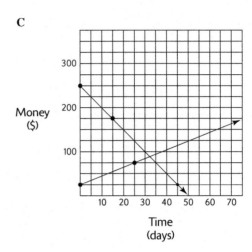

B

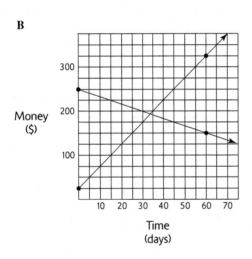

D

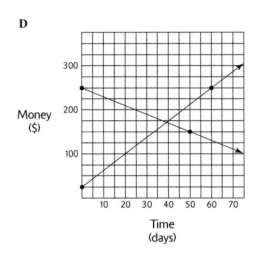

GO ON TO THE NEXT PAGE

40 Fifty TV sets were randomly pulled from the factory conveyor belt after their assembly was completed. Five would not turn on, 10 had minor defects that could be quickly repaired, and the other 35 operated as expected. Which of the following statements regarding the reported data is *not* a valid conclusion?

F Twice as many TV sets were defective as inoperable.

G If 200 TV sets were randomly tested, it would be reasonable to expect 40 to have minor defects.

H The number of TV sets that operated was more than twice the number that either did not operate or had minor defects.

J If 100 TV sets were randomly tested, it would be reasonable to expect about 30 to have minor defects.

41 A farmer has enclosed 2 fields with fences as shown in the diagram below.

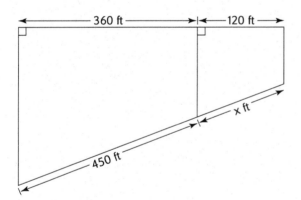

Find the length of the section of fence marked x.

A 113 ft
B 150 ft
C 210 ft
D 300 ft

42 Tom has 3 fewer CDs than Luke. Manuel has twice as many CDs as Tom. If the three boys have a total of 39 CDs, which equation can be used to determine the number of CDs Luke has?

F $x + (\frac{x}{3}) + 2x = 39$
G $x + (x - 3) + (\frac{x}{2}) = 39$
H $x + (x - 3) + 2x = 39$
J $x + (x - 3) + 2(x - 3) = 39$

43

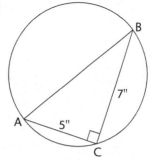

Find the approximate length of diameter AB of the circle.

A 4.9 in
B 8.6 in
C 9.0 in
D 74.0 in

44 On the side of many office water coolers is a dispenser containing paper cups shaped like the one below.

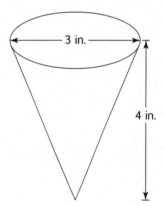

Find the approximate volume of this conical drinking cup.

F 37.68 in^3
G 12.56 in^3
H 9.42 in^3
J 6.28 in^3

GO ON TO THE NEXT PAGE

45 Find the slope and y-intercept of the line containing the point $(3, -2)$ and having the same y-intercept as $3x - 2y = 12$.

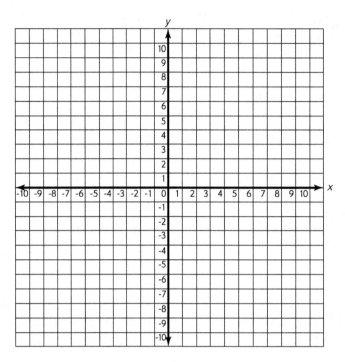

A $m = \dfrac{4}{3}$
   $b = -6$

B $m = \dfrac{-8}{3}$
   $b = -6$

C $m = \dfrac{-14}{3}$
   $b = 12$

D $m = -2$
   $b = 4$

GO ON TO THE NEXT PAGE

46 A 3-dimensional object has the dimensions as shown by the front, top and side views below.

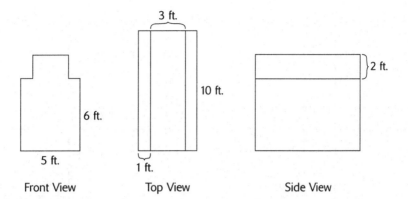

| Front View | Top View | Side View |

What is the volume of this 3-dimensional object?

F 300 ft³

G 360 ft³

H 412 ft³

J 546 ft³

47 An electronics supplier sells small quantities of a metal to be used in making electrical components. The costs for various weights of this metal are shown in the table.

Weight (w)	Cost (c)
.02 g	$.09
.11 g	$.27
.35 g	$.75
.48 g	$1.01

If w is the weight of the metal and c is the cost to purchase that weight, which of the following best shows the relationship between the weight and the cost?

A $w = 2c + .05$

B $c = 10w - .02$

C $w = \dfrac{c - .01}{2}$

D $c = 2w + .05$

48 Which expression is the simplified form of $(-5x^3y^{-5})(3x^{-7}y^{-8})$?

F $\dfrac{-y^3}{15x^4}$

G $\dfrac{-15}{x^{21}y^{40}}$

H $\dfrac{-15y^3}{x^4}$

J $\dfrac{-x^4}{15y^3}$

49 Find the solution set of the equation $4(2x - 5)^2 = 64$.

A $\left\{\dfrac{5}{2}, \dfrac{9}{2}\right\}$

B $\left\{\dfrac{11}{2}, \dfrac{5}{2}\right\}$

C $\left\{\dfrac{1}{2}, \dfrac{9}{2}\right\}$

D $\left\{\dfrac{7}{2}, \dfrac{11}{2}\right\}$

GO ON TO THE NEXT PAGE

50 Which graph shows the set of ordered pairs (x,y) for which $x + y > 5$?

F

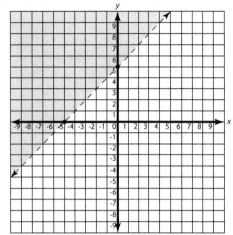

H

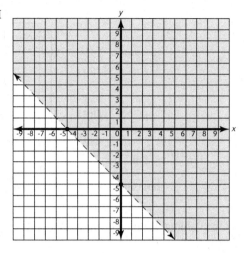

G

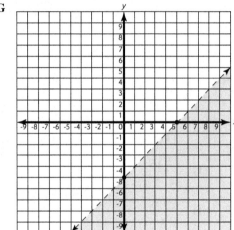

J

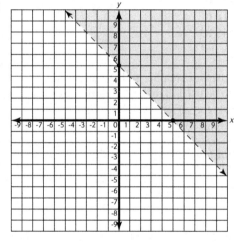

GO ON TO THE NEXT PAGE

51 Which equation represents the total area, *A*, of the figure below?

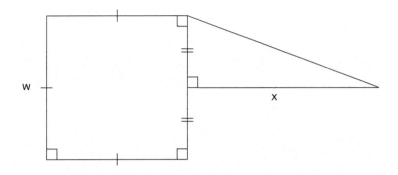

A $w^2 + (\frac{xw}{2})$

B $w^2 + (\frac{xw}{4})$

C $4w + x$

D $w^2 + xw$

52 From a piece of square metal, 12 inches on a side, a metal fabricator needs to cut out a circle of radius 6 inches and 4 small squares, 3 inches on a side. Why is this not possible?

F The area of the circle is greater than the area of the large square piece of metal

G There will not be enough metal left to cut out the 4 squares once the circle has been cut out.

H A circle cannot be cut from a square piece of metal.

J The perimeter of the 4 small squares is greater than the circumference of the circle.

53 Find the *y*-intercept of the function whose graph is shown below.

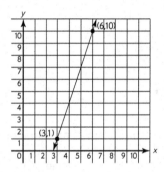

A −5

B −8

C −15

D −24

GO ON TO THE NEXT PAGE

Practice Test 1

54 The figures below illustrate a sequence of circles and triangles.

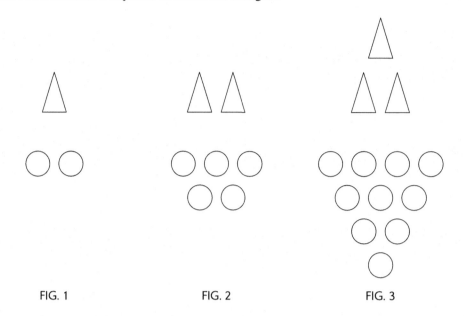

FIG. 1   FIG. 2   FIG. 3

Which equation relates c, the number of circles to t, the number of triangles?

F $t = c^2 - 1$

G $c = t^2 + 1$

H $t = \dfrac{(c - 1)}{3}$

J $c = 2t + 1$

55 The daily temperatures for a period of one week were recorded and the results are shown below.

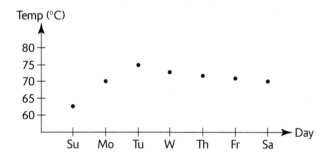

Which conclusion regarding the data above is most accurate?

A   The average daily temperature for the week was above 75°.

B   The daily temperature increased throughout the week.

C   The daily temperature changed more than 10° between 2 consecutive days at least once during the week.

D   The daily temperature increased in the beginning of the week and then leveled off toward the end of the week.

GO ON TO THE NEXT PAGE

56 Figure *PQRS* has vertices *P* (4,1), *Q* (8,4), *R* (5,8), and *S* (1,5). Which of the following is the correct name of figure *PQRS*?

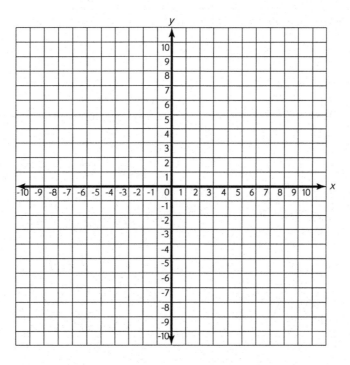

   F   Square

   G   Rhombus

   H   Rectangle

   J   Trapezoid

57 Thomas builds wooden furniture and works, at most, 40 hours each week. It takes him 2.5 hours to make a chair, and 3 hours to make a table. Which of the following best represents the time each week it takes Thomas to build *c* chairs and *t* tables?

   A $(2.5 + 3)ct = 40$

   B $2.5c + 3t \leq 40$

   C $3t > 40 - 2.5c$

   D $2.5c < 3t + 40$

58 What is the slope of the line having the equation $5y = -2(x - 3)$?

   F   5

   G $\dfrac{6}{5}$

   H $\dfrac{-2}{5}$

   J -2

GO ON TO THE NEXT PAGE

59 A weather balloon is released into the earth's atmosphere from sea level. As the balloon travels from sea level, where the temperature is 20°C, to an altitude of 12 kilometers, the temperature decreases linearly to –60° C, then increases linearly to 2°C at an altitude of 50 km, and decreases again, linearly, to –87°C at an altitude of 80 km above sea level. Which graph best illustrates this temperature change in the atmosphere?

A
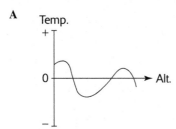

C
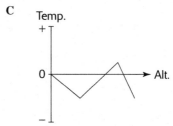

B
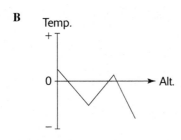

D
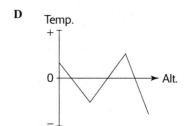

60 The velocity of an object dropped from a skyscraper is dependent on the time for which the object falls through the air. This relationship is shown in the table below.

Falling Time(s)	Velocity (ft/s)
2	64
3	96
5	160

At what velocity would you reasonably expect an object to be falling after falling for 4.5 seconds?

F   112 ft/s
G   121 ft/s
H   128 ft/s
J   144 ft/s

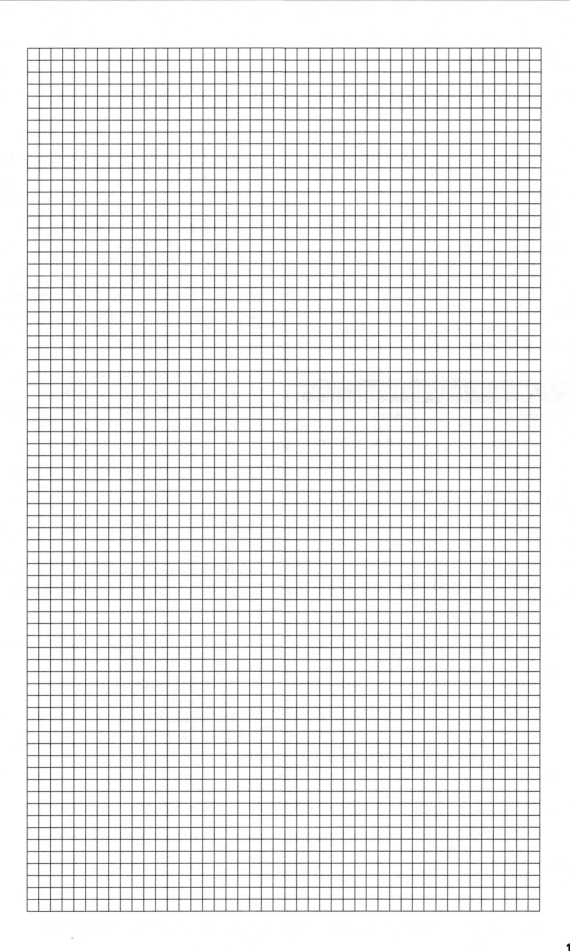

Social Studies

Directions: Read each question and then choose the best answer. Carefully fill in the correct answer on your answer document.

1 As a result of the Spanish-American War, the United States acquired which territory from Spain?

   A   Philippines
   B   Cuba
   C   Virgin Islands
   D   Hawaiian Islands

Use the chart and your knowledge of social studies to answer the following question.

Amending the Constitution	
To Propose	**To Ratify**
⅔ vote of both houses of Congress	¾ of state legislatures
Convention called by ⅔ of state legislatures	Conventions in ¾ of the states

2 Which of the following statements about the amendment process is correct?

   F   Only Congress can propose amendments.
   G   States can have a role in both proposing and ratifying amendments.
   H   Amendments do not go into effect until approved by state legislatures.
   J   Getting an amendment through Congress is easy.

3 The New Deal attempted to increase farm prices by—

   A   tariffs on agricultural imports
   B   improving farm efficiency
   C   cutbacks in farm production
   D   soil erosion programs

Use the excerpt and your knowledge of social studies to answer the following question.

> To be fearful of investing Congress, constituted as that body is, with ample authority for national purposes, appears to me the very climax of popular absurdity and madness.
>
> —*George Washington, 1786*

4 According to George Washington, Congress does not have enough power under—

   F   the new state constitutions
   G   the United States Constitution
   H   the Declaration of Independence
   J   the Articles of Confederation

5 The introduction of the assembly line in 1913 allowed Henry Ford to—

   A   increase the price of his cars
   B   pay his workers less
   C   cut production costs
   D   increase fuel efficiency

6 Supporters of states' rights are likely to emphasize which provision of the Constitution?

   F   Tenth Amendment
   G   necessary and proper clause
   H   supremacy clause
   J   Fourteenth Amendment

GO ON TO THE NEXT PAGE

Use the photograph and your knowledge of social studies to answer the following question.

7 The photograph of the Japanese internment camp at Manzanar during World War II best supports which statement?

   A   Internees lived in an area suitable for growing crops.

   B   Internees had the opportunity to ski, hike, and mountain climb.

   C   Internees were put in camps in remote and isolated areas.

   D   Internees were housed near major urban areas for security reasons.

8 Which of the following lists is in the correct sequence?

   F   Declaration of Independence
         Articles of Confederation
         U.S. Constitution
         Bill of Rights

   G   Articles of Confederation
         U.S. Constitution
         Bill of Rights
         Declaration of Independence

   H   Declaration of Independence
         Bill of Rights
         U.S. Constitution
         Articles of Confederation

   J   Declaration of Independence
         Bill of Rights
         Articles of Confederation
         U.S. Constitution

9 Merchants and scholars helped spread the ideas of the Renaissance from—

   A   Italy to Northern Europe

   B   Italy to the Americas

   C   France to Eastern Europe

   D   Holland and Germany to Italy

GO ON TO THE NEXT PAGE

Use the excerpt and your knowledge of social studies to answer the following question.

> Limitations of this kind can be preserved in practice no other way than through the medium of the courts of justice, whose duty it must be to declare all such acts contrary to the . . . constitution void.
>
> —*Alexander Hamilton, Federalist 78*

10 The power of the federal courts Alexander Hamilton is referring to is better known as

    F appellate jurisdiction

    G indictment

    H judicial review

    J original jurisdiction

11 When it was established in 1949, the purpose of the North Atlantic Treaty Organization (NATO) was to—

    A prevent Germany from controlling Europe

    B deter an attack on Europe by the Soviet Union

    C respond to ethnic violence around the world

    D provide economic aid to Western Europe

12 Early factories during the Industrial Revolution were located near

    F natural gas supplies

    G railroads

    H population centers

    J rivers and streams

13 The launch of Sputnik, the first satellite, in 1957 made many Americans feel that—

    A the U.S. was falling behind the Soviet Union in technology

    B the U.S. should reduce spending on space exploration

    C peace between the U.S. and the Soviet Union was essential

    D science could solve the world's problems

14 The main purpose for the construction of the Panama Canal was to—

    F get miners to the California gold fields

    G increase trade between American Atlantic and Pacific ports

    H provide jobs for Americans who were out of work

    J protect the west coast of the U.S. from attack

15 As a vertical combination, the Carnegie Steel Company owned steel mills and

    A textile mills

    B oil refineries

    C coal mines

    D lumber yards

GO ON TO THE NEXT PAGE

Use the diagram and your knowledge of social studies to answer the following question.

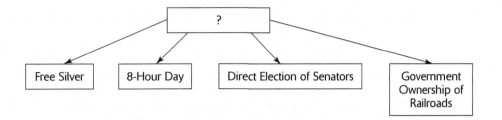

16 In the late 19th century, all of these issues were associated with the—

   F Populist Party
   G American Federation of Labor
   H Know-Nothing Party
   J Free Soil Party

17 Labor unions supported limits on immigration to the United States because they felt that—

   A immigrants took jobs from American workers
   B immigrants were dangerous radicals
   C immigrants never became citizens
   D immigrants were poor and illiterate

18 During the early 1950s, Senator Joseph McCarthy gained national attention through his investigations of—

   F organized crime
   G wasteful defense spending
   H Communists in the government
   J the civil rights movement

19 The invention of the cotton gin by Eli Whitney in 1793 led to—

   A the growth of cotton production in the North
   B the expansion of slavery in the South
   C the development of railroads in the South
   D the gradual emancipation of the slaves in the South

20 At the beginning of the 20th century, the Open Door Policy referred to—

   F unlimited immigration to the U.S.
   G U.S. trade with China
   H improved relations between the U.S. and South America
   J ending the power of political machines

GO ON TO THE NEXT PAGE

Use the map and your knowledge of social studies to answer the following question.

Gains and Losses of Seats in the House of Representatives
Between 1990 and 2000 Census

States that gain 2 seats
States that gain 1 seat
States that lose 2 seats
States that lose 1 seat
States that stay the same

21 Based on the map, which is a valid statement?

A The Northeast and Midwest are gaining in population.

B Population growth is occurring across the South.

C There is a population shift to the South and West.

D The population of the Great Plains is growing significantly.

Use the excerpt and your knowledge of social studies to answer the following question.

> Our purpose and our only purpose is to vindicate the right of parents to guard the religion of their children against efforts made in the name of science to undermine faith in supernatural religion.
>
> —*William Jennings Bryan, 1925*

22 What issue is Bryan referring to in this speech?

F the growing independence of women

G the impact of new technology such as the radio

H the popularity of revival meetings

J the teaching of evolution

GO ON TO THE NEXT PAGE

Use the photograph and your knowledge of social studies to answer the following question.

23 The photograph shows Charles Lindbergh and his wife, Anne Morrow Lindbergh, in 1927. Lindbergh was famous for—

    A   shooting down the most enemy planes in World War I

    B   making the first trans-Atlantic flight with a woman passenger

    C   flying across the Pacific Ocean from Los Angeles to Tokyo

    D   flying nonstop from New York to Paris solo

GO ON TO THE NEXT PAGE

Use the table and your knowledge of social studies to answer the following question.

Ranking of U.S. Cities, 1810 and 1860	
1810	*1860*
New York	New York
Philadelphia	Philadelphia
Baltimore	Baltimore
Boston	Boston
Charleston	New Orleans
New Orleans	Cincinnati
Salem	St. Louis
Providence	Chicago
Richmond	Buffalo
Albany	Newark

24 What conclusion can be drawn from the table about urbanization before the Civil War?

   F The Northeast no longer had the most large cities.

   G Cities were developing faster in the Midwest than the South.

   H There was no change in the pattern of urbanization between 1810 and 1860.

   J New Jersey was the fastest growing state.

25 The event that led to the buildup of American combat troops in Vietnam was the—

   A Gulf of Tonkin Resolution

   B Yalta Conference

   C Battle of Dien Bien Phu

   D War Powers Act

26 George Washington was appointed Commander-in-Chief of the American forces during the Revolutionary War by the—

   F Continental Congress

   G Virginia House of Burgesses

   H state militias

   J U.S. Senate

Use the excerpt and your knowledge of social studies to answer the following question.

> A free Negro of the African race, whose ancestors were brought to this country and sold as slaves, is not a "citizen" within the meaning of the Constitution of the United States.
>
> —Dred Scott *v.* Sanford, *1857*

27 This controversial Supreme Court decision was effectively overturned by which constitutional amendment?

   A Fifteenth Amendment

   B Fourteenth Amendment

   C Eighteenth Amendment

   D Twelfth Amendment

28 The Truman Doctrine was a response to—

   F a strike in the steel industry

   G Congress' failure to enact Medicare

   H the beginning of the Cold War

   J the integration of the armed forces

GO ON TO THE NEXT PAGE

29 The demand for automobiles in the 1920s—

   A increased the market for steel

   B encouraged automobile workers to join unions

   C led to more imports from Asia

   D encouraged the use of public transportation

30 What technical problem did Thomas Edison face when he opened the first electric power plant in 1882?

   F There were not enough customers.

   G The price of electricity was very high.

   H Electricity could not be transmitted over long distances.

   J There were no appliances that used electricity.

31 In passing the Civil Rights Act of 1964, Congress prohibited discrimination in

   A housing

   B affirmative action plans

   C workers' salaries

   D public accommodations

Use the excerpt and your knowledge of social studies to answer the following question.

> On the first day of January, A.D. 1863, all persons held as slaves within any state or designated part of a state, the people whereof shall then be in rebellion against the United States, shall be then, thenceforward, and forever free.
>
> —*Emancipation Proclamation*

32 What did the Emancipation actually do?

   F It freed all slaves, North and South.

   G It recognized that African Americans were equal before the law.

   H It gave free African Americans the right to vote.

   J It freed all slaves in states fighting against the U.S.

33 The issue that caused the Nullification Crisis of 1832–1833 was—

   A tariff policy

   B slavery

   C taxation

   D Indian removal

34 The construction of the Suez Canal in 1869 increased shipping between—

   F the Mediterranean Sea and the Atlantic Ocean

   G the Atlantic and Pacific oceans

   H the Mediterranean Sea and the Indian Ocean

   J the Persian Gulf and the Arabian Sea

GO ON TO THE NEXT PAGE

Use the chart and your knowledge of social studies to answer the following question.

Popular Vote for President

Election of 1824		Election of 1828	
Andrew Jackson	153,544	Andrew Jackson	647,286
John Quincy Adams	108,740	John Quincy Adams	508,064
Henry Clay	47,136		
William Crawford	46,618		

35 What was the cause of the more than tripling of the popular vote between the two elections?

   A   African Americans were given the right to vote.

   B   Many states allowed women to vote.

   C   The voting age was lowered to 21.

   D   Property qualifications for voting were ending.

Use the excerpt and your knowledge of social studies to answer the following question.

> A general association of nations must be formed under specific covenants for the purpose of affording mutual guarantees of political independence and territorial integrity to great and small states alike.
>
> —*President Woodrow Wilson, 1918*

36 In this speech, President Wilson is proposing the creation of the—

   F   International Monetary Fund

   G   League of Nations

   H   United Nations

   J   Southeast Asia Treaty Organization

37 Which of the following New Deal agencies provided jobs for young, out-of-work men?

   A   Federal Communications Commission

   B   Civilian Conservation Corps

   C   Securities and Exchange Commission

   D   Social Security Administration

38 Which provision of the Constitution did the Seventeenth Amendment change?

   F   the method of electing senators

   G   the number of senators from each state

   H   the term of senators

   J   the minimum age of senators

GO ON TO THE NEXT PAGE

Use the diagram and your knowledge of social studies to answer the following questions.

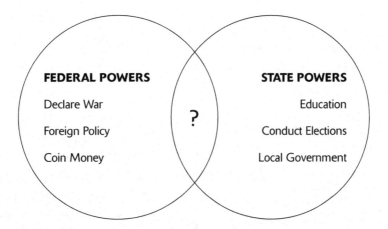

FEDERAL POWERS

Declare War

Foreign Policy

Coin Money

?

STATE POWERS

Education

Conduct Elections

Local Government

39 Which powers do both the states and the federal government share?

    A   establish post offices

    B   regulate interstate trade

    C   levy taxes

    D   create marriage laws

40 In addition to those listed in the diagram, states have the power to—

    F   enter into a treaty

    G   license doctors

    H   tax imports

    J   create an army

41 As a result of the national quotas included in U.S. immigration laws in the 1920s—

    A   the total number of immigrants to the U.S. increased

    B   the number of immigrants from Southern and Eastern Europe declined

    C   immigration from Asia was allowed to continue

    D   all immigration to the U.S. came to an end

GO ON TO THE NEXT PAGE

42 Which is the best source to use about the origins of the Cold War?

    F commercial internet site on the Cold War

    G a recent book by a historian on the Cold War

    H the memoirs of President Harry Truman

    J a biography of Joseph Stalin

Use the excerpt and your knowledge of social studies to answer the following question.

> . . . ask not what your country can do for you—ask what you can do for your country.
> —*President John F. Kennedy, 1961*

43 What federal program best represents President Kennedy's call to public service?

    A War on Poverty

    B Peace Corps

    C Alliance for Progress

    D NASA

44 Which issue would interest the World Trade Organization?

    F high unemployment in the U.S. automobile industry

    G high inflation in Mexico

    H tariffs on steel imported into the U.S.

    J growing budget deficits in several African countries

45 As a result of the Battle of Midway—

    A Germany declared war on the U.S

    B the Japanese threat to Hawaii ended

    C Japan was able to attack the west coast of the U.S

    D the U.S. recaptured the Philippine Islands

46 In the period after the Civil War, the federal government helped the railroads by—

    F regulating the rates railroads charged

    G lowering protective tariffs

    H creating the Department of Transportation

    J providing the railroads with public lands

47 Although the Tennessee Valley Authority brought many benefits to the people of the region, its projects also contributed to

    A environmental pollution

    B higher unemployment

    C higher prices for electricity

    D increased flood danger

GO ON TO THE NEXT PAGE

Use the chart and your knowledge of social studies to answer the following question.

PERCENTAGE OF WHITE SOUTHERNERS BY NUMBER OF SLAVES OWNED

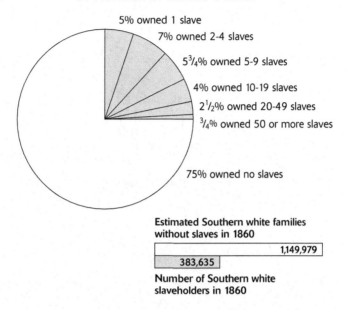

5% owned 1 slave

7% owned 2-4 slaves

$5^3/_4$% owned 5-9 slaves

4% owned 10-19 slaves

$2^1/_2$% owned 20-49 slaves

$^3/_4$% owned 50 or more slaves

75% owned no slaves

Estimated Southern white families without slaves in 1860

1,149,979

383,635

Number of Southern white slaveholders in 1860

48 Which of the following statements best describes the information in the chart?

    F The average white Southerner was able to afford one slave.

    G Plantations with many slaves were common.

    H The number of slaves varied from state to state in the South.

    J The majority of slave owners owned less than 10 slaves.

Use the excerpt and your knowledge of social studies to answer the following question.

> The help being daily extended by neighbors, by local, and national agencies, by municipalities, by industry and by a great multitude of organizations . . . is many times any appropriation yet proposed. The opening of the doors of the federal treasury is likely to stifle this giving . . .
>
> —*President Herbert Hoover, 1931*

49 According to his statement to the press, President Hoover believed that—

    A Congress should spend more money on relief

    B states should provide work for the unemployed

    C private charity was doing a good job during the Depression

    D local government had to do more to help the poor

GO ON TO THE NEXT PAGE

Use the map and your knowledge of social studies to answer the following question.

The Black Death in Europe, 1347–1350

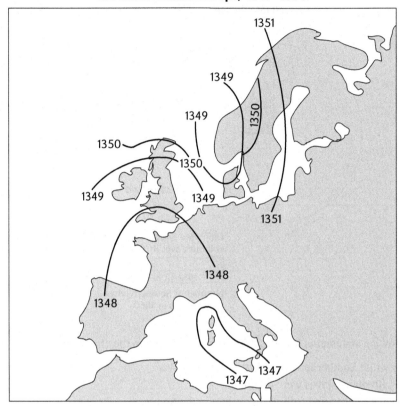

50 What conclusion can you come to from the map about the spread of the Black Death?

    F   The plague spread from northern to southern Europe.

    G   The plague spread from the interior of Europe to the port cities.

    H   The plague spread primarily north and east.

    J   There is no pattern to the way the plague spread.

GO ON TO THE NEXT PAGE

Use the chart and your knowledge of social studies to answer the following question.

American Foreign Policy in the 1920s

1921	1924	1928	1929
Washington Naval Conference	Dawes Plan on Reparations	Kellog-Briand Pact	Young Plan on Reparations

51 Based on the timeline, which statement best characterizes American foreign policy in the decade after World War I?

A The U.S. was determined to keep Germany weak.

B The U.S. was involved in an arms race with the other world powers.

C The U.S. was engaged in world affairs.

D The U.S. was concerned about developments in Africa.

Use the excerpt and your knowledge of social studies to answer the following question.

> After several consecutive bumper crops from 1752 on, maize has become one of the mountain farmers' very source of [food] and has been grown by every household.
>
> —*Report from China, 1866*

52 The report on agricultural production in a Chinese province shows that—

F maize can grow in any place in the world

G there was direct trade between Asia and Africa

H maize gradually spread to Asia from the Western Hemisphere

J the price of maize was very low

53 The GI Bill of Rights contributed directly to the economic expansion after World War II by—

A providing veterans with loans to buy homes and businesses

B increasing the benefits for disabled veterans

C guaranteeing veterans' entrance into the colleges of their choice

D offering life insurance at a reasonable price

54 The tactic that Cesar Chavez used to get national attention on the problems of farm workers was—

F burning fields

G boycotts

H legal action

J confrontations with police

GO ON TO THE NEXT PAGE

Use the graph and your knowledge of social studies to answer the following question.

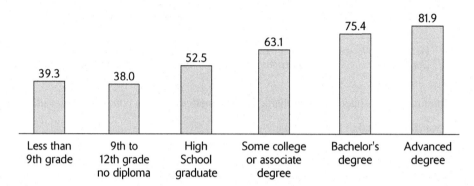

Voting by Educational Attainment: 2000
(Percent who voted of the voting-age citizen population)

Source: U.S. Census Bureau, Current Population Survey, November 2000.

55 What conclusions about voting patterns can you draw from the graph?

   A College students are more likely to vote than senior citizens.

   B Education is a key factor in voting.

   C African Americans vote more than whites.

   D Voter participation is declining.

Science

Directions: Read each question and select the best answer. Then fill in the correct answer on your answer document.

GO ON TO THE NEXT PAGE

FORMULA CHART
for Grade 11 Science Assessment

Density = $\dfrac{\text{mass}}{\text{volume}}$ $\qquad\qquad\qquad\qquad\qquad\qquad$ $D = \dfrac{m}{v}$

$\begin{pmatrix}\text{heat gained or}\\ \text{lost by water}\end{pmatrix} = \begin{pmatrix}\text{mass in}\\ \text{grams}\end{pmatrix}\begin{pmatrix}\text{change in}\\ \text{temperature}\end{pmatrix}\begin{pmatrix}\text{specific}\\ \text{heat}\end{pmatrix}$ $\qquad$ $Q = (m)(\Delta T)(C_p)$

Speed = $\dfrac{\text{distance}}{\text{time}}$ $\qquad\qquad\qquad\qquad\qquad\qquad$ $s = \dfrac{d}{t}$

Acceleration = $\dfrac{\text{final velocity} - \text{initial velocity}}{\text{change in time}}$ $\qquad$ $a = \dfrac{V_f - V_i}{\Delta t}$

Momentum = mass × velocity $\qquad\qquad\qquad\qquad$ $p = mv$

Force = mass × acceleration $\qquad\qquad\qquad\qquad$ $F = ma$

Work = force × distance $\qquad\qquad\qquad\qquad\qquad$ $W = Fd$

Power = $\dfrac{\text{work}}{\text{time}}$ $\qquad\qquad\qquad\qquad\qquad\qquad$ $P = \dfrac{W}{t}$

% efficiency = $\dfrac{\text{work output}}{\text{work input}} \times 100$ $\qquad\qquad$ $\% = \dfrac{W_O}{W_I} \times 100$

Kinetic energy = $\dfrac{1}{2}$ (mass × velocity^2) $\qquad\qquad$ $KE = \dfrac{mv^2}{2}$

Gravitational potential energy = mass × acceleration due to gravity × height $\quad$ $GPE = mgh$

Energy = mass × (speed of light)^2 $\qquad\qquad\qquad$ $E = mc^2$

Velocity of a wave = frequency × wavelength $\qquad$ $v = f\lambda$

Current = $\dfrac{\text{voltage}}{\text{resistance}}$ $\qquad\qquad\qquad\qquad\qquad$ $I = \dfrac{V}{R}$

Electrical power = voltage × current $\qquad\qquad\qquad$ $P = VI$

Electrical energy = power × time $\qquad\qquad\qquad\qquad$ $E = Pt$

Constants/Conversions
g = acceleration due to gravity = 9.8 m/s^2
c = speed of light = 3 × 10^8 m/s
speed of sound = 343 m/s at 20°C
1 cm^3 = 1 mL
1 wave/second = 1 hertz (Hz)
1 calorie (cal) = 4.18 joules
1000 calories (cal) = 1 Calorie (Cal) = 1 kilocalorie (kcal)
newton (N) = kgm/s^2
joule (J) = Nm
watt (W) = J/s = Nm/s
volt (V) $\qquad$ ampere (A) $\qquad$ ohm (Ω)

GO ON TO THE NEXT PAGE

Periodic Table of the Elements

1 IA	2 IIA	3 IIIB	4 IVB	5 VB	6 VIB	7 VIIB	8	9 VIII	10	11 IB	12 IIB	13 IIIA	14 IVA	15 VA	16 VIA	17 VIIA	18 VIIIA

Atomic Number — 14
Symbol — Si
Atomic Mass — 28.086
Name — Silicon

1 H 1.008 Hydrogen																	2 He 4.0026 Helium
3 Li 6.941 Lithium	4 Be 9.012 Beryllium											5 B 10.81 Boron	6 C 12.011 Carbon	7 N 14.007 Nitrogen	8 O 15.999 Oxygen	9 F 18.998 Flourine	10 Ne 20.179 Neon
11 Na 22.990 Sodium	12 Mg 24.305 Magnesium											13 Al 26.982 Aluminum	14 Si 28.086 Silicon	15 P 30.974 Phosphorus	16 S 32.066 Sulfur	17 Cl 35.453 Chlorine	18 Ar 39.948 Argon
19 K 39.098 Potassium	20 Ca 40.08 Calcium	21 Sc 44.956 Scandium	22 Ti 47.88 Titanium	23 V 50.942 Vanadium	24 Cr 51.996 Chromium	25 Mn 54.938 Manganese	26 Fe 55.847 Iron	27 Co 58.933 Cobalt	28 Ni 58.69 Nickel	29 Cu 63.546 Copper	30 Zn 65.39 Zinc	31 Ga 69.72 Gallium	32 Ge 72.61 Germanium	33 As 74.922 Arsenic	34 Se 78.96 Selenium	35 Br 79.904 Bromine	36 Kr 83.80 Krypton
37 Rb 85.468 Rubidium	38 Sr 87.62 Strontium	39 Y 88.906 Yttrium	40 Zr 91.224 Zirconium	41 Nb 92.906 Niobium	42 Mo 95.94 Molybdenum	43 Tc (98) Technetium	44 Ru 101.07 Ruthenium	45 Rh 102.906 Rhodium	46 Pd 106.42 Palladium	47 Ag 107.868 Silver	48 Cd 112.41 Cadmium	49 In 114.82 Indium	50 Sn 118.71 Tin	51 Sb 121.763 Antimony	52 Te 127.60 Tellurium	53 I 126.904 Iodine	54 Xe 131.29 Xenon
55 Cs 132.905 Cesium	56 Ba 137.33 Barium	57 La 138.906 Lanthanum	72 Hf 178.49 Hafnium	73 Ta 180.948 Tantalum	74 W 183.84 Tungsten	75 Re 186.207 Rhenium	76 Os 190.23 Osmium	77 Ir 192.22 Iridium	78 Pt 195.08 Platinum	79 Au 196.967 Gold	80 Hg 200.59 Mercury	81 Tl 204.383 Thallium	82 Pb 207.2 Lead	83 Bi 208.980 Bismuth	84 Po (209) Plutonium	85 At (210) Astatine	86 Rn (222) Radon
87 Fr (223) Francium	88 Ra 226.025 Radium	89 Ac 227.028 Actinium	104 Rf (261) Rutherfordium	105 Db (262) Dubnium	106 Sg (263) Seaborgium	107 Bh (262) Bohrium	108 Hs (265) Hassium	109 Mt (266) Meitnerium	110 (269)								

Mass numbers in parentheses are those of the most stable or most common isotope.

Lanthanide Series

58 Ce 140.12 Cerium	59 Pr 140.908 Praseodymium	60 Nd 144.24 Neodymium	61 Pm (145) Promethium	62 Sm 150.36 Samarium	63 Eu 151.97 Europium	64 Gd 157.25 Gadolinium	65 Tb 158.925 Terbium	66 Dy 162.50 Dysprosium	67 Ho 164.930 Holmium	68 Er 167.26 Erbium	69 Tm 168.934 Thulium	70 Yb 173.04 Ytterbium	71 Lu 174.967 Lutetium

Actinide Series

90 Th 232.038 Thorium	91 Pa 231.036 Protactinium	92 U 238.029 Uranium	93 Np 237.048 Neptunium	94 Pu (244) Plutonium	95 Am (243) Americium	96 Cm (247) Curium	97 Bk (247) Berkelium	98 Cf (251) Californium	99 Es (252) Einsteinium	100 Fm (257) Fermium	101 Md (258) Mendelevium	102 No (259) Nobelium	103 Lr (262) Lawrencium

GO ON TO THE NEXT PAGE

1 Since severe weather can occur quickly and without warning, it is important that students know the procedures to follow if severe weather occurs during a field study. If lightning occurs during a field investigation, the students should first—

   A look for shelter below isolated trees

   B cover themselves with tarps

   C attempt to find shelter inside a sturdy building

   D try to hide under cars or tractors

2 Scientists are continually trying to develop an effective vaccine against HIV, the virus that causes AIDS. One approach has been a drug whose components are protease inhibitors, which interfere with virus replication. Which of the following best summarizes the reasons for this approach?

   F An HIV enzyme forms new copies of the virus in an undetermined way.

   G Stopping the spread of AIDS is most important.

   H HIV is most easily fought before it invades the body.

   J HIV reproduces very rapidly within cells of the immune system.

3 Which of the following groups of elements contain members with the most similar properties?

   A K, Ca, Sc

   B H, Li, Na

   C Mn, Fe, C

   D Be, Mg, Ca

4 Two students are working in a laboratory as shown above. Their assignment is to neutralize a standard solution of sulfuric acid and record the amount of solution necessary. The students are probably using a burette to measure out the required liquid because—

   F it is easy to use

   G only two students are necessary to use the equipment

   H it is the safest tool to use when adding sulfuric acid

   J it measures out extremely precise amounts of liquid

GO ON TO THE NEXT PAGE ⟩

5 A student needed to dilute a strong solution of nitric acid. The best way to do this would be to—

A add distilled water to the acid while constantly stirring

B add hot water to the acid to allow it to dilute more quickly

C divide the acid into small quantities, adding water slowly to each quantity

D add the nitric acid to the water while constantly stirring

Whole Puffs Cereal

Nutrition Facts
Serving 1/2 cup (30g)
Servings per Container about 20

Amounts Per Serving

Total Fat   1g
   Saturated Fat   0g
   Polyunsaturated Fat   0g
   Monounsaturated Fat   0g
Cholesterol   0mg
Sodium   130mg
Potassium   210mg
Total Carbohydrate   24g
   Dietary Fiber   14g
   Soluble Fiber   1g
   Sugars   0g
   Other Carbohydrate   10g
Protein   2g

---

6 The recommended daily allowance for Sodium is 2400–2600mg, for potassium 3000–3500mg, and for dietary fiber 20–25g. Based on the information above, two servings a day for a total of 60g would provide—

F more sodium than is recommended

G less potassium than sodium

H more dietary fiber than is recommended

J more potassium than is recommended

GO ON TO THE NEXT PAGE

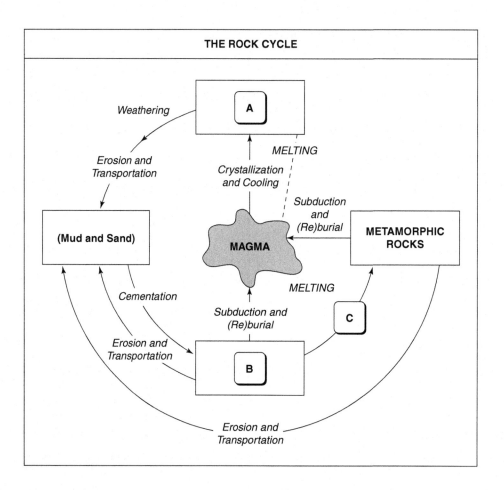

THE ROCK CYCLE

7 Based on the diagram of the rock cycle, what geologic process corresponds with the arrow labeled "C" in the diagram?

- **A** weathering
- **B** erosion and transportation
- **C** compaction and cementation
- **D** heat and pressure

8 Within a natural community of many different plant and animal species, which of the following is most likely to be true?

- **F** Competition between two species will upset the delicate natural balance.
- **G** Each species occupies its own niche in the environment.
- **H** The largest carnivore will command the greatest territory.
- **J** Owls hunt at night and therefore do not compete with nocturnal animals.

GO ON TO THE NEXT PAGE

**Time Required for Water to Freeze to Ice
Experimental Data**

Container	A	B	C
Volume of water (mL)	10	20	45
Temperature (°C)	-10	-10	-10
Time Required (hours)	1	1.5	2.0

9 The outcome of an experiment is shown in the table above. The table shows the times required for water to freeze to ice from three different sized containers using the same temperature. Which of the following is the best question to ask before developing a hypothesis to explain the outcome of this experiment?

A Why does the higher temperature slow the rate of freezing?

B How does the rate of freezing change with the different size of the containers?

C How long would it take for 70 mL of water to freeze at −15° ?

D What is the freezing point of water?

10 An object is moving at 50 m/s and has a momentum of 20 kg × m/s. The mass of the object is—

F 100 kg

G 20 kg

H 5.0 kg

J 0.4 kg

11 In the following classification levels, which level has the most members?

A phylum

B species

C kingdom

D order

12 Which of the following will not increase the rate at which a solid dissolves in a liquid?

F heating the solution

G cooling the solution

H making the solute particles smaller

J shaking the solution

13 A recent ad in a popular magazine claimed that patients could begin to regrow hair in a week by taking a patented medication, available without a prescription, and it cost only $10 a bottle. Which of the following data would be important in testing the claim?

A The price of $10 a bottle

B The fact that it was available without a prescription

C The fact that the medication was patented

D How many people were used in testing the claim

GO ON TO THE NEXT PAGE

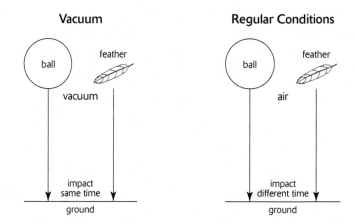

14 In an experiment, feathers and lead balls fell at the same rate when in a vacuum. When dropped in regular conditions, the lead balls fell at a faster rate. Which of the following can be concluded from this experiment?

   F   Distance of the fall has a major effect on the falling rate.
   G   Shape of the object has no effect on the falling rate.
   H   Air resistance has a major effect on the falling rate.
   J   Lead balls always fall at a faster rate than feathers.

Plant Group	Chlorophyll	Leaves	Seeds	Flowers
fungi	yes	no	yes	yes
algae	yes	yes	no	no
ferns	yes	yes	no	no
gymnosperms	no	yes	yes	yes

15 Four of the five plant groups are given above. From the table above, which of the following plant groups is correctly associated with its characteristics?

   A   fungi
   B   algae
   C   ferns
   D   gymnosperms

GO ON TO THE NEXT PAGE

THE CELL

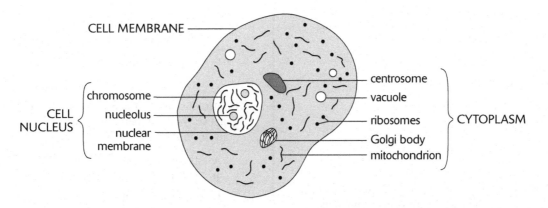

16 The cytoplasm is one of the three essential subdivisions of any cell. Using the diagram above, which of the following best describes the basic characteristics of this essential subdivision?

    F   The cytoplasm varies in consistency from fluid to a semi-solid.
    G   The cytoplasm is a constant fluid.
    H   The cytoplasm is composed of only two items.
    J   The cytoplasm occurs within the nucleus.

17 For small changes to accumulate eventually into a new life form, each single change or variation in an organism would have to be—

    A   frequent
    B   inheritable
    C   mechanical
    D   probable

18 During the process of photosynthesis, which of the following is produced?

    F   water
    G   carbon dioxide
    H   sunlight
    J   oxygen

GO ON TO THE NEXT PAGE

$$\Box Fe + \Box O_2 \longrightarrow \Box Fe_2O_3$$

19 What are the coefficients that will balance the equation above?

    A 2, 1, 1
    B 2, 3, 1
    C 3, 2, 2
    D 4, 3, 2

20 A solution with a volume of 65.2 mL has a density of 1.2 g/mL. What is the mass in grams of the solution? Record and bubble in your answer to the nearest tenth on the answer document.

water

21 Arminta can float in a swimming pool as shown above. What property of water explains her ability to float?

    A buoyancy
    B mobility
    C surface tension
    D viscosity

GO ON TO THE NEXT PAGE

Insects Offered to Monkey as Food

	Eaten by Monkey	Rejected by Monkey
Insects of Bright Colors	23	120
Insects of Dull Colors	83	18

22 The chart above summarizes a study of 244 species of insects offered to a monkey as food. Which of the following is the most likely interpretation of the results of the study in terms of animals adapting to their environment?

    F Insects have adapted to have dull colors to avoid being eaten.

    G Some insects of bright colors have likely adapted to have bitter tastes.

    H Color as a variable is not sufficient in explaining the monkey's behavior.

    J Monkeys have adapted to eat most species of insects.

23 The group of elements lithium, sodium, and potassium would be described as—

    A highly reactive gases

    B unreactive gases

    C highly reactive metals

    D slightly reactive metals

24 Which of the following factors most clearly separates a bread mold from a cactus plant?

    F the ability to reproduce

    G body functions such as respiration and transpiration

    H the ability to manufacture food

    J a microscopic cell structure

ELECTROLYSIS

Decomposition of Water by Electric Current

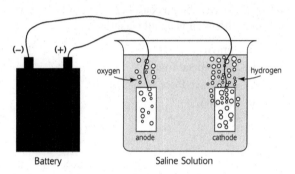

25 The diagram above shows the decomposition of water by an electric current. If you examine the diagram carefully, you will see more bubbles of hydrogen than of oxygen. What is the best explanation for this reaction?

    A The cathode material is considerably more porous than the anode material.

    B Hydrogen gas is less dense than oxygen gas, so hydrogen bubbles rise faster.

    C Some oxygen is dissolved into the solution, while all the insoluble hydrogen escapes.

    D The water that is being decomposed has twice as much hydrogen as oxygen.

GO ON TO THE NEXT PAGE

26 Enzymes are special proteins that speed up specific biochemical reactions within an organism. An example of an enzyme reaction is—

   F   digestion of fats
   G   tanning of skin
   H   sneezing
   J   oxygenation of blood

Use the information below and your knowledge of science to answer questions 27–28.

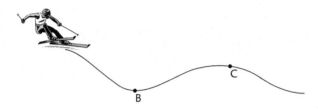

27 The skier is able to coast between points B and C even though it is uphill because of—

   A   gravity
   B   centripetal force
   C   cohesive force
   D   inertia

28 The force that opposes motion between the skier's skis and the surface of the snow is—

   F   inertia
   G   friction
   H   centripetal force
   J   centrifugal force

29 Which of the following does the circulatory system not provide?

   A   transport of nutrients
   B   transport of wastes
   C   transport of gases
   D   transport of nerve impulses

30 When completely immersed in water, a piece of glass—

   F   appears bent by refraction
   G   seems to weigh less
   H   decreases in density
   J   increases in density

GO ON TO THE NEXT PAGE

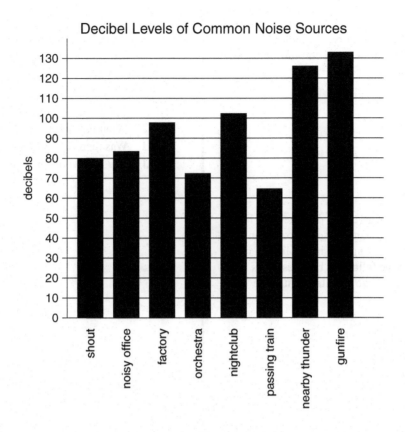

Decibel Levels of Common Noise Sources

31 The graph above shows the average decibel levels associated with various common sources of noise. Only two noise sources in the graph exceed the hearing pain threshold. The hearing pain threshold is approximately—

A 90 decibels
B 100 decibels
C 120 decibels
D 130 decibels

32 Acids have all of the following properties in common except—

F they neutralize bases
G they have a sour taste
H they turn red litmus paper blue
J they react with active metals to release hydrogen gas

33 Oxygen enters into the blood at the—

A esophagus
B throat
C heart
D lungs

GO ON TO THE NEXT PAGE

34 A mammalian cell contains 24 chromosomes in its normal diploid state. After two generations of division by mitosis, how many chromosomes will be present in each new cell?

   F 6
   G 12
   H 24
   J 48

35 Termites have tiny, one-celled parasites that live inside their intestines, and these protozoa can digest cellulose, allowing termites to live on dead wood. Which of the following best describes the relationship between the termite and its tiny inhabitants?

   A parasitism
   B commensalism
   C predation
   D mutualism

36 If a recent study by NASA showed that small amounts of oxygen were found on a distant planet, then which of the following questions would be relevant in determining whether or not plants once lived on this planet?

   F What does the planet look like?
   G What types of plants occur on the planet?
   H Was there ever water on the planet?
   J Are herbivores present?

GO ON TO THE NEXT PAGE

37 Josephine uses a fixed pulley and exerts a 7.2-Newton force to raise a 6.5-Newton box. What is the efficiency of the pulley?

   A 7%

   B 14%

   C 90%

   D 100%

38 Which class of compounds explains why children resemble their parents?

   F carbohydrates

   G lipids

   H nucleic acids

   J proteins

39 Table salt is a compound made up of sodium and chlorine atoms. What type of bonding exists between these atoms?

   A covalent

   B ionic

   C metallic

   D molecular

GO ON TO THE NEXT PAGE

An Aerosol Can

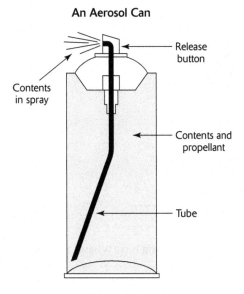

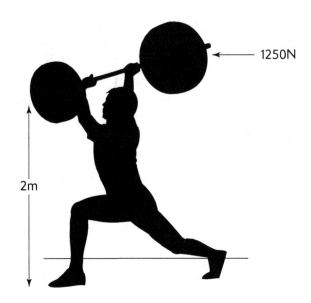

40 Which of the following processes causes the ingredients of the aerosol can to spray out when the top button is depressed?

   F the change from a gaseous to a liquid state

   G the expansion of gas by being heated

   H the movement of molecules toward lower pressure

   J the swelling of atoms to a larger size

41 Most natural organisms depend on other organisms in the food chain for nutrition. Which of the following organisms is most independent in obtaining nourishment?

   A bighorn sheep

   B codfish

   C cougar

   D palm tree

42 As shown in the picture above, a weightlifter lifts a 1,250 Newton barbell a distance of 2 meters in 3 seconds. Approximately how much power was used to lift the barbell?

   F 833 watts

   G 2,500 watts

   H 7,500 watts

   J 8,333 watts

43 The movement of wind is an example of—

   A radiation

   B conduction

   C convection

   D combustion

GO ON TO THE NEXT PAGE

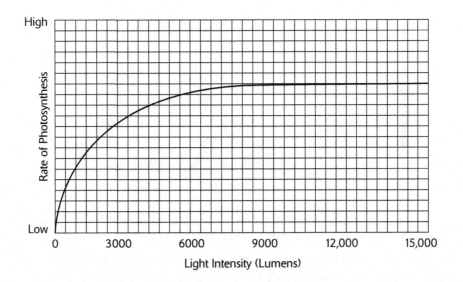

44 The graph above shows the effects of light intensity and temperature on the rate of photosynthesis in land plants. What does the graph above tell about the effect of light intensity on the rate of photosynthesis?

  F   As light intensity increases, the rate of photosynthesis decreases.

  G   As light intensity increases, the rate of photosynthesis increases.

  H   As light intensity increases, the rate of photosynthesis increases until around 9,000 lumens, above which level of light the rate does not increase.

  J   There is no relationship between light intensity and the rate of photosynthesis.

GO ON TO THE NEXT PAGE

THE HUMAN EYE

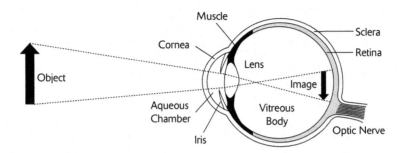

45 From the diagram, it appears that the image of the object is upside down. Which of the following is the best explanation of why we see the image in the correct position?

   A   The image is actually transposed twice as it crosses through the vitreous body.

   B   The image is not actually transposed on the retina, merely slightly refocused.

   C   The image is transposed onto the retina, but the brain makes the proper adjustment as it reads the impulses.

   D   The optic nerve transposes the upside down images before they reach the brain.

46 The magnification of images by a lens is due to—

   F   dispersion

   G   focusing

   H   reflection

   J   refraction

47 Most ecosystems consist of several food chains. These food chains interlink to form complex food webs. Food webs are formed because—

   A   some animals eat only one specific food.

   B   most animals eat more than one specific food.

   C   plants produce their own food.

   D   one specific food can supply several essential nutrients.

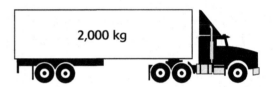

48 What is the momentum of a 2,000-kilogram truck that is moving at a speed of 10 meters per second?

   F   20 kg × m/s

   G   200 kg × m/s

   H   10,000 kg × m/s

   J   20,000 kg × m/s

49 Which of the following biological processes is most helpful in explaining the metabolism of an amoeba?

   A   photosynthesis

   B   reproduction

   C   respiration

   D   secretion

GO ON TO THE NEXT PAGE ▷

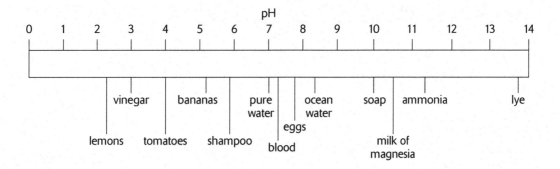

50 According to the pH scale above, shampoo is a—

   F   weak acid

   G   strong acid

   H   weak base

   J   strong base

51 | Regina shouts "Hello," to a friend across the street.

Which of the following would be the best explanation of the physical process that enables Regina's friend to hear her shout?

   A   Tiny particles move from Regina's mouth to her friend's ear.

   B   The molecules in the atmosphere are temporarily deformed.

   C   Movement is generally from high pressure toward low pressure.

   D   A pattern of vibrations is set up in the air.

52 The similar arrangement of bones within a person's arm and a whale's flipper suggests that—

   F   coincidences can occur

   G   people evolved from fishes

   H   people are meant to swim

   J   people and whales have a common ancestor

53 Which factor aided the evolution of the finch as it evolved from the same ancestor into many species in the Galapagos Islands?

   A   the threat of predators

   B   the closeness to other species of finches

   C   the isolation of the islands

   D   the large number of birds that already existed on the islands

GO ON TO THE NEXT PAGE

The Number of Amino Acid Differences in Hemoglobin Molecules						
	Horse	**Cow**	**Sheep**	**Pig**	**Rabbit**	**Mouse**
Horse	0	18	18	17	25	23
Cow	18	0	13	17	26	20
Sheep	18	13	0	18	29	24
Pig	17	17	18	0	26	24
Rabbit	25	26	29	26	0	28
Mouse	23	20	24	24	28	0

54 The chart shows the number of amino acid differences between the hemoglobin molecules in selected animals. Using only the data given in the chart, which of the following two animals are most similar?

F horse and cow

G cow and sheep

H sheep and pig

J pig and rabbit

55 Some boxes and bottles have labels that read: "Keep in a cool, dry place." "Do not open near flame." "Keep away from excessive heat." "Do not expose to light."

Which of the following is the best explanation for the use of these labels?

A These warnings tell you that undesirable chemical changes might take place if the instructions are not followed.

B These warnings notify you of the proper disposal methods for these materials.

C These labels have little value but are required by law to be placed on certain containers.

D These warnings are included to make sure the user is properly informed of the correct uses of these materials.

Reviewing Practice Test 1

Review your simulated TAKS Practice Examination by following these steps:

1. Check the answers you marked on your answer sheet against the Answer Key that follows. Put a check mark in the box following any wrong answer.
2. Fill out the Review Chart (p. 208).
3. Read all the explanations (pp. 209–236). Go back to review any explanations that are not clear to you.
4. Finally, fill out the Reasons for Mistakes chart on p. 208.

Don't leave out any of these steps. They are very important in learning to do your best on the TAKS.

Special note for the English Language Arts, Open-ended answers and Essay:

Have an English teacher, tutor, or someone else with good writing skills read and evaluate your essay and open-ended answers by using the checklists given. Using the evaluation checklists will give you a general feeling of how you did on these question types. *Note:* Your essay and open-ended answers will actually be scored by specially trained readers.

Answer Key for Practice Test 1

English Language Arts

Reading and Written Composition

1 B	**10** H	**19** D	**28** J
2 F	**11** A	**20** F	**29–31** Use the Checklist for the Open-Ended Answers on p. 27 to evaluate your answers.
3 C	**12** G	**21** A	
4 G	**13** A	**22** H	
5 A	**14** J	**23** C	
6 J	**15** C	**24** F	**Essay** Use the Checklist for the Essay on p. 33 to evaluate your essay.
7 C	**16** G	**25** B	
8 J	**17** B	**26** G	
9 B	**18** G	**27** C	

Revising and Editing

32 H	**37** A	**42** H	**47** C
33 C	**38** F	**43** B	**48** H
34 G	**39** D	**44** H	**49** B
35 B	**40** J	**45** A	**50** G
36 H	**41** D	**46** G	**51** C

Mathematics

1	C	16	G	31	D	46	G
2	H	17	C	32	G	47	D
3	D	18	G	33	C	48	H
4	G	19	B	34	J	49	C
5	B	20	F	35	C	50	J
6	G	21	$m = 3$	36	H	51	B
7	D	22	J	37	C	52	G
8	F	23	C	38	H	53	B
9	A	24	H	39	A	54	G
10	J	25	D	40	J	55	D
11	A	26	H	41	B	56	F
12	H	27	B	42	J	57	B
13	D	28	H	43	B	58	H
14	G	29	C	44	H	59	B
15	B	30	F	45	A	60	J

Social Studies

1	A	15	C	29	A	43	B
2	G	16	F	30	H	44	H
3	C	17	A	31	D	45	B
4	J	18	H	32	J	46	J
5	C	19	B	33	A	47	A
6	F	20	G	34	H	48	J
7	C	21	C	35	D	49	C
8	F	22	J	36	G	50	H
9	A	23	D	37	B	51	C
10	H	24	G	38	F	52	H
11	B	25	A	39	C	53	A
12	J	26	F	40	G	54	G
13	A	27	B	41	B	55	B
14	G	28	H	42	H		

Science

1	C	**15**	C	**29**	D	**43**	C
2	J	**16**	F	**30**	G	**44**	H
3	D	**17**	B	**31**	C	**45**	C
4	J	**18**	J	**32**	H	**46**	J
5	D	**19**	D	**33**	D	**47**	B
6	H	**20**	78.2 grams	**34**	H	**48**	J
7	D	**21**	A	**35**	D	**49**	C
8	G	**22**	G	**36**	H	**50**	F
9	B	**23**	C	**37**	C	**51**	D
10	J	**24**	H	**38**	H	**52**	J
11	C	**25**	D	**39**	B	**53**	C
12	G	**26**	F	**40**	H	**54**	G
13	D	**27**	D	**41**	D	**55**	A
14	H	**28**	G	**42**	F		

Review Chart

Use your marked Answer Key to fill in the following Review Chart for the multiple-choice questions.

	Possible	Completed	Right	Wrong
English Language Arts	48			
Mathematics	60			
Social Studies	55			
Science	55			

Reasons for Mistakes

Fill out the following chart only after you have read all the explanations that follow. This chart will help you spot your strengths and weaknesses and your repeated errors or trends in types of errors.

	Total Missed	Simple Mistake	Misread Problem	Lack of Knowledge
English Language Arts				
Mathematics				
Social Studies				
Science				
TOTALS				

Examine your results carefully. Reviewing the above information will help you pinpoint your common mistakes. Focus on avoiding your most common mistakes as you practice. If you are missing a lot of questions because of "Lack of Knowledge," you should go back and review the basics.

Answers and Explanations for Practice Test 1

English Language Arts

Reading and Written Composition

1 B By this point in the selection, the reader knows that this is an Indian household. This sentence, particularly because of the reference to the *freeway,* establishes that the historical time in which the passage takes place is the present or fairly close to the present, as freeways are a twentieth-century phenomenon.

2 F The story is told from the first person (I) point of view. These are the author's words and thoughts exclusively. That point of view allows the reader to understand the writer's (or character's) perceptions.

3 C There is no dialogue (the actual, quoted words of the characters) in this selection. The absence of dialogue (as well as the first person point of view) emphasizes the writer's thoughts and feelings, not those of the others involved. The passage does, however, often describe the physical environment, consistently use the present tense, and mention many everyday, normal, occurrences, such as children splashing in the creek, people sitting in lawn chairs, and a man taking a nap.

4 G The paragraph states that the stones will be the heat source for the sweat lodge, and they are being *fired* (fuel is being applied to them) in the fire that is burning.

5 A These paragraphs describe the author's preparations for the ceremony. But nothing indicates that these preparations are specifically required by the leader (**B**). She seems to know without being told what she needs to do—talk to the man who will put the ceremony together about the help she needs, tie the prayer ties, and collect wood, meat, and bread.

6 J The author seems quite calm (*composed*) and comfortable with her preparations and with the ceremony itself. She may perhaps be worried about something, since she does indicate she needs *help,* but nothing in the passage suggests that her worry is so great that she is *haunted* by it, that is, that she is obsessed with it.

7 C Everything the author says about the purpose of the sweat lodge ceremony leads to answer **C,** although that purpose is not stated directly in the terms of answer **C.** She says the ceremony includes *not just our own prayers and stories of what brought us to it, but also includes the unspoken records of history, the mythic past, and all the other lives connected to ours, our families, nations, and all other creatures.* She refers to the fact that by the end of the ceremony *it is as if skin contains land and birds . . . the animals and ancestors move into the human body, into skin and blood . . . land merges with us . . . stones come to dwell inside the person.* Although *healing* is mentioned, from all that is said, the healing is a mental one rather than a physical one (**D**).

8 J The details presented about the house give you the answer to this question. The wringer washer (an old fashioned washing machine) is in the kitchen, not in a separate laundry room as in some larger houses. There are two beds in the living room for travelers to use. The best word to describe this house, then, is *modest,* in this sense meaning unpretentious, free from showy extravagance. Although the house is modest, it could not be appropriately described as *primitive* (**G**), which would suggest a living space without any modern conveniences. And although a number of people seem to be in the house, it isn't a *chaotic* environment—normal household things are going on, cooking, and eating, and talking.

9 B Personification is the assigning of human characteristics to the nonhuman—animals, plants, objects, and so forth. The willows are said to *remember* things—as would a human—*their lives rooted in ground, the sun their leaves took in,* the *minerals and water* that *rose up their trunks.* They are depicted as not only alive but also as having thoughts. The personification here is directly connected to a major theme of the passage—that we, our environment, and our past are all one interconnected community.

10 H In Indian communities, reading is sometimes suspect (not trusted, suspicious) because it isn't considered traditional. But in the next room, a television is playing in the man's house, and television could certainly never be thought of as traditional either. They laugh because it's obviously inconsistent to look down on nontraditional reading while watching nontraditional TV.

11 A The title of the selection and its last line are both *all my relations.* The relations are not only American Indians (**B**), people who help her (**C**), or other people in general (**D**). Instead, the relations are between an individual and all else in the world, past and present, that is, something larger.

12 G This is a difficult question because choices **F, H,** and **J** all deal in part with the theme of the passage, the idea of oneness with all things, that everything in the world is part of us and part of our family. But although the other answers are connected in part with that idea, choices **F** and **H** specifically have to do with the ceremony itself, and choice **J,** while it approaches the idea of oneness with the stones, is about them only, not all other things in the world. But the sentence *There is no real aloneness* most completely speaks to the idea that all is one.

13 A The soldiers had been *in the bush* for two months before they were given *a week's standdown.* That is, they have been taken out of the combat area and allowed to rest and recuperate for a week. The day they make their calls home is the *final day* of that rest period and the day before they will return to the fighting.

14 J The term *legs* is used by the Pfc (private first class) as a name for the four soldiers and other soldiers like them. Even if you haven't come across the term used in this way before, you can figure out what it probably refers to from context. It's used in the same way that phrases such as *lend a hand* or *he needed another pair of eyes* is used. In both cases, a part of the body refers both to a whole person and to the role that they play—in one case, helping by using the hands and in the other, looking at something carefully by using the eyes. Here, the soldiers are thought of simply as pairs of legs, men who walk and march and move along through the battle. It's an unpleasant thing to be thought of as no more than one of your body parts and suggests that you aren't worth much except for that single function. Oscar reacted to that suggestion when he *shook his head* (a negative reaction) and *murmured* the word to himself.

15 C The word *pensive* means thoughtful (thinking and considering, not thoughtful, in the sense of being attentive to someone else's feelings). It often suggests thoughtfulness with a touch of sadness. Paragraph 32 consists of two sentences. The second sentence begins with *Then,* which suggests that there is a contrast to come—a contrast with the sentence that has just gone before. The second sentence says they would then *chuckle* or *grin,* indicating they are outgoing and happy, so *amused* (**A**) would not be a good contrast. Although being *judgmental* (**C**) might be considered a negative feeling and being happy a positive one, these terms don't really contrast with one another. But the happy, outgoing feeling indicated by a chuckle or grin does contrast with the idea of being quietly thoughtful.

16 G These paragraphs are almost completely dialogue, the words of the soldiers. There is nothing in the words themselves that suggests chaos or destruction (**H**), and the author does not describe their thoughts (**J**) in these paragraphs, only their actions and their words. But much of their speech is in sentence fragments, as is that of most real-life people who are having an informal conversation with one another.

17 B There is no suggestion that the soldiers are uninterested or bored, choices **A** and **C.** There also is no reason to think that *only* a call home will make this a good time for them. But it is reasonable to infer that when something as frightening and dangerous as fighting and perhaps dying faces them again very soon, it would be difficult for them to thoroughly enjoy their rest period.

18 G Sentence **F** refers to the general environment, not specifically the calls home. Sentence **H** describes the Pfc, who is not emotionally involved in these particular calls. Sentence **J** describe Oscar's, Eddie's, and the Pfc's reaction to the fact that Paul could not connect his call. But sentence **G** directly deals with the emotion of one of the soldiers, Eddie, after he has completed his call home. His eyes are shiny because he is near tears.

19 D Eddie's mother, according to him, *almost passes out* because he's called. She immediately fears that he's been shot. He is both amused that she is so rattled by the idea that she perhaps thinks he's actually dead and is somehow still calling from Graves Registration. It's clear that Eddie knows that his mother cares a great deal about him. Choice **C** is incorrect because we really don't know if he's talked with everyone in his family, although he doesn't mention anyone he might have missed speaking to.

20 F To Paul, the kitchen, and indeed all the details of his home, symbolize for him his family. The house is much more than simply a shelter (**J**) and is much more specific to him than the United States in general (**G**). All these details are important to him because they remind him of his home.

21 A A sentence in paragraph 2 identifies the theme: *There was singing and dancing, and afterward there was homesickness.* Homesickness is a yearning for home and family and one's accustomed environment. It is this homesickness that makes the calls home so important to these soldiers. In many stories, theme is not so clearly stated as it is here.

22 H All of these paragraphs are composed of Paul's thoughts. Even though we have had some of his thoughts presented elsewhere, the bulk of the story so far has been about Paul's companions. But these long paragraphs, completely concerned with Paul, himself, clearly establish him as the main character in the story. Choice **J** is incorrect because the reader empathizes primarily with Paul, and the story is told from his perspective, not that of the families left behind.

23 C Most of the story is about the anticipation of making a call home. Paul's friends successfully do so. As the phone is ringing at his home, Paul makes many plans for what he will say to his family and he is full of joy at the idea. It is only with Doc's comment *Tough luck* that the reader realizes that Paul's call didn't connect with his family.

24 F The author in "All My Relations" comes to see all of her environment as part of her "family." The world contains all of her relations. Although it isn't stated directly, Paul seems to think of his family in a more restricted sense—his immediate blood relatives to whom he wants to speak on the phone. Both characters need help (**G**), have understanding people around them (**H**), and use modern mechanical devices (**J**). (Although the ceremony in "All My Relations" doesn't involve modern devices, the group does drive to the ceremony in an automobile.)

25 B In "All My Relations," the sweat lodge ceremony is meant to remind the participants that they are not alone in the world but rather are part of everything around them. The author says, *this is the purpose of the ceremony.* In "Calling Home," Paul is homesick—he feels alone, separated from his home and family, and the telephone calls are looked forward to because they can heal some of that hurt.

26 G The word *State* lets you eliminate option **H.** (The Palmetto State is South Carolina, although you don't need to know that to answer the question.). A U.S. department would be unlikely to specifically address a single state's foster care program, and the Department of Education would be involved with school concerns rather than foster care. A political action committee (**F**) (PAC) is most likely to be involved in political fundraising. The visual representation isn't directly concerned with adoption (**J**), but rather with foster care, the placement of children with caregivers until either their parents are again able to care for them or until they are later adopted. But a state Department of Social Services would be very likely to promote interest in foster care so as to find these children the temporary homes they need.

27 C Foster care is the care of children who are not blood relatives of the caregivers. The words *No Bounds,* that is, no restrictions, suggest that love can exist outside the traditional idea of family as parents and their natural children.

28 J Option **F** isn't the best answer here because it isn't at all clear that these children have no home. It's more likely that the picture is of children who *do* have a home, with foster parents. The picture shows a happy scene in which the children seem to be well cared for. And nothing in the picture suggests hard work (**G**), although that logically would be involved in caring for children. While the picture, especially the smiles of the children, is pleasant to see (**H**), the primary purpose of the presentation is most likely to promote foster care—to find foster parents for children who need them.

Revising and Editing

32 H The first two descriptions of *words* are *uncommon* and *unlikely to be understood.* Each uses an adjective. The third descriptive phrase in the series should be parallel in form with the first two. But as it stands, the third phrase uses a noun, *meaning,* rather than an adjective. Changing *a meaning that is vague* both makes the series parallel and removes unnecessary words.

33 C This question tests number agreement of a verb with its subject. In *whether you, the listener, understands it,* the *understands* does not agree with its subject, *you.* It should be *you . . . understand it.* This problem is hard to see because the phrase *the listener* comes between the subject and the verb. *Depends* is correctly singular and shouldn't be changed (option **B**). When two subjects are joined by an *or,* the verb agrees with the nearer subject. In this case, both subjects are singular. This is a difficult question.

34 G The sentence *She had no way to understand what language is* further explains why Helen Keller was cut off from the rest of the world, a fact introduced in sentence 6. If the new sentence were inserted after sentence 5, there would be no clear reference to the pronoun *she* because Keller has not been mentioned yet. And it would make no sense to insert the sentence either after sentence 7 or at the end of the paragraph because the topic has changed to Keller's growing ability to communicate, not her lack of ability.

35 B Two independent sentences joined by a conjunction, such as *and,* should be separated by a comma. In this case, without the comma, a reader might read the sentence as *communicate with her and Keller,* as though someone is speaking to two people, which isn't what the sentence means.

36 H The sentence begins with quotation marks (") and should end with them, since the end of the sentence marks the end of Keller's direct speech. Notice that when an item within quotation marks is set off as *'w-a-t-e-r'* is here, single quotation marks are used.

37 A *Messing around with* is very informal usage. It might be appropriate if you were trying to reproduce the flavor of someone's speech, but in this report, it doesn't at all agree in tone with the rest of the language. *Using* is better. *Effect*, the noun, rather than *affect,* the verb, is correct here (choice **B**).

38 F What *this* refers to is unclear. The main topic of sentence 11 is *bureaucratese,* and it makes the meaning of sentence 12 clearer to specifically mention that.

39 D Choice **A** both leaves out information and changes the meaning of the sentences. It's not computers and electronics themselves that are full of jargon, it's the *industries* (and their words). Choice **B** is wordy and incorrectly joins two complete sentences (not connected by a conjunction) with a comma. Choice **C** creates a sentence fragment by following the semicolon with a phrase rather than a sentence. Choice **D** is clear, concise, and correctly punctuated and includes all of the information given in the original two sentences.

40 J Sentence 19 mentions the *term for "good"* and a *point* to be illustrated. So the sentence sensibly belongs after the point to be illustrated and before any further discussion of the term for *good.* The *point* is that teenagers construct their own language, which is discussed in sentence 20, so the best placement of sentence 19 is after sentence 20.

41 D Sentence 24 is correct. No change is needed.

42 H The term *catering business* is not a proper noun; it is simply the general name of a type of business (such as *plumbing business* or *furniture store*). So *catering* shouldn't be capitalized.

43 B Consuela's words, immediately following sentence 4, begin with *Because.* So sentence 4 should logically provide a question she's answering. Choices **A** and **D** don't include such a question. Choice **C** does mention a question, but **C** isn't as good an answer as **B** because **B** provides the specific question and makes sense with all of Consuela's comments that follow.

44 H Sentence 9 begins *But even when the flowers die.* In the sentence Luis wants to add, Consuela talks about the flowers dying (when she snips them off with her scissors), so the new sentence makes the most sense after sentence 8 and before sentence 9.

45 A *It's,* meaning *it is,* is correct here, not *its,* the possessive. *A lot* (two words) is correct (not *alot,* one word). The comma after *work* is correct to separate the direct quotation from *I said.*

46 G This is a direct question that Luis is asking Consuela. It needs a question mark, not a period. The quotation marks are correct.

47 C Since adding peat, compost, and fertilizer is the way the dirt is fed, the ideas in sentence 14 can be effectively combined with those in sentence 13. Doing so also makes the two sentences less wordy (by replacing the *I found out from her* with *She told me* and deleting one *she has* and one *and*). There are problems in all of the other options, in addition to their sense and style. **A** has a sentence fragment in *To feed the dirt.* The whole of **B** is a sentence fragment. And **D** joins the two complete sentences with a comma rather than the needed semicolon.

48 **H** Sentences 13 through 15 deal with what must be done to the dirt in the garden. Consequently, there is nothing that the *them* in sentence 16 can clearly refer to. Adding *the plants* makes the meaning of the sentence clear. It doesn't make sense to change *deer* to *animals* because a *squirrel* is an animal and has already been mentioned (although changing *deer* to *other animals* could be acceptable, depending on the meaning intended).

49 **B** Sentences 18 and 22 both talk about other gardens and they should go together. But sentence 18 does not fit as well after sentence 22 as before it because sentence 18 introduces the idea of Consuela's visits to gardens other than her own.

50 **G** In this sentence, *her* should be *herself.* Pronouns ending in *self* (singular) or *selves* (plural) are called reflexive pronouns. They refer to another noun or pronoun in the sentence. Here *herself* refers to *She* at the beginning of the sentence. If you were to use *her* rather than *herself* in this sentence, the sentence would suggest that another woman, someone other than Consuela, is being discussed.

51 **C** To avoid confusion, a modifier, a word or phrase that describes something else in the sentence, should come as close to the word it modifies as possible. In this case, *to discover new plants,* refers to something *she* does—*visits.* Choice **C** places *to discover to plants* immediately before *she visits,* making the meaning clear. The placement of the phrase in the original sentence makes it seem as though the reason the *gardens are open to the public* is *to discover new plants,* which isn't the sense of the sentence. All the other choices have problems. Choices **A** and **D** make it seem as though the St. Louis Botanical Garden is a plant. Choice **B** is a sentence fragment.

Mathematics

1 **C**

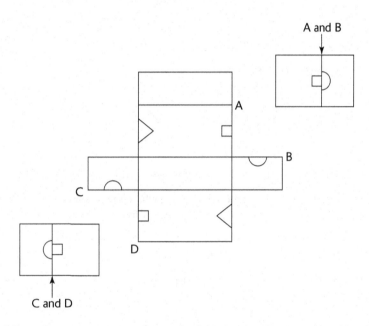

When the unfolded figure is cut out and the "flaps" are folded up, points A and B will coincide and the half-circle and the square will touch. Likewise, points C and D will coincide—the half-circle and the square will again touch. So choice **C** is the best answer.

2 H

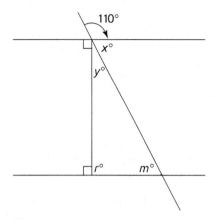

In the diagram, $x + 110 = 180$, so $x = 70$. Since $x + y = 90$, $y = 20$. r must be 90 since it is adjacent to another right angle along a straight line. So we now have:

$$r + y + m = 180$$

$$\downarrow \quad \downarrow$$

$$90 + 20 + m = 180$$

$$110 + \quad m = 180$$

$$m = 70$$

Therefore, the 3 angles are 90°, 70°, and 20°, answer choice **H**.

3 D You want 2 CDs and 3 DVDs to sell for $19.00:

$$2c + 3d = 19.00$$

You also want 3 CDs and 1 DVD to sell for $14.50:

$$3c + 1d = 14.50$$

Your answer should consist of these 2 equations, and this pair corresponds to choice **D.**

4 G For equations of the form $y = x^2 + k$, k is the y-intercept (where the graph crosses the y-axis) of the parabola. Changing from $y = x^2 - 3$ to $y = x^2 + 6$ will move the y-intercept from -3 <u>up</u> to $+6$; so choice **G** is the best answer.

5 B If the temperature drops, you subtract; if the temperature rises, you add. So starting with a temperature of T you have: Start at T; dropped 37; rose 15; ended at -12. As an equation you can write this as:

$$T - 37 + 15 = -12$$

$$T - 22 = -12$$

$$T = 10$$

So the original temperature was 10°. Correct answer is choice **B.**

6 G Lines which are parallel have the same slope. Written in slope-intercept form, $y = mx + b$, m is the slope. The line with equation $y = 2x + 3$ has slope 2.

With slope $= \frac{rise}{run}$, you are looking for a rise (or vertical change) or 2 and a run (horizontal change) of 1. From a given point on the line, you want to go "up 2 and over 1" to arrive at another point on the line, as in choice **G.**

7 D Adding up all types of vehicles sold, you get $75 + 15 + 30 + 45 + 60 = 225$ vehicles total. 45 pickups represent $\frac{45}{225}$ or $\frac{1}{5}$ of the total vehicle sales. Since there are 360° in a circle, the central angle for the pickups should be $\frac{1}{5}$ of 360°, or 72°. Choice **D** is correct.

Note: You also could have solved the following proportion: $\frac{45}{225} = \frac{x}{360}$ to get $x = 72$.

8 F Another name for the average is the arithmetic mean, or just <u>mean</u>, as in choice **F.**

9 A Using the ruler, the dimensions were measure and are noted on the diagram below.

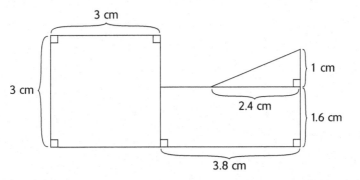

Total Area = area of square + area of rectangle + area of triangle

$$= 3(3) + (3.8)(1.6) + \frac{1}{2}(2.4)(1)$$

$$= 9 + 6.08 + 1.2$$

$$= 16.28$$

So an approximation of 16.3 cm², choice **A,** is appropriate.

10 J The price of one pound of potatoes multiplied by the number of pounds purchased will give the total price—thus, choice **J** is correct.

11 A To ride 1 mile, you will be charged (4.25) dollars; to ride 2 miles, you will be charged (4.25)2 dollars; to ride 7 miles, we will be charged (4.25)7 dollars. So to ride *m* miles, we will be charged (4.25)*m* dollars.

Adding the initial fee of $3.70 of getting into the cab, the total charge will be:

$C = 3.70 + 4.25m$

The correct answer is choice **A.**

12 H The volume of the chocolate cube = 24 × 24 × 24 = 13,824 cm³

$$\text{The volume of the sphere} = \frac{4}{3}\pi r^3$$

$$= \frac{4}{3}(3.14)\left(2^3\right)$$

$$= 33.4933 \, cm^3$$

Next, we divide the volume of the cube by the volume of the sphere to get:

$$\frac{13,824}{33.4933} = 412.739$$

So she can make about 412 spheres—choice **H.**

13 D Two polygons are similar if their corresponding angles are congruent and their corresponding sides are proportional (have = ratio).

In choice **D,** the sides are $\frac{3}{9}$ and $\frac{9}{27}$; both of these ratios equal $\frac{1}{3}$.

14 G A triangular pyramid has a triangular base.

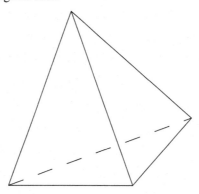

Counting vertices (corners), you get 4.

Counting faces (flat surfaces), you get 4.

Counting edges (line segments), you get 6.

So the correct answer is choice **G.**

15 B To find the x-intercepts, you set $y = 0$ and then solve for x.

$$y = x^2 - x - 20$$
$$0 = x^2 - x - 20$$

Next, factor the right-hand side to get

$$0 = (x - 5)(x + 4)$$

Set each factor to $= 0$ and then solve for x:

$$x - 5 = 0 \text{ or } x + 4 = 0$$
$$x = 5 \text{ or } x = -4$$

Therefore, choice **B** is correct.

16 G Using the equation $y = \frac{1}{3} f$ and the data from choice **G**, substituting 30 for f you get:

$$y = \frac{1}{3}(30) = 10$$

So 30 feet does correspond to 10 yards.

17 C For each hour he works, Ramon saves 20% of $7.00, or $1.40 per hour. So to purchase a $77 coat from his savings, he will need to work $\frac{\$77}{\$1.40/\,hr} = 55$ hours; thus choice **C** is correct.

18 G The cost of a container of Brand Q is $5.75. The cost of a container of Brand E is $4.25. The difference between the 2 prices is $1.50, which represents a savings of $1.50. Brand Q costs $5.75, so $\frac{\$1.50}{\$5.75} = .2608 = 26.08\%$. The correct answer is choice **G.**

19 B P(5,7), Q(–6,3), and R(2,–3) are the locations of the 3 cities—see the figure below.

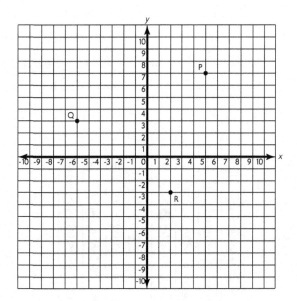

To find the coordinates of city M, you use the midpoint formula and the coordinates of cities P and R to find:

$$M = \left(\frac{5+2}{2}, \frac{7+^-3}{2} \right) = (3.5, 2)$$

To find the distance from city Q to city M, you use the distance formula and the coordinates of cities Q (–6,3) and M (3.5,2).

$$
\begin{aligned}
\text{Distance } QM &= \sqrt{(-6-3.5)^2 + (3-2)^2} \\
&= \sqrt{(-9.5)^2 + (1)^2} \\
&= \sqrt{90.25 + 1} \\
&= \sqrt{91.25} \\
&= 9.55
\end{aligned}
$$

So answer **B** is correct.

20 F Since the perimeter of the square is 32 feet, the length of one side is $\frac{32}{4} = 8$ feet.

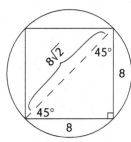

The diameter of the circle divides the square into two $45° - 45° - 90°$ triangles. Using the pattern for the ratios of the sides for that type of triangle ($x: x: x\sqrt{2}$), the hypotenuse of the right triangle (or in this case, the diameter of the circle) would be $8\sqrt{2}$. Therefore the radius would be half of that, $4\sqrt{2}$ or approximately 5.65. Answer **F** is the best choice.

21

$$2m + 14 = 3m - 7 + 6m$$

$$2m + 14 = 9m - 7 \qquad \text{combined the like terms on the right}$$

$$14 = 7m - 7 \qquad \text{subtracted } 2m \text{ from each side}$$

$$21 = 7m \qquad \text{added 7 to each side}$$

$$3 = m \qquad \text{divided each side by 7}$$

Be sure to grid your answer correctly.

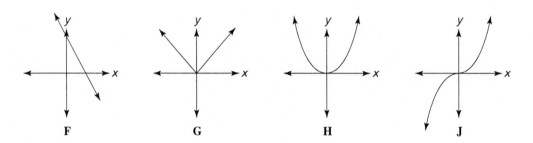

22 J

As x increases, you want y to increase also. As you move from left to right along the x-axis (x is increasing), you want the graph to move upward all the time (meaning y is also increasing). Choice F moves down (decreases) consistently, while choices G and H move down (decrease) and then up (increase). Choice J moves consistently upward (y increases). Therefore the correct answer is **J**.

23 C To graph the inequality $3x + 2y < 18$, you first find the x and y intercepts of the graphs of the equation $3x + 2y = 18$. To find the $x =$ intercept, set $y = 0$ and solve for x:

$$3x + 2y = 18$$

$$3x + 2(0) = 18$$

$$3x + 0 = 18$$

$$3x = 18$$

$$x = 6$$

The x-intercept is 6, so the graph crosses the x-axis at 6. To find the y-intercept, set $x = 0$ and solve for y:

$$3x + 2y = 18$$

$$3(0) + 2y = 18$$

$$0 + 2y = 18$$

$$2y = 18$$

$$y = 9$$

The y-intercept is 9, so the graph crosses the y-axis at 9.

Next, connect the x-intercept of 6 and the y-intercept of 9 to get the diagram below, where the equation $3x + 2y = 18$ is graphed.

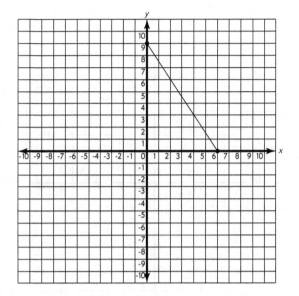

Since the inequality is $3x + 2y < 18$, your answer should appear under, or below, this line. The only point among the 4 choices that is under the line is (2,5), answer **C.**

24 H If 2 angles are supplementary, the sum of their measure is 180°. So,

$$m\angle C + m\angle D = 180$$
$$\downarrow \qquad \downarrow$$
$$c + \quad d = 180$$
$$d = 180 - c$$

This corresponds to choice **H.**

25 D $(3x - 4)2x - (4x - 3)(x - 1)$

$= 6x^2 - 8x - [4x^2 - 4x - 3x + 3]$	distributed both terms
$= 6x^2 - 8x - [4x^2 - 7x + 3]$	combined like terms within the brackets
$= 6x^2 - 8x - 4x^2 + 7x - 3$	distributed the "–" sign within the brackets
$= 2x^2 - x - 3$	combined like terms

Therefore, choice **D** is correct.

26 H From the bar graph, you have the following responses:

$$50 \text{ Independents}$$
$$25 \text{ No Choice}$$
$$100 \text{ Republicans}$$
$$\underline{+75 \text{ Democrats}}$$
$$150 \text{ total responses}$$

For the phone survey, 75 of the 250 people most agreed with the Democrats ($\frac{75}{250} = \frac{3}{10}$), so you would expect about $\frac{3}{10}$ of the city's 10,000 residents to agree with the Democrats. $\frac{3}{10}$ of 10,000 is 3,000. Therefore, choice **H** is correct.

Note: You could also have solved the proportion $\frac{75}{250} = \frac{d}{10,000}$ to get $d = 3,000$.

27 B A reflection across a line is comparable to "flipping" the figure over the line—the new image is also sometimes called a "mirror image." To rotate a figure through an angle $x°$ around a point P, you rotate the figure counterclockwise $x°$, with the figure fixed at point P, but the remainder of the figure moving counterclockwise. A translation "slides" the figure left, right, up or down.

The result of the indicated transformation is shown below:

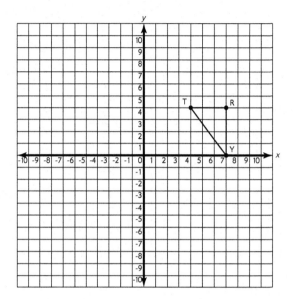

Therefore, answer **B** is correct.

28 H You first note that as x increases, y also increases; so you would expect the equation relating them to be $y = mx$, with m greater than 1.

Solving for m, you get $\frac{y}{x} = m$. Choosing the first entry in your table, you have $m = \frac{2,585}{1,100} = 2.35$. Therefore your equation is $y = 2.35x$, answer choice **H.**

29 C

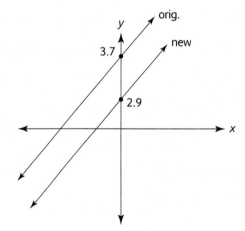

For the slope-intercept form, $y = mx + b$, m is the slope and b in the y-intercept, the place where the graph of the equation crosses the y-axis. If we decrease the y-intercept of the equation $y = 7.2x + 3.7$, the graph of the new equation will just move down the y-axis (note that in this case, decreasing the y-intercept caused an increase in the x-intercept). But the new line will have the same slope, and will be parallel to the original line. Thus, choice **C** is correct.

30 **F** The volume of the rectangular solid with length L, width W, and height H, can be found by volume = L × W × H. With a volume of 144, we have 144 = L × W × H.

Since the new solid has $\frac{1}{2}$ the length ($\frac{1}{2}$ L), $\frac{1}{3}$ the width ($\frac{1}{3}$ W), and $\frac{1}{4}$ the height ($\frac{1}{4}$ H), the volume of the new solid is

$$\left(\frac{1}{2}L\right)\left(\frac{1}{3}W\right)\left(\frac{1}{4}H\right)$$

$$=\left(\frac{1}{2}\right)\left(\frac{1}{3}\right)\left(\frac{1}{4}\right)\times L\times W\times H$$

$$=\left(\frac{1}{24}\right)\times L\times W\times H$$

$$=\left(\frac{1}{24}\right)\times 144 = 6\,in^3$$

This is answer choice **F.**

31 **D** Sharon's pay raise is just the difference between her new and old salary. So, her pay raise = 28,800 − 24,300. You want to compare this pay raise to her old salary, so you now have $\dfrac{28,800-24,300}{24,300}$, but this will give you a decimal answer. To change this to a percent you need to multiply by 100. So the correct answer is $\dfrac{(28,800-24,300)}{24,300}\times 100$, which corresponds to answer choice **D.**

32 **G** In step 1, you have 3 dots. In step 2, you have 5 dots (notice that 5 − 3 = 2). In step 3, you have 9 dots (notice that 9 − 5 = 4). Since the difference between the number of dots between consecutive steps is a multiple of 2 (or power of 2), you should try expressions like, $2n$, $2n + 1$, $2n$, $2n − 1$, and so on. Also, notice that:

$$3 = 2^1 + 1 = \text{step 1 dots}$$

$$5 = 2^2 + 1 = \text{step 2 dots}$$

$$9 = 2^3 + 1 = \text{step 3 dots}$$

So you would expect step n to have $2^n + 1$ dots, as in answer choice **G.**

33 **C** If c is the number of cars Jorge details each week, then his fixed costs for the week are $600 + 5c$ dollars. Charging $55 to detail a car, he makes $55c$ dollars a week. To "break even" you have:

$$55c = 60 + 5c$$

$50c = 600$ subtracted $5c$ from each side

$c = 12$ divided each side by 50

Therefore, Jorge must detail 12 cars each week before he can make a profit. **C** is the correct answer.

34 **J** The triangle in this question is a 30°-60°-90° triangle.

With the $x : x\sqrt{3} : 2x$ ratio of sides for the 30°-60°-90° triangle, you have $x = 150$, so $x\sqrt{3} = 150\sqrt{3} \approx 259.80$. Therefore, answer **J** of 260 feet is a good approximation.

35 **C** Let x = number of student tickets sold (at $4 each). Then $327 − x$ = number of adult tickets sold (at $7 each):

money from students + money from adults = money total

$4x + 7(327 − x) = 1{,}683$

$4x + 2289 − 7x = 1{,}683$ distributed on the left

$2289 − 3x = 1683$ combined like terms of the left

$−3x = −606$ subtracted 2,289 from each side

$x = 202$ divided both sides by −3

Therefore, 202 students attended the showing. Choice **C** is correct.

36 H For the equation $y = ax^2$, the value of a affects how wide or narrow the graph (a parabola) opens. For example, $y = 2x^2$ opens wider than $y = y = \frac{1}{3}x^2$, but $y = 2x^2$ opens narrower than $y = 5x^2$. If the value of a in $y = a x^2$ is negative, the parabola opens downward rather than upward.

You are looking for functions for which the $|a|$ increases in value as in choice **H.**

37 C For 2 rectangles to be similar, the ratios of their corresponding sides have to be equal; for example, $\frac{length}{width} = \frac{7}{5}$ for both rectangles.

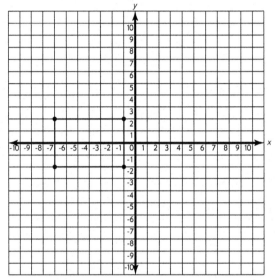

The ratio of $\frac{length}{width} = \frac{3}{2}$ for the given rectangle. In choice **C**, the ratio of $\frac{length}{width} = \frac{6}{4} = \frac{3}{2}$. So the given rectangle and the rectangle in grid H are similar. Thus, **C** is the correct answer.

38 H Lines which are parallel have equal slope. The slope of a line with equation $y = mx + b$ is m; so the slope of the given line, $y = \frac{2}{3}x$, is $\frac{2}{3}$. You are looking for the line having $slope = \frac{rise}{run} = \frac{vertical\ change}{horizontal\ change} = \frac{2}{3}$ as you travel from the point $(0,-2)$ up the line and to the right (up 2, right 3; up 2, right 3, and so on). Graph **H** meets these conditions.

39 A One investment starts at \$250 and decreases at the rate of \$2 per day; this can be interpreted as a "slope" of –2. You want the $\frac{money\ decrease}{time\ increase} = ^-2$.

In grid A, you could start at 250 on the vertical axis, go down 2 squares (– \$50) and over 5 squares (25 days) and get a slope of $\frac{-50}{25} = ^-2$.

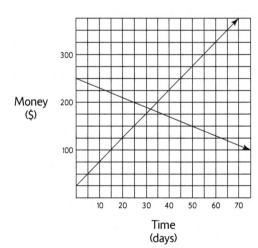

Money
($)

Time
(days)

The second investment starts at \$25 and increases at the rate of \$5 per day. This can be interpreted as a "slope" of 5. You want the $\frac{money\ increase}{time\ increase}$ = 5. Again, in grid A, you could start at 25 on the vertical axis, go up 3 squares (\$75) and over 3 squares (15 days) and get a slope of $\frac{75}{15}$ = 5. The point where the 2 lines cross would correspond to the time at which the 2 investments have the same value. The correct answer is **A.**

40 J The date shows:

$$5 \text{ TV sets not operable}$$
$$10 \text{ TV sets with minor defects}$$
$$\underline{+35 \text{ TV sets with no problems}}$$
$$50 \text{ TV sets total}$$

Going through choices **F** through **J** one at a time, you have:

F: True → 10 is twice 5

G: True → 10 of 50 is $\frac{1}{5}$ and $\frac{1}{5}$ of 200 = 40

H: True → 35 is greater than 2(10 + 5)

J: False → 10 of 50 is $\frac{1}{5}$ and $\frac{1}{5}$ of 100 = 20, not 30 as stated.

Therefore, choice **J** is not a valid conclusion.

41 B

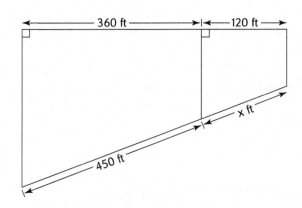

When 3 parallel lines intersect 2 transversals, the segments formed on the transversals are proportional. In the case of our diagram, that means $\frac{120}{360} = \frac{x}{450}$. You have 2 methods from which to choose to solve this:

Method A: $\frac{120}{360} = \frac{x}{450}$. Since 120 is $\frac{1}{3}$ of 360 on the left, x should be $\frac{1}{3}$ of the 450 on the right; so x would be 150.

Method B: $\frac{120}{360} = \frac{x}{450}$. You could just "cross multiply and divide" to solve the proportion to get

$$360x = (120)(450)$$
$$360x = 540,000$$
$$x = 150$$

The correct answer is **B.**

42 J Let x = number of CDs for Luke. Then,

$$x - 3 = \text{number of CDs for Tom}$$
$$2(x - 3) = \text{number of CDs for Manuel}$$

Next: Luke's CDs + Tom's CDs + Manuel's CDs = Total CDs. So $x + (x - 3) + 2(x - 3) = 39$. Thus, choice **J** is correct.

43 B Using the Pythagorean theorem, you have:

$$d^2 = 5^2 + 7^2$$
$$d^2 = 25 + 49$$
$$d^2 = 74$$
$$d = \sqrt{74} \approx 8.60.$$

Choice **B** is the best approximation.

44 H The formula for the volume of a cone is $V = \frac{1}{3}\pi r^2 h$. Since the diameter of the cup is 3 inches, its radius is only 1.5 inches. Then the cup has a volume of

$$V = \frac{1}{3}(3.14)(1.5)^2(4)$$
$$= 9.42\,\text{in}^3$$

So the correct answer is choice **H.**

45 A To find the y-intercept of the graph of the equation $3x - 2y = 12$, let $x = 0$ and solve for y.

$$3x - 2y = 12$$
$$3(0) - 2y = 12$$
$$0 - 2y = 12$$
$$-2y = 12$$
$$y = -6$$

So, the y-intercept is –6. The line must contain the point (3,–2) and have a y-intercept of –6. Counting the slope from –6 on the y-axis, go up 4 and over 3 to arrive at the point (3,–2); thus, the slope is $\frac{4}{3}$. So $m = \frac{4}{3}$ and $b = -6$. Choice **A** is correct answer.

46 G

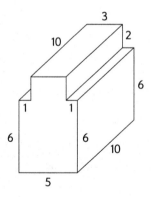

The complete 3D object appears in the figure above. You can find the volume of this object by finding the sum of the volumes of the larger "base" rectangular solid and the smaller "upper" rectangular solid. Each volume is found by: Volume = (length)(width)(height).

Volume of "base" = (5)(10)(6) = 300

Volume of "upper" = (10)(3)(2) = 60

Their sum, 300 + 60 = 360 cu. ft., is the combined volume of the 3D object. This is choice **G.**

47 D For the last 2 entries in the table, the cost is a bit more than twice the weight. So let's try $c = 2w +$ "something." For the first table entry, with $w = .02$ and $c = .09$, substitute this data into our "guess" equation:

$$c = 2w + ?$$

$$.09 = 2(.02) + ?$$

$$.09 = .04 + ?$$

$$.05 = ?$$

So, the equation $c = 2w + .05$ appears to work. As a quick double check, be sure this equation works for other data in the table also. **D** is the correct answer.

48 H $(-5x^3y^{-5})(3x^{-7}y^8)$

$$= (-5)(3)(x^3x^{-7})(y^{-5}y^8)$$

$$= -15\,x^{-4}y^3 \qquad \text{for } x \text{ (added exponents } 3 + -7 = -4)$$
$$\text{for } y \text{ (added exponents } -5 + 8 = 3)$$

$$= \frac{-15y^3}{x^4}$$

The correct answer is choice **H.**

49 C $4(2x - 5)^2 = 64$

$$(2x - 5)^2 = 16 \qquad \text{divided both sides by 4}$$

$$(2x - 5) = \pm 4 \qquad \text{took square root of both sides}$$

This breaks down into 2 separate equations as follows:

$$2x - 5 = {}^-4 \qquad\qquad 2x - 5 = 4$$
$$2x = 1 \qquad OR \qquad 2x = 9$$
$$x = \frac{1}{2} \qquad\qquad x = \frac{9}{2}$$

So the solution set of the given equation is: $\{\frac{1}{2}, \frac{9}{2}\}$, choice **C.**

50 J Starting with the inequality $x + y > 5$, you solve for y to get: $y > -x + 5$. Next, sketch the graph of $y = -x + 5$. This is a line having y-intercept 5 and a slope of -1 (or $\frac{-1}{1}$). Start at 5 on the y-axis, go down 1 space, right 1 space, and so on, to get the graph of $y = -x + 5$. To get the solution of the inequality $y > -x + 5$, shade above the line, as in choice **J.**

51 B

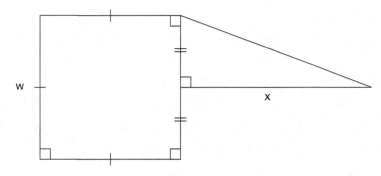

Total area = area of square + area of triangle

$$= (w)(w) + \frac{1}{2}(x)\left(\frac{w}{2}\right)$$

$$= w^2 + \frac{xw}{4}$$

Therefore, choice **B** is the correct answer.

52 G Once the circle has been cut out, there is no way to cut a square, 3 inches on a side, from each corner of the remaining material. **G** is therefore the correct answer.

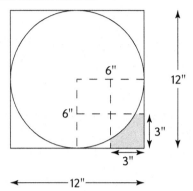

53 B Using the given points (6,10) and (3,1), you can compute the slope of the line containing them:

$$m = \frac{1-10}{3-6} = \frac{-9}{-3} = 3$$

Using the slope, $m = 3$, and the point (3,1), you can substitute into the point-slope of a linear equation to get:

$$y - 1 = 3(x - 3)$$

$$y - 1 = 3x - 9 \qquad \text{distributed on the right}$$

$$y = 3x - 8 \qquad \text{added 1 to both sides}$$

The equation above is now in slope-intercept form, with y-intercept of –8, choice **B.**

54 G In table form, you have the corresponding number of circles and triangles in each figure.

Number of Triangles (t)	Number of Circles (c)
1	2
2	3
3	10

For $t = 1$: $1^2 + 1 = 2$

For $t = 2$: $2^2 + 1 = 3$

For $t = 3$: $3^2 + 1 = 10$

In each case, the formula to get from number of triangles to number of circles seems to be $c = t^2 + 1$, so answer **G** is correct.

55 D Going through the choices one at a time, you have:

A: False → since the temperature never got above 75, the average could not be that large

B: False → daily temperature did <u>not</u> decrease consistently—it increased a bit and then decreased

C: False → between consecutive days, the difference <u>never</u> exceeded 10°

D: True → accurately describes the data shown on the graph

The correct answer is **D.**

56 F With vertices P(4,1), Q(8,4), R(5,8), and S(1,5), the points are plotted below.

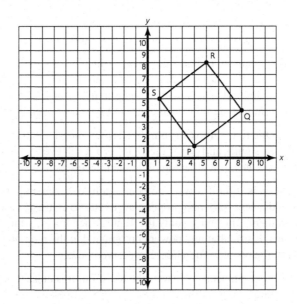

After connecting the points in the order P to Q to R to S, it can be seen that PQRS is a square—all sides are equal and all angles are right angles. Answer **F** is correct.

57 B To build c chairs would take $2.5c$ hours. To build t tables would take $3t$ hours. If Thomas has at most ($\leq$) 40 hours to build the furniture, chair building time + table building time ≤ 40, $2.5c + 3t \leq 40$, which corresponds to answer choice **B**.

58 H To find the slope to the line having equation $5y = -2(x - 3)$, you solve for y to put the equation in slope-intercept form.

$$5y = -2(x - 3)$$
$$5y = -2x + 6 \qquad \text{distribute on the right}$$
$$y = (\frac{-2}{5})x + \frac{6}{5} \qquad \text{divided both sides by 5}$$

In the slope-intercept form, $y = mx + b$, m is the slope. So the slope of our line is $\frac{-2}{5}$, choice **H**.

59 B You can exclude **A** since its graph is not changing linearly (straight line segments). Graph **C** needs to start at 20 and not at 0 on the TEMP axis; for graph **D**, the high point to the right should be lower than the starting point on the left. Thus, graph **B** is the best illustration of the given data.

60 J The relationship between velocity and falling time is just 32 to 1. In other words, the velocity after t seconds of falling is just $32t$ ft/sec. So after 4.5 seconds, the velocity should be velocity $= 32t = 32(4.5) = 144$ ft./sec., which is choice **J**.

Social Studies

1 A Although the United States had a great deal of influence over Cuba after the war, Cuba remained an independent country. The U.S. bought the Virgin Islands from Denmark in 1917. The Hawaiian Islands were formally annexed by the U.S. during the Spanish-American War, but the islands were not a Spanish colony. You should be able to get to the correct answer by the process of elimination.

2 G The states are key to the ratification process either through their legislatures or state conventions, but they also can call for a convention for the purpose of proposing amendments. This understanding will help you eliminate choices **F** and **H**. The chart provides no information to you about how easy or hard it is to get an amendment proposal through the Congress.

3 C American farmers were faced with the problem of overproduction that led to sharply falling prices. The Agricultural Adjustment Act (1933) paid farmers to reduce the amount of wheat, corn, and other commodities, including livestock, they raised. The law was declared unconstitutional by the Supreme Court but it established the policy of the federal government subsidizing farmers to limit production.

4 J The date of Washington's statement should be a giveaway. This is before the U.S. Constitution was written (1787), and therefore the Congress he referred to must be under the Articles of Confederation. Neither the new state constitutions nor the Declaration of Independence mention the Congress. Washington believed the country needed a stronger national government, and presided over the Federal Convention that wrote the Constitution.

5 C The assembly lined reduced the time it took to complete an automobile, making it cheaper to produce. The price of a Ford Model T dropped significantly over the years as a result even though Ford paid his workers high wages. Fuel efficiency was not a concern with automobile manufacturers at the time.

6 F You can approach the question is several ways. The Fourteenth Amendment puts restrictions on state action to protect individual rights; both the necessary and proper clause (elastic clause) and the supremacy clause stress the authority of the federal government. This leaves only the Tenth Amendment, which was added to the Constitution specifically to protect the states. It says that any powers not granted to the federal government or denied to the states belong to the states or to the people. These are the reserved powers.

7 C You need to analyze the photograph itself to answer the question. It is clear that Manzanar is located in a rather desolate valley far from large cities. Although the Eastern Sierra Nevada mountains of California in the background are a winter and summer recreational area, the Japanese and Japanese Americans at Manzanar were internees and could not leave the camp.

8 F Declaration of Independence (1776), Articles of Confederation (1781), U.S. Constitution (1787), Bill of Rights (1791). Remember that the Articles of Confederation were the first written constitution of the United States, and obviously comes before the U.S. Constitution. The Bill of Rights is the first ten amendments to the Constitution, and were approved after the Constitution was in effect.

9 A This question is about the diffusion of ideas. You should be aware that the Renaissance, the "rebirth" in interest in the world of ancient Greece and Rome, began in Italy in the 14th to 15th centuries and then spread to Northern Europe. Holland and Germany were important centers of the Northern Renaissance. Although the Renaissance overlaps with the Age of Exploration, neither Native Americans nor Europeans settling in the Western Hemisphere were much interested in Renaissance ideas.

10 H Judicial review means that the federal courts, ultimately the Supreme Court, can declare a law passed by Congress unconstitutional. Although this power is not specifically mentioned in the Constitution, Hamilton's argument in the Federalist Papers indicates that the framers felt it was implied. The principle of judicial review is clearly stated in the 1803 Supreme Court decision *Marbury* v. *Madison*.

11 B NATO is a military alliance that was created after the Soviet Union closed all roads, canals, and railroads linking western Germany and Berlin in 1948. Although it did respond to ethnic violence in the Balkans in the 1990s, its original purpose was to prevent an attack by the Soviet Union during the Cold War.

12 J The source of energy to drive the machines in the early American factories was waterpower. One of the reasons that New England—Connecticut, Massachusetts, and Rhode Island—was an important center of industrialization in the late 18th and early 19th centuries was that the region had numerous waterfalls and rivers on which the factories could rely.

13 A Sputnik led to increased spending on the American space program, and the beginning of the space race with the Soviet Union. Funding also increased for science and mathematics education to close the technology gap that Americans believed existed between the two countries.

14 G Construction of the Panama Canal began in 1904, long after the California gold rush. While Americans provided the engineering know-how, most of the workers were actually from the British West Indies. There was certainly a military aspect to building the canal, but the key reason was to promote trade.

15 **C** This is a definition question. A vertical combination is a company that controls a product from the time it is a raw material to its sale to the consumer. In a sense, the question is: what do you need to make steel? The only answer that makes sense in this context is coal mines. Coke, a key ingredient in steel making, comes from coal. Carnegie also bought barges and railroads to transport the raw materials he needed.

16 **F** Although the Populist party grew out of the farmers' movement, it did try to reach out to other "exploited" groups such as workers as well as reformers. The party's 1892 platform was an attempt to broaden its base of support. The AF of L was only concerned with the bread and butter issues of workers. Both the Free Soil party and the Know-Nothing party were minor third parties before the Civil War, and are easily eliminated by the timeframe of the question.

17 **A** All of the other answers are concerns that were generally raised against immigrants during the 19th and early 20th century. For labor unions, however, the central question was competition for jobs since immigrants were usually willing to work for less money. Immigration restriction was a demand of the American Federation of Labor even though its leader, Samuel Gompers, was an immigrant himself.

18 **H** As the Cold War began in the late 1940s and early 1950s, many Americans became afraid that Communists, agents of the Soviet Union, were trying to subvert the government. Senator Joseph McCarthy was the leader of this campaign. His unsupported attacks on people who he claimed were Communists became known as McCarthyism.

19 **B** The cotton gin allowed landowners in the South to increase cotton production at a time when demand was high in both the North and Great Britain. Cotton was a labor-intensive crop like tobacco and that labor was provided by slaves. As cotton production spread across the Deep South and into Texas in the first half of the 19th century, so did slavery. You should be aware that the climate and soil in the North did not support cotton, that the cotton gin had little direct impact on the railroads, and that slaves in the South were not fully free until after the Civil War (1861–1865).

20 **G** If you know that the Open Door refers to a foreign policy issue, you can eliminate choices **F** and **J.** At the time, our relations with Latin America were not good. After the Spanish-American War, the U.S. had significant control over Cuba and had taken Puerto Rico as a territory. We encouraged and supported a Panamanian revolt against Columbia so that we could build the Panama Canal. President Theodore Roosevelt made it clear we had the right to intervene in the affairs of countries in the Western Hemisphere. The Open Door Policy stated that the U.S. supported free trade for all nations with China and the territorial integrity of China following the Boxer Rebellion.

21 **C** The key information is that the number of seats a state has in the House of Representatives is based on population. The seats are reapportioned after every decennial census, and the number of representatives a state has increases, decreases or remains the same. The trend is clear with the increase in representation for North Carolina, Georgia, Florida, Texas, Arizona, California, and Nevada. The Great Plains states show no significant population growth, while the fact that Mississippi lost a seat, indicates that its population declined.

22 **J** William Jennings Bryan, three-time Democratic candidate for the presidency, was also a noted evangelical Christian. He participated on the prosecution team during the trial of John Scopes in 1925 for violating the Tennessee law that prohibited the teaching of evolution. This was the so-called "Monkey Trial." The references to science and religion in the excerpt should help you eliminate at least choices **A** and **C.**

23 **D** Charles Lindbergh was one the most popular heroes in the 1920s for his solo flight across the Atlantic Ocean in 1927. His plane, *The Spirit of St. Louis,* can be seen in the background of the photograph. The fact that Lindbergh's wife is in the picture is not relevant.

24 **G** Three Midwest cities—Cincinnati, St. Louis, and Chicago—that were not ranked in 1810 are on the list in 1860; New Orleans is the only ranked Southern city. It is clear that the largest cities in the country are in the Northeast, and the table provides no information about population growth by state.

25 **A** The Yalta Conference took place in February 1945, and dealt with post–World War II issues. Both the Battle of Dien Bien Phu and the War Powers Act are related to Vietnam but not to the American military buildup. Dien Bien Phu was a major defeat for the French in 1954 and convinced them to give up their control of Indochina. The War Powers Act (1973) limits the authority of the president to commit American troops to combat, and was a response to the Vietnam experience. The Gulf of Tonkin Resolution (1964) gave President Lyndon Johnson broad power to use military force to protect American troops in the region.

26 F When it convened in May 1775, the Second Continental Congress assumed the powers of a government. It created a postal system, sent ambassadors to Europe to seek foreign support, and appointed George Washington to head the Continental army. Although Washington was a Virginian, the House of Burgesses, as the Virginia colonial legislative was called, did not have the authority to make the appointment nor did the state militias. The Continental Congress is the only recognized legislative institution; the Senate was established under the U.S. Constitution, which was not written until 1787.

27 B The question you need to ask yourself is which amendment to the Constitution deals with slavery and citizenship. Slavery should immediately bring to mind the three amendments passed after the Civil War—13th (1865), 14th (1868), and 15th (1870) Amendments—and help you eliminate choices **C** and **D.** The Fifteenth Amendment granted African Americans the right to vote. It is the Fourteenth Amendment that defines as a citizen "[a]ll persons born or naturalized in the United States . . . "

28 H All of the possible answers relate to events during the Truman Administration (1945–1953), but you should realize that the Truman Doctrine is related to American foreign policy. Under the Truman Doctrine, the U.S. pledged to support "free peoples" struggling against an armed minority or outside pressure. It was issued in response to the Communist insurgency in Greece and pressure that the Soviet Union was putting on Turkey, and was an important milestone at the start of the Cold War.

29 A The automobile was an important factor in the strong economy during the 1920s. As demand for cars increased, demand for the materials needed to make them increased as well—the steel, rubber, and glass industries prospered during the decade. Union membership generally declined during the 1920s; the U.S. was the leading automobile producer in the world at the time and it is safe to say there were no imports from Asia. Public transportation remained critical for intra-urban travel, but if anything, with more cars on the road, fewer people were using buses and subways.

30 H Edison's first power plant, the Pearl Street Station in New York, operated on direct current (dc) that lost a considerable amount of energy when transported over power lines; the development of alternating current (ac) generation by Nikola Telsa allowed the transmission of electricity over long distances. The main purpose of the Pearl Street Station was to provide the electricity to light homes and businesses that used Edison's electric lightbulb.

31 D Discrimination in housing was not addressed by Congress until the Civil Rights Act of 1968. The Equal Pay Act of 1963 required employers to pay the same salary to workers doing the same job under the same working conditions. Affirmative action plans were first introduced by the federal government for federal agencies, and did not require legislation. Public accommodations included hotels, motels, and restaurants.

32 J Although it had a tremendous effect on all slaves as word about it spread through the South, the practical effect of the Emancipation Proclamation was more limited. By its own terms, it only applied to slaves in states that were "in rebellion against the United States." Slaves held in the border states that remained part of the Union—Delaware, Maryland, Kentucky, and Missouri—were not impacted. The Emancipation Proclamation also allowed African Americans to serve in the army, but did not provide for either equality before the law or voting rights.

33 A In 1828, Congress passed a tariff that significantly raised duties on imported goods. Southerners called it the "Tariff of Abominations" because the duties made manufactured products needed by the South more expensive. John C. Calhoun wrote the South Carolina Exposition and Protest in response, which argued that the states had the right to "nullify" (refuse to obey) a law they considered unconstitutional. In 1832, South Carolina nullified a new tariff that actually reduced duties somewhat and threatened secession if the federal government tried to collect the tariff in the state. South Carolina backed down when President Andrew Jackson threatened the use of force and lower duties were adopted by Congress.

34 H This question requires that you know where the Suez Canal is located. Completed in 1869 in Egypt, the canal allows ships to pass from the Mediterranean Sea into the Red Sea. From here, ships can travel into the Indian Ocean. The Strait of Gibraltar provides access from the Mediterranean to the Atlantic; the Panama Canal links the Atlantic and the Pacific Oceans; the Strait of Hormuz connects the Persian Gulf to the Arabian Sea.

35 D The number of eligible voters increased significantly between the elections of 1824 and 1828 as states changed their constitutions to eliminate property qualifications for voting. This trend continued as the country moved toward universal white male suffrage over the next decade. Many states in the North denied free African Americans the right to vote at this time, and it was not until the Fifteenth Amendment (1870) that their voting rights were protected by the Constitution. Women officially voted for the first time in territorial elections in Wyoming in 1869. The voting age for men was always 21.

36 G The excerpt is taken from President Wilson's famous statement of American aims during the First World War—the Fourteen Points—in which he called for the creation of what became known as the League of Nations. The Treaty of Versailles that ended war included provisions for establishing the League; the Treaty was not approved by the Senate, and the U.S. never became a member of the League. All of the other international organizations listed were established after World War II. The United Nations, of course, is the successor to the League. It should be obvious that the International Monetary Fund does not deal with issues of "political independence" and "territorial integrity." Wilson is clearly referring to a much broader organization than the Southeast Asia Treaty Organization (SEATO), which, in any event, was a product of the Cold War.

37 B The Civilian Conservation Corps (CCC) specifically provided jobs for young men between the ages of 18 and 25. They planted trees, created trails and campgrounds, and did other forestry work throughout the south and west. The CCC camps were organized on a quasi-military basis, and the men were required to send part of their monthly pay back home to their families.

38 F Under the Constitution as ratified, senators were chosen by their respective state legislatures. This was an indirect process, i.e., the people elected the members of the state legislature and then the legislature selected the two senators. The Seventeenth Amendment (1913) provided for the direct election of senators, expanding considerably the role of the people in the political process.

39 C The diagram indicates that there are powers that the federal and state governments share under our system. These are known as concurrent powers. Only the federal government can establish post offices and regulate interstate commerce under the Constitution, while marriage laws are the responsibility of the states. But both the federal government and the states can require you pay taxes. There is a federal income tax and most states have a state income tax as well or have a broad range of other taxing authority.

40 G This question is asking what the states can and cannot do. Under the Constitution, the states are actually prohibited from having their own foreign policy, taxing goods coming into the state, or establishing an army. The states, not the federal government, however, license professionals working in the state, including physicians, lawyers, and teachers.

41 B The quotas limited immigration for each country to a percentage of its nation living in the U.S. The laws were intended to limit the number of immigrants from Southern and Eastern Europe, i.e., Italians, Poles, Russians, who were often stereotyped as dangerous radicals. A ceiling was set on the total number of immigrants who could enter the U.S. annually, but immigration was not prohibited altogether. The Chinese Exclusion Act of 1882 remained in effect and the 1924 law ended Japanese immigration.

42 H You would likely use all the sources. The internet is a valuable research tool, but students should be a little wary of commercial sites; a university or government site is better. The best source, however, would be the only primary source listed—President Truman's memoirs. This would provide an eyewitness account of key events—the Potsdam Conference with Stalin, the decision to use the atomic bomb against Japan, the Berlin airlift.

43 B The Peace Corps is the only program among the possible answers that was based on volunteerism. It sent American men and women to developing countries around the world for a two-year period to establish schools and medical clinics, to help with agricultural and water projects, and a broad range of other assistance programs. The emphasis was on people to people contact, and the Peace Corps continues to represent the U.S. in numerous countries today.

44 H The World Trade Organization (WTO) is responsible for promoting the free flow of goods and services between countries; high tariffs are contrary to free trade. When the Bush administration raised tariffs on steel imports to the U.S. to protect the American steel industry, the WTO condemned the U.S. action.

45 B The Battle of Midway took place in June 1942. The U.S. was at war with Germany a few days after the Japanese attack on Pearl Harbor. American forces did not recapture of the Philippines until early 1945. Midway was a major defeat for the Japanese, and its forces never did attack the west coast. You should come up with the correct answer by the process of elimination.

46 J Under the Pacific Railway Act, the railroad companies received over 125 million acres of public land to build the trans-continental lines that connected the east with the west coast. Lowering tariffs would have little direct impact on the railroads, and regulating what they could charge would not be considered help. Demands of farmers for lower rates ultimately lead to the creation of the Interstate Commerce Commission in 1887. The Department of Transportation was not established until 1966.

47 A The Tennessee Valley Authority (TVA) was a New Deal program that built dams and hydroelectric plants throughout a seven-state region that included Kentucky, Tennessee, Alabama, Mississippi, Georgia, North Carolina, and Virginia. The TVA provided jobs, led to lower electricity prices, and helped with flood control. Environmental problems were raised, however, by strip-mining and coal-burning power plants.

48 J The pie chart clearly shows that the overwhelming majority of Southerners on the eve of the Civil War were not slave owners. It is also clear that large plantations that relied on many slaves were rare, and the data does not address the number of slaves by state. Coming up with the right answer is just a matter of doing some simple addition.

49 C As the Depression worsened across the country, President Hoover was reluctant to direct federal assistance for those Americans who needed help. In this statement, he recognizes that private charity—neighbors, local agencies, industry, and "a great multitude of organizations"—is providing significant amounts of money. He is silent on the question of the states making work for the unemployed, and sees federal contributions to the problem as counterproductive.

50 H The lines showing the spread of the plague between 1347 and 1350 show a clear pattern. The plague entered Western Europe from the Mediterranean and moved north, and spreading from the ports into the interior. The plague also moved east, reaching into Russia by 1351.

51 C The failure of the U.S. to join the League of Nations is usually seen as a sign that the U.S. was isolationist in the 1920s. But the U.S. was engaged with other countries to help prevent the outbreak of another world conflict. This was the purpose of the Washington Naval Conference, a step toward disarmament, the Dawes and Young Plans on reparations, and the signing of the Kellog-Briand Pact that outlawed war as an instrument of foreign policy.

52 H The report on agricultural production in a Chinese province shows that maize, which was first grown in northern Mexico, had spread to Asia by the 18th century. The question is about the diffusion of agricultural products through global interconnections. Although the exact route maize took from the Western Hemisphere to Asia is not clear, you should be able to get the answer if you knew that maize (Indian corn) was indigenous to Mexico.

53 A The GI Bill of Rights (1944) provided veterans of the World War II financial assistance to help them buy homes, start businesses or farms, go to college or get technical training. It did not guarantee their admission to any college they wanted. The fact that the veterans had the means to buy homes obviously stimulated the construction industry to meet that demand. This fact plus the new businesses started by the veterans had a positive effect on the economy.

54 G Like other civil rights groups, the farm workers used a variety of nonviolent forms of protest. The most effective was the nationwide boycott of table grapes that Cesar Chavez began in 1966. The boycott lasted until 1970 when grape growers signed a new contract with the farm workers union.

55 B It should be clear what information the graph provides and what it doesn't. The graph provides no information on voting patterns of African Americans and whites, nor does it address voter participation over time. You may know that older Americans are more likely to vote than those 18 to 25, but the graph does not address age. It is clear, however, that the more education a person has, the more likely it is for that person to vote.

Science

1 C A sturdy building would offer the best safe shelter from the lightning.

2 J HIV reproduces within cells of the immune system, making 1 to 10 billion new copies of itself every day.

3 D Families or groups (elements in the same vertical column) have similar properties. Even though H, Li, Na are in the same group, hydrogen is a nonmetal, while Li and Na are metals.

4 J Since the students are required to record the amount of solution, they are probably using a burette because it measures out extremely precise amounts of liquid. The burette has markings on it to the nearest 0.1 mL. A stopcock at the bottom can be adjusted to deliver liquids down to the drop level. The correct answer is **J.** Note that choice **H** is incorrect since the students aren't adding sulfuric acid.

5 D A rule of safe laboratory procedure is to always *add the acid to the water.* If you were to add water to acid, it could overheat and spatter.

6 H Since one serving (30g) provides 14g of dietary fiber, then two servings (60g) will provide 28g of dietary fiber. This is more than the daily recommended allowance of 20 to 25g per day.

7 D The arrow labeled "C" in the diagram shows metamorphic rocks being formed. Metamorphic rocks are formed by the application of heat or pressure to pre-existing rocks.

8 G In a natural community, a balance usually develops, allowing organisms to exist and reproduce. Each plant and animal occupies its own niche. Choice **F** is incorrect because competition is an ongoing natural process. Choice **J** is incorrect because owls *are* nocturnal animals.

9 B Before developing a hypothesis to explain the outcome, the correlation between the volume of water and the time required should be noted. So the best question would be "How does the rate of freezing change with the different size of the containers?"

10 J The formula including momentum, velocity, and mass is:

$$momentum = mass \times velocity$$

Since you are looking for mass, you could rearrange the formula as follows:

$$\frac{momentum}{velocity} = mass$$

Now plugging in the values gives

$$\frac{20}{50} = mass$$

Since $\frac{20}{50} = .4$, the mass is .4 kg.

11 C Since kingdom is the highest taxonomic level and therefore the most general term, it would contain the most members.

12 G Cooling a solution actually slows down the rate at which a solid dissolves.

13 D The number of people used in testing a product is important. Generally, the larger the size of the experimental group, the more reliable the conclusions are. Control groups are also important in comparing results.

14 H With objects of different shapes and weight, air resistance (wind, friction) has an effect on the falling rate. In a vacuum, there is no air resistance so any two objects would fall equal distances at equal times.

15 C The more primitive groups are algae and fungi. These plants lack true roots, stems, and leaves. Fungi lack chlorophyll. The more advanced plants possess roots, stems, and leaves. Ferns are green plants that lack seeds and reproduce by means of spores. This allows ferns to reproduce without fertilization. The gymnosperms are cone-bearing plants (angiosperms—flowering plants—are omitted) that possess chlorophyll.

16 F The cytoplasm in either plant or animal cells varies in consistency from fluid to semi-solid. The diagram helps you eliminate choices **G, H,** and **J.**

17 B To answer this question, you must analyze the question carefully. Notice the important phrase—"changes to accumulate." Only changes that could be inherited would accumulate (add up). Over many generations, the many small changes would persist and result in a large overall change of the organism.

18 J Oxygen and glucose are produced during photosynthesis.

19 D Balancing this equation may take a little trial and error. Notice on the left you have O_2 and on the right O_3, so you will probably need to multiply the O_2 by 3 and the O_3 by 2 to get 6 Os on each side. But if you multiply the O_3 by 2 on the right, then you are also multiplying the Fe_2 by 2, giving you 4Fe. So you will need to multiply Fe on the left by 4. The balanced equation is $4Fe + 3O_2 \rightarrow 2Fe_2O_3$.

20 78.2 grams. The formula involving density, mass, and volume is

$$density = \frac{mass}{volume}$$

Rearranging the formula gives *volume* × *density* = *mass*. Now substituting in the values gives $65.2 \times 1.2 = 78.24$. But since the question asks for an answer to the nearest tenth, the answer is **78.2.**

21 A Buoyancy is the power of a fluid to exert an upward force on any body placed in the fluid. The force equals the weight of the fluid moved out of the way by the body. When Arminta gets into the swimming pool, she moves away water that weighs as much as she does, so she floats. Choice **C** is wrong because most of her body is below the surface.

22 G Adaptations enable organisms to better survive in an environment. It is to the advantage of each insect species to avoid being eaten, and many have adapted by having bright colors for protection. From the information presented, one could logically assume that monkeys have learned that insects with bright colors taste bad. Even insects that don't taste bad would then find that bright colors are helpful protection.

23 C They are highly reactive metals, the alkali metals of the first column of the periodic table. Other alkali metals of higher atomic numbers are rubidium and cesium.

24 H Molds are not green plants (producers) but are fungi and lack true leaves, roots, and stems. Molds do not contain chlorophyll and therefore cannot manufacture food. However, because molds are a life form, basic life elements such as reproduction, respiration, and cellular structure can be eliminated as correct choices, leaving the ability to manufacture food as the correct answer.

25 D The diagram shows the decomposition of water by an electric current (electrolysis). The purpose of an electrolytic experiment is to break down water into its elements, hydrogen and oxygen. Each molecule of water contains two hydrogen atoms and one oxygen atom. So the decomposition of water gives off twice as much hydrogen as oxygen.

26 F Enzymes aid in the digestion of fats, helping to speed up the breakdown of fats into glucose.

27 D Inertia is the tendency of an object to resist any change in its motion. If an object is moving, it tends to keep moving at the same speed and in the same direction unless a force acts on it. This is also known as Newton's First Law of Motion. In other words, the velocity of the object remains constant unless a force changes it. If an object is at rest, it tends to remain at rest.

28 G Friction is the force that opposes motion between two surfaces that are touching each other.

29 D The circulatory system transports nutrients obtained through digestion, delivers oxygen and removes carbon dioxide, and transports wastes to the kidneys. The nervous system transports nerve impulses.

30 G The force of buoyancy diminishes the apparent weight by the weight of water displaced by the glass object. You know from swimming that submerged objects (including people) seem to weigh less.

31 C To answer this question, you must be able to read the graph and understand the information included. Notice that the decibels of noise are listed along the left-hand side in increases of 10. The common sources of noise are listed along the bottom of the graph. Since only two noise sources here are greater than the hearing pain threshold, it must be less than 125 decibels but greater than 100 decibels. Of the choices, the best approximation is 120 decibels, which is, in fact, the normal hearing pain threshold.

32 H Bases turn red litmus paper blue. Acids turn blue litmus paper red.

33 D The lungs are the organs that exchange oxygen gas for carbon dioxide gas.

34 H Each new cell has the same number of chromosomes as the original cell. So, there will be 24 chromosomes in each of the new cells.

35 **D** Both creatures benefit from their association. The termite gets food from the cellulose that is digested by its tiny inhabitants. Those little parasites get much of their food from the termite. Such a relationship of benefit to both animals is called mutualism.

36 **H** Water is required for plants to grow. Even if there is evidence of carbon dioxide in the atmosphere, the origin may not be from plants. If water never occurred on the planet, then plants (as we know them) would not be able to grow.

37 **C** Some of the energy put into a machine is lost as thermal energy as a result of friction. So the work put out by a machine is always less than the work put into the machine. Efficiency is a measure of how much of the work put into a machine is changed to useful work put out by a machine. The higher the efficiency of a machine, the greater the amount of work input is changed to useful work output.

In a fixed pulley, the resistance distance equals the effort distance, $d_r = d_e$. Use the following formula to solve the problem:

$$Efficiency = \frac{work\ out}{work\ in} \times 100\%$$

$$= \frac{F_{resistance} \times D_{resistance}}{F_{effort} \times D_{effort}} \times 100\%$$

$$= \frac{6.5\,N}{7.2\,N} \times 100\%$$

$$= 90\%$$

38 **H** Nucleic acids, including DNA and RNA, are composed of long molecules and used to store genetic information.

39 **B** Ionic bonding exists in compounds containing both a metal (sodium) and a nonmetal (chlorine). In ionic bonding, the metallic atom gives up electrons, and the nonmetallic atom receives them. The transfer of electrons creates ions (charged atoms) of opposite charges. The attraction between opposite charges keeps the compound bonded together.

40 **H** Inside the aerosol can is the actual product and a compressed gas. That gas is stored under high pressure. Pressing the top button allows the gas to escape toward lower pressure in the surrounding air. As gas escapes to the lower pressure, it also pushes out the product (such as paint or hairspray).

41 **D** The palm tree is most independent. Green plants get their energy from sunlight and store that energy as sugar. Animals cannot be independent because they get their energy by eating plants (as sheep do) or other animals (as codfish and cougars do).

42 **F** The problem is solved according to the following steps:

$$Work = Force \times Distance$$

$$= 1,250\ Newton \times 2\ meters$$

$$= 2,500\ Newton\ meters = 2,500\ Joules$$

$$Power = \frac{Work}{Time} = \frac{2,500\ Joules}{3\ seconds} \cong 833\ watts$$

43 **C** Movement of wind is an example of convection. Convection, the most efficient way of transferring heat, is the upward movement of a warm liquid or gas. Air above the equator is warmer than the air at any other place on Earth, and it rises. Air at the poles, however, is much cooler than it is anywhere else. This cold, dense air sinks and moves along the Earth's surface away from the poles.

44 **H** Above 9,000 lumens, there are biological factors that limit the rate of photosynthesis.

45 **C** When the retina gets the image, it has been transposed (turned upside down). The optic nerve sends the image as it is to the brain. The brain makes the adjustment by transposing the image so that it is right side up.

46 **J** A lens magnifies images by refracting (bending) light rays. A focus is a position where the image is well defined. Dispersion separates white light into its component colors, because each color is refracted differently.

47 B Because most animals eat more than one specific food, complex food webs are needed to show the different foods that the animals eat.

48 J Momentum is a property a moving object has due to its mass and velocity. Momentum can be calculated using the following formula:

$$momentum = mass \times velocity$$

or

$$p = m \times v$$

The unit for momentum is kg × m/s. Momentum of an object does not change unless its mass, or velocity, or both, change. Momentum also can be transferred from one object to another as when billiard balls collide.

In this problem, $p = 2000$ kg × 10 m/s = 20,000 kg × m/s.

49 C Respiration is the central life process during metabolism. Oxygen is taken in, allowing stored chemical energy to be released. Respiration takes place within a cell. Photosynthesis (**A**) is the process opposite to respiration. In respiration, an individual inhales air rich in oxygen and exhales air rich in carbon dioxide. In photosynthesis, green plants take carbon dioxide and water from the atmosphere and release oxygen, water, and glucose as by-products.

50 F Solutions with a pH lower than 7 are acidic, with 0 being the strongest acid. Solutions with a pH greater than 7 are basic, with 14 being the strongest base. Solutions with a pH of 7 are neutral (pure water). Since the scale shows shampoo at a pH close to 6, shampoo would be a weak acid.

51 D To answer this question, you must understand her vocal cords vibrate and start the air vibrating. Another way to say this is "a pattern of vibrations is set up in the air."

52 J The proper inference is that human beings and whales have a common ancestor, the bone structure being inherited from some earlier mammal. The possibility that people evolved from fishes is not suggested by the human/whale similarity, for whales are not fishes but mammals.

53 C Isolation, such as that on islands, gives an opportunity for characteristics to concentrate and become established in a given population.

54 G Since the numbers in the chart are the number of differences between the hemoglobin molecules of two animals, the most similar animals will have the smallest number on the chart. The zeros don't count because they are where a row and a column are the same animal. The smallest number for two animals is 13, the cow and the sheep.

55 A Excessive heat, dampness, or exposure to light or flame might cause the materials to spoil or react in an undesirable and sometimes dangerous way. Notice that the labels mentioned do not discuss the *uses* of the materials.

Answer Document for Practice Test 2

English Language Arts

1 Ⓐ Ⓑ Ⓒ Ⓓ	6 Ⓕ Ⓖ Ⓗ Ⓙ	11 Ⓐ Ⓑ Ⓒ Ⓓ	16 Ⓕ Ⓖ Ⓗ Ⓙ	21 Ⓐ Ⓑ Ⓒ Ⓓ	26 Ⓕ Ⓖ Ⓗ Ⓙ
2 Ⓕ Ⓖ Ⓗ Ⓙ	7 Ⓐ Ⓑ Ⓒ Ⓓ	12 Ⓕ Ⓖ Ⓗ Ⓙ	17 Ⓐ Ⓑ Ⓒ Ⓓ	22 Ⓕ Ⓖ Ⓗ Ⓙ	27 Ⓐ Ⓑ Ⓒ Ⓓ
3 Ⓐ Ⓑ Ⓒ Ⓓ	8 Ⓕ Ⓖ Ⓗ Ⓙ	13 Ⓐ Ⓑ Ⓒ Ⓓ	18 Ⓕ Ⓖ Ⓗ Ⓙ	23 Ⓐ Ⓑ Ⓒ Ⓓ	28 Ⓕ Ⓖ Ⓗ Ⓙ
4 Ⓕ Ⓖ Ⓗ Ⓙ	9 Ⓐ Ⓑ Ⓒ Ⓓ	14 Ⓕ Ⓖ Ⓗ Ⓙ	19 Ⓐ Ⓑ Ⓒ Ⓓ	24 Ⓕ Ⓖ Ⓗ Ⓙ	
5 Ⓐ Ⓑ Ⓒ Ⓓ	10 Ⓕ Ⓖ Ⓗ Ⓙ	15 Ⓐ Ⓑ Ⓒ Ⓓ	20 Ⓕ Ⓖ Ⓗ Ⓙ	25 Ⓐ Ⓑ Ⓒ Ⓓ	

29 _____

_____

_____

_____

_____

30 _____

_____

_____

_____

_____

31 _____

_____

_____

_____

_____

32 Ⓕ Ⓖ Ⓗ Ⓙ	36 Ⓕ Ⓖ Ⓗ Ⓙ	41 Ⓐ Ⓑ Ⓒ Ⓓ	46 Ⓕ Ⓖ Ⓗ Ⓙ	51 Ⓐ Ⓑ Ⓒ Ⓓ
33 Ⓐ Ⓑ Ⓒ Ⓓ	37 Ⓐ Ⓑ Ⓒ Ⓓ	42 Ⓕ Ⓖ Ⓗ Ⓙ	47 Ⓐ Ⓑ Ⓒ Ⓓ	
34 Ⓕ Ⓖ Ⓗ Ⓙ	38 Ⓕ Ⓖ Ⓗ Ⓙ	43 Ⓐ Ⓑ Ⓒ Ⓓ	48 Ⓕ Ⓖ Ⓗ Ⓙ	
35 Ⓐ Ⓑ Ⓒ Ⓓ	39 Ⓐ Ⓑ Ⓒ Ⓓ	44 Ⓕ Ⓖ Ⓗ Ⓙ	49 Ⓐ Ⓑ Ⓒ Ⓓ	
	40 Ⓕ Ⓖ Ⓗ Ⓙ	45 Ⓐ Ⓑ Ⓒ Ⓓ	50 Ⓕ Ⓖ Ⓗ Ⓙ	

Use a lined 8½ × 11 sheet of paper to write your essay.

CUT HERE

Answer Document for Practice Test 2

Mathematics

1 Ⓐ Ⓑ Ⓒ Ⓓ								22 Ⓕ Ⓖ Ⓗ Ⓙ	41 Ⓐ Ⓑ Ⓒ Ⓓ
2 Ⓕ Ⓖ Ⓗ Ⓙ								23 Ⓐ Ⓑ Ⓒ Ⓓ	42 Ⓕ Ⓖ Ⓗ Ⓙ
3 Ⓐ Ⓑ Ⓒ Ⓓ								24 Ⓕ Ⓖ Ⓗ Ⓙ	43 Ⓐ Ⓑ Ⓒ Ⓓ

21 (grid-in fields with bubbles 0–9)

1 Ⓐ Ⓑ Ⓒ Ⓓ
2 Ⓕ Ⓖ Ⓗ Ⓙ
3 Ⓐ Ⓑ Ⓒ Ⓓ
4 Ⓕ Ⓖ Ⓗ Ⓙ
5 Ⓐ Ⓑ Ⓒ Ⓓ
6 Ⓕ Ⓖ Ⓗ Ⓙ
7 Ⓐ Ⓑ Ⓒ Ⓓ
8 Ⓕ Ⓖ Ⓗ Ⓙ
9 Ⓐ Ⓑ Ⓒ Ⓓ
10 Ⓕ Ⓖ Ⓗ Ⓙ
11 Ⓐ Ⓑ Ⓒ Ⓓ
12 Ⓕ Ⓖ Ⓗ Ⓙ
13 Ⓐ Ⓑ Ⓒ Ⓓ
14 Ⓕ Ⓖ Ⓗ Ⓙ
15 Ⓐ Ⓑ Ⓒ Ⓓ
16 Ⓕ Ⓖ Ⓗ Ⓙ
17 Ⓐ Ⓑ Ⓒ Ⓓ
18 Ⓕ Ⓖ Ⓗ Ⓙ
19 Ⓐ Ⓑ Ⓒ Ⓓ
20 Ⓕ Ⓖ Ⓗ Ⓙ

22 Ⓕ Ⓖ Ⓗ Ⓙ
23 Ⓐ Ⓑ Ⓒ Ⓓ
24 Ⓕ Ⓖ Ⓗ Ⓙ
25 Ⓐ Ⓑ Ⓒ Ⓓ
26 Ⓕ Ⓖ Ⓗ Ⓙ
27 Ⓐ Ⓑ Ⓒ Ⓓ
28 Ⓕ Ⓖ Ⓗ Ⓙ
29 Ⓐ Ⓑ Ⓒ Ⓓ
30 Ⓕ Ⓖ Ⓗ Ⓙ
31 Ⓐ Ⓑ Ⓒ Ⓓ
32 Ⓕ Ⓖ Ⓗ Ⓙ
33 Ⓐ Ⓑ Ⓒ Ⓓ
34 Ⓕ Ⓖ Ⓗ Ⓙ
35 Ⓐ Ⓑ Ⓒ Ⓓ
36 Ⓕ Ⓖ Ⓗ Ⓙ
37 Ⓐ Ⓑ Ⓒ Ⓓ
38 Ⓕ Ⓖ Ⓗ Ⓙ
39 Ⓐ Ⓑ Ⓒ Ⓓ
40 Ⓕ Ⓖ Ⓗ Ⓙ

41 Ⓐ Ⓑ Ⓒ Ⓓ
42 Ⓕ Ⓖ Ⓗ Ⓙ
43 Ⓐ Ⓑ Ⓒ Ⓓ
44 Ⓕ Ⓖ Ⓗ Ⓙ
45 Ⓐ Ⓑ Ⓒ Ⓓ
46 Ⓕ Ⓖ Ⓗ Ⓙ
47 Ⓐ Ⓑ Ⓒ Ⓓ
48 Ⓕ Ⓖ Ⓗ Ⓙ
49 Ⓐ Ⓑ Ⓒ Ⓓ
50 Ⓕ Ⓖ Ⓗ Ⓙ
51 Ⓐ Ⓑ Ⓒ Ⓓ
52 Ⓕ Ⓖ Ⓗ Ⓙ
53 Ⓐ Ⓑ Ⓒ Ⓓ
54 Ⓕ Ⓖ Ⓗ Ⓙ
55 Ⓐ Ⓑ Ⓒ Ⓓ
56 Ⓕ Ⓖ Ⓗ Ⓙ
57 Ⓐ Ⓑ Ⓒ Ⓓ
58 Ⓕ Ⓖ Ⓗ Ⓙ
59 Ⓐ Ⓑ Ⓒ Ⓓ
60 Ⓕ Ⓖ Ⓗ Ⓙ

Social Studies

1 Ⓐ Ⓑ Ⓒ Ⓓ
2 Ⓕ Ⓖ Ⓗ Ⓙ
3 Ⓐ Ⓑ Ⓒ Ⓓ
4 Ⓕ Ⓖ Ⓗ Ⓙ
5 Ⓐ Ⓑ Ⓒ Ⓓ
6 Ⓕ Ⓖ Ⓗ Ⓙ
7 Ⓐ Ⓑ Ⓒ Ⓓ
8 Ⓕ Ⓖ Ⓗ Ⓙ
9 Ⓐ Ⓑ Ⓒ Ⓓ
10 Ⓕ Ⓖ Ⓗ Ⓙ

11 Ⓐ Ⓑ Ⓒ Ⓓ
12 Ⓕ Ⓖ Ⓗ Ⓙ
13 Ⓐ Ⓑ Ⓒ Ⓓ
14 Ⓕ Ⓖ Ⓗ Ⓙ
15 Ⓐ Ⓑ Ⓒ Ⓓ
16 Ⓕ Ⓖ Ⓗ Ⓙ
17 Ⓐ Ⓑ Ⓒ Ⓓ
18 Ⓕ Ⓖ Ⓗ Ⓙ
19 Ⓐ Ⓑ Ⓒ Ⓓ
20 Ⓕ Ⓖ Ⓗ Ⓙ

21 Ⓐ Ⓑ Ⓒ Ⓓ
22 Ⓕ Ⓖ Ⓗ Ⓙ
23 Ⓐ Ⓑ Ⓒ Ⓓ
24 Ⓕ Ⓖ Ⓗ Ⓙ
25 Ⓐ Ⓑ Ⓒ Ⓓ
26 Ⓕ Ⓖ Ⓗ Ⓙ
27 Ⓐ Ⓑ Ⓒ Ⓓ
28 Ⓕ Ⓖ Ⓗ Ⓙ
29 Ⓐ Ⓑ Ⓒ Ⓓ
30 Ⓕ Ⓖ Ⓗ Ⓙ

31 Ⓐ Ⓑ Ⓒ Ⓓ
32 Ⓕ Ⓖ Ⓗ Ⓙ
33 Ⓐ Ⓑ Ⓒ Ⓓ
34 Ⓕ Ⓖ Ⓗ Ⓙ
35 Ⓐ Ⓑ Ⓒ Ⓓ
36 Ⓕ Ⓖ Ⓗ Ⓙ
37 Ⓐ Ⓑ Ⓒ Ⓓ
38 Ⓕ Ⓖ Ⓗ Ⓙ
39 Ⓐ Ⓑ Ⓒ Ⓓ
40 Ⓕ Ⓖ Ⓗ Ⓙ

41 Ⓐ Ⓑ Ⓒ Ⓓ
42 Ⓕ Ⓖ Ⓗ Ⓙ
43 Ⓐ Ⓑ Ⓒ Ⓓ
44 Ⓕ Ⓖ Ⓗ Ⓙ
45 Ⓐ Ⓑ Ⓒ Ⓓ
46 Ⓕ Ⓖ Ⓗ Ⓙ
47 Ⓐ Ⓑ Ⓒ Ⓓ
48 Ⓕ Ⓖ Ⓗ Ⓙ
49 Ⓐ Ⓑ Ⓒ Ⓓ
50 Ⓕ Ⓖ Ⓗ Ⓙ

51 Ⓐ Ⓑ Ⓒ Ⓓ
52 Ⓕ Ⓖ Ⓗ Ⓙ
53 Ⓐ Ⓑ Ⓒ Ⓓ
54 Ⓕ Ⓖ Ⓗ Ⓙ
55 Ⓐ Ⓑ Ⓒ Ⓓ

Science

1 Ⓐ Ⓑ Ⓒ Ⓓ
2 Ⓕ Ⓖ Ⓗ Ⓙ
3 Ⓐ Ⓑ Ⓒ Ⓓ
4 Ⓕ Ⓖ Ⓗ Ⓙ
5 Ⓐ Ⓑ Ⓒ Ⓓ
6 Ⓕ Ⓖ Ⓗ Ⓙ
7 Ⓐ Ⓑ Ⓒ Ⓓ
8 Ⓕ Ⓖ Ⓗ Ⓙ
9 Ⓐ Ⓑ Ⓒ Ⓓ
10 Ⓕ Ⓖ Ⓗ Ⓙ
11 Ⓐ Ⓑ Ⓒ Ⓓ
12 Ⓕ Ⓖ Ⓗ Ⓙ
13 Ⓐ Ⓑ Ⓒ Ⓓ
14 Ⓕ Ⓖ Ⓗ Ⓙ
15 Ⓐ Ⓑ Ⓒ Ⓓ
16 Ⓕ Ⓖ Ⓗ Ⓙ
17 Ⓐ Ⓑ Ⓒ Ⓓ
18 Ⓕ Ⓖ Ⓗ Ⓙ
19 Ⓐ Ⓑ Ⓒ Ⓓ

20 (grid-in fields with bubbles 0–9)

21 Ⓐ Ⓑ Ⓒ Ⓓ
22 Ⓕ Ⓖ Ⓗ Ⓙ
23 Ⓐ Ⓑ Ⓒ Ⓓ
24 Ⓕ Ⓖ Ⓗ Ⓙ
25 Ⓐ Ⓑ Ⓒ Ⓓ
26 Ⓕ Ⓖ Ⓗ Ⓙ
27 Ⓐ Ⓑ Ⓒ Ⓓ
28 Ⓕ Ⓖ Ⓗ Ⓙ
29 Ⓐ Ⓑ Ⓒ Ⓓ
30 Ⓕ Ⓖ Ⓗ Ⓙ
31 Ⓐ Ⓑ Ⓒ Ⓓ
32 Ⓕ Ⓖ Ⓗ Ⓙ
33 Ⓐ Ⓑ Ⓒ Ⓓ
34 Ⓕ Ⓖ Ⓗ Ⓙ
35 Ⓐ Ⓑ Ⓒ Ⓓ
36 Ⓕ Ⓖ Ⓗ Ⓙ
37 Ⓐ Ⓑ Ⓒ Ⓓ
38 Ⓕ Ⓖ Ⓗ Ⓙ
39 Ⓐ Ⓑ Ⓒ Ⓓ
40 Ⓕ Ⓖ Ⓗ Ⓙ

41 Ⓐ Ⓑ Ⓒ Ⓓ
42 Ⓕ Ⓖ Ⓗ Ⓙ
43 Ⓐ Ⓑ Ⓒ Ⓓ
44 Ⓕ Ⓖ Ⓗ Ⓙ
45 Ⓐ Ⓑ Ⓒ Ⓓ
46 Ⓕ Ⓖ Ⓗ Ⓙ
47 Ⓐ Ⓑ Ⓒ Ⓓ
48 Ⓕ Ⓖ Ⓗ Ⓙ
49 Ⓐ Ⓑ Ⓒ Ⓓ
50 Ⓕ Ⓖ Ⓗ Ⓙ
51 Ⓐ Ⓑ Ⓒ Ⓓ
52 Ⓕ Ⓖ Ⓗ Ⓙ
53 Ⓐ Ⓑ Ⓒ Ⓓ
54 Ⓕ Ⓖ Ⓗ Ⓙ
55 Ⓐ Ⓑ Ⓒ Ⓓ

CUT HERE

Practice Test 2

English Language Arts

Reading and Written Composition

Reading

Directions: Read the two selections and the viewing and representing piece. Then answer the questions that follow.

Kate Chopin, in the late 1800s, wrote many tales about the lives of the Creoles of Louisiana. In her short story "Regret," Chopin captures the sound of their speech, which contains many words derived from their French ancestry and a dialect unique to the area. Some French words used include Dieu sait *(God knows),* maman *(mother),* terrassent *(tiring),* bonté! *(goodness!), and* Croque-mitaine *(bogeyman) and* Loup-garou *(werewolf), both scary figures of stories. The dialect is reproduced with spellings different from standard English or shortened words, such as* 'em *for them,* otha *for other, or* chil'ren *for children.*

Regret
By Kate Chopin

1   Mamzelle Aurélie possessed a good strong figure, ruddy cheeks, hair that was changing from brown to gray, and a determined eye. She wore a man's hat about the farm, and an old blue army overcoat when it was cold, and sometimes top-boots. Mamzelle Aurélie had never thought of marrying. She had never been in love. At the age of twenty she had received a proposal, which she had promptly declined, and at the age of fifty she had not yet lived to regret it.

2   So she was quite alone in the world, except for her dog Ponto, and the negroes who lived in her cabins and worked her crops, and the fowls, a few cows, a couple of mules, her gun (with which she shot chicken-hawks), and her religion. One morning Mamzelle Aurélie stood upon her gallery, contemplating, with arms akimbo, a small band of very small children who, to all intents and purposes, might have fallen from the clouds, so unexpected and bewildering was their coming, and so unwelcome. They were the children of her nearest neighbor, Odile, who was not such a near neighbor, after all.

3   The young woman had appeared but five minutes before, accompanied by these four children. In her arms she carried little Élodie; she dragged Ti Nomme by an unwilling hand; while Marcéline and Marcélette followed with irresolute steps. Her face was red and disfigured from tears and excitement. She had been summoned to a neighboring parish by the dangerous illness of her mother; her husband was away in Texas—it seemed to her a million miles away; and Valsin was waiting with the mule-cart to drive her to the station.

4   "It's no question, Mamzelle Aurélie; you jus' got to keep those youngsters fo' me tell I come back. Dieu sait, I wouldn' botha you with 'em if it was any otha way to do! Make 'em mine you, Mamzelle Aurélie; don' spare 'em. Me, there, I'm half crazy between the chil'ren, an' Léon not home, an' maybe not even to fine po' maman alive encore!"—a harrowing possibility which drove Odile to take a final hasty and convulsive leave of her disconsolate family.

My notes about what I am reading

$\boxed{\text{GO ON TO THE NEXT PAGE} \triangleright}$

My notes about what I am reading

5   She left them crowded into the narrow strip of shade on the porch of the long, low house; the white sunlight was beating in on the white old boards; some chickens were scratching in the grass at the foot of the steps, and one had boldly mounted, and was stepping heavily, solemnly, and aimlessly across the gallery. There was a pleasant odor of pinks in the air, and the sound of negro laughter was coming across the flowering cotton-field.

6   Mamzelle Aurélie stood contemplating the children. She looked with a critical eye upon Marcéline, who had been left staggering beneath the weight of the chubby Élodie. She surveyed with the same calculating air Marcélette mingling her silent tears with the audible grief and rebellion of Ti Nomme. During those few contemplative moments she was collecting herself, determining upon a line of action, which should be identical with a line of duty. She began by feeding them. If Mamzelle Aurélie's responsibilities might have begun and ended there, they could easily have been dismissed; for her larder was amply provided against an emergency of this nature. But little children are not little pigs: they require and demand attentions, which were wholly unexpected by Mamzelle Aurélie, and which she was ill prepared to give.

7   She was, indeed, very inapt in her management of Odile's children during the first few days. How could she know that Marcélette always wept when spoken to in a loud and commanding tone of voice? It was a peculiarity of Marcélette's. She became acquainted with Ti Nomme's passion for flowers only when he had plucked all the choicest gardenias and pinks for the apparent purpose of critically studying their botanical construction.

8   "'T'ain't enough to tell 'im, Mamzelle Aurélie," Marcéline instructed her; "you got to tie 'im in a chair. It's w'at maman all time do w'en he's bad: she tie 'im in a chair." The chair in which Mamzelle Aurélie tied Ti Nomme was roomy and comfortable, and he seized the opportunity to take a nap in it, the afternoon being warm.

9   At night, when she ordered them one and all to bed as she would have shooed the chickens into the henhouse, they stayed uncomprehending before her. What about the little white nightgowns that had to be taken from the pillow-slip in which they were brought over, and shaken by some strong hand till they snapped like ox-whips? What about the tub of water which had to be brought and set in the middle of the floor, in which the little tired, dusty, sun-browned feet had every one to be washed sweet and clean? And it made Marcéline and Marcélette laugh merrily—the idea that Mamzelle Aurélie should for a moment have believed that Ti Nomme could fall asleep without being told the story of Croque-mitaine or Loup-garou, or both; or that Élodie could fall asleep at all without being rocked and sung to.

10   "I tell you, Aunt Ruby," Mamzelle Aurélie informed her cook in confidence; "me, I'd rather manage a dozen plantation' than fo' chil'ren. It's terrassent! Bonté! Don't talk to me about chil'ren!"

11   "'T'ain' ispected sich as you would know airy thing 'bout 'em, Mamzelle Aurélie. I see dat plainly yistiddy w'en I spy dat li'le chile playin' wid yo' baskit o'keys. You don' know dat makes chillun grow up hard-headed, to play wid keys? Des like it make 'em teeth hard to look in a lookin'-glass. Them's the things you got to know in the raisin' an' manigement o' chillun."

12   Mamzelle Aurélie certainly did not pretend or aspire to such subtle and far-reaching knowledge on the subject as Aunt Ruby possessed, who had "raised five an' buried six" in her day. She was glad enough to learn a few little mother-tricks to serve the moment's need.

13   Ti Nomme's sticky fingers compelled her to unearth white aprons that she had not worn for years, and she had to accustom herself to his moist kisses—the expressions of an affectionate and exuberant nature. She got down her sewing-basket, which she

GO ON TO THE NEXT PAGE

seldom used, from the top shelf of the armoire, and placed it within the ready and easy reach which torn slips and buttonless waists demanded. It took her some days to become accustomed to the laughing, the crying, the chattering that echoed through the house and around it all day long. And it was not the first or the second night that she could sleep comfortably with little Élodie's hot, plump body pressed close against her, and the little one's warm breath beating her cheek like the fanning of a bird's wing. But at the end of two weeks Mamzelle Aurélie had grown quite used to these things, and she no longer complained.

14   It was also at the end of two weeks that Mamzelle Aurélie, one evening, looking away toward the crib where the cattle were being fed, saw Valsin's blue cart turning the bend of the road. Odile sat beside the mulatto, upright and alert. As they drew near, the young woman's beaming face indicated that her homecoming was a happy one.

15   But this coming, unannounced and unexpected, threw Mamzelle Aurélie into a flutter that was almost agitation. The children had to be gathered. Where was Ti Nomme? Yonder in the shed, putting an edge on his knife at the grindstone. And Marcéline and Marcélette? Cutting and fashioning doll-rags in the corner of the gallery. As for Élodie, she was safe enough in Mamzelle Aurélie's arms; and she had screamed with delight at sight of the familiar blue cart, which was bringing her mother back to her.

16   The excitement was all over, and they were gone. How still it was when they were gone! Mamzelle Aurélie stood upon the gallery, looking and listening. She could no longer see the cart; the red sunset and the blue-gray twilight had together flung a purple mist across the fields and road that hid it from her view. She could no longer hear the wheezing and creaking of its wheels. But she could still faintly hear the shrill, glad voices of the children.

17   She turned into the house. There was much work awaiting her, for the children had left a sad disorder behind them; but she did not at once set about the task of righting it. Mamzelle Aurélie seated herself beside the table. She gave one slow glance through the room, into which the evening shadows were creeping and deepening around her solitary figure. She let her head fall down upon her bended arm, and began to cry. Oh, but she cried! Not softly, as women often do. She cried like a man, with sobs that seemed to tear her very soul. She did not notice Ponto licking her hand.

Better Safer Warmer

By Cynthia Kaplan

1   It happened very suddenly and was, perhaps, the most violent act in which I have ever participated. A space became available and we had to grab it or risk waiting maybe six or eight months for another. I don't know why I thought there would be more warning. It's not like they call you up and say we're expecting Mrs. Feingold to sign off in about two months so you should start to get ready. Mrs. Feingold or whomever just dies and they clean up her room and they call you. That's it. So my parents and I packed up my grandmother's winter clothing, a few pictures and books and some of her music, and tore her out of the ground like a mandrake root, and although she came willingly the silent scream was there, not so silent; I could hear it, we all could. Despite our best efforts to prepare her, there was no way she could have known what was happening. And despite our best intentions, here is what *was* happening: Come, put on your coat, get in the car, you will never see this place, your home, again. Sorry, sorry, sorry.

GO ON TO THE NEXT PAGE >

2   At first she was excited. She was finally out of the apartment, out and on her way to, where? Well, to the good new place, we said. To the place near Mom and Dad. With a piano. None of us could say nursing home. But then after half an hour in the car she stopped wanting information and started wanting soup. When we got to The Place everyone gave my grandmother the big welcome. They gave her soup. They gave us all soup. We walked her around the common rooms and garden, which were beautiful. Nurses and aides and administrators made a fuss over her, which she loves. She was bubbly and charming and spoke nonsense and everyone thought she was adorable. My parents and I made furtive eye contact; it was going so well, but still, all I could think was: Just wait.

3   We went to her room, or rather her *half* room. It was small and the wallpaper was a psychedelic flower pattern that it seemed to me could itself induce dementia. The furniture was old and the bed creaky and hospital-like. I went out into the hall and cried. There was a roommate who was incensed to find people in her room. We drew the curtains that divided the space. At least my grandmother had the window half, looking out onto the garden. At least, at least. She had not shared a room with anyone besides her husband in seventy years. Now she was going to share it with a mean stranger. I went into the hall again and cried. My grandmother was taken off for evaluations of some kind. We waited in her room in a state of what can only be described as wistful dread. Surely the other shoe was going to drop.

4   It did. My grandmother returned distraught, furious. She hates to be poked and prodded and questioned and she was ready to go home. She said: "Get me out of here. You have to take me out of here. I've had enough. You can just kill me if you want but I won't stay here. I'll just lay down on the floor. That's all. I'll just lay down on the floor and die."

5   Now we had to explain to her why she wasn't going home, why she had to stay tonight, and maybe for a while. We didn't mention forever; what a ridiculous, damaging concept *that* is. My father left the room for a few minutes, maybe to figure out what would be the best thing to say, maybe to cry. While he was gone the roommate poked her head through the curtain and said, "It's a nice place, really." But my grandmother was inconsolable. My father came back and said quietly, "Mom, you have to stay." That was it for me and I went back out into the hall.

6   Somehow, a few weeks went by. At least one of us has seen her every day, even though she doesn't always know our names and will probably not remember that we were there. We walk with her in the garden. We sit and people-watch. We talk her into playing the piano in the lobby. (She complains that it is not as nice as hers, and she's right.) We have endless conversations with her aide and nurse and social worker so they'll know what she likes and doesn't like, who she is, so they'll understand her. My brother has come with his children, and even my mother-in-law, way above and beyond the call of duty, has visited.

7   She is still very confused by her surroundings, calls everyone names behind their backs (actually, she barely waits until they are out of view, much less out of earshot) and thinks the social worker is someone she knows from the beach. Sometimes when we arrive she seems all right, sometimes she collapses into our arms, lost and distraught. Each day she takes her clothes out of the drawers and the closet, folds them beautifully, packs what she can into the small straw bag I brought for her piano music, then leaves the rest piled on the bed and dresser. She carries her pocketbook everywhere and sometimes tries to go out the emergency door. She talks incessantly of going home (who wouldn't?), of getting on the train she sometimes hears in the distance and going back to her apartment.

8   This will change, we know. In time she will make friends and have activities. (Okay, she'll never have activities, she hates activities.) She will be cared for around the clock by professionals who are trained to meet the needs of people with Alzheimer's. We tell her: Stay for now, stay for the winter, it's better, safer, warmer, whatever. We tell her what we hope she'll understand. But she is planning a breakout, I think. *Dear Sarah,* (Who?) *Send help. I need help. Help please.* She has written this on a paper towel and put it in her pocketbook. She is our hostage. As I said, it feels like the most violent act in which I have ever participated. I would take it back, if I could.

GO ON TO THE NEXT PAGE

Don't make *them* pay tomorrow for what *you* didn't do today.

NALIC
Life Insurance

North American
Life Insurance Cooperative

**Use "Regret" (pp. 239–241)
to answer questions 1–13.**

---

1 In paragraphs 1 and 2, Mamzelle Aurélie is characterized as a woman who—

A loves children and often takes care of them for her neighbor

B is angry and distrustful of everyone around her

C lives in a chaotic, disordered environment

D is independent and capable

2 Mamzelle Aurélie is asked to take care of the children because—

F she is alone in the world

G Odile's mother is ill

H Valsin can no longer care for them

J the children will be a help with chores

3 The cook's advice about raising children is intended by the author to have what effect?

A It is meant to be amusing to the reader.

B It is meant to illustrate the cook's skill in dealing with children.

C The advice shows the insecurities of the cook.

D It suggests that Mamzelle Aurélie is more proficient at raising children than is the cook.

4 Read the following dictionary entry.

beat \bēt\ *v* **1.** to stir vigorously **2.** to strike against **3.** to achieve victory **4.** to avoid blame

Which definition best matches the use of the word *beating* in paragraph 5?

F Definition 1

G Definition 2

H Definition 3

J Definition 4

GO ON TO THE NEXT PAGE

Practice Test 2

5 Paragraph 6 is mainly about—

    A the grief of the children

    B the fact that the children will take more care than Mamzelle Aurélie anticipated

    C the difficulty of planning meals for the group

    D the caring behavior of the children toward one another

6 In paragraph 6, the word *larder* means—

    F medical supplies

    G pigpen

    H toy chest

    J pantry

7 Which line from the story serves as an example of irony?

    A *Her face was red and disfigured by tears and excitement.*

    B *She began by feeding them.*

    C *The chair in which Mamzelle Aurélie tied Ti Nomme was roomy and comfortable, and he seized the opportunity to take a nap in it, the afternoon being warm.*

    D *It took her some days to become accustomed to the laughing, the crying, the chattering that echoed through the house and around it all day long.*

8 The author uses the examples in paragraph 9 to—

    F suggest that Mamzelle Aurélie is learning more about the fact that "little children are not little pigs"

    G contrast the needs of these children with those of other children

    H illustrate Mamzelle Aurélie's great irritation at her responsibility

    J make it clear that the children are not being well cared for

9 In the next to last sentence of paragraph 13, Élodie's breath is compared to "the fanning of a bird's wing." The author uses this description to—

    A emphasize the delicate nature of babies

    B imply that Mamzelle Aurélie is enjoying this experience

    C portray the child as fussy and difficult

    D illustrate Mamzelle Aurélie's inability to sleep because of her responsibilities

10 The author's description of the physical environment in paragraph 16 serves to—

    F establish a peaceful tone

    G contrast with Mamzelle Aurélie's feelings

    H parallel the environment at the beginning of the story

    J mirror Mamzelle Aurélie's emotional environment

GO ON TO THE NEXT PAGE

11 Mamzelle Aurélie, at the beginning of the story and at the end of the story, respectively, feels—

   A   a sense of duty/loneliness

   B   pain/relief

   C   patient/impatient

   D   content/ill

12 The last sentence of the story says "She did not notice Ponto licking her hand." The author uses this sentence to indicate that—

   F   Ponto has been neglected while the children were there

   G   the dog misses the children now that they are gone

   H   Mamzelle Aurélie is so disturbed that she doesn't notice her surroundings

   J   Mamzelle Aurélie is so tired from her ordeal taking care of the children that she cannot bring herself to clean up the mess they left behind.

13 Which word in paragraph 1 foreshadows the end of the story?

   A   changing

   B   never

   C   declined

   D   yet

**Use "Better Safer Warmer" (pp. 241–242)
to answer questions 14–23.**

---

14 In paragraph 1, the author uses a simile—

   F   to explain why the grandmother had to be moved so quickly

   G   because Mrs. Feingold's emotions cannot otherwise be known

   H   to compare the parents' actions to the author's actions

   J   to describe the experience of being removed from one's home

15 The last sentence of paragraph 3, *Surely the other shoe was going to drop,* contributes to the tone of the passage by—

   A   foreshadowing the fact that the grandmother will constantly try to pack her clothes to go home

   B   creating a context in which the grandmother will eventually come to enjoy her new environment

   C   emphasizing a feeling of dread

   D   suggesting to the reader that dealing with old age is a universal problem

GO ON TO THE NEXT PAGE

16 Which line from the selection best illustrates the emotions of the author?

    F   *I would take it back, if I could.*

    G   *I'll just lay down on the floor and die.*

    H   *Well, to the good new place, we said.*

    J   *This will change, we know.*

17 Paragraphs 6 and 7 are mainly about—

    A   the grandmother's successful adaptation to her new home

    B   the grandmother's day-to-day life

    C   the author's visits to the grandmother

    D   the family's efforts to get back to normal routines

18 Which of these is a major theme in the essay?

    F   The inevitability of growing old

    G   The sorrow caused by doing something that must be done

    H   The deplorable state of the care of old people

    J   The responsibilities of children to their parents

19 The words *silent scream* in paragraph 1 are called an oxymoron, a figure of speech in which the two words contradict one another. The author uses this oxymoron to—

    A   show the reader that the grandmother is exercising self-control

    B   refer to the grandmother's later scream *Get me out of here*

    C   convey the emotions of the family as they hurry the grandmother into the car

    D   suggest the depth of the grandmother's despair at being moved

20 Which of these is the best summary of the selection?

    F   The author removes her grandmother from her home and places her in a nursing facility. She visits often and hopes that her grandmother will adapt to the home.

    G   A woman with Alzheimer's is taken to a nursing facility because she can no longer care for herself. She is not happy there but everyone feels that she will eventually accept the new surroundings.

    H   A grandmother with Alzheimer's is taken by her son and granddaughter to a nursing home. Her behavior and conversation suggest she's having difficulty with the transition, and she and her family are emotionally upset at the ordeal.

    J   The author describes taking her grandmother from her own home to a nursing home. She also describes the other people in the home, the routines there, and the staff. In addition she tells of the family's visits to the home.

GO ON TO THE NEXT PAGE

21 In paragraph 7, the author uses the question *who wouldn't?* to—

   A remind the reader that Alzheimer's causes similar reactions in those who have it

   B indicate that any family would do as much as this one has

   C imply that not only old people would react in this way

   D intentionally change the emphasis of the essay from a universal problem to that of a specific person

22 The point of view from which the essay is written—

   F lets the reader hear the thoughts of the grandmother

   G makes it harder for the author to explain the loss of reasoning ability in those who are senile

   H reminds the reader that people are more alike than they are different

   J better allows the reader to understand the emotions of the author

23 Which of the following words from paragraph 1 and paragraph 8 best show the connection between the main ideas of the paragraphs?

   A *I could hear it / it's better, safer, warmer*

   B *we had to grab it or risk waiting / In time she will make friends*

   C *Mrs. Feingold or whomever just dies / Okay, she'll never have activities*

   D *the most violent act in which I have ever participated / I would take it back, if I could*

**Use "Regret" and "Better Safer Warmer" (pp. 239–242)
to answer questions 24 and 25.**

---

24 Mamzelle Aurélie in "Regret" and Cynthia Kaplan, the author of "Better Safer Warmer," are alike in that—

   F their love of their families leads to their difficulties

   G they have substituted one hope for another by the end of the story and the essay

   H they would probably change something in their lives if they could

   J they both exhibit an ability to completely control their emotions

25 Unlike the conflict in "Regret," the conflict in "Better Safer Warmer" is—

   A resolved by the end

   B between two women

   C present throughout

   D internal

GO ON TO THE NEXT PAGE

239

Practice Test 2

**Use the visual representation on page 243
to answer questions 26–28.**

---

26 What element in the visual representation suggests a positive outcome?

   F The clasped hands

   G The words *them* and *you*

   H R.I.P.

   J The lily

27 The primary purpose of this representation is to—

   A remind people that they will one day die

   B promote behavior that will lead to a long life

   C convince people that they should plan to care for their family financially

   D urge people to make funeral arrangements ahead of time

28 The emotions aroused by this presentation are primarily those of—

   F tenderness and passion

   G concern and fear

   H sadness and grief

   J acceptance and patience

GO ON TO THE NEXT PAGE

Directions: Answer the following questions in the space provided on the answer document.

29 In "Regret," why does Mamzelle Aurélie cry *like a man, with sobs that seemed to tear her very soul*? Support your answer with evidence from the selection.

30 For what reason might the author have called this essay "Better Safer Warmer"? Support your answer with evidence from the selection.

31 What is similar about the author's purpose in both "Regret" and "Better Safer Warmer"? Support your answer with evidence from the selections.

BE SURE YOU HAVE WRITTEN YOUR ANSWERS
ON THE ANSWER DOCUMENT.

GO ON TO THE NEXT PAGE >

Practice Test 2

Written Composition

> Write an essay explaining how a person's choice
> either to do something or not to do something
> may later result in regret.

The information in the box below will help you remember what you should think about when you write your composition.

REMEMBER TO

- write on the topic given
- make your writing thoughtful and interesting
- check that each sentence you write adds to your composition as a whole
- make sure that your ideas are clear and easy for the reader to follow
- write about your ideas in detail so that the reader can better understand what you are trying to say
- proofread your writing to correct errors in spelling, capitalization, punctuation, grammar, and sentence structure

GO ON TO THE NEXT PAGE

USE THIS PREWRITING PAGE TO
PLAN YOUR COMPOSITION.

MAKE SURE THAT YOU WRITE YOUR COMPOSITION ON
THE LINED SPACES IN THE ANSWER DOCUMENT.

GO ON TO THE NEXT PAGE

At this point during an actual exam, you would be given 3 sample revising and editing questions. After completing these 3 samples, you would be directed to stop, raise your hand, and wait for the test administrator to assist you before continuing to the next section.

Revising and Editing

Directions: Read the following passages and mark your answers on the answer sheet. Remember that you are NOT permitted to use dictionaries or other reference materials on this section of the test.

Levonne has written this report for a history assignment. She has asked you to read the report and think about the corrections and improvements she needs to make. When you finish reading the report, answer the multiple-choice questions that follow.

Groundhog Day

(1) My friend and I were sitting in the park one bright fall day eating our lunch when I see movement out of the corner of my eye. (2) I looked around quickly and spied a fat, brown rump protruding from behind a tree. (3) Then the animal waddled out as fast as it seemed to be able to go and ran for the next tree, where it again put its head and middle behind the trunk. (4) But there was it's rump, still in plain sight. (5) It seemed to think, like an ostrich, that if its head wasn't seen, the rest of it wouldn't be either! (6) It was, I later learned, a groundhog.

(7) The groundhog (*Marmota monax*), is also called a woodchuck. (8) It is a commonly seen mammal (phylum Chordata) and is a rodent and a member of the squirrel family. (9) The name "woodchuck" comes from an Indian word for the animal (Wojak). (10) The name "Groundhog" is based on the animal's chunky appearance, waddle, and habit of living in the ground.

(11) Groundhog Day is celebrated in the United States on February second. (12) Legend has it that if it comes out of his burrow on that day and sees his shadow—that is, if the sun is out—there will be six more weeks of winter. (13) If, however, he doesn't see his shadow, there will be an early spring.

(14) The Groundhog Day legend is based on this Scottish rhyme: "If Candlemas Day is bright and clear, there will be two winters in the year." (15) It also may be based on simaler rhymes from England and Germany. (16) Candlemas Day occurs at the midpoint between the winter solstice and the spring equinox.

(17) The headquarters for the Groundhog Day celebration is in Punxutawney, Pennsylvania. (18) There they hold a celebration each year with their resident groundhog named Punxutawney Phil. (19) This tradition goes back to 1887 and

GO ON TO THE NEXT PAGE

records have been kept of Phil's predictions ever since. (20) Each February second, at a sight in Punxutawney called Gobbler's Knob, Phil is put into a heated burrow made especially for the celebration. (21) At 7:25 a.m. in the morning, he's pulled out to see whether he sees his shadow or not. (22) There are many festivities in the town celebrating the event and tourists flock there to see it and join in the fun. (23) There was a movie called *Groundhog Day,* starring Bill Murray, made in 1993 in which Murray's character wakes up and it is Groundhog Day over and over again. (24) Phil even has his own Web site, PunxutawneyPhil.com.

32 What change should be made in sentence 1?

    F   Change *I* to **me**
    G   Insert a comma after *park*
    H   Change *when* to **then**
    J   Change *see* to **saw**

33 What change, if any, should be made in sentence 4?

    A   Change *But* to **Instead**
    B   Change *it's* to **its**
    C   Change *plain* to **plane**
    D   Make no change

34 What is the most effective way to rewrite the ideas in sentences 7 and 8?

    F   The groundhog (*Marmota monax*) is a commonly seen mammal (phylum Chordata), it is also called a woodchuck and is a rodent, it is also a member of the squirrel family.
    G   The groundhog (*Marmota monax*), also called a woodchuck, is a commonly seen mammal (phylum Chordata) and is a rodent and a member of the squirrel family.
    H   The woodchuck, or groundhog, (*Marmota monax*) is a commonly seen mammal (phylum Chordata). Because it is a rodent and a member of the squirrel family.
    J   Also called a woodchuck (*Marmota monax*), the groundhog is a commonly seen mammal, phylum Chordata; rodents and squirrels.

35 What change, if any, should be made in sentence 10?

    A   Change *Groundhog* to **groundhog**
    B   Change *is based* to **is being based**
    C   Change *animal's* to **animals**
    D   Make no change

36 What change, if any, should be made in sentence 12?

    F   Change *if it* to **if he**
    G   Change *if it* to **if the groundhog**
    H   Change *is out* to **was out**
    J   Make no change

37 What change, if any, should be made in sentence 15?

    A   Change *It* to **They**
    B   Change *may be* to **is**
    C   Change *simaler* to **similar**
    D   Make no change

GO ON TO THE NEXT PAGE

38 What change should be made in sentence 19?

    F Change *goes* to **gos**

    G Insert a comma after *1887*

    H Change *have been kept* to **are kept**

    J Change *ever* to **every**

39 What change, if any, should be made in sentence 20?

    A Change *sight* to **site**

    B Delete the comma after *Knob*

    C Change *especially* to **espeshally**

    D Make no change

40 What change, if any, should be made in sentence 21?

    F Delete *in the morning*

    G Change *whether* to **weather**

    H Change *his* to **a**

    J Make no change

41 What is the most effective way to improve the organization of the fifth paragraph (sentences 17–24)?

    A Move sentence 19 to the beginning of the paragraph

    B Move sentence 19 to the end of the paragraph

    C Delete sentence 22

    D Delete sentence 23

GO ON TO THE NEXT PAGE

Emma has written this report for her speech class. As a member of Emma's peer-editing group, you have been asked to read the report and think about the corrections and improvements she should make. When you finish reading the report, answer the questions that follow.

Stage Fright

(1) When appearing before an audience, stage fright is extreme nervousness of a performer or speaker. (2) Everyone seems to be afflicted by the malady at one time or another. (3) It's been reported that Mel Gibson was so excruciatingly nervous before his first school performance that he had to play the part sitting down because his stage fright made his legs too weak to stand up on. (4) In young Roger Corman's acting class, he was so nervous appearing before the class he appeared on stage with his back to them, and when he was asked to turn around, he did so, but with his eyes closed. (5) After Jennifer Anniston accepted an award for her acting in *Friends,* she said about her acceptance speech, "I forgot the cast!—I'm just terrified—I have stage fright unless I have something written for me to say—I couldn't speak—I'm a blithering idiot."

(6) Most stage fright is caused by fear of failure. (7) It can also be a result of some physical ailment—for example, coming down with the flu or you just ate something that doesn't agree with you. (8) Stage fright might also be a result of not rehearsing enough for what you're going to present or simply a lack of self-esteem or confidence in your abilities. (9) It seems to have no basis at all. (10) It's just there, as is the case with many accomplished, professional performers.

(11) Symptoms of stage fright can include upset stomach, shaking hands or legs, sweating, chills, racing heartbeat, headache, or a dry mouth. (12) It can result in suddenly forgetting your speech, or your lines in a play, or the words to the song you were going to sing. (13) These are not pleasant things to deal with.

(14) While you might have to live with the fact that you are sometimes going to get stage fright, there are things you can do to lesson it or turn it to your advantage. (15) Since stage fright happens in your mind, even though it has physical results sometimes, you have to deal with it in your head. (16) Practice (so you're sure you're prepared) and concentration (so the sight of the audience doesn't confuse you to the point you forget what you're doing) is helpful. (17) Another that has been suggested is pretending you're just talking with your friends instead of a roomful of strangers. (18) You can also pick out one member of the audience pretending you're speaking or performing just for that person. (19) It has even been said that picturing the audience in their underwear will help because it makes them seem like just plain people and not threats, people who will enjoy and except your talent and efforts.

GO ON TO THE NEXT PAGE

42 What is the most effective way to rewrite sentence 1?

- **F** Extreme nervousness appearing before an audience is stage fright.
- **G** Stage fright, extreme nervousness appearing before an audience by a performer or speaker.
- **H** Stage fright is extreme nervousness of a performer or speaker when appearing before an audience.
- **J** Extreme nervousness happens sometimes when a performer appears before an audience or a speaker appears before an audience.

43 Emma wants to add the following sentence in the first paragraph (sentences 1–5).

You might think that a seasoned performer would be immune from stage fright, but that isn't the case.

Where should this sentence be inserted?

- **A** At the beginning of the paragraph
- **B** After sentence 1
- **C** After sentence 2
- **D** After sentence 4

44 What change, if any, should be made in sentence 7?

- **F** Delete *also*
- **G** Change the dash after *ailment* to a semicolon
- **H** Change *coming down* to **come down**
- **J** Change *you just ate* to **eating**

45 Which transition should be added to the beginning of sentence 9?

- **A** Nevertheless,
- **B** Likewise,
- **C** At times,
- **D** Furthermore,

46 What change, if any, should be made in sentence 12?

- **F** Change *can result* to **results**
- **G** Change *forgetting* to **forgeting**
- **H** Change *were going to sing* to **will have sung**
- **J** Make no change

GO ON TO THE NEXT PAGE

47 What change, if any, should be made in sentence 14?

   A   Change *that* to **which**
   B   Change *lesson* to **lessen**
   C   Change *your* to **you're**
   D   Make no change

48 What change, if any, should be made in sentence 16?

   F   Insert *absolutely* before **sure**
   G   Change *audience* to **audiense**
   H   Change *is* to **are**
   J   Make no change

49 The meaning of sentence 17 can be clarified by changing *Another* to—

   A   Another strategy
   B   Other results
   C   A way
   D   A stage fright

50 What change, if any, should be made in sentence 18?

   F   Change *out* to **on**
   G   Change *pretending* to **and pretend**
   H   Insert a comma after *speaking*
   J   Make no change

51 What change, if any, should be made in sentence 19?

   A   Change *It has* to **They have**
   B   Insert a comma after *because*
   C   Change *except* to **accept**
   D   Make no change

Practice Test 2

BE SURE YOU HAVE RECORDED ALL OF YOUR ANSWERS
ON THE ANSWER DOCUMENT.

Mathematics

Directions: Read each question and then carefully fill in the correct answer on your answer document. If a correct answer is not here, then mark the letter of the choice for "Not Here."

GO ON TO THE NEXT PAGE

Mathematics Chart

LENGTH

Metric	Customary
1 kilometer = 1000 meters	1 mile = 1760 yards
1 meter = 100 centimeters	1 mile = 5280 feet
1 centimeter = 10 millimeters	1 yard = 3 feet
	1 foot = 12 inches

CAPACITY AND VOLUME

Metric	Customary
1 liter = 1000 milliliters	1 gallon = 4 quarts
	1 gallon = 128 ounces
	1 quart = 2 pints
	1 pint = 2 cups
	1 cup = 8 ounces

MASS AND WEIGHT

Metric	Customary
1 kilogram = 1000 grams	1 ton = 2000 pounds
1 gram = 1000 milligrams	1 pound = 16 ounces

TIME

1 year = 365 days

1 year = 12 months

1 year = 52 weeks

1 week = 7 days

1 day = 24 hours

1 hour = 60 minutes

1 minute = 60 seconds

Inches

Centimeters

GO ON TO THE NEXT PAGE

Mathematics Chart

Perimeter	rectangle	$P = 2l + 2w$ or $P = 2(l + w)$
Circumference	circle	$C = 2\pi r$ or $C = \pi d$
Area	rectangle	$A = lw$ or $A = bh$
	triangle	$A = \frac{1}{2} bh$ or $A = \frac{bh}{2}$
	trapezoid	$A = \frac{1}{2}(b_1 + b_2)h$ or $A = \frac{(b_1 + b_2)h}{2}$
	circle	$A = \pi r^2$
Surface Area	cube	$S = 6s^2$
	cylinder (lateral)	$S = 2\pi rh$
	cylinder (total)	$S = 2\pi rh + 2\pi r^2$ or $S = 2\pi r(h + r)$
	cone (lateral)	$S = \pi rl$
	cone (total)	$S = \pi rl + \pi r^2$ or $S = \pi r(l + r)$
	sphere	$S = 4\pi r^2$
Volume	prism or cylinder	$V = Bh*$
	pyramid or cone	$V = \frac{1}{3} Bh*$
	sphere	$V = \frac{4}{3} \pi r^3$

*B represents the area of the Base of a solid figure.

Pi	π	$\pi \approx 3.14$ or $\pi \approx \frac{22}{7}$
Pythagorean Theorem		$a^2 + b^2 = c^2$
Distance Formula		$d = \sqrt{(x_2 - x_1)^2 + (y_2 - y_1)^2}$
Slope of a Line		$m = \frac{y_2 - y_1}{x_2 - x_1}$
Midpoint Formula		$M = \left(\frac{x_2 + x_1}{2}, \frac{y_2 + y_1}{2}\right)$
Quadratic Formula		$x = \frac{-b \pm \sqrt{b^2 - 4ac}}{2a}$
Slope-Intercept Form of an Equation		$y = mx + b$
Point-Slope Form of an Equation		$y - y_1 = m(x - x_1)$
Standard Form of an Equation		$Ax + By = C$
Simple Interest Formula		$I = prt$

GO ON TO THE NEXT PAGE

1 The Hutchinson family plans to construct a circle graph, which shows how they spend their money each month. Their expenses for a typical month are summarized in the table below.

Typical Monthly Expenses	
Rent	$875
Car Payment	$375
Food	$500
Entertainment	$250
Utilities	$125
Savings	$375

The section of the circle graph representing the Car Payment should have what central angle?

A 6.67°
B 15°
C 27°
D 54°

GO ON TO THE NEXT PAGE

2 Which of the graphs below shows a line parallel to the graph of the equation $y = -3x + 2$?

F

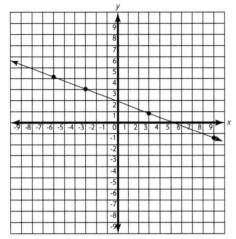

H

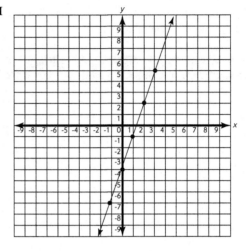

G

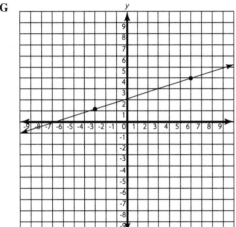

J

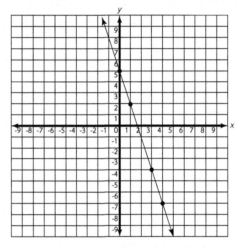

GO ON TO THE NEXT PAGE

3 A door manufacturer has received a custom order to construct a window in the shape of a regular pentagon as shown below. The window will consist of 5 equal-sized triangular pieces of glass. What are the measurements of the three angles in each piece of glass?

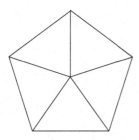

   A   60°, 60°, 60°
   B   72°, 54°, 54°
   C   36°, 72°, 72°
   D   90°, 45°, 45°

4 What effect will there be on the graph of $y = x^2 + 7$ when it is changed to $y = x^2 + 2$?

   F   The graph is congruent and its vertex moves up the y-axis
   G   The curve translates in its positive x direction
   H   The graph is congruent and its vertex moves down the y-axis
   J   The curve translates in the negative x direction

5 At the snack bar in a movie theater, the cost of two medium sodas and a large popcorn is $5.25. The cost of three medium sodas and two large popcorns is $9.25. To determine s, the cost of one medium soda, and p, the cost of one large popcorn, which pair of equations can be used?

   A $2s + 2p = 5.25$
         $3s + p = 9.25$

   B $2s + p = 5.25$
         $3s + 2p = 9.25$

   C $3s + p = 5.25$
         $2s + 2p = 9.25$

   D $2s + p = 5.25$
         $3s + 3p = 9.25$

GO ON TO THE NEXT PAGE

6 The net below shows the surface of a 3-dimensional figure.

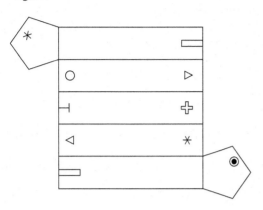

Which 3-dimensional figure does this net represent?

F

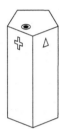

G

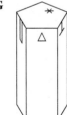

H

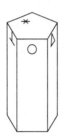

J

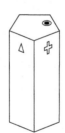

7 To make a long-distance phone call with the AP&P phone company, a customer pays \$.49 to connect with an operator and an additional \$.17 for each minute the call lasts. Which equation best shows the relationship between the cost, p, of the phone call, and the numbers of minutes, m, for which the call lasts?

A $p = .49 + .17$

B $p = .49m + .17m$

C $p = .49 + .17m$

D $p = .49m + .17$

8 Gerhardt found that 10 quarters weigh 57 grams. To find the number of quarters, q, that weigh a total of w grams, he can—

F multiply q by w

G divide w by the weight of 1 quarter

H divide w by q

J multiply q by the weight of 1 quarter

9 An elementary school principal examines the math scores of his first through sixth grade students. Which statistical measure of the data would describe the math score for which there are the same number of students above or below this score?

A mean

B median

C mode

D range

GO ON TO THE NEXT PAGE

10 A metal fabricator buys cylindrical metal rods with dimensions as shown in the diagram below.

1.5 in

48 in

After melting the cylindrical rod, he pours the liquid metal into molds to form rectangular blocks which will be 1/2 inch × 3 inches × 5 inches. About how many blocks can be made from each rod?

   F   9
   G   45
   H   60
   J   90

11 Use the ruler on the Mathematics Chart to measure the appropriate dimensions of the figure to the nearest tenth of a centimeter.

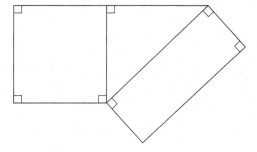

Which of the following gives the approximate area of the figure above?

   A   15.9 cm^2
   B   16.4 cm^2
   C   17.1 cm^2
   D   21.1 cm^2

12 Rafael needs to maintain an 84% average on his 3 tests this quarter to keep his "B" grade. He earned an 85% on his first test, and a 73% on his second. What score does he need on his third test in order to maintain his "B" grade?

   F   50%
   G   80.7%
   H   87%
   J   94%

13 Janell makes 30% commission as a computer salesperson. With monthly expenses of $750 for rent, $152 for utilities, and $250 for food, how many $960 computers does she need to sell each month to cover her monthly expenses?

   A   3
   B   4
   C   32
   D   70

Practice Test 2

GO ON TO THE NEXT PAGE

14 A linear function which relates the number of days, d, to the number of weeks, w, is $d = 7w$. Which of the following illustrates the same linear function?

F

d	w
14	2
28	3
35	5

G

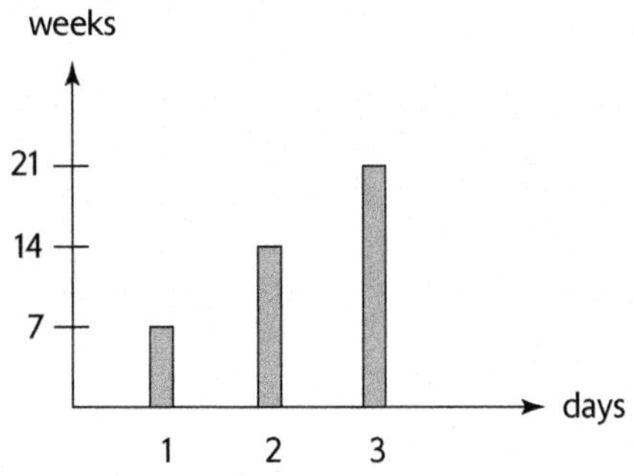

H If today is Tuesday, then three weeks from today will also be Tuesday.

J

w	d
7	1
14	2
21	3

15 If a hexagonal prism has a hexagonal top and a hexagonal bottom, how many faces, edges, and vertices does a hexagonal prism have?

A 7 faces, 12 edges, 7 vertices
B 7 faces, 6 edges, 7 vertices
C 8 faces, 6 edges, 12 vertices
D 8 faces, 18 edges, 12 vertices

16 Sylvia bought a box containing 5 brand P ballpoint pens for $4.95. She later found that had she shopped around, she could have purchased a box of brand T ballpoint pens for only $3.75. In buying the brand P pens, Sylvia spent approximately what percent more than she would have had she bought the box of brand T pens?

F 24%
G 32%
H 76%
J 120%

17 What are the y-intercepts of the graph of the equation $x = y^2 + 2y - 24$?

A $y = 4, y = 6$
B $y = -4, y = 6$
C $y = 4, y = -6$
D $y = -4, y = -6$

GO ON TO THE NEXT PAGE

18 Which of the following choices include a pair of similar polygons?

F

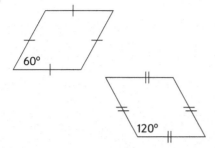

H

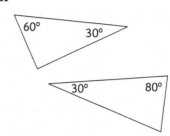

G

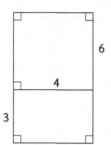

J

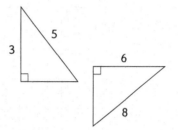

GO ON TO THE NEXT PAGE

Practice Test 2

19 Tanya went to the supermarket to buy magazines and notebooks. She bought x magazines costing $6 each, and y notebooks costing $3 each. Excluding tax, she spent less than $24.

Graph the inequality $6x + 3y < 24$ on the grid below.

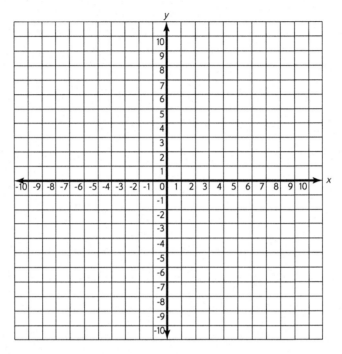

Which point represents a possible number of magazines and notebooks purchased by Tanya?

   A (1,8)

   B (3,4)

   C (2,6)

   D (2,3)

20 Which of the equations describes the relationship in which y decreases as x increases?

   F $y = 3x$

   G $y = x^3$

   H $y = -2x$

   J $y = x^2$

21 Solve for w in the equation $3w + 10 - 7w = 2w - 14$.

Record your answer and fill in the bubbles on your answer document. Be sure to use correct place value.

GO ON TO THE NEXT PAGE

22 ∠A is acute and m∠A = a. ∠B is obtuse and m∠B = b. Which of the following statements could be true?

    F $0 < a+b < 90$

    G $a + b > 270$

    H $a - b > 0$

    J $a = \dfrac{b}{2}$

23 The length of a rectangular room is 20 ft, while its diagonal measure is 25 ft. Find the perimeter of the room.

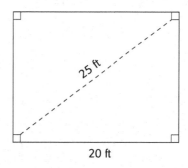

20 ft

    A   15 ft

    B   35 ft

    C   70 ft

    D   300 ft

GO ON TO THE NEXT PAGE

Practice Test 2

24 Coordinate grids are often placed over maps to help identify specific locations. With a coordinate grid placed over a map, three cities are located at points E(–3,5), F(7,2), and G(–1,4). A fourth city, M, is located at a point midway between cities E and G. Which of the following is the best approximation, in coordinate units, of the distance between cities F and M?

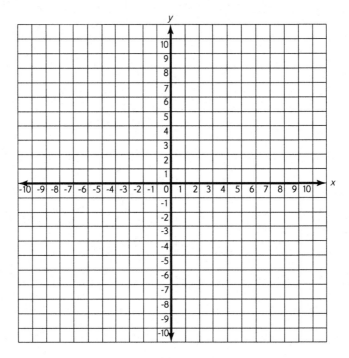

F   8.14

G   9.34

H   66.25

J   87.25

25 Which statement best describes the effect on the graph of the function $y = 2.5x + 4.3$, if 2.9 is added to its slope?

A   Graph of new function is perpendicular to graph of original function.

B   The y-intercept increases.

C   The x-intercept increases.

D   Slope of new line is less than slope of original line.

26 Using the table below, find the equation that describes y, the total cost of buying paint, as a function of x, the number of 1 gallon cans of paint purchased.

Gallons of Paint (x)	Total Cost (y)
3	$58.50
7	$136.50
12	$234.00

F $x = .15y$

G $y = 19.50x$

H $y = .05x$

J $x = 19.50y$

GO ON TO THE NEXT PAGE

27 As they exited their polling sites on election day, a random sample of voters across a city were asked to choose their favorite sport to watch on TV. The results are shown below.

Based on the data displayed above, how many of the city's 12,000 residents are likely to watch golf on TV?

A 3,000
B 2,000
C 300
D 200

GO ON TO THE NEXT PAGE

28 From the top of a 210-ft tall building, the angle of depression to a car on the ground is 60°.

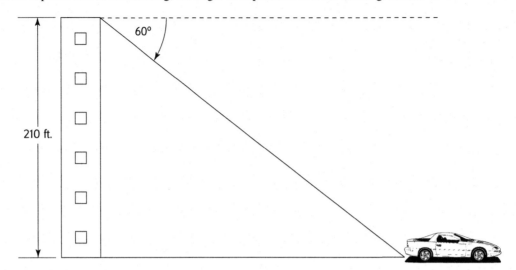

What is the approximate horizontal distance from the base of the building to the car?

F 121 ft

G 182 ft

H 210 ft

J 364 ft

GO ON TO THE NEXT PAGE

29 Figure *FGHM* is shown on the coordinate plane.

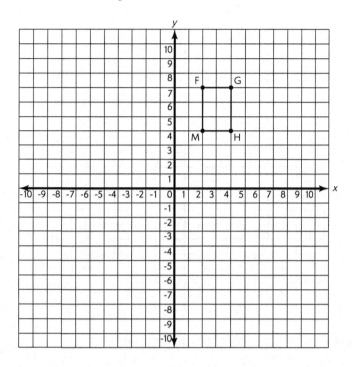

The transformation, which rotates figure FGHM 180° around *M*, then reflects this image across the line $x = -1$, will create a new figure with point G's image laying at which of the following points?

A (4,–3)
B (–1,6)
C (–2,1)
D (5,–4)

30 Which expression is equivalent to
$(2c - 3) 4c - (3c - 4)(c - 1)$?

F $5c^2 - 5c - 4$
G $5c^2 - 19c + 4$
H $5c^2 - 12c - 4$
J $-3c^2 - 10c + 4$

31 Susan buys colored T-shirts from her supplier for $2.25 each. After silk-screening faces of famous entertainers on the T-shirts, she sells each T-shirt for $4.00. How many T-shirts does she need to sell in order to make a profit of at least $150?

A 24
B 38
C 67
D 86

32 Listed below are the first 4 terms of a patterned sequence.

1	3	7	15
Term 1	Term 2	Term 3	Term 4

Which of the following represents the value of the nth term of the sequence?

F $2n - 1$
G $2^n - 1$
H $2n$
J 2^n

GO ON TO THE NEXT PAGE

33 A triangle with vertices (–2,6), (–6,6), and (–6,2) is shown below.

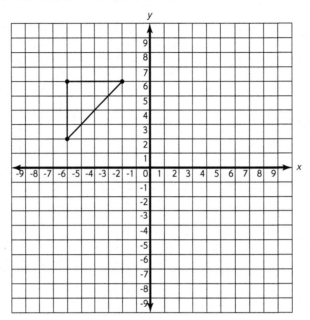

Which triangle below is similar to the triangle in the figure above?

A

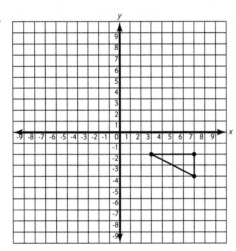

C

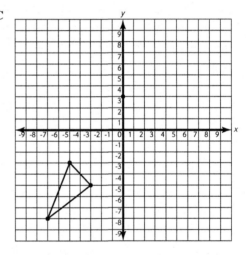

B

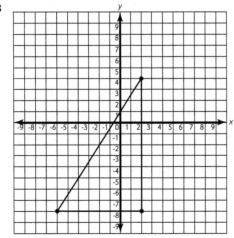

D

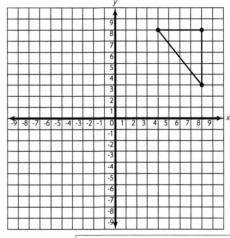

GO ON TO THE NEXT PAGE

34 Which represents the graph of the line containing the point (3,0) and perpendicular to $y = \left(\frac{3}{2}\right)x$?

F

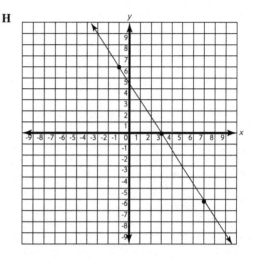

H

G

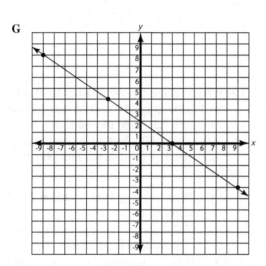

J

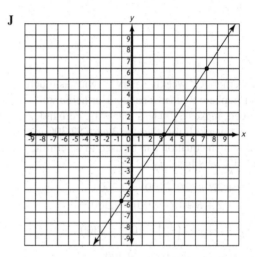

35 A right circular cylinder has a volume of 64π cm^3. If the radius at the base and the height of the cylinder are each reduced to half their original sizes, what will be the volume of this new right circular cylinder?

  A 8π cm^3

  B 11π cm^3

  C 16π cm^3

  D 32π cm^3

36 Mrs. Gardiner's front lawn is a square 30 feet on a side. After digging up some of the lawn and putting in a 5-foot wide border around the yard for flowerbeds, her lawn was reduced to a square, 20 feet on a side. Which expression can be used to determine the percent decrease in the area of Mrs. Gardiner's lawn?

  F $\left(\dfrac{(30-20)}{20}\right) \times 100$

  G $\left(\dfrac{(30 \times 30 - 20 \times 20)}{(30 \times 30)}\right) \times 100$

  H $\left(\dfrac{(30 \times 30 - 20 \times 20)}{(20 \times 20)}\right) \times 100$

  J $\left(\dfrac{(30-20)}{30}\right) \times 100$

GO ON TO THE NEXT PAGE

37 Find the approximate height *PR* of trapezoid *TRAZ*.

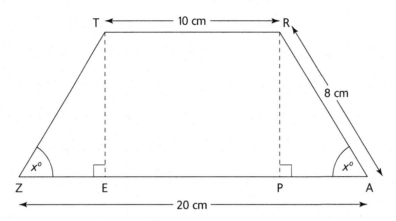

   A   6.0 cm
   B   6.2 cm
   C   9.4 cm
   D   39.0 cm

38 Mrs. Fernandez' weekly salary is twice as much as her nephew Reuben's salary. Her neighbor, Maureen, makes $100 less than Mrs. Fernandez does per week. If together the 3 earn $2,300 in a week, which equation can be used to determine Reuben's weekly salary?

   F $R + 2R + (2R - 100) = 2,300$
   G $R + 2 + R + (R - 100) = 2,300$
   H $R + \left(\dfrac{R}{2}\right) + \left(\left(\dfrac{R}{2}\right) - 100\right) = 2300$
   J $2R + R + (R - 100) = 2,300$

39 When 100 teachers were asked to identify their favorite beverage, 50 said "coffee," 25 said "soda," 15 replied "tea," and the remaining 10 responded with "milk." Which of the following conclusions is valid based on the data reported about beverage choice?

   A   Twice as many teachers favored soda, as did coffee.
   B   If 500 teachers were asked, it would be reasonable to expect about 100 to prefer milk.
   C   If 50 teachers were asked, it would be reasonable to expect about 25 to prefer coffee.
   D   As many teachers preferred soda or tea as those who preferred coffee.

GO ON TO THE NEXT PAGE

40 A national brand of potato chips is sold in a cylindrical container with dimensions as shown below.

Find the approximate volume of this potato chip container.

   F   236 cm^3
   G   707 cm^3
   H   942 cm^3
   J   2,826 cm^3

GO ON TO THE NEXT PAGE

41 A light on top of an 18-ft pole shines on a man 6 ft tall, creating a 5-ft long shadow on the ground.

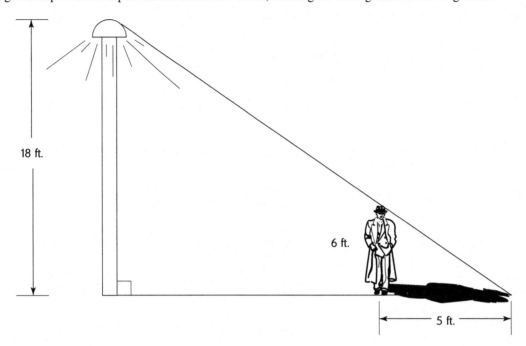

18 ft.

6 ft.

5 ft.

Find the distance from the man to the base of the light pole.

A   10 ft
B   12 ft
C   15 ft
D   17 ft

GO ON TO THE NEXT PAGE

42 An accountant for a small company notes that its checking account currently has a balance of $1,200 and money is being paid out in checks at the rate of $20 per hour. The company's saving account has a current balance of $200 with money being deposited into savings at the rate of $8 per hour. Which graph shows when the checking and savings account will have the same balance?

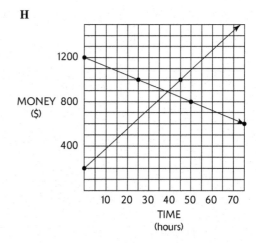

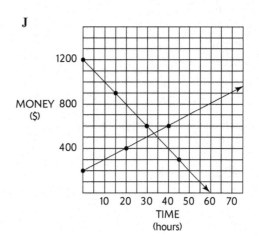

43 Find the solution set of the equation $9(4x + 3)^2 = 36$.

  A $\left\{-\frac{1}{4}, -\frac{5}{4}\right\}$

  B $\left\{-\frac{3}{4}, -\frac{1}{4}\right\}$

  C $\left\{-\frac{3}{4}, -\frac{5}{4}\right\}$

  D $\left\{\frac{15}{2}, -\frac{3}{4}\right\}$

44 A snack shop in the park sold a combined total of 136 chilidogs and hamburgers on Saturday, taking in $288. If chilidogs cost $1.50 and hamburgers cost $3, how many hamburgers were sold that day?

  F 42

  G 56

  H 80

  J 94

GO ON TO THE NEXT PAGE ▷

Practice Test 2

45 The front, top, and side views of a 3-dimensional object are shown below. What is the volume of the 3-dimensional object?

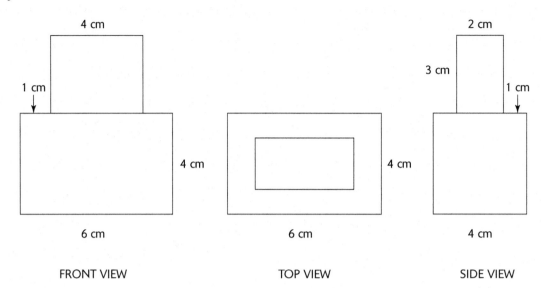

FRONT VIEW	TOP VIEW	SIDE VIEW

    A   84 cm^3

    B   96 cm^3

    C   120 cm^3

    D   192 cm^3

46 Which expression is the simplified form of $(7w^{-4}c^3)(-4w^7c^5)$?

    F $\dfrac{-28w^3}{c^2}$

    G $\dfrac{-w^3}{28c^2}$

    H $\dfrac{-28}{w^{28}c^{15}}$

    J $\dfrac{-28c^2}{w^3}$

47 A company offers paid vacations to its workers based on how many years they have been employed by the company. The days of paid vacation for various years of employment are shown in the table below:

Length of Employment (y)	Paid Vacation (d)
3	7
6	16
10	28
15	43

If y is the number of years a person has been employed at this company, and d is the number of days of paid vacation per year, which of the following best shows the relationship between the years of employment and the days of paid vacation?

    A $y = 3d - 2$

    B $d = 3y - 2$

    C $y = d - 10$

    D $d = 2y + 6$

GO ON TO THE NEXT PAGE

48 Find the slope and y-intercept of the line containing the point $(-3,4)$ and having the same y-intercept as $2x - 3y = 6$.

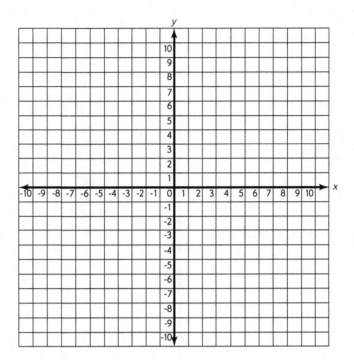

F $m = -\dfrac{2}{3}$

       $b = 2$

G $m = -\dfrac{1}{4}$

       $b = -2$

H $m = 2$

       $b = 6$

J $m = -2$

       $b = -2$

GO ON TO THE NEXT PAGE

49 Which of the following is the *y*-intercept of the function whose graph is shown below?

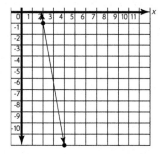

   A 3

   B 5

   C 7

   D 9

50 From a rectangular piece of cardboard 15 cm by 4 cm, Sean wants to cut out 4 equal size circles having radius 2 cm. Which statement explains why this cannot be done?

   F Circles cannot be cut from a rectangular piece of cardboard.

   G The sum of the circumferences of the 4 circles is greater than the perimeter of the rectangular piece of cardboard.

   H The sum of the area of 4 circles is less than the area of the rectangular piece of cardboard.

   J The cardboard is not long enough to cut out 4 equal circles of radius 2 cm.

GO ON TO THE NEXT PAGE

51 Which graph shows the set of ordered pairs (x, y) for which $x + y < -4$?

A

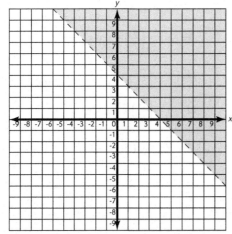

C

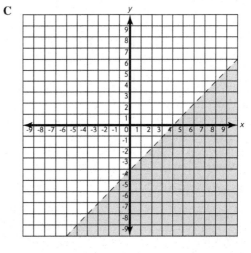

B

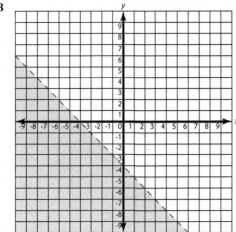

D

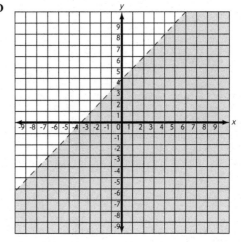

Practice Test 2

52 A casino game pays the customer a specific amount of money based on what number shows on a die that tossed.

# Tossed	1	2	3	4	5	6
$ Paid	1	3	5	7	9	11

Which equation relates p, the money paid, to n, the number tossed on the dice?

F $p = 2n + 1$

G $n = 2p + 1$

H $p = 2n - 1$

J $n = \left(\dfrac{p}{2}\right) + 1$

GO ON TO THE NEXT PAGE ▷

53 Which equation represents the total area, A, of the figure below?

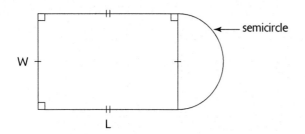

A $LW + \left(\dfrac{\pi}{2}\right)W^2$

B $W + 2L + 2\pi W$

C $LW + \left(\dfrac{\pi}{8}\right)W^2$

D $LW + \pi W$

54 Which of the following correctly lists the functions in order from the widest to the narrowest graph?

F $y = -\left(\dfrac{1}{3}\right)x^2,\ y = \left(\dfrac{6}{5}\right)x^2,\ y = -2x^2,\ y = 4x^2$

G $y = -7x^2,\ y = 4x^2,\ y = \left(\dfrac{3}{4}\right)x^2,\ y = -\left(\dfrac{5}{3}\right)x^2$

H $y = \left(\dfrac{3}{4}\right)x^2,\ y = -\left(\dfrac{7}{3}\right)x^2,\ y = 4x^2,\ y = -9x^2$

J $y = 5x^2,\ y = -2x^2,\ y = -\left(\dfrac{5}{4}\right)x^2,\ y = \left(\dfrac{1}{3}\right)x^2$

GO ON TO THE NEXT PAGE

55 Water is being pumped into an empty tank at a constant rate; all of a sudden the pump shuts off. After a short delay, most of the water in the tank has to be drained off in order to repair the pump. After another short delay, the pump is repaired; water starts pumping back into the tank. The pump then stops when the tank reaches capacity. Which of the following graphs best illustrates the given scenario?

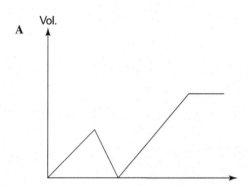

A

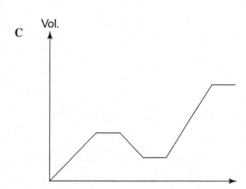

C

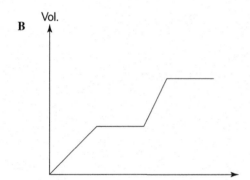

B

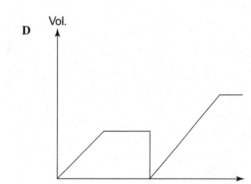

D

Practice Test 2

GO ON TO THE NEXT PAGE

56 Figure RSTU has vertices R (2,1), S (10,7), T (7,8), and U (3,5). Which of the following is the correct name of the figure RSTU?

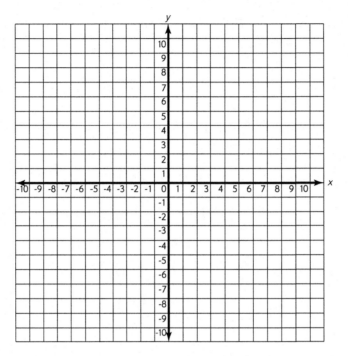

F   Rectangle
G   Rhombus
H   Square
J   Trapezoid

GO ON TO THE NEXT PAGE

57 Marissa has 2 part-time jobs. As a college student she needs to find time to earn at least $800 each month. When she works as a waiter, she earns $6/hour, but when she works as a graphic artist, she earns $10/hour. Which of the following best represents the time each month Marissa can work as a waitress for w hours and graphic artist for g hours?

   A $6(w + g) = 800$

   B $6w < 800 + 10g$

   C $10w > 800 - 6g$

   D $6w + 10g \geq 800$

58 The pressure on an object underwater depends on the depth of the object. The data in the table below demonstrates this relationship.

Depth (ft)	Pressure (lb/sq. ft)
10	620
25	1,600
150	9,600

What is the water pressure of an object at a depth at 80 ft?

   F 715 lb/sq. ft

   G 3,542 lb/sq. ft

   H 4,960 lb/sq. ft

   J 11,324 lb/sq. ft

59 Find the slope of the line having the equation $-2y = 3(x - 4)$.

   A -2

   B $-\dfrac{3}{2}$

   C $\dfrac{3}{2}$

   D 3

Practice Test 2

GO ON TO THE NEXT PAGE

60 The bar graph below shows the monthly sales for a period of 6 months for an auto parts store.

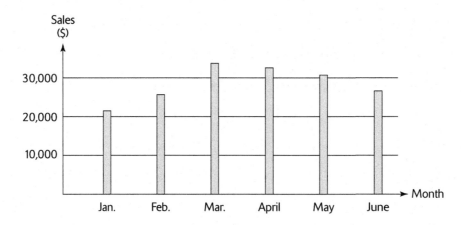

Which conclusion regarding the data above is most accurate?

   F   Monthly sales increased throughout the first half of the year.

   G   Monthly sales increased at the beginning of the year and then decreased toward the middle of the year.

   H   Monthly sales for this period were never above $30,000 in a given month.

   J   The average monthly sales were between $10,000 and $20,000.

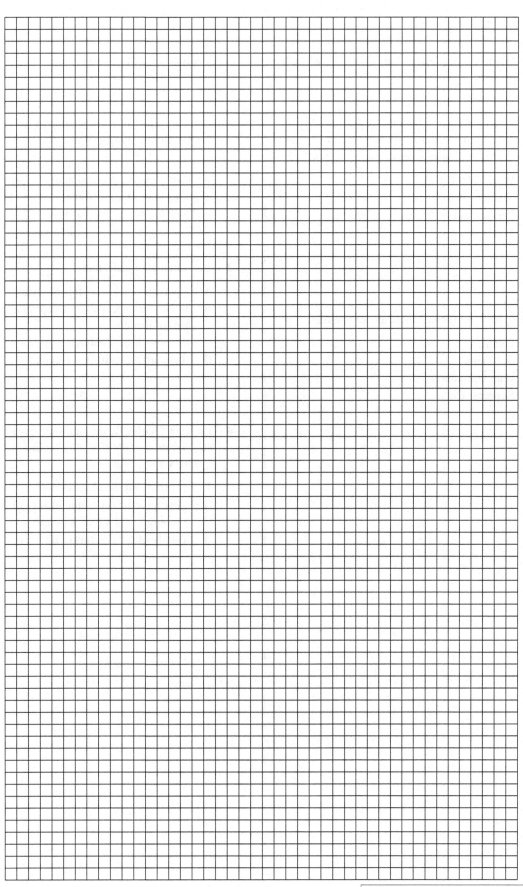

GO ON TO THE NEXT PAGE

Social Studies

Directions: Read each question and then choose the best answer. Carefully fill in the correct answer on your answer document.

1 The War Powers Act, which limits the authority of the president to commit American troops overseas without congressional approval, was a response to

  A World War I
  B Vietnam War
  C Persian Gulf War
  D World War II

2 The NAACP was most successful in advocating civil rights for African Americans before the

  F Congress
  G president
  H state legislatures
  J Supreme Court

Use the excerpt and your knowledge of social studies to answer the following question.

> The most stringent protection of free speech would not protect a man falsely shouting fire in a theater, and causing a panic.
>
> —Schenck *v.* United States, *1919*

3 This statement means that—

  A a person can say anything he/she wants.
  B freedom of speech is not guaranteed in the Bill of Rights.
  C the government can tell a person what to say.
  D there are limits to free speech.

4 Historian Charles Beard published his *Economic Interpretation of the Constitution* in 1913. This is a primary source for—

  F an article on the Constitution.
  G a book on the economic history of the U.S.
  H a biography of Charles Beard.
  J a study of the reforms of the Progressive Era.

GO ON TO THE NEXT PAGE

Use the map and your knowledge of social studies to answer the following question.

Major West African Trade Routes in the Late Middle Ages

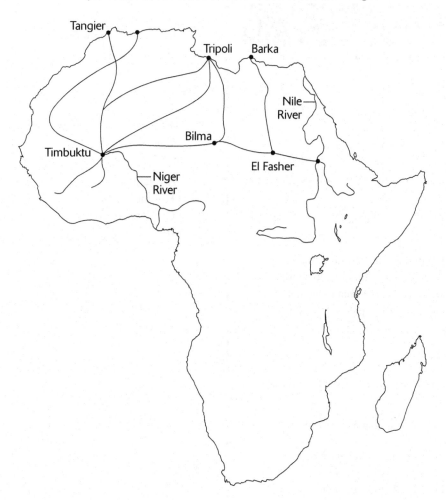

5 Given the geography of the region, what conclusion can you draw from the map?

    A   The Sahara was not an obstacle to human activity.

    B   The Sahara was wetter in the late Middle Ages than today.

    C   The major trading centers in West Africa were in the rain forest.

    D   Gold was a major export from West Africa.

6 Under the Articles of Confederation—

    F   amendments required the approval of all the states.

    G   the president was more powerful than the Congress.

    H   judges were appointed by the Congress.

    J   Congress did not have the authority to declare war.

7 NAFTA established a free trade zone between—

    A   U.S., Canada, European Union

    B   U.S., Mexico, Brazil

    C   U.S., Canada, Mexico

    D   Canada, Mexico, Argentina

GO ON TO THE NEXT PAGE

Use the table and your knowledge of social studies to answer the following question.

African American Population by Region, 1910-1930 (in thousands)			
Region	*1910*	*1920*	*1930*
Northeast	484	679	1,146
North Central	543	793	1,262
South	8,749	8,912	9,362
West	52	79	120

Source: U.S. Bureau of the Census. Historical Statistics of the United States, Colonial Times to 1970.

8 The cause of the significant increase in the black population in the North and West was—

   F   a jump in immigration from Africa

   G   a rise in the African American birth rate

   H   a successful Back to Africa movement

   J   black migration from the rural South

9 Which of the following is an example of checks and balances?

   A   The Senate confirms a nominee for the Supreme Court.

   B   The president signs a treaty on behalf of the U.S.

   C   Congress passes a new tax law.

   D   The president delivers the state of the union address to Congress.

10 The Equal Rights Amendment, which was approved by the Congress, but failed to get ratified by the states, was intended to protect—

   F   the elderly

   G   women

   H   religious minorities

   J   Native Americans

11 The new weapon that was a factor in the decision of the U.S. to declare war on Germany in 1917 was the—

   A   tank

   B   submarine

   C   mustard gas

   D   airplane

GO ON TO THE NEXT PAGE

Use the information in the box and your knowledge of social studies to answer the following question.

New Technology

- Email
- Cellular Phones
- Fax Machines
- Cable Television

---

12 Which of the following best describes the new technology?

F Information Superhighway

G Communications Revolution

H Electronics Today

J Computer Future

13 Demographically, the greatest impact of the Great Biological Exchange, the diffusion of plants and animals between the Old World and the New that began with Columbus, was—

A the introduction of the horse to the Western Hemisphere

B changes in the diet of Europeans

C the dying off of the Native American population

D the decline in the world slave trade

Use the excerpt and your knowledge of social studies to answer the following question.

Our skilled men are the tool makers, the experimental workmen, the machinists, and the patternmakers . . . they should not be wasted on doing what the machines they contrive can do better.

—Henry Ford, 1922

---

14 From this statement, you can conclude that the workers on the Ford assembly line were—

F paid low wages

G highly trained

H recent immigrants

J unskilled

15 The policy of Vietnamization adopted by President Nixon in 1969 resulted in—

A a quick end to the war in Vietnam

B the Chinese sending supplies to Vietnam

C the release of American prisoners of war

D the gradual withdrawal of U.S. troops

Practice Test 2

GO ON TO THE NEXT PAGE

Use the graph and your knowledge of social studies to answer the following question.

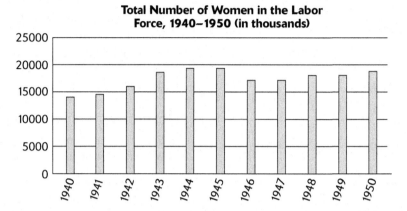

Total Number of Women in the Labor Force, 1940–1950 (in thousands)

Source: US Bureau of the Census. Historical Statistics of the United States, Colonial Times to 1970.

16 What factor contributed to the decline in women in the labor force after 1944?

    F   GI Bill of Rights

    G   War contracts were canceled.

    H   Demand for consumer products increased.

    J   The Baby Boom

GO ON TO THE NEXT PAGE

Use the map and your knowledge of social studies to answer the following question.

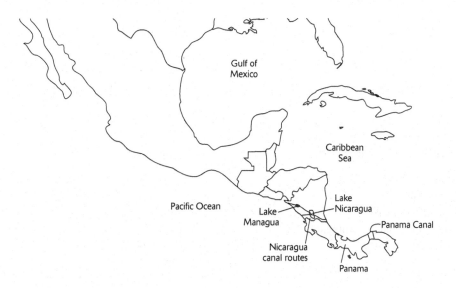

17 Before the Panama Canal was built, Nicaragua was considered the possible site for a canal linking the Atlantic and Pacific Oceans. What advantage did Nicaragua have?

   A The route was shorter.
   B Nicaragua was closer to the U.S.
   C The route could take advantage of large lakes.
   D The route was not a sea level.

18 Ancient Egypt was protected from invaders by which natural barrier?

   F Nile River
   G Atlas Mountains
   H Libyan Desert
   J Sinai Peninsula

19 American colonists were strongly opposed to the Stamp Act because they claimed—

   A it would destroy the postal system
   B the tax was too high
   C Parliament did not have power to tax the colonies
   D it would hurt stamp collectors in the colonies

GO ON TO THE NEXT PAGE

Use the excerpt and your knowledge of social studies to answer the following question.

> Attaching a peace sign to a flag, refusing to salute the flag, and displaying a red flag, we have held, all may find shelter under the First Amendment.
>
> —Texas *v.* Johnson, *1989*

20 What part of the First Amendment was the Supreme Court referring to in this decision?

   F   freedom of speech

   G   right to assemble

   H   freedom of the press

   J   right to petition the government

21 The "second front" that the Soviet Union demanded from 1941 to take pressure off Russian troops was opened by—

   A   the invasion of North Africa in November 1942

   B   the Normandy invasion of June 1944

   C   the Battle of the Bulge in December 1944

   D   the 1943 invasion of Sicily and Italy

GO ON TO THE NEXT PAGE

Use the photograph and your knowledge of social studies to answer the following question.

22 Settlers on the Great Plains built sod houses like the one shown in the photograph because—

   F   there were few trees on the prairie

   G   lumber was needed for barns and other farm buildings

   H   sod offered better protection from Indian attacks

   J   the climate was dry with frequent droughts

23 When North Korea invaded South Korea in June 1950, the U.S. sent troops to defend South Korea based on—

   A   a declaration of war by Congress

   B   obligations under the North Atlantic Treaty Organization (NATO)

   C   a request from the Soviet Union

   D   a resolution of the U.N. Security Council

GO ON TO THE NEXT PAGE

Use the advertisement and your knowledge of social studies to answer the following question.

24 The purpose of this 1920s brochure for an all-electric range was to—

    F   encourage energy conservation

    G   persuade women to spend more time with their children

    H   inform consumers that electrical appliances were safe

    J   promote the greater use of electricity

GO ON TO THE NEXT PAGE

Use the diagram and your knowledge of social studies to answer the following question.

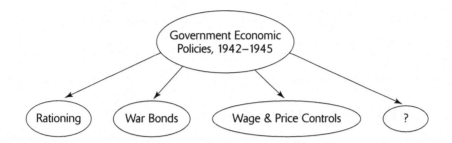

25 Which of the following answers best completes the diagram?

   A   Ban on Unions

   B   Raise Income Taxes

   C   Black Market

   D   High Tariffs

26 Prohibition, which became law with the ratification of the 18th Amendment, led to—

   F   an increase in alcoholism

   G   a breakdown of law and order

   H   a rising divorce rate

   J   more incidents of family violence

27 Which event occurred before the American colonies declared their independence from Great Britain?

   A   The Constitution is ratified.

   B   France helps the Americans during the war with Great Britain.

   C   The First Continental Congress meets.

   D   The Bill of Rights goes into effect.

GO ON TO THE NEXT PAGE

Use the excerpt and you knowledge of social studies to answer the following question.

> No free man shall be taken or imprisoned . . . except by the legal judgement of his peers or by the law of the land.
>
> —*Magna Carta, 1215*

28 What right, protected by the U.S. Constitution, does the excerpt refer to?

    F   No cruel or unusual punishment

    G   No unreasonable search or seizure

    H   Trial by jury

    J   No double jeopardy

29 The mathematical formula $E = MC^2$, which means that a small amount of matter can release a tremendous amount of energy, was important in the development of—

    A   transistors

    B   computer chips

    C   nuclear energy

    D   solar power

GO ON TO THE NEXT PAGE

Use the graph and your knowledge of social studies to answer the following question.

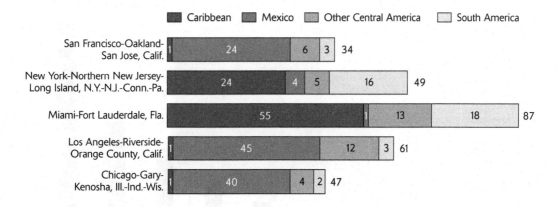

Percent of the Foreign-Born Population From Latin America by Subregion for Selected Metropolitan Areas: 2000

■ Caribbean ■ Mexico ■ Other Central America □ South America

San Francisco-Oakland-San Jose, Calif.: 1, 24, 6, 3 — 34
New York-Northern New Jersey-Long Island, N.Y.-N.J.-Conn.-Pa.: 24, 4, 5, 16 — 49
Miami-Fort Lauderdale, Fla.: 55, 1, 13, 18 — 87
Los Angeles-Riverside-Orange County, Calif.: 1, 45, 12, 3 — 61
Chicago-Gary-Kenosha, Ill.-Ind.-Wis.: 1, 40, 4, 2 — 47

30 Which of the following conclusions is valid based on the data?

F The majority of foreign-born residents of Southern California are from Mexico.

G The overwhelming major of foreign-born residents in South Florida are from South America.

H A significant number of Caribbean immigrants settle on the West Coast.

J The Midwest mainly attracts large numbers of immigrants from South America.

31 What do the Progressive Era, the New Deal, and World War II have in common?

A Civil rights for all Americans were expanded.

B The power of the federal government increased.

C Democrats controlled the White House.

D The economy of the country was sound.

32 Limiting the number of terms a member of Congress can serve requires a—

F constitutional amendment

G federal law

H executive order of the president

J Supreme Court decision

Use the excerpt and your knowledge of social studies to answer the following question.

> Is it possible and probable that millions of men can make effective progress in economic lines if they are deprived of political rights, made a servile caste, and allowed only the most meager chance for developing their exceptional men?
>
> —*W. E. B. Du Bois,* The Souls of Black Folk, *1903*

33 In his criticism of Booker T. Washington, Du Bois emphasized that the most important issue for African Americans was—

A vocational training

B better jobs

C returning to Africa

D civic equality

GO ON TO THE NEXT PAGE ▷

Practice Test 2

Use the graph and your knowledge of social studies to answer questions 34 and 35.

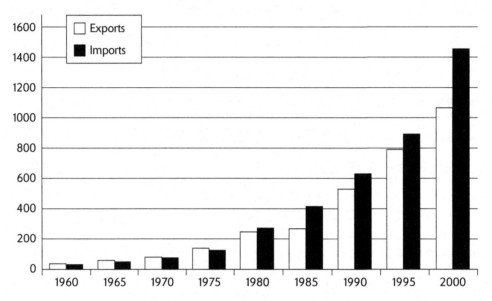

U.S. Imports and Exports, Select Years, 1960-2000 (in billions of dollars)

34 Based on the data, the U.S. first had an unfavorable balance of trade in the—

    F   1960s

    G   1970s

    H   1980s

    J   1990s

GO ON TO THE NEXT PAGE

35 What conclusions can you draw about the American economy based on the graph?

  A American participation in international trade expanded considerably.

  B The American economy was consistently strong.

  C International efforts to promote free trade failed.

  D The most important American import during the period was oil.

Use the excerpt and your knowledge of social studies to answer the following question.

> In the field of world policy I would dedicate this nation to the policy of good neighbor—the neighbor who resolutely respects himself and, because he does, respects the rights of others.
>
>   *—President Franklin Roosevelt, 1933*

36 The foreign policy shift that President Roosevelt announced applied to which part of the world?

  F Europe

  G Latin America

  H Africa

  J Asia

37 The energy crisis of the 1970s led to

  A declining prices for oil and natural gas

  B lower rates of inflation

  C a recession in energy-producing states

  D an emphasis on alternative energy sources

Practice Test 2

GO ON TO THE NEXT PAGE

Use the photograph and your knowledge of social studies to answer the following question.

38 Conditions like these during the 1930s led to a significant migration of Americans to the—

    F   Southwest

    G   Northeast

    H   Midwest

    J   West Coast

GO ON TO THE NEXT PAGE

39 At the end of World War I, the U.S. Senate rejected the Treaty of Versailles that included the creation of the League of Nations because—

   A League membership was too expensive

   B it feared the League would limit American foreign policy

   C membership required recognizing the Soviet Union

   D it wanted the headquarters of the League to be in New York

Use the table and your knowledge of social studies to answer the following question.

1912 Presidential Election Results			
Candidate	*Party*	*Popular Vote*	*Electoral Vote*
Woodrow Wilson	Democrat	6,296,547	435
Theodore Roosevelt	Progressive	4,118,547	88
William Howard Taft	Republican	3,486,720	8
Eugene V. Debs	Socialist	900,672	–
Eugene W. Chafin	Prohibition	200,275	–

40 Woodrow Wilson was elected president in 1912 largely because—

   F African Americans voted for him in large numbers

   G the Republican vote was split between Roosevelt and Taft

   H the Socialists took votes away from the Republicans

   J he won the electoral votes in California

GO ON TO THE NEXT PAGE

Use the excerpt and your knowledge of social studies to answer the following question.

> He had made our judges dependent on his will alone for the tenure of their offices and the amount and payment of their salaries.
>
> —*Declaration of Independence, 1776*

41 How does the U.S. Constitution deal with the issue of political influence over judges?

- **A** All judges are elected by the people.
- **B** Federal judges are appointed for a four-year term.
- **C** Federal judges serve for life.
- **D** Federal judges cannot be removed from office.

42 Which of the following is a problem the Social Security system faces today?

- **F** The number of people paying into the system is increasing.
- **G** Social Security does not provide enough money for retirement.
- **H** There is too much money in the Social Security Trust Fund.
- **J** The number of people eligible for benefits is increasing.

43 What impact did the improvements in urban transportation have on cities in the late 19th century?

- **A** People could live farther from their work.
- **B** Mass transit encouraged the construction of skyscrapers.
- **C** Immigrants became concentrated in specific neighborhoods.
- **D** More people left the farms for the cities.

GO ON TO THE NEXT PAGE

Use the excerpt and your knowledge of social studies to answer the following question.

That the several acts and parts of acts of the Congress of the United States, purporting to be laws for the imposing of duties . . . on the importation of foreign commodities . . . are unauthorized by the Constitution of the United States.

—*South Carolina Ordinance of Nullification, 1832*

44 According to the nullification doctrine, the states—

  F   can challenge a federal law in the courts
  G   must accept any law passed by the Congress
  H   can declare a federal law unconstitutional
  J   urge Congress to pass laws fair to all parts of the country

Key Events

- Japan invades Manchuria
- Hitler comes to power in Germany
- Civil war breaks out in Spain
- Germany and the Soviet Union sign a non-aggression pact

45 These events are significant because they led up to—

  A   the Cold War
  B   World War II
  C   World War I
  D   the Great Depression

Practice Test 2

GO ON TO THE NEXT PAGE

Use the map and your knowledge of social studies to answer questions 46 and 47.

Right to Vote for Women

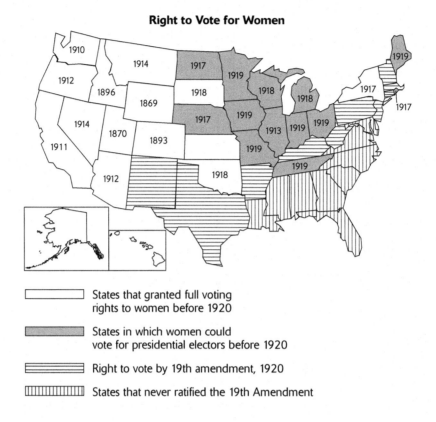

States that granted full voting
rights to women before 1920

States in which women could
vote for presidential electors before 1920

Right to vote by 19th amendment, 1920

States that never ratified the 19th Amendment

46 The region of the country least supportive of women's rights was—

   F   the West
   G   the Midwest
   H   New England
   J   South

47 Which of the following conclusions can be drawn
from the map?

   A   A constitutional amendment was not
necessary to give all women the right to vote.
   B   States set the qualifications for voting.
   C   World War I had no impact on extending the
right to vote.
   D   The 19th Amendment was not enforced in
parts of the country.

GO ON TO THE NEXT PAGE

Use the excerpt and your knowledge of social studies to answer the following question.

> We are determined to keep out of the war, yet we cannot ensure ourselves against the disastrous effects of war and the dangers of involvement. We are adopting such measures as will minimize our risk of involvement but we cannot have complete protection . . .
>
> —*President Franklin Roosevelt, 1937*

48 The measures President Roosevelt referred to included the—

F Selective Service Act

G Lend-Lease Act

H Neutrality Acts

J Destroyer-Naval Base Deal

49 Which region of the U.S. is matched with the correct agricultural product?

A cotton—Northwest

B corn—New England

C wheat—Great Plains

D tobacco—West

Use the excerpt and your knowledge of social studies to answer the following question.

> The enumeration in the Constitution of certain rights shall not be construed to deny or disparage others retained by the people.
>
> —Ninth Amendment to the U.S. Constitution

50 What other rights, not mentioned in the Constitution, do the American people have?

F right of privacy

G freedom of religion

H freedom of speech

J trial by jury

51 Rosa Parks is associated with ending discrimination against African Americans in—

A education

B public transportation

C voter registration

D employment

GO ON TO THE NEXT PAGE >

Practice Test 2

Use the chart and your knowledge of social studies to answer the following question.

Sequence of Events—Road to the Civil War

John Brown's raid at Harper's Ferry	Election of Abraham Lincoln	South Carolina secedes	Confederate States of America	?

52 Which completes the sequence?

    F   Virginia secedes from the Union.

    G   Confederate forces attack Fort Sumter.

    H   Uncle Tom's Cabin is published.

    J   The border states secede from the Union.

Use the excerpt and your knowledge of social studies to answer the following question.

> All citizens of the United States who are otherwise qualified to vote at any election by the people of any state, territory, district, county, city, parish, township, school district, municipality or other territorial subdivision, shall be entitled and allowed to vote in such elections . . .
>
> —*Voting Rights Act, 1965*

53 This legislation made which constitutional amendment truly effective?

    A   13th Amendment

    B   14th Amendment

    C   15th Amendment

    D   17th Amendment

Use the excerpt and your knowledge of social studies to answer the following question.

> Wherefore, Richard M. Nixon, by such conduct, warrants impeachment and trial, and removal from office.
>
> —*House Judiciary Committee, 1974*

54 The House Judiciary Committee reached this conclusion after examining Nixon's role in the—

    F   Watergate break-in

    G   Iran-Contra affair

    H   expansion of the war in Vietnam

    J   Kent State protests

55 During the early Depression, many banks failed because—

    A   currency was not backed by gold

    B   deposits were stolen by criminals

    C   people did not believe their money was safe

    D   the federal government refused to help the banks

Science

Directions: Read each question and select the best answer. Then fill in the correct answer on your answer document.

GO ON TO THE NEXT PAGE

FORMULA CHART
for Grade 11 Science Assessment

Density = $\dfrac{\text{mass}}{\text{volume}}$ $D = \dfrac{m}{v}$

$\left(\begin{array}{c}\text{heat gained or}\\ \text{lost by water}\end{array}\right) = \left(\begin{array}{c}\text{mass in}\\ \text{grams}\end{array}\right)\left(\begin{array}{c}\text{change in}\\ \text{temperature}\end{array}\right)\left(\begin{array}{c}\text{specific}\\ \text{heat}\end{array}\right)$ $Q = (m)(\Delta T)(C_p)$

Speed = $\dfrac{\text{distance}}{\text{time}}$ $s = \dfrac{d}{t}$

Acceleration = $\dfrac{\text{final velocity} - \text{initial velocity}}{\text{change in time}}$ $a = \dfrac{V_f - V_i}{\Delta t}$

Momentum = mass × velocity $p = mv$

Force = mass × acceleration $F = ma$

Work = force × distance $W = Fd$

Power = $\dfrac{\text{work}}{\text{time}}$ $P = \dfrac{W}{t}$

% efficiency = $\dfrac{\text{work output}}{\text{work input}} \times 100$ $\% = \dfrac{W_O}{W_I} \times 100$

Kinetic energy = $\dfrac{1}{2}$ (mass × velocity²) $KE = \dfrac{mv^2}{2}$

Gravitational potential energy = mass × acceleration due to gravity × height $GPE = mgh$

Energy = mass × (speed of light)² $E = mc^2$

Velocity of a wave = frequency × wavelength $v = f\lambda$

Current = $\dfrac{\text{voltage}}{\text{resistance}}$ $I = \dfrac{V}{R}$

Electrical power = voltage × current $P = VI$

Electrical energy = power × time $E = Pt$

Constants/Conversions
g = acceleration due to gravity = 9.8 m/s²
c = speed of light = 3×10^8 m/s
speed of sound = 343 m/s at 20°C
1 cm³ = 1 mL
1 wave/second = 1 hertz (Hz)
1 calorie (cal) = 4.18 joules
1000 calories (cal) = 1 Calorie (Cal) = 1 kilocalorie (kcal)
newton (N) = kgm/s²
joule (J) = Nm
watt (W) = J/s = Nm/s
volt (V)   ampere (A)   ohm (Ω)

Centimeters
0
1
2
3
4
5
6
7
8
9
10
11
12
13
14
15
16
17
18
19
20

GO ON TO THE NEXT PAGE

Periodic Table of the Elements

Key:
Atomic Number — 14
Symbol — Si
Atomic Mass — 28.086
Name — Silicon

1 IA	2 IIA	3 IIIB	4 IVB	5 VB	6 VIB	7 VIIB	8	9 VIII	10	11 IB	12 IIB	13 IIIA	14 IVA	15 VA	16 VIA	17 VIIA	18 VIIIA
1 H 1.008 Hydrogen																	2 He 4.0026 Helium
3 Li 6.941 Lithium	4 Be 9.012 Beryllium											5 B 10.81 Boron	6 C 12.011 Carbon	7 N 14.007 Nitrogen	8 O 15.999 Oxygen	9 F 18.998 Flourine	10 Ne 20.179 Neon
11 Na 22.990 Sodium	12 Mg 24.305 Magnesium											13 Al 26.982 Aluminum	14 Si 28.086 Silicon	15 P 30.974 Phosphorus	16 S 32.066 Sulfur	17 Cl 35.453 Chlorine	18 Ar 39.948 Argon
19 K 39.098 Potassium	20 Ca 40.08 Calcium	21 Sc 44.956 Scandium	22 Ti 47.88 Titanium	23 V 50.942 Vanadium	24 Cr 51.996 Chromium	25 Mn 54.938 Manganese	26 Fe 55.847 Iron	27 Co 58.933 Cobalt	28 Ni 58.69 Nickel	29 Cu 63.546 Copper	30 Zn 65.39 Zinc	31 Ga 69.72 Gallium	32 Ge 72.61 Germanium	33 As 74.922 Arsenic	34 Se 78.96 Selenium	35 Br 79.904 Bromine	36 Kr 83.80 Krypton
37 Rb 85.468 Rubidium	38 Sr 87.62 Strontium	39 Y 88.906 Yttrium	40 Zr 91.224 Zirconium	41 Nb 92.906 Niobium	42 Mo 95.94 Molybdenum	43 Tc (98) Technetium	44 Ru 101.07 Ruthenium	45 Rh 102.906 Rhodium	46 Pd 106.42 Palladium	47 Ag 107.868 Silver	48 Cd 112.41 Cadmium	49 In 114.82 Indium	50 Sn 118.71 Tin	51 Sb 121.763 Antimony	52 Te 127.60 Tellurium	53 I 126.904 Iodine	54 Xe 131.29 Xenon
55 Cs 132.905 Cesium	56 Ba 137.33 Barium	57 La 138.906 Lanthanum	72 Hf 178.49 Hafnium	73 Ta 180.948 Tantalum	74 W 183.84 Tungsten	75 Re 186.207 Rhenium	76 Os 190.23 Osmium	77 Ir 192.22 Iridium	78 Pt 195.08 Platinum	79 Au 196.967 Gold	80 Hg 200.59 Mercury	81 Tl 204.383 Thallium	82 Pb 207.2 Lead	83 Bi 208.980 Bismuth	84 Po (209) Polonium	85 At (210) Astatine	86 Rn (222) Radon
87 Fr (223) Francium	88 Ra 226.025 Radium	89 Ac 227.028 Actinium	104 Rf (261) Rutherfordium	105 Db (262) Dubnium	106 Sg (263) Seaborgium	107 Bh (262) Bohrium	108 Hs (265) Hassium	109 Mt (266) Meitnerium	110 (269)								

Mass numbers in parentheses are those of the most stable or most common isotope.

Lanthanide Series

58 Ce 140.12 Cerium	59 Pr 140.908 Praseodymium	60 Nd 144.24 Neodymium	61 Pm (145) Promethium	62 Sm 150.36 Samarium	63 Eu 151.97 Europium	64 Gd 157.25 Gadolinium	65 Tb 158.925 Terbium	66 Dy 162.50 Dysprosium	67 Ho 164.930 Holmium	68 Er 167.26 Erbium	69 Tm 168.934 Thulium	70 Yb 173.04 Ytterbium	71 Lu 174.967 Lutetium

Actinide Series

90 Th 232.038 Thorium	91 Pa 231.036 Protactinium	92 U 238.029 Uranium	93 Np 237.048 Neptunium	94 Pu (244) Plutonium	95 Am (243) Americium	96 Cm (247) Curium	97 Bk (247) Berkelium	98 Cf (251) Californium	99 Es (252) Einsteinium	100 Fm (257) Fermium	101 Md (258) Mendelevium	102 No (259) Nobelium	103 Lr (262) Lawrencium

Practice Test 2

GO ON TO THE NEXT PAGE

1 Which physical property is most commonly used to separate a solution of alcohol and water into its two liquid components?

A density
B surface tension
C viscosity
D volatility

The Gill of a Fish

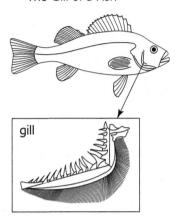

gill

2 Which part of the human body does about the same job as the gills of a fish?

F ears
G esophagus
H lungs
J neck

GO ON TO THE NEXT PAGE

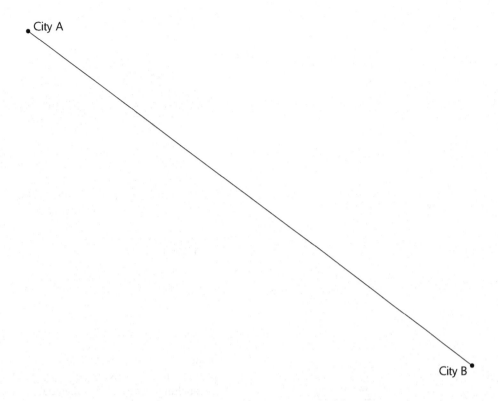

City A

City B

3 The diagram above shows the distance on a map from City A to City B. A bicycle rider starts his bicycle trip at City A, rides to City B, and then rides back to City A. In the diagram, 1cm equals a distance of 3 miles.

Using the ruler supplied on the Formula Chart, determine the speed of the bicycle if the entire trip took 6 hours.

 A   7.5 miles per hour
 B   10 miles per hour
 C   15 miles per hour
 D   20 miles per hour

4 Viruses are intracellular parasites. Which of these objects could not be a host for a virus?

 F   horse
 G   lobster
 H   protein
 J   yellow pine

5 Fluorine, chlorine, and bromine are known as halogens. They are—

 A   nonmetals and are too reactive to occur on their own in nature
 B   metals and are too reactive to occur on their own in nature
 C   nonmetals and are almost totally unreactive
 D   transition metals and are reactive

GO ON TO THE NEXT PAGE

Practice Test 2

6 The gray squirrel, *Sciurus carolinensis*, is most closely related to the—

F red squirrel, Tamiasciurus hudsonicus
G spotted ground squirrel, Spermophilus spilosoma
H southern flying squirrel, Glaucomys sabrinus
J fox squirrel, Sciurus niger

7 The correct formula for zinc carbonate is—

A Zn_2CO
B $ZnCO_2$
C $ZnCO_3$
D Zn_3CO_2

8 The experiment above was set up to show which of the following energy transformations?

F Mechanical energy is converted to heat energy.
G Chemical energy is converted to electrical energy.
H Electromagnetic energy is converted to light energy.
J Electromagnetic energy is converted to heat energy.

9 Near the end of a daily swim, a swimmer pushes to swim faster and increases from 1.1 m/s to 1.3 m/s during the last 20 seconds of his workout. What is his acceleration during this interval?

A 0.001 m/s^2
B 0.01 m/s^2
C 0.1 m/s^2
D 1.0 m/s^2

10 In trying to stop the rusting process, chemists look for something to keep the oxygen in the air from touching wet iron. This material, however, could not combine with or damage the iron. Paint is most commonly used to stop rusting, but sometimes using paint is not practical. For example, many tools should not be painted. Which of the following materials would be best to stop the rusting of tools?

F baking powder
G oil
H alcohol
J window cleaner

GO ON TO THE NEXT PAGE

11 The wave nature of light is demonstrated by passing two flashlight beams of light through each other. The outcome is—

A each beam bends lightly

B the light beam particles collide and scatter the light

C there is no scattering of particles and the beams remain intact

D one light beam merges with the other

12 Heating chemicals in a closed or corked test tube should never be done because—

F expanding gas inside may cause the test tube to explode

G test tubes stoppers do not fit perfectly

H the stopper is not meant to withstand the heat

J expanding gas inside may leak out through a faulty stopper

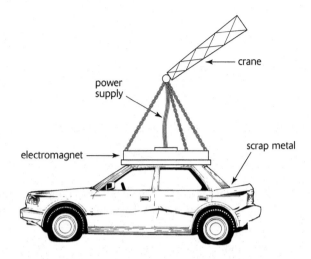

13 How would the operator of the large electromagnetic crane most easily get the magnet to let go of the car?

A by joggling the crane to shake off the car

B by sending electricity through the coil in the other direction

C by throwing a switch to interrupt the current

D by turning on an opposing electromagnet

Practice Test 2

GO ON TO THE NEXT PAGE

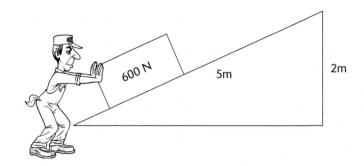

14 Johnny pushes a 600 Newton box up a ramp or inclined plane with a force of 300 Newtons. The ramp is 2 meters high and 5 meters long. What is the efficiency of the inclined plane?

    F   40%

    G   80%

    H   90%

    J   100%

15 In mammals, oxygen is carried to the body tissue by means of the—

    A   circulatory system

    B   respiratory system

    C   digestive tract

    D   nervous system

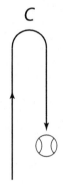

16 The diagram above shows the conservation of energy when a ball is thrown vertically into the air. Which of the following statements accurately describes the condition of the ball when it is thrown perfectly straight up but before it reaches the peak of its upward flight at point C?

    F   The ball has no potential energy but increasing kinetic energy.

    G   The ball has maximum potential energy.

    H   The ball has decreasing kinetic energy and increasing potential energy.

    J   The ball has increasing kinetic energy and decreasing potential energy.

GO ON TO THE NEXT PAGE

17 Fungi are decomposers that are important in natural recycling. A fungus that is a parasite would most likely feed on which of the following?

A an individual's skin
B moldy bread
C a decomposing tree
D slime on a bathroom wall

$$H_2SO_4 + 2KOH \rightarrow K_2SO_4 + H_2O$$

18 What is the coefficient of H_2O when the equation above is balanced?

F 1
G 2
H 3
J 4

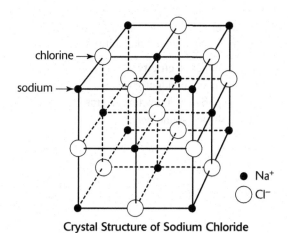

chlorine →
sodium →

● Na^+
○ Cl^-

Crystal Structure of Sodium Chloride

19 The diagram shows the crystal structure of sodium chloride—ordinary table salt—with the atoms greatly magnified to show their arrangement. Table salt is made up of equal numbers of sodium and chlorine atoms. Based on the diagram, which of the following statements is valid?

A Atoms of the opposite charge are closer than atoms of the same charge.
B Each atom can vibrate in only three directions.
C The crystal faces of the structure are slightly rounded.
D The pattern cannot be continued in all directions.

20 An object that is moving at 40 m/s has a momentum of 10 kg × m/s. What is the mass of the object in kilograms? Record and bubble in your answer to the nearest hundredth on the answer document.

21 Hydrochloric acid and sulfuric acid both contain—

A chlorine
B hydrogen
C oxygen
D sulfur

GO ON TO THE NEXT PAGE ▷

Practice Test 2

The carbon cycle

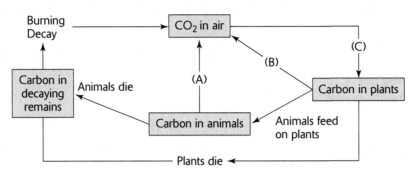

22 The diagram above shows the various interrelationships that take place during the carbon cycle. Which of these shows the process of photosynthesis?

   F   A
   G   B
   H   C
   J   Not shown

23 Fruit flies are often used instead of other flies in the study of gene mutation probably because—

   A   they are rare
   B   they breed quickly
   C   they seldom have changes in their genes
   D   they have genetic characteristics that are easy to see

24 Tap water is composed of water and dissolved minerals which give it the ability to—

   F   conduct electricity
   G   stop any conductivity
   H   vaporize at a low temperature
   J   enhance sound waves

GO ON TO THE NEXT PAGE

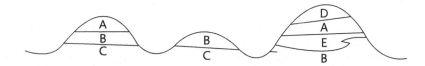

25 Five sedimentary formations are labeled in the cross-section through three hills shown above. Which formation is the youngest?

   A A

   B B

   C C

   D D

26 Sound travels at a speed of 330 meters per second. If a firecracker explodes 3,630 meters away from you, how long does it take for the sound of the explosion to reach you?

   F 0.11 seconds

   G 3 seconds

   H 6 seconds

   J 11 seconds

GO ON TO THE NEXT PAGE

Table			
Homologous series	Number of carbon atoms		
	meth- 1	eth- 2	prop- 3
alkane	CH_4 methane	C_2H_6 ethane	C_3H_8 propane
alkene	———	C_2H_4 ethene	C_3H_6 propene
alcohol	CH_3OH methanol	CH_3CH_2OH ethanol	$CH_3CH_2CH_2OH$ propanol

27 The table shows three examples of homologous series—alkanes, alkenes, and alcohols. Based on the table, alcohols differ from alkanes and alkenes in that alcohols must contain—

    A more carbon atoms than hydrogen atoms

    B more hydrogen atoms than carbon atoms

    C fewer carbons atoms than all other atoms

    D atoms other than carbon and hydrogen

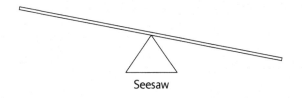

Seesaw

28 The diagram above illustrates a seesaw. A seesaw is an example of a(n) —

    F lever

    G inclined plane

    H wedge

    J pulley

29 An experiment is conducted in which five circular holes of equal size are cut into a large plastic bottle. The holes are arranged from top to bottom, with each hole exactly one inch from the next. The holes are covered with tape, and the bottle is filled with water. The tape is then removed. Which of the following can be a predicted outcome based on the information given and your knowledge of science?

    A Water from each hole will squirt out the same distance from the bottle.

    B Water from the top hole will squirt out farther than that from the bottom hole.

    C Water from the bottom hole will squirt out farther than that from any other hole.

    D Water from all five holes rapidly being released will cause the bottle to collapse.

GO ON TO THE NEXT PAGE

30 Which optical process explains why a teaspoon appears to be bent when it is immersed halfway into a cup of weak tea?

F absorption
G emission
H reflection
J refraction

Properties of the Four Alkali Metals

Metal Element	Melting Point in °C	Boiling Point in °C
cesium	29	670
lithium	186	1336
potassium	62	760
rubidium	39	700

31 The chart above shows some of the properties of four alkali metals. As a general rule in chemistry, the bonds between atoms are strongest in solids and weakest in gases. The strength of a bond varies inversely with the size of atoms. Strong bonds go with small atoms, and weak bonds go with large atoms. Which of the following alkali elements has the largest atoms?

A cesium
B lithium
C potassium
D rubidium

32 On the pH scale, how many times stronger is a pH of 2 than a pH of 5?

F 3
G 10
H 100
J 1,000

33 The tumbleweed almost never grows anywhere but on plowed fields, overgrazed ranges, or along roads.

Which of the following explains the relationship of the tumbleweed to its environment?

A It can't compete with established plants.
B It destroys the natural environment.
C It is a delicate, endangered species.
D It requires an unusually dry environment.

Distribution of Water Near Earth's Surface

Location of Water	Percent
Oceans	97.1
Saltwater lakes	0.008
Freshwater lakes	0.009
Rivers and streams	0.0001
Polar ice caps	2.24
Underground water	0.61
Water vapor in air	0.001
Total Water	100.0

34 Pollution is a threat to all of the types of water shown in the chart. Which of the following is less than 1.00 percent, yet once polluted, can spread pollution in an unseen and unpredictable way?

F oceans
G rivers and streams
H underground water
J freshwater lakes

GO ON TO THE NEXT PAGE

35 Reusable safety goggles that form a seal around the eyes should always be—

    A   disinfected before being used by another student

    B   disposed of after the second usage

    C   equipped with side shields for extra protection

    D   cleaned daily with a soapy water solution

36 Alice picks up a hot plate. The type of energy transfer from the plate to her hand is—

    F   radiation

    G   conduction

    H   convection

    J   combustion

37 The basic building blocks for proteins are—

    A   amino acids

    B   carbohydrates

    C   minerals

    D   phosphates

Use the information below and your knowledge of science to answer questions 38–39.

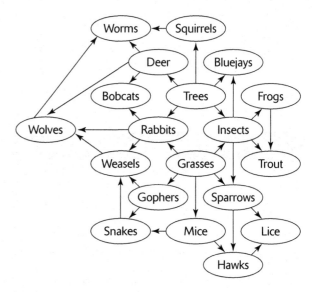

(The diagram above shows the feeding relationships in one woodland community. The arrows point toward the dependent organism. For example, frogs eat insects.)

38 Which of the following animals are natural enemies of snakes?

    F   gophers and mice

    G   hawks and weasels

    H   mice and hawks

    J   weasels and gophers

GO ON TO THE NEXT PAGE

39 A campaign by chicken farmers to eradicate weasels throughout the area could lead indirectly to—

   A   a decrease of hawks
   B   a decrease of snakes
   C   an increase of blue jays
   D   an increase of bobcats

40 As a covered kettle of vegetable soup continues to boil gently on the stove, what happens to the temperature of the soup?

   F   It falls very slowly.
   G   It remains the same.
   H   It rises very slowly.
   J   It rises rapidly.

41 Although forest fires can be devastating, the major benefit of forest fires is probably that—

   A   young trees are given the opportunity to grow quickly because old, tall trees have been cleared allowing sunlight through
   B   old trees have additional room to grow, become lush, and spread their branches
   C   animals move to a new location to balance the ecology
   D   seeds that are naturally scattered are not eaten by birds

GO ON TO THE NEXT PAGE

Use the information given below and your knowledge of science to answer questions 42–43.

Table 1					Table 2	
Study Number	Date	Richter scale magnitude	Effect		Magnitude	Description
1	Jan. 12	3.2	noticed only by a few people		less than 3.0	detected by instruments only
2	Jan. 18	4.5	woke up those asleep		3.0 – 3.4	weak
3	Jan. 23	2.1	detected by seismograph only		3.5 – 3.9	slight
4	Mar. 2	6.8	houses collapsed		4.0 – 4.4	moderate
5	Mar. 4	5.7	walls cracked		4.5 – 4.8	fairly strong
6	May 25	4.1	objects moved		4.9 – 5.4	strong
7	Jun. 4	3.7	heavy truck-type vibrations		5.5 – 6.0	very strong
8	Jul. 17	6.1	chimneys collapsed		6.1 – 6.5	destructive
9	Sep. 4	7.4	buildings and pipelines destroyed		6.6 – 7.0	ruinous
10	Sep. 5	8.4	city totally destroyed		7.1 – 7.3	disastrous
11	Oct. 15	7.1	landslides and ground cracked		7.4 – 8.1	calamitous
12	Dec. 1	5.0	objects fell off shelves		greater than 8.1	catastrophic

A researcher conducted studies of twelve different earthquakes on twelve different dates as shown in Table 1. Table 2 gives descriptions for ranges of magnitudes.

42 According to the information given in the twelve studies, the effects caused by heavy truck could—

 F   be detected only by instruments

 G   be considered a slight vibration

 H   wake up those who are asleep

 J   crack thin walls

43 Which of the following could reasonably be assumed from the information given?

 A   Moderate quakes always occur in January.

 B   No walls crack during strong quakes.

 C   In a disastrous quake, chimneys are destroyed.

 D   The highest magnitude quakes always occur in September throughout the world.

44 Which of the following organs is not part of the circulatory system?

 F   aorta

 G   capillary

 H   heart

 J   trachea

GO ON TO THE NEXT PAGE

Liquid	Molecular Weight	Viscosity (millipoises)		
		0°C	20°C	40°C
Water	16	17.92	10.05	6.56
Ethanol	46	17.73	12.01	8.34
Pentane	72	3.11	2.43	2.03
Benzene	78	9.12	6.52	5.03
Sulfuric acid	98	13.29	10.04	8.19
Heptane	100	5.24	4.09	3.41
Octane	114	7.06	5.42	4.33
Mercury	201	16.84	15.47	14.83

45 The table shows the results of experiments that measured the viscosities of liquids at three different temperatures. According to the data in the table, which of the following liquids has the highest viscosity at normal room temperature?

A   ethanol

B   mercury

C   sulfuric acid

D   water

46 The greatest percent carbohydrate content by mass would be in—

F   a food containing 10 grams of carbohydrate and with a net mass of 20 grams

G   a food containing 10 grams of carbohydrate and with a net mass of 25 grams

H   a food containing 10 grams of carbohydrate and with a net mass of 50 grams

J   a food containing 20 grams of carbohydrate and with a net mass of 100 grams

47 | A car is driven at high speeds for a long time. The size of the tires temporarily increases.

Which of the following is the best explanation for this occurrence?

A   Gases can be compressed to small volumes by pressure.

B   As temperature of a gas increases, the volume increases.

C   When the pressure exerted on a gas is greatest, the volume is greatest.

D   A compressed gas pushes out equally in all directions.

GO ON TO THE NEXT PAGE >

Practice Test 2

Characteristics of Some Major Groups of Animals			
Animal Group	**Mobility (ability to move)**	**Symmetry (evenly proportioned)**	**Further Description**
Arthropods	high	bilateral	organism divided into segments and organism covered with external skeleton
Chordates	high	bilateral	organism has internal skeleton
Coelenterates	none	radial	cavity surrounded by tentacles
Echinoderms	slight	five-fold	organism has heavy protective skeleton
Mollusks	slight	bilateral	organism has one or two hard shells

48 The chart above shows characteristics of some major groups of animals. Bees, spiders, and lobsters have bodies with many common features. Which of the following is the best classification for all three of these animals?

   F   arthropods

   G   chordates

   H   coelenterates

   J   echinoderms

49 In a food chain, one species eats another, which in turn, is eaten by another species. Green plants begin any food chain because they—

   A   need water to survive

   B   are eaten by many different species of animal

   C   are the only organisms that can make their own food

   D   get their energy from the sun and color from chlorophyll

GO ON TO THE NEXT PAGE

Deer Population in Northern Arizona from 1905 to 1935

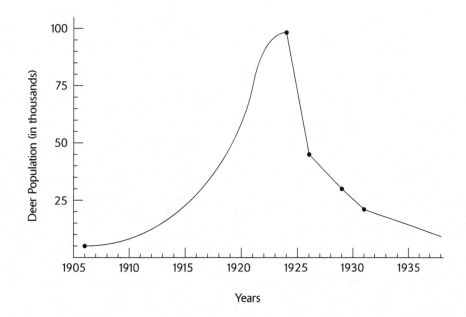

50 The graph shows the deer population in northern Arizona from 1905 to 1935. What was the approximate increase in deer population from 1907 to 1923?

  F 9,300

  G 24,000

  H 93,000

  J 123,000

GO ON TO THE NEXT PAGE

51 A 500 Newton passenger is inside a 24,500 Newton elevator that rises 30 meters in exactly 1 minute. How much power is needed for the elevator's trip?

   A   1,250 watts

   B   12,500 watts

   C   125,000 watts

   D   1,250,000 watts

52 A dog and its fleas is one example of—

   F   commensalism

   G   parasitism

   H   predation

   J   mutualism

In trying to classify living organisms, scientists in the 1970s made detailed comparisons of the amino acid sequences of a protein called cytochrome c. This protein exists in slightly different forms, yet performs a similar function of energy transportation in hundreds of different species. The assumption is that those sequences resembling each other the most indicate closely related species. The following chart shows the sequence of the first twenty-five amino acids for cytochrome c.

Amino-Acid Sequences 1-25 for Cytochrome c

Tuna	GDVAKGKKTFVQKCAQCHTVENGGK
Moth	GNADNGKKIFVQRCAQCHTVEAGGK
Dog	CDVEKGKKIFVQKCAQCHTVEKGGK
Wheat	GNPDAGAKIFKTKCAQCHTVDAGAG

53 According to the information above, which two organisms are the most closely related?

   A   tuna and moth

   B   dog and wheat

   C   moth and dog

   D   dog and tuna

54 Which characteristic of a wave must change in order to affect the pitch of a sound?

   F   amplitude

   G   wavelength

   H   frequency

   J   crest

55 Which of the following are cold-blooded animals?

   A   penguins

   B   cats

   C   lizards

   D   whales

Reviewing Practice Test 2

Review your simulated TAKS Practice Examination by following these steps:

1. Check the answers you marked on your answer sheet against the Answer Key that follows. Put a check mark in the box following any wrong answer.
2. Fill out the Review Chart (p. 335).
3. Read all the explanations (pp. 336–366). Go back to review any explanations that are not clear to you.
4. Finally, fill out the Reasons for Mistakes chart on p. 335.

Don't leave out any of these steps. They are very important in learning to do your best on the TAKS.

Special note for the English Language Arts, Open-ended answers and Essay:

Have an English teacher, tutor, or someone else with good writing skills read and evaluate your essay and open-ended answers by using the checklists given. Using the evaluation checklists will give you a general feeling of how you did on these question types. Note that your essay and constructed answers will actually be scored by trained readers.

Answer Key for Practice Test 2

English Language Arts

Reading and Written Composition

1 D	**10** J	**19** D	**28** G
2 G	**11** A	**20** H	**29–31**—Use the Checklist for the Open-Ended Answers on p. 27 to evaluate your answers.
3 A	**12** H	**21** C	
4 G	**13** D	**22** J	
5 B	**14** J	**23** D	
6 J	**15** C	**24** H	**Essay**—Use the Checklist for the Essay on p. 33 to evaluate your essay.
7 C	**16** F	**25** C	
8 F	**17** B	**26** F	
9 B	**18** G	**27** C	

Revising and Editing

32 J	**37** C	**42** H	**47** B
33 B	**38** G	**43** D	**48** H
34 G	**39** A	**44** J	**49** A
35 A	**40** F	**45** C	**50** G
36 G	**41** D	**46** J	**51** C

Mathematics

1 D	**16** G	**31** D	**47** B
2 J	**17** C	**32** G	**48** J
3 B	**18** F	**34** G	**49** D
4 H	**19** D	**35** A	**50** J
5 B	**20** H	**36** G	**52** H
6 J	**21** $4 = w$	**37** B	**53** C
7 C	**22** J	**38** F	**54** J
8 G	**23** C	**39** C	**55** C
9 B	**24** G	**40** G	**56** J
10 G	**25** A	**41** A	**57** D
11 A	**26** G	**42** G	**58** H
12 J	**27** B	**43** A	**59** B
13 B	**28** F	**44** G	**60** G
14 H	**29** C	**45** C	
15 D	**30** F	**46** F	

Social Studies

1 B	**15** D	**29** C	**43** A
2 J	**16** G	**30** F	**44** H
3 D	**17** C	**31** B	**45** B
4 H	**18** H	**32** F	**46** J
5 A	**19** C	**33** D	**47** B
6 J	**20** F	**34** H	**48** H
7 C	**21** B	**35** A	**49** C
8 J	**22** F	**36** G	**50** F
9 A	**23** D	**37** D	**51** B
10 G	**24** J	**38** J	**52** G
11 B	**25** B	**39** B	**53** C
12 G	**26** G	**40** G	**54** F
13 C	**27** C	**41** C	**55** C
14 J	**28** H	**42** J	

Science

1	D	**15**	A	**29**	C	**43**	C
2	H	**16**	H	**30**	J	**44**	J
3	C	**17**	A	**31**	A	**45**	B
4	H	**18**	G	**32**	J	**46**	F
5	A	**19**	A	**33**	A	**47**	B
6	J	**20**	.25 kg	**34**	H	**48**	F
7	C	**21**	B	**35**	A	**49**	C
8	G	**22**	H	**36**	G	**50**	H
9	B	**23**	D	**37**	A	**51**	B
10	G	**24**	F	**38**	G	**52**	G
11	C	**25**	D	**39**	D	**53**	D
12	F	**26**	J	**40**	G	**54**	H
13	C	**27**	D	**41**	A	**55**	C
14	G	**28**	F	**42**	G		

Review Chart

Use your marked Answer Key to fill in the following Review Chart for the multiple-choice questions.

	Possible	*Completed*	*Right*	*Wrong*
English Language Arts	48			
Mathematics	59			
Social Studies	55			
Science	55			

Reasons for Mistakes

Fill out the following chart only after you have read all the explanations that follow. This chart will help you spot your strengths and weaknesses and your repeated errors or trends in types of errors.

	Total Missed	*Simple Mistake*	*Misread Problem*	*Lack of Knowledge*
English Language Arts				
Mathematics				
Social Studies				
Science				
TOTALS				

Examine your results carefully. Reviewing the above information will help you pinpoint your common mistakes. Focus on avoiding your most common mistakes as you practice. If you are missing a lot of questions because of "Lack of Knowledge," you should go back and review the basics.

Answers and Explanations for Practice Test 2

English Language Arts

Reading and Written Composition

1 D The first paragraph uses words such as *strong, ruddy,* and *determined* to describe Mamzelle Aurélie. She is not married by choice and is sure of herself. The best choice for this characterization is *independent* and *capable.* There is no suggestion that she has had much to do with children in the past or that she has ever taken care of these children before.

2 G Paragraph 3 tells you that "She [Odile] had been summoned to a neighboring parish by the dangerous illness of her mother." Valsin is not the children's father, but simply the driver of the cart, and there is no suggestion that he would normally take care of the children. Odile's request that Mamzelle Aurélie take care of the children is prompted by Odile's trip, not by any concern that Mamzelle Aurélie is alone.

3 A The conversation between the cook, Aunt Ruby, and Mamzelle Aurélie is an amusing one. The cook has some rather odd and superstitious ideas in that she thinks playing with keys will make a child hard-headed or looking in a mirror will harden a child's teeth—information Mamzelle Aurélie takes as absolute truth, since Ruby has "raised five an' buried six."

4 G The sentence containing the word is "the white sunlight was beating in on the white old boards." *Stir vigorously, achieve victory,* and *avoid blame* make no sense in describing what sunlight might do. But sunlight could be described as *striking* the old boards.

5 B Paragraph 6 describes Mamzelle Aurélie as she looks at the children who have just been left with her. She's trying to determine just what it is that she should do with and for them. And she is, perhaps, just beginning to see that it may, indeed, be more than she might have anticipated—"they require and demand attentions which were wholly unexpected."

6 J A *larder* is a *pantry*—a place to keep food and kitchen supplies. The sentence before the one in which *larder* appears says "She began by feeding them." The next sentence goes on to suggest that if feeding them were her only responsibility, she would have no trouble because her "larder was amply provided against an emergency of this nature."

7 C Irony is a situation in which a result is *not* what could reasonably be expected, given the cause. You'd normally expect that a child tied to a chair would respond by crying, or screaming, or displaying some other negative reaction. It's ironic that Ti Nomme took a nice nap instead.

8 F The examples in paragraph 9 are all of the particular requirements these children seem to have. They have to have their "little white nightgowns," which must be shaken out just right "till they snapped like ox-whips." They have to be bathed in a tub of water and have their feet washed "sweet and clean." And Ti Nomme must have his bedtime stories. Mamzelle Aurélie is realizing that, indeed, "children are not little pigs." They require a great deal more care than little pigs do. There isn't anything here that suggests that Mamzelle Aurélie is irritated or that she isn't taking care of the children properly.

9 B The phrase "like the fanning of a bird's wing" is a simile that refers to the baby's warm breath. The fanning of a bird's wing would produce a very gentle flow of air, one that would be quite pleasant on one's cheek. The author uses the phrase here to suggest that the experience of having the gently breathing baby in bed next to Mamzelle Aurélie is pleasing to her. She is clearly beginning to enjoy having the children with her.

10 J The physical environment after the children have left is described as *still*. The sun is going down, producing a *blue-gray twilight* and a *purple mist*. The voices of the children are now only *faint*. This environment suggests loss and sadness and mirrors exactly what Mamzelle Aurélie is feeling, which becomes clear in the last paragraph as she sobs.

11 A At the beginning of the story, Mamzelle Aurélie has agreed to take care of the children for Odile, but there is no sense that she is particularly happy with the situation, only that she thinks it's her duty to do this. But at the end of the story, after she has become happy with and has learned to count on the children's company, she is terribly lonely after they leave her.

12 H Mamzelle Aurélie is extremely upset and sad after the children leave. She is so disturbed that she doesn't even notice her dog licking her hand.

13 D The last line of the first paragraph says "At the age of twenty she had received a proposal, which she had promptly declined, and at the age of fifty she had not yet lived to regret it." By the end of the story, she has learned the pleasure of having children in her life, but she cannot change her decision now. The *yet* of the sentence in the first paragraph foreshadows the fact that she will, by the end of the story, regret the fact that her decision as a young woman means that she will never have the joy of her own family.

14 J The simile in the first paragraph is *tore her out of the ground like a mandrake root.* An author uses a simile, a comparison using *like,* to suggest a similarity between two things that otherwise might seem dissimilar. In the sentence in which the simile occurs, the author compares the family's removal of the grandmother from her home to the *violent* act of yanking a plant out of the ground by its roots. The simile suggests further that the grandmother herself must feel like this savaged plant because her "roots" have been in this home for most of her life. The fact that the root in question is a *mandrake* root refers to the *silent scream* of the next sentence because a mandrake root is said to grow in the form of a human (who could scream), but you don't have to know this fact to answer this question.

15 C The phrase *waiting for the other shoe to drop* refers to being convinced that something else, usually something bad, is going to happen and waiting in fear till that occurs. (In the same way, you'd perhaps hear someone taking off shoes and dropping the first one to the floor. You'd know the person would eventually drop the other one also.) In paragraph 2, the author describes the grandmother as being *bubbly and charming,* but after seeing the room where she'll live and the *mean stranger,* the author is convinced that soon the *other shoe was going to drop,* that is, that the grandmother will no longer be charming but will react negatively. The tone produced by the phrase is one of *dread.*

16 F The essay is primarily about the emotional impact on a family and on the person in question of being moved from a lifelong home and placed in a care facility. The question, however, asks what illustrates the *author's* emotions, not the grandmother's or those of the rest of the family. *I would take it back, if I could* sums up the author's overall feeling about this traumatic event.

17 B In paragraphs 6 and 7, the author describes the family's visits and conversations and the grandmother's behavior—her day-to-day life.

18 G The author says *I would take it back, if I could.* She feels great sorrow and regret that she had to do this thing to her grandmother, even though it seemed to have been absolutely necessary. Although *responsibilities* (**J**) are involved, they are not the main thrust of the essay, nor is growing old (**F**) or the care of old people in general (**H**).

19 D An oxymoron, as does a simile, compares seemingly unlike things in order to suggest something new about them. Other oxymorons are, for example, *cold fire* or, in a less serious usage, *jumbo shrimp.* The term *silent scream* makes us think of people who are so distraught, so emotionally devastated, that they are unable even to make a sound and instead scream inside their heads, a scream nobody can hear except themselves. Here, that person is the author's grandmother.

20 H The central facts of the essay concern the moving of the grandmother, her reaction to the move, and the emotional effects of the move on the author and her family. The other choices, while they are not untrue, don't address all three of these important issues.

21 C The question *who wouldn't?* refers to the grandmother's talking *incessantly of going home.* The author is suggesting that it would be strange if *anyone* in this situation *didn't* talk about going home, not only old people.

22 J The essay is written in the first person point of view. That is, the author speaks of herself as *I.* In this point of view, the author can know only her own thoughts, not those of others—although she can speculate on them and suggest what they are or might be. This point of view is particularly effective in allowing the reader to understand the author's emotions.

23 D These words (*the most violent act in which I have ever participated / I would take it back, if I could*) from paragraph 1 and paragraph 8, when combined, effectively summarize the main point of the essay and best connect the main points of the two paragraphs. The author has been part of something that she terms a *violent* act, an act she wishes she could take back—but an act that was seemingly necessary and that she can't take back now.

24 H Both Mamzelle Aurélie and the author of "Better Safer Warmer" would probably change something in their lives if they could. Mamzelle Aurélie would probably have children of her own, and Cynthia Kaplan would wish to change the fact that her grandmother had to be taken from her home. But neither can change these things. Choice **F** is incorrect because Mamzelle Aurélie has no family that we know about. Choice **G** is incorrect because the only hopes we know about are perhaps Mamzelle Aurélie's hope that she can successfully take care of the children and Cynthia Kaplan's hope that her grandmother will adapt to her new home. But neither of these hopes change. Neither woman can completely control her emotions (**J**); they both cry.

25 C A conflict in a literary piece may be internal or external—that is, within a character or between two characters. Here, in *both,* the conflict is internal. Both women are trying to deal with their own reactions to their life situations. *Neither* conflict is resolved by the end. But the conflicts are *unlike* in that Mamzelle Aurélie's conflict is not present at the beginning, at least not that we are aware of. But Cynthia Kaplan's conflict is present throughout.

26 F The clasped hands in the logo of the company suggest something positive. A handshake usually has a connotation of agreement, friendship, peace, and so forth. In this case, the picture works in two ways: it echoes the idea of "Cooperative" in the company name, and it suggests that the viewer of the ad will agree with the message of the ad—and will agree to buy insurance. You might think that the letters R.I.P., which stand for rest in peace, suggest something positive because of the word *peace,* but since they are used only for someone who has died, they don't indicate something people would generally look forward to.

27 C This is an ad by the North American Life Insurance Cooperative. The purpose of life insurance is to leave money to someone after one dies. The purpose of the ad is to convince people that they should buy life insurance in order to make their families (or perhaps others who depends on them) financially secure.

28 G The ad is designed to make people think about a future after they have died. The emotions it promotes are those of concern (for those left behind—*them*) after one (*you*) is gone and can no longer provide for them. The presentation is meant to instill fear that those left behind will be poor and uncared for if the viewer of this ad doesn't buy life insurance.

Revising and Editing

32 J The verb in the first part of the sentence, *were,* is in the past tense. The second verb should agree with that— *saw* rather than *see. I* is correct as the subject of the sentence (**F**).

33 B The possessive for *it* is *its,* with no apostrophe. *It's* is a contraction meaning *it is. Instead* at the beginning of the sentence doesn't make sense because it suggests something that is the opposite of what has been said just before, and that isn't the case here. *Plain,* meaning *clear,* is the correct word in this sentence, not *plane* (which is an aircraft).

34 G The original sentence 7 is a sentence fragment; it has no main verb. Choice **G** combines sentence 7 with sentence 8 in a way that is both clear and correctly punctuated. Choice **F** uses commas to separate three complete sentences rather than semicolons. Choice **H** creates another sentence fragment in *Because it is . . .* Choice **J** incorrectly uses a semicolon and doesn't clearly express the meaning of the original sentences.

35 A Throughout the report, the word *groundhog* is not capitalized, and there is no reason to do so because it is not a proper noun.

36 G In the original sentence, the *it* in the phrase *if it comes out* does not have a clear reference because *groundhog* has not been mentioned in this sentence, or even in this paragraph. In addition, *it* is used in this phrase, but *his* is used thereafter. The two don't agree. Choice **F** fixes the *it/his* problem, but it doesn't change the fact that the reference is unclear. Choice **G** takes care of both problems.

37 C This is a spelling error. The word is spelled *similar,* not *simaler.*

38 G There are two independent sentences here joined by the conjunction *and*. The correct joining punctuation is a comma after *1887*.

39 A The sense of the sentence is that the celebration is held at a particular place; a synonym for *place* is *site*. *Sight* means *something seen*. The comma is correct after the introductory phrase, and *especially* is correctly spelled.

40 F You can say *At 7:25 a.m.* or you can say *At 7:25 in the morning*. To say both *a.m.* and *in the morning* is unnecessarily repeating information, so one of them should be deleted. The only choice given is to delete *in the morning*.

41 D The entire paragraph is about the celebration held in Punxutawney, Pennsylvania, and about the groundhog named Punxutawney Phil. The sentence about the movie, although it's called *Groundhog Day,* is not clearly connected to the topic of the paragraph, and the organization would be improved if it were deleted. If the writer wished to discuss that movie and its connection to the celebration, it would best be handled in a separate paragraph.

42 H The problem with the original sentence is that it contains a dangling modifier in *When appearing before an audience*. The phrase comes immediately before *stage fright,* but it doesn't make sense that the *stage fright* is appearing before an audience. The phrase needs to be moved near *performer or speaker,* which it should modify. Choices **F** and **G** are both sentence fragments. In addition, **F** leaves out the person who is nervous, the performer or speaker. Choice **J** is wordy and doesn't mention stage fright, the topic of the report, at all.

43 D The paragraph introduces the concept of stage fright and then goes on to mention some anecdotes about nervous actors. The new sentence specifically talks about *seasoned performers,* but the first two stories about actors have to do with *young* performers—the first with schoolboy Mel Gibson and the second with *young* Roger Corman in an *acting class*. It's clear, though, that Anniston is a *seasoned performer* because she's accepting an award for a television performance. So the best place for a sentence introducing stage fright in a seasoned performer is before the sentence about Anniston (after sentence 4).

44 J The two items that follow *for example* should be parallel in form, but *coming down with the flu* and *you just ate something* are not parallel. Choice **J** fixes the problem with the parallel *coming down with the flu* and *eating something*.

45 C Sentences 6, 7, and 8 give reasons that a person might have stage fright. But sentence 9 seems to say that there is no reason for stage fright, contradicting what has just been said. Adding *At times* clarifies the meaning and makes good sense in this context.

46 J The sentence is correct as it is. Each of the other choices introduces an error. Choice **F** isn't right because it changes the meaning of the sentence, suggesting that stage fright always has these effects.

47 B The word should be *lessen* (to reduce), not *lesson* (something studied).

48 H This sentence has a compound subject—*practice* and *concentration*—so it requires a plural verb—*are*. This error is easy to miss because the subject and verb are separated by the material in parentheses.

49 A Sentence 16 talks about ways to deal with stage fright. A synonym for *way,* in this meaning, is *strategy*. In sentence 17, *Another* has nothing to refer to, so it isn't clear—the reader asks *Another what?* Adding the word *strategy* clarifies the meaning.

50 G The phrase *pretending you're speaking* seems here to refer to *one member of the audience,* when it actually should refer to *you*. Changing *pretending* to *and pretend* gives the sentence a compound verb, with both verbs clearly referring to *you*.

51 C The word *except,* as a verb, means *to leave out, to omit*. As a preposition, *except* means *excluding*. Neither meaning is appropriate in this sentence. The word *accept,* a verb meaning *to receive with approval,* is correct here.

Mathematics

1 D Finding the sum of the monthly expenses, you get

$$875 + 375 + 500 + 250 + 125 + 375 = 2{,}500.$$

The car payment is then $\frac{375}{2500}$ or $\frac{3}{10}$ of the monthly expenses. Since there are 360° in a circle, the central angle for the car payment should be $\frac{3}{10}$ of 360, or 54°.

Answer **D** is correct. Note: You could also have solved the proportion $\frac{375}{2500} = \frac{x}{360}$ to get $x = 54$.

2 J Lines which are parallel have the same slope. Written in slope-intercept form, $y = mx + b$, m is the slope. The line with equation $y = -3x + 2$ has a slope of –3.

With slope $= \frac{\text{rise}}{\text{run}} = \frac{\text{vertical change}}{\text{horizontal change}} = \frac{-3}{1}$, you are looking for a line, as in choice **K,** where from a given point on the line you go "down 3 and over 1" to arrive at another point on the line.

3 B

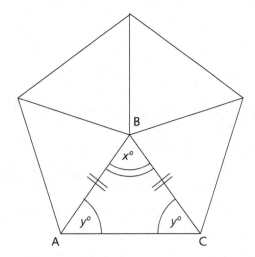

The regular pentagon can be divided into 5 equal isosceles triangles. The central angle, labeled x, can be found by $\frac{360}{5} = 72$. Since $\triangle ABC$ is isosceles with AB = AC, $\angle BAC = \angle BCA$ (both labeled as y). Then,

$$x + y + y = 180$$
$$72 + 2y = 180$$
$$2y = 108$$
$$y = 54$$

So the 3 angles of $\triangle ABC$ are 72°, 54°, and 54° as in answer choice **B.**

4 H For $y = x^2 + k$, k is the y-intercept (where graph crosses the y-axis) of the parabola. Changing from $y = x^2 + 7$ to $y = x^2 + 2$ will move the y-intercept from +7 down to +2.

So choice **H** is the best answer.

5 B Buying 2 sodas and 1 popcorn will cost $5.25.

$$2s + 1p = 5.25$$

Buying 3 sodas and 2 popcorns will cost $9.25.

$$3s + 2p = 9.25$$

Practice Test 2

Your answer should consist of these 2 equations:

$$2s + p = 5.25$$

$$3s + 2p = 9.25$$

This pair corresponds to choice **B.**

6 J When the net is cut out and the "flaps" are folded up, points A and A' will coincide, likewise points B and B', and C and C'. The • will match up with the large "+" sign. Next the △ will match up with side BC as in figure choice **J.**

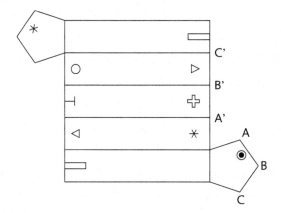

7 C A one-minute call will cost us (.17). A two-minute call will cost us (.17)2. A fifteen-minute call will cost us (.17)15. So, a call lasting for *m* minutes will cost us (.17)*m*.

Adding the initial connect charge of $.49, your total charge will be: $p = .49 + .17m$, choice **C.**

8 G If you divided the total weight of a bunch of quarters by weight of one quarter, you will get the number of quarters. So choice **G** is correct.

9 B To find the score for which the same number of students score above and below this, you are looking for the middle or <u>median</u> score. Thus correct choice is **B.**

10 G The volume of a cylinder is:

$$V = \pi r^2 h$$

$$= (3.14)(1.5)^2(48)$$

$$= 339.12 \; in^3$$

The volume of the rectangular block is:

$$V = (length)(width)(height)$$

$$= (.5)(3)(5)$$

$$= 7.5 \; in^3$$

Next, you divide the volume of the cylinder by the volume the block to get:

$$\frac{339.12}{7.5} = 45.216$$

So, he can pour about 45 full blocks. Correct answer is **G.**

11 A Consider the dimensions of the diagram.

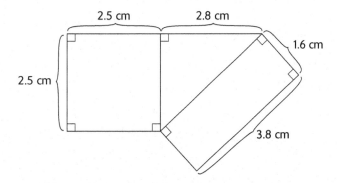

Total Area = area of square + area of triangle + area of rectangle

$$=(2.5)(2.5)+\frac{1}{2}(2.8)(2.5)+(3.8)(1.6)$$
$$=6.25+3.5+6.08$$
$$=15.83$$

So an approximate area of $15.8cm^2$, choice **A,** is appropriate.

12 J To find the average of 3 test scores, you find their sum and divide this by 3. Letting t be the third test score, you have:

$$\frac{(85+73+t)}{3}=84$$
$$85+73+t=252 \quad \textit{multiplied both sides by } 3$$
$$158+t=252$$
$$t=94 \quad \textit{subtracted } 158 \textit{ from both sides}$$

So Rafael needs a 94% on his next test. Choice **J** is the correct answer.

13 B Janell's monthly expenses total:

$$750+152+250=\$1,152$$

She makes 30% of $960 = \$288$ for each computer she sells.

So she needs to sell $\dfrac{\$1152}{\$288 \text{ per computer}} = 4$ computers to cover her monthly expenses. Choice **B.**

14 H With $d=7w$, one week is 7 days, 2 weeks is 14 days, 3 weeks is 21 days. So 3 weeks (or 21 days) from Tuesday, it will again be a Tuesday. Choice **H** is the correct answer.

15 D

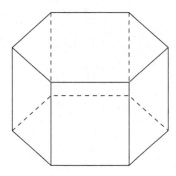

A hexagonal prism has a hexagonal top and a hexagonal bottom, with rectangular lateral faces.

Counting vertices (corners), you get 12.

Counting edges (line segments), you get 18.

Counting faces (flat surfaces), you get 8.

So the correct answer is choice **D.**

16 G

$$\begin{array}{r} \text{cost of Brand P } \$4.95 \\ -\text{cost of Brand T } \$3.75 \\ \hline \text{difference of } \$1.20 \end{array}$$

When compared to Brand T, $\frac{\$1.20}{\$3.75} \approx 0.32 = 32\%$, so choice **G** is best answer.

17 C To find the y-intercepts, you set $x = 0$ and then solve for y.

$$x = y^2 + 2y - 24$$
$$0 = y^2 + 2y - 24$$
$$0 = (y + 6)(y - 4) \qquad \text{factored the right side}$$
$$y + 6 = 0 \text{ or } y - 4 = 0 \qquad \text{set each factor} = 0 \text{ and then solve for } y$$
$$y = -6 \text{ or } y = 4$$

Choice **C** is correct.

18 F Two polygons are similar if their corresponding angles are congruent and their corresponding sides are proportional (have = ratio). In choice **F,** the 2 rhombuses each have 4 = sides, so their sides are proportional. In any parallelogram (and a rhombus is a type of parallelogram) adjacent angles are supplementary. So the angles of each rhombus are 60°, 120°, 60°, and 120°.

Correct answer is choice **F.**

19 D To graph the inequality $6x + 3y < 24$, you first find the x and y intercepts of the graph of the equation $6x + 3y = 24$.

To find the x-intercept, set $y = 0$ and solve for x.

$$6x + 3y = 24$$
$$6x + 3(0) = 24$$
$$6x + 0 = 24$$
$$6x = 24$$
$$x = 4 \qquad \text{divided both sides by 6}$$

The graph crosses the x-axis at 4.

To find the y-intercept, set $x = 0$ and solve for y.

$$6x + 3y = 24$$
$$6(0) + 3y = 24$$
$$0 + 3y = 24$$
$$3y = 24$$
$$y = 8 \qquad \text{divided both sides by 3}$$

The graph crosses the y-axis at 8.

Next, connect the x-intercept of 4 and the y-intercept of 8 to get the diagram below, where the equation $6x + 3y = 24$ is graphed.

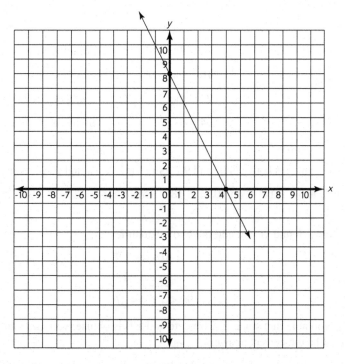

Since your inequality is $6x + 3y < 24$, your answer should appear under, or below this line. The only point among the 4 choices that is under the line is $(2,3)$, answer **D**.

20 H As x increases, you want y to decrease. You should first make a chart for each of the equations and then plug in simple values as follows:

F	G	H	J
$y = 3x$	$y = x^3$	$y = -2x$	$y = x^2$

x	y		x	y		x	y		x	y
0	0		0	0		0	0		0	0
1	3		1	1		1	-2		1	1
2	6		2	8		2	-4		2	4

From these charts you can quickly see that **H** is the only chart that shows x increasing and y decreasing. If you would have included a few more points and plotted them on a graph you would see the general features of the graph of each equation as follows:

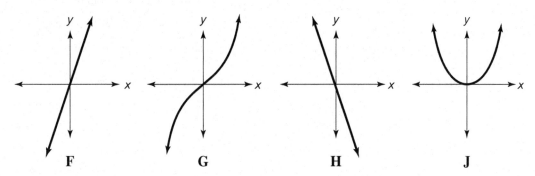

Practice Test 2

As you move from left to right along the x-axis (x increases), you want the graph to move downward all of the time. Choice **J** moves downward, but then goes back up. Choice **H** moves consistently downward (y decreases). Correct answer is therefore choice **H**.

21 **4**

$$3w + 10 - 7w = 2w - 14$$

$$10 - 4w = 2w - 14 \qquad \text{combine like terms on the left}$$

$$10 = 6w - 14 \qquad \text{add } 4w \text{ to both sides}$$

$$24 = 6w \qquad \text{add 14 to both sides}$$

$$4 = w \qquad \text{divide both sides by 6}$$

Be sure to grid your answer correctly.

22 **J** The measure of an acute angle is between 0° and 90°. Since m∠A = a and ∠A is acute, you know that $0 < a < 90$.

The measure of an obtuse angle is between 90° and 180°. Since m∠B = b and ∠B is obtuse, you know that $90 < b < 180$.

To eliminate answer choices **F** and **G** you add the two inequalities:

$$0 < a < 90$$
$$+\ 90 < b < 180$$

$$\text{to get} \quad 90 < a + b < 270$$

To eliminate choice **H**, you note that since ∠A is acute and ∠B is obtuse, you know that $b > a$, so that $b - a > 0$. Therefore, choice **J** must be the correct answer.

23 **C** To find the perimeter of the rectangle, you need to know its length and its width. The length and the diagonal are given. To determine the width you use the Pythagorean Theorem to get:

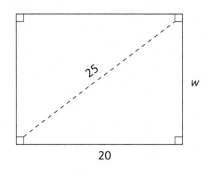

$$w^2 + 20^2 = 25^2$$

$$w^2 + 400 = 625$$

$$w^2 = 225 \qquad \text{subtracted 400 from both sides}$$

$$w = 15 \qquad \text{took square root of both sides}$$

Or you could use the 3-4-5 right triangle pattern, noting that the diagonal is 5(5) and the length is 5(4), the width must be 5(3), or 15.

The perimeter can be found by:

$$\text{perimeter} = 2(\text{length}) + 2(\text{width})$$

$$= 2(20) + 2(15)$$

$$= 40 + 30$$

$$= 70$$

So choice **C** is correct.

24 G The 3 cities have coordinates: E(3,5), F(7,2), and G(–1,4)

To find the coordinates of city M, you use the midpoint formula and the coordinates of cities E and G; you find that
$M = \left(\dfrac{-3 + -1}{2}, \dfrac{5 + 4}{2} \right) = (-2, 4.5)$.

To find the distance from city F to city M, you use the distance formula and the coordinates of F(7,2) and M(–2, 4.5).

$$\text{distance FM} = \sqrt{\left(7 - {}^-2\right)^2 + \left(2 - 4.5\right)^2}$$
$$= \sqrt{9^2 + (-2.5)^2}$$
$$= \sqrt{81 + 6.25}$$
$$= \sqrt{87.25}$$
$$\approx 9.34$$

So answer **G** is a good approximation.

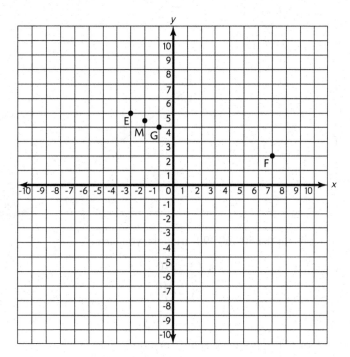

25 A For the slope-intercept form, $y = mx + b$, m is the slope, and b is the y-intercept, the place where the graph crosses the y-axis.

So $y = -2.5x + 4.3$ has slope –2.5 and y-intercept 4.3.

If you add 2.9 to the slope –2.5, you get a new slope of .4. Your new equation is $y = .4x + 4.3$.

Note that your two slopes, $-2.5 = \dfrac{-5}{2}$ and $.4 = \dfrac{2}{5}$, are "opposite reciprocals"; therefore, they represent slopes of lines that are perpendicular. Choice **A** is then correct.

Practice Test 2

26 **G** Noting that as x increases, y also increases, you would expect the equation relating them to be $y = mx$, with m greater than 1. Solving for m, you get $\frac{y}{x} = m$.

Choosing the first entry in your table you have: $m = \frac{y}{x} = \frac{58.50}{3} = 19.50$.

Therefore, your equation is $y = 19.50x$. **G** is the correct answer.

27 **B** For the circle graph, you have: $60 + 45 + 30 + 45 = 180$ total responses.

Those who like to watch GOLF represent $\frac{30}{180} = \frac{1}{6}$ of those who gave their preference.

So you would expect $\frac{1}{6}$ of the city's 12,000 residents to prefer to watch GOLF on TV.

$\frac{1}{6}$ of 12,000 is 2,000. So answer choice **B** is correct.

28 **F** The triangle in this diagram is a 30°-60°-90° triangle.

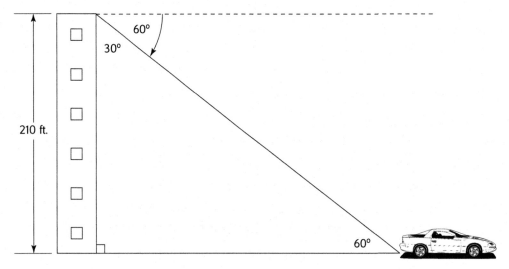

With the $x : x\sqrt{3} : 2x$ side ratios for the 30°-60°-90° triangle, you have:

$$x\sqrt{3} = 210$$
$$x = \frac{210}{\sqrt{3}}$$
$$\approx 121.24$$

Therefore, answer choice **F** of 121 ft. is a good approximation.

29 **C** To rotate a figure through an angle of $x°$, around a point P, you rotate counterclockwise $x°$, with the figure fixed at point P, but the remainder of the figure rotating counterclockwise.

A reflection across a line is comparable to "flipping" the figure over the line to form what is often called its "mirror image."

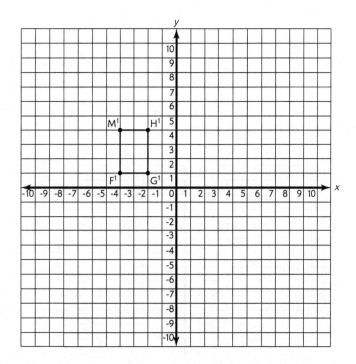

So point G will end up at the point with coordinates $(-2,1)$. Choice **C** is the answer.

30 **F** $(2c - 3)4c - (3c - 4)(c - 1)$

$= 8c^2 - 12c - [3c^2 - 3c - 4c + 4]$	distribute both terms
$= 8c^2 - 12c - [3c^2 - 7c + 4]$	combine like terms within the brackets
$= 8c^2 - 12c - 3c^2 + 7c - 4$	distribute the "–" sign through the brackets
$= 5c^2 - 5c - 4$	combine like terms

Correct answer choice is **F.**

31 **D** If Susan buys a T-shirt for $2.25 and then sells it for $4.00, her profit per T-shirt is $4.00 – $2.25 = $1.75.

If t is the number of T-shirts sold, you need to solve the inequality

$$1.75t \geq 150 \quad \text{"at least" means greater than or equal to}$$
$$t \geq 85.71$$

Since she cannot sell a fraction or a T-shirt, Susan needs to sell 86 T-shirts in order of profit at least $150. Correct answer is **D.**

32 **G**

term 1	term 2	term 3	term 4
1	3	7	15

You notice that as you move from term 1 to term 4, the difference between consecutive terms is 2, then 4, and then 8. These differences are all powers of 2, so an expression containing 2^n seems reasonable. Notice also that:

$$2^1 - 1 = 2 - 1 = 2 \qquad \text{term 1}$$
$$2^2 - 1 = 4 - 1 = 3 \qquad \text{term 2}$$
$$2^3 - 1 = 8 - 1 = 7 \qquad \text{term 3}$$
$$2^4 - 1 = 16 - 1 = 15 \qquad \text{term 4}$$

The power of 2 used is the same as the term number in each case. So it looks like term n should be equal to $2^n - 1$. Thus, answer **G** is correct.

33 B For 2 right triangles (with no other angle measures given) to be similar, the ratios of the corresponding sides forming the right angles must be equal.

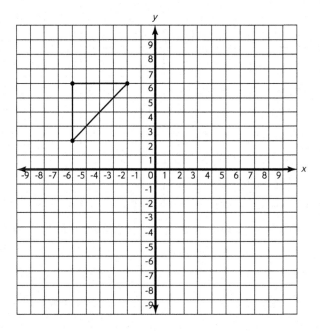

For the given figure $\dfrac{\text{short side of right triangle}}{\text{long side of right triangle}} = \dfrac{4}{6} = \dfrac{2}{3}$.

In answer choice **B,** the ratio of $\dfrac{\text{short side of right triangle}}{\text{long side of right triangle}} = \dfrac{8}{12} = \dfrac{2}{3}$.

So the given right triangle and the one in grid **B** are similar. **B** is therefore the correct answer.

B

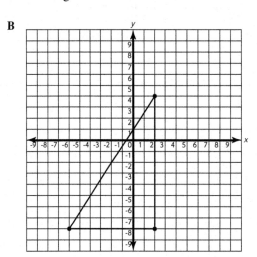

34 **G** Lines which are perpendicular have slopes which are opposite reciprocals. The slope of $y = \frac{3}{2} x$ is $\frac{3}{2}$; so the line which is perpendicular would have slope $\frac{-2}{3}$.

You are looking for the line with slope = $\frac{\text{vertical change}}{\text{horizontal change}} = \frac{-2}{3}$ as you travel from the point (3,0) down the line and to the right (down 2 and right 3, down 2 and right 3, etc.).

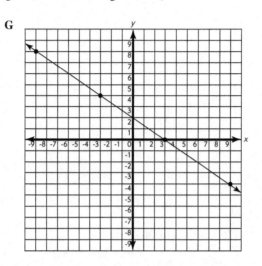

G

Graph **G** meets these conditions.

35 **A** The volume of a right circular cylinder is found by the formula:

$$V = \pi r^2 h$$

So you know that $64\pi = \pi r^2 h$ for your cylinder.

Since the new cylinder has half the radius ($\frac{1}{2} r$) and half the height ($\frac{1}{2} h$), the volume of the new cylinder is:

$$\pi \left(\frac{1}{2} r \right)^2 \left(\frac{1}{2} h \right)$$

$$= \pi \left(\frac{1}{4} \right) r^2 \left(\frac{1}{2} \right) h$$

$$= \left(\frac{1}{4} \right) \left(\frac{1}{2} \right) \left(\pi r^2 h \right)$$

$$= \left(\frac{1}{8} \right) (64\pi)$$

$$= 8\pi$$

So the volume of the new cylinder is $8\pi cm^3$. Choice **A** is correct.

Practice Test 2

36 G Below are diagrams of Mrs. Gardiner's old and new gardens.

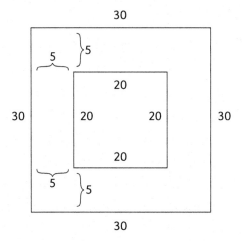

Area of the old garden is 30×30.

Area of the new garden is 20×20.

Her garden area was reduced by $(30 \times 30 - 20 \times 20)$.

Comparing this decrease to the old area, you have: $\dfrac{(30 \times 30 - 20 \times 20)}{30 \times 30}$

But since this will give us a decimal answer, you need to multiply by 100 to get a percent. So the correct answer is $\dfrac{(30 \times 30 - 20 \times 20)}{30 \times 30} \times 100$, which is answer choice **G.**

37 B

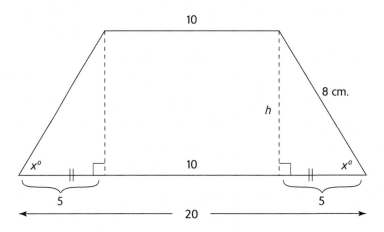

Using the Pythagorean Theorem, you get:

$$h^2 + 5^2 = 8^2$$
$$h^2 + 25 = 64$$
$$h^2 = 39 \quad \textit{subtracted 25 from both sides}$$
$$h = \sqrt{39} \approx 6.25$$

So choice **B** contains the best approximation of the height of the trapezoid.

38 **F** Let R = Reuben's weekly salary, then $2R$ = Mrs. Fernandez' weekly salary, and $2R - 100$ = Maureen's weekly salary.

Next, you know that Reuben's salary + Mrs. Fernandes' salary + Maureen's salary = 2,300:

$$R + 2R + 2R - 100 = 2,300$$

Therefore, **F** is the correct answer choice.

39 **C** The data shows:

$$50 \text{ coffee}$$
$$25 \text{ soda}$$
$$15 \text{ tea}$$
$$+ 10 \text{ milk}$$
$$\overline{100 \text{ total responses}}$$

Going through the choices one at a time, you have:

A: False → 25 is not twice 50

B: False → 10 of 100 is $\frac{1}{10}$ and $\frac{1}{10}$ of 500 = 50, not 100 as stated

C: True → 50 of 100 is $\frac{1}{2}$ and $\frac{1}{2}$ of 50 = 25

D: False → 25 + 15 does not equal 50

Choice **C** is correct.

40 **G** The formula for the volume of a right circular cylinder is $V = \pi r^2 h$

Since the diameter of the cylinder is 6 cm., its radius is 3 cm. Then the volume is: $V = (3.14)(3^2)(25) = 706.5 cm^3$

So $707 cm^3$, choice **G,** is a good approximation.

41 **A**

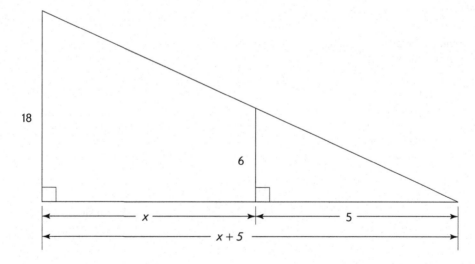

Two similar right triangles are formed so their corresponding sides are proportional (have = ratio). Comparing the height to the base for each right triangle, you have the proportion:

$$\frac{18}{x+5} = \frac{6}{5}$$

$$6(x+5) = (18)(5) \quad \text{cross multiply}$$

$$6x + 30 = 90 \qquad \text{distribute on the left; do the multiplication on the right}$$

$$6x = 60 \qquad \text{subtract 30 from each side}$$

$$x = 10 \qquad \text{divide both sides by 6}$$

Correct answer is **A.**

42 G The checking account starts with a balance of $1,200 and decreases at a rate of $20 per hour; this can be thought of as a "slope" of –20. You want the $\frac{\text{money decrease}}{\text{time increase}} = {}^-20$

In grid G, starting with 1200 on the vertical axis, you can go down 3 squares (–$300) and then over 3 squares (15 hours) to get a slope of $\frac{-300}{15} = {}^-20$

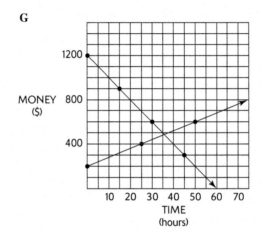

G

The savings account starts with a balance of $200 and increases at a rate of $8 per hour; this can be thought of as a "slope" of +8.

You want $\frac{\text{money increase}}{\text{time increase}} = +8$

Again, in grid B, starting at 200 on the vertical axis, you can go up 2 squares ($200) and over 5 squares (25 hours) to get a slope of $\frac{200}{25} = 8$

The point at which these 2 lines cross would correspond with the time at which the 2 accounts had the same balance. So the correct answer is choice **G.**

43 A

$$9(4x + 3)^2 = 36$$

$$(4x + 3)^2 = 9 \qquad \text{divided both sides by 9}$$

$$4x + 3 = \pm 2 \qquad \text{took square root of both sides}$$

You separate this into 2 equations:

$$4x + 3 = -2 \qquad\qquad 4x + 3 = 2$$

$$4x = -5 \qquad \text{or} \qquad 4x = -1$$

$$x = \frac{-5}{4} \qquad\qquad x = \frac{-1}{4}$$

So the solution set of this equation is: $\left\{\frac{-5}{4}, \frac{-1}{4}\right\}$, answer choice **A.**

44 **G** Let h = number of hamburgers sold (at $3 each), then $136 - h$ = number of chilidogs sold (at $1.50 each). Finally, the money from hamburgers + money from chilidogs = total money.

$$3h + 1.5(136 - h) = 288$$

$$3h + 204 - 1.5h = 288 \qquad \text{distributed the 1.5 on the left side}$$

$$1.5h + 204 = 288 \qquad \text{combined like terms on the left}$$

$$1.5h = 84 \qquad \text{subtracted 204 from both sides}$$

$$h = 56 \qquad \text{divided both sides by 1.5}$$

So 56 hamburgers were sold in the snack shop that Saturday. Answer **G** is correct.

45 **C**

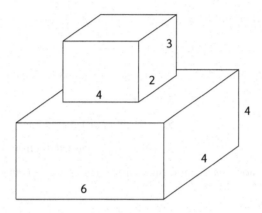

The 3D object appears above with its dimensions. By adding the volumes of the lower and upper rectangular solids, you can find the volume of the combined 3D solid. With volume = (length)(width)(height) you have:

volume upper = $(6)(4)(4) = 96$

volume lower = $(4)(2)(3) = 24$

Their sum, $96 + 24 = 120 \ cm^3$, is the volume of the 3D object. Choice **C** is the correct answer.

46 **F**

$$\left(7w^{-4}c^3\right)\left(-4w^7c^{-5}\right)$$

$$=(7)(-4)\left(w^{-4}w^7\right)\left(c^3c^{-5}\right)$$

$$=-28w^3c^{-2} \qquad \text{added exponents} -4 + 7 = 3 \text{ for } w;$$

$$\qquad\qquad\qquad \text{added exponents } 3 + {}^-5 = -2 \text{ for } c$$

$$=\frac{-28w^3}{c^2} \qquad \text{note that } c^{-2} = \frac{1}{c^2}$$

Therefore choice **F** is correct.

47 **B** For the first 2 entries in the table, the number of days seems to be a little less than 3 times the number of years. So, let's try $d = 3y -$ "something."

For the first table entry, with $d = 7$ and $y = 3$, substitute this data into your "guess" equation:

$$d = 3y - ?$$

$$7 = 3(3) - ?$$

$$7 = 9 - ?$$

$$2 = ?$$

Therefore, your equation seems to be: $d = 3y - 2$. As a quick double check, be sure this equation works for other data in the table also. Choice **B** is correct.

48 J To find the *y*-intercept of the graph of the equation, set $x = 0$ and solve for *y*.

$$2x - 3y = 6$$

$$2(0) - 3y = 6$$

$$0 - 3y = 6$$

$$-3y = 6$$

$$y = -2 \qquad \text{divided both sides by } -3$$

The *y*-intercept is –2. The line must have *y*-intercept of –2 and contain the point (–3,4). Counting the slope from –2 on the *y*-axis, go up 6 and left 3 to arrive at point (–3,4). Thus the slope is $\dfrac{vertical\ change}{horizontal\ change} = \dfrac{6}{-3} = -2$. So $m = -2$ and $b = -2$, answer choice **J.**

49 D Using the given points (4,–11) and (2,–1) you can compute the slope of the line containing them:

$$m = \frac{-1 - {}^-11}{2 - 4} = \frac{10}{-2} = -5$$

Using the slope, $m = -5$ and the point (2,–1), substituting into the point-slope form a linear equation gives:

$$y - (-1) = -5(x - 2)$$

$$y + 1 = -5x + 10 \qquad \text{distributed the } -5 \text{ on the right side}$$

$$y = -5x + 9 \qquad \text{subtracted 1 from both sides}$$

The equation above is now in slope-intercept form, with *y*-intercept of 9, as in choice **D.**

50 J

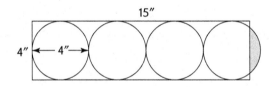

As seen in the figure above, the 15 cm. long piece of cardboard is not long enough to cut 4 circles having a radius of 2 cm.; this would give diameters of 4 cm., and 4(4) is greater than 15. Answer is choice **J.**

51 B Starting with the inequality $x + y < -4$, you solve for *y* to get $y < -x - 4$. Next, you sketch the graph of the equation $y = -x + 4$. This is a line having a *y*-intercept of –4 and a slope of –1 (or $\frac{-1}{1}$). Start at –4 on the *y*-axis, go down 1 space and then right 1 space, etc., to get the graph of $y = -x - 4$.

To get the solution of $y < -x - 4$, shade below the line, as in choice **B.**

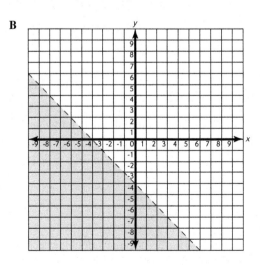

52 H Using the given data, you note that:

for $n = 1$: $2(1) - 1 = 1$

for $n = 2$: $2(2) - 1 = 3$

for $n = 3$: $2(3) - 1 = 5$

It appears that $p = 2n - 1$ is the equation relating the number tossed on the die to the money paid out in the game. So, choice **H** is correct.

53 C

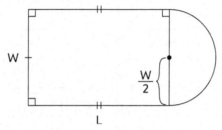

Total Area = area of rectangle + $\frac{1}{2}$ area of circle

$$= LW + \frac{1}{2} \pi \left(\frac{w}{2}\right)^2$$

$$= LW + \frac{1}{2} \pi \frac{w^2}{4}$$

$$= LW + \frac{\pi w^2}{8}$$

So correct answer is choice **C**.

54 J For the equation $y = ax^2$, the value of $|a|$ affects how narrow or wide the graph (a parabola) opens. For example, $y = 2x^2$ opens wider than $y = y = \frac{1}{3}x^2$, but opens narrower than $y = 5x^2$. If the value of "a" in $y = ax^2$ is negative, the parabola opens downward instead of upward.

You are looking for functions in which the $|a|$ decreases in value as in choice **J**.

55 C Graph A has no "leveling off" of the volume when short delays in the pumping took place. Graph B shows no drop in volume when the tank was partially drained. Graph D does not show the second delay in pump action where the graph should be horizontal for a short span of time. Therefore, **C** is the best graph illustrating the given scenario.

Practice Test 2

56 J

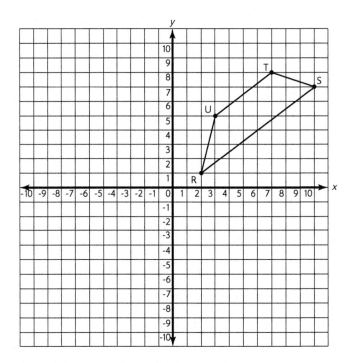

After plotting and then connecting the points in the RSTU order, it can be seen that the figure is a trapezoid—only 2 parallel sides. Therefore, answer **J** is correct.

57 D Working as a waiter for w hours will earn Marissa $6w$ dollars. Working as a graphic artist for g hours, she earns $10g$ dollars. If she needs to earn at least ($\geq$) $800, you must have:

$$\text{waitress money} + \text{graphic artist money} \geq 800$$

$$6w + 10y \geq 800$$

Therefore, choice **D** is correct.

58 H It appears that the pressure is 62 times the depth in each case. So for a depth of 50 feet, the pressure should be $62(80) = 4{,}960$ lb./sq.ft. as in answer choice **H.**

59 B To find the slope of the line with equation $-2y = 3(x - 4)$ you solve for y to write the equation in slope-intercept form:

$$-2y = 3(x - 4)$$
$$-2y = 3x - 12 \qquad \textit{distributed } 3 \textit{ on the right side}$$
$$y = \frac{-3}{2}x + 6 \qquad \textit{divided both sides by } -2$$

In the $y = mx + b$ form, m is the slope; so the slope of your line is $\frac{-3}{2}$, choice **B.**

60 G Checking each choice one at a time:

F: False $\rightarrow$ Sales increased for the first quarter (Jan. to March) but not all the way through June.

G: True $\rightarrow$ Accurately describes rise and fall of sales for the first half of the year.

H: False $\rightarrow$ Sales above $30,000 per month in March, April, and May.

J: False $\rightarrow$ Since all 6 months exceeded $20,000 in sales, average sales would be greater than $20,000 per month.

Correct answer is choice **G.**

Social Studies

1 B As opposition to the war in Southeast Asia grew, there was strong sentiment in Congress to "prevent another Vietnam." Congress reasserted its power to declare war through the War Powers Act that sets a 60-day limit on the ability of the president to send troops into combat without further congressional action.

2 J The NAACP used the courts to fight for civil rights from its beginnings. In 1915, the Supreme Court struck down the so-called "grandfather clause" that was used to deny African Americans the right to vote. The NAACP won numerous cases challenging segregation in public education, including the landmark case *Brown* v. *Board of Education* in 1954 that overturned the "separate but equal" doctrine.

3 D During World War I, Congress passed the Espionage and Sedition Acts that effectively restricted the right to criticize the government or the army. The excerpt is an illustration of the "clear and present danger" test that makes it clear that freedom of speech is not absolute. The decision also indicates that constitutional rights can be restricted during war.

4 H Beard's work is a secondary source on the Constitution or American economic history. Although he is considered a Progressive historian, it is hard to see how *An Economic Interpretation* could throw any light on early 20th-century reforms. Beard's biographer would examine all his published writings along with his correspondence to get a full picture of him as a historian.

5 A There is no indication that the Sahara was wetter 500 to 600 years ago; major trading cities like Timbuktu are located in the savanna between the desert and the forest zone. Gold and ivory indeed were the major exports, but have nothing to do with the geography of the region.

6 F There was no executive or judicial branch provided for under the Articles of Confederation. While Congress had limited authority over states, it did have the power to declare war and make peace. The requirement that changes to the Articles required the unanimous vote of the states was ignored by the framers of the Constitution. The terms of the Constitution provided its own ratification, and a less rigorous amendment process.

7 C NAFTA stands for the North American Free Trade Agreement, which went into effect in 1994. Its three participants are the countries of North America—United States, Canada, Mexico. President George W. Bush is interested in creating a free trade area of the Americas to include the entire Western hemisphere.

8 J There was no large-scale immigration from Africa during the period. Although Marcus Garvey's Universal Negro Improvement Association actively promoted the establishment of a black homeland in Africa during the 1920s, the plan did not attract many African Americans. If the population changes were due to an increase in the birth rate, the increase in the South would have been greater. Between the 1910 and 1930 census, African Americans in the South moved to the cities in the Northeast and Midwest both to escape discrimination and to take advantage of the job opportunities. Northern factories hired large numbers of blacks during World War I.

9 A Under the appointment power, the president names all federal judges, including the justices of the Supreme Court. These are considered the most important appointments the president makes because they can affect the direction of the entire judicial system. Before a presidential nominee can take office, he/she must be approved by the Senate. Although rare, the Senate has failed to confirm a president's Supreme Court choice.

10 G The first Equal Rights Amendment was proposed in 1923 by the National Woman's Party, but found little support even among women's groups. Congress passed a new Equal Rights Amendment in 1972 that would have prohibited discrimination based on sex. Although the amendment was approved by the majority of the states, it fell three states short of the three-fourths needed for ratification by the 1982 deadline set by the Congress. Religious minorities are protected under the First Amendment; the status of civil rights for homosexuals remains controversial at the state and federal levels.

11 B While all of the weapons listed were used during World War I, only the submarine was a factor in the decision of the U.S. to declare war on Germany. In the Spring of 1916, Germany agreed to warn merchant ships before a submarine attack through the Sussex Pledge. Less than a year later (February 1917), Germany announced the resumption of unrestricted submarine warfare. In his war message to Congress in April, President Woodrow Wilson specifically mentioned the German decision on the use of her submarine fleet.

12 G The term "Information Superhighway" refers to the Internet. Computers are only relevant to email among the examples. All of the new technology allow people to communicate faster and more effectively than ever before. Cable television, for example, has led to 24-hour all-news channels.

13 C The Europeans brought a wide variety of diseases to the Western Hemisphere to which the Native Americans had no immunity. These diseases included measles and smallpox, and had a devastating effect on the indigenous population. Death rates of upward of 90% were not uncommon in certain regions; in the Caribbean Islands, the Spaniards brought in slaves from Africa to work the sugar cane plantations in the early 16th century because the Native American tribes were effectively wiped out by disease.

14 J From Henry Ford's statement, it should be clear that assembly line workers were not highly skilled. The quote says nothing of the ethnic background of these workers, and you should know that Ford workers were some of the highest paid in the industry. The men on the assembly line earned $5 a day in the early 20th century in an attempt to keep the workforce stable and discourage the formation of labor unions.

15 D Beginning in 1969, the number of American troops in Vietnam were gradually reduced and the fighting increasingly became the responsibility of the South Vietnamese army. This was the essence of Nixon's Vietnamization policy. The Chinese, although they supported North Vietnam, never committed troops to the fighting, and the war did drag on until 1973. The exchange of prisoners of war took place after the cease-fire agreement was in place in January 1973.

16 G As the war wound down, defense contracts were cancelled, and many workers, men and women, were laid off. The total labor force shrank from war time highs in 1945, and unemployment was a major concern in the first year of the peace. There is no direct connection between the other choices and the drop in the number of women working. It should be understood that many women took jobs in defense-related industries knowing that the work was just "for the duration"—as long as the war lasted.

17 C The possible Nicaragua canal route was not shorter than a canal across the isthmus of Panama, and the fact that Nicaragua was closer to the U.S. is obviously irrelevant. The map makes it very clear that possible route was designed to utilize Lake Managua and Lake Nicaragua. Locks were built for the Panama Canal because the route ultimately chosen was not at sea level.

18 H The Nile River was the lifeblood of Egypt and the geographic feature that united the country. The Atlas Mountains are in North Africa, but far from Egypt and have no relation to its history. The Sinai Peninsula was a major trade and invasion route. Of the possible choices, only the Libyan Desert to the west of the Nile River valley can be considered an effective natural barrier to attack.

19 C The Stamp Act (1765) placed a direct tax on printed materials, ranging from newspapers to playing cards. The issue was not how high or low the tax was, but whether Parliament had the power to tax the colonies at all. It was the Stamp Act that raised the cry, "No taxation without representation." Since the colonies were not represented in Parliament, Parliament could not impose such a tax on them. The British unsuccessfully responded to this argument with the claim of "virtual representation"—the idea that Parliament acts in the name of all British subjects no matter where they live. The colonial opposition to the Stamp Act was so intense that Parliament was forced to repeal it in 1766.

20 F *Texas* v. *Johnson* is a landmark case involving the burning of an American flag during a protest against the policies of the Reagan administration. The Supreme Court ruled that burning the flag was protected under the First Amendment as symbolic speech. Even if you do not know the facts of the case, it is clear from the excerpt from the decision that the Court was dealing with actions with respect to the flag that fell under the First Amendment. The only choice that makes sense is freedom of speech.

21 B The 1944 Normandy invasion, known as Operation Overlord, was the attack on German-occupied Western Europe that the Soviet Union hoped would relieve the pressure on the Russian army fighting the Germans on the eastern front. The invasions of North Africa as well as Sicily and Italy, while critical to the Allied war effort, were not considered as important by the Soviet Union as the cross-Channel invasion of France. The Battle of the Bulge refers to the German offensive in Belgium and northern France in late 1944.

22 F The Great Plains were a vast grassland, and trees were scarce. Sod houses were built from "bricks" made of the heavy top soil. The Great Plains, which was also known as the Great American Desert, does have a dry climate and is subject to frequent droughts; these facts, however, have nothing to do with sod houses. Whether or not sod provided better protection against attacks by Native Americans or the limited amount of lumber was used for other structures, the fact is that sod houses were constructed because there were few trees.

23 D The Security Council approved a resolution proposed by the United States that called on member states of the United Nations to come to the assistance of South Korea, the clear victim of aggression. The Security Council was able to pass the resolution because the Soviet Union was boycotting its session over the refusal of the U.N. to recognize the People's Republic of China. South Korea was outside of the scope of NATO's responsibilities, and Congress was never asked for a declaration of war.

24 J An important theme of the electric utility industry during the 1920s was that electrical appliances allowed women to have more leisure time; having an all-electric range frees a housewife from the drudgery of cooking. The purpose of the advertisement is not to convince women to spend more time with their children, but to suggest that if they had an all-electric range they would have more time with their children. The more electric ranges sold, the more electricity consumers would use. This is called "load promotion" in the industry.

25 B The income tax rate and the number of people eligible to pay taxes were increased to pay for the war. While there were some restrictions on strike activities, unions were not banned. A black market that sold rationed products existed during the war, but was certainly not encouraged by the federal government. Protective tariffs were irrelevant during the war given the sharp reduction in international trade.

26 G Prohibition, a ban on the manufacture, sale, and distribution of alcohol, was a goal of reformers since the first half of the 19th century. It ultimately failed because many Americans simply ignored the law, not enough money was put into enforcement, and police and government corruption was widespread. The 18th Amendment actually did reduce alcohol consumption. Divorce and family violence were associated with drinking, and were two problems that Prohibition was intended to address.

27 C This is a basic chronology question that can be approached in several ways. The colonies declared independence in 1776. The Constitution was ratified in 1788, and since the Bill of Rights is the first ten amendments to the Constitution, it had to go into effect after 1788. The Battle of Saratoga took place in 1778, which gives you the First Continental Congress as the correct answer. If you know that it was the Second Continental Congress that actually declared independence, you may have a quicker route to the right choice.

28 H All of the rights listed in the possible choices are protected either in the Constitution as ratified or the Bill of Rights. The key phrase in the excerpt is "the legal judgment of his peers." This clearly refers to a trial. Trial by jury is provided for in Article III of the Constitution, which deals with the judiciary, and in the Seventh Amendment for most civil cases.

29 C The famous mathematical formula was developed by Albert Einstein in 1905, and was essential to the development of nuclear power. You may well remember that Einstein wrote a letter to President Franklin Roosevelt just before World War II broke out in Europe in 1939 warning about the possibility that Germany could develop an atomic bomb. The letter ultimately led to the Manhattan Project, the crash American-led program to design and test an atomic bomb that got under way in 1942.

30 F This question involves reading the graph. Clearly, most of the immigrants in South Florida come from the Caribbean area. By the same token, Caribbean immigrants represent a small percentage of the foreign-born population in either Southern California or the San Francisco Bay area. The smallest percentage of foreign-born immigrants in the Midwest is from South America.

31 B The common thread is clearly that the power of the federal government expanded. During the Progressive Era, the regulatory authority of the federal government increased through such legislation as the Pure Food and Drug Act and the Meat Inspection Act as well as the creation of the Federal Reserve System. The federal government expanded its authority during the Depression to address the economic and human crisis the country faced—large-scale public works projects and programs such as the Tennessee Valley Authority and Social Security are good examples. During World War II, it was the federal government that mobilized the economy and the American people for war with Germany and Japan.

32 F Many states and local governments have limited the number of terms an elected official—mayor, member of the city council or state legislature, governor—can serve. The Supreme Court has ruled, however, that since the terms of senators and representatives are specified in the Constitution, terms limits can only be accomplished through the amendment process. Congress cannot impose term limits on itself, and an executive order or Supreme Court action would violate the principle of the separation of powers.

33 D Booker T. Washington, the founder of the Tuskegee Institute, stressed the importance of African Americans achieving economic independence through the skilled trades. He downplayed the fight against racial discrimination. For Du Bois, there could be no economic progress unless blacks won the civil rights battle.

34 H A country has an unfavorable balance of trade when imports exceed exports. If you know this fact, the graph is rather clear that the shift occurred in the 1980s and continued.

35 A The graph only addresses total imports and exports. While it may seem logical that oil was the most important import, this is not a conclusion you can draw from the data. Trade balance is just one element of the overall economy. The fact is that during the period covered, the U.S. experienced several significant recessions as well as stagflation—high inflation and high unemployment. The growth in the import/export numbers indicates that world trade was expanding. The expansion might not have been as significant if high tariffs were in place.

36 G Under the Roosevelt Corollary to the Monroe Doctrine, the U.S. frequently intervened in the internal affairs of countries in the Caribbean and Central America—Haiti and Nicaragua are notable examples. The Good Neighbor Policy rejected intervention throughout Latin America, and included such specific steps as the withdrawal of American troops from Haiti. The only "neighbor" of the U.S. among the choices is Latin America.

37 D At the heart of the energy crisis was the 1973 Arab oil embargo and oil price increases by OPEC. As the price of oil increased, prices of other goods increased as well, i.e., inflation. High oil prices were actually a boon to energy-producing states like Texas and Oklahoma. The energy policy that President Jimmy Carter developed to respond to the crisis included increasing reliance on solar, geothermal, and wind energy.

38 J You should immediately recognize that the photograph shows Dust Bowl conditions on the Great Plains. Many farmers lost everything because of the Dust Bowl, and left their homes to start over in California and other West Coast states. John Steinbeck captured the lives of these migrants in his 1939 novel *The Grapes of Wrath*.

39 B The major issue during the debate in the Senate over the treaty was whether the U.S. could maintain an independent foreign policy. Senators like Henry Cabot Lodge of Massachusetts were concerned that the U.S. would be drawn into a war it did not want by the terms of the Covenant of the League of Nations that was part of the treaty.

40 G When former President Teddy Roosevelt became dissatisfied with his hand-picked successor, William Howard Taft, he decided to challenge him for the Republic nomination in 1912. When Taft won the nomination, Roosevelt ran as a third party candidate as a Progressive. The election results make it clear that had the Republicans been able to decide on a single candidate, they would have easily kept control of the White House. To the extent that African Americans could and did vote in 1912, they voted Republican—the party of Lincoln.

41 C Article III of the Constitution provides that federal judges serve "in good behavior" and that their compensation will not be reduced. In the Federalist Papers, "in good behavior" was interpreted to mean that federal judges serve for life as a means of guaranteeing their political independence.

42 J The baby boom generation is fast approaching retirement age, and will significantly increase the number of Americans eligible for Social Security. The so-called "graying of America" means that while more and more people are entitled to benefits, the number of workers paying into the Social Security Trust Fund is shrinking.

43 A Urban transportation systems refer to street cars, trolleys, and subways during this period. As cities grew, the creation and extension of mass transit allowed people to live farther and farther from the central city where most jobs remained. Skyscrapers allowed cities to grow up as well as out as urbanization continued, but they had nothing to do with mass transit. The invention of the elevator and steel frame construction made skyscrapers possible.

44 **H** While the fairness to the South of tariffs Congress adopted was an issue for South Carolina, the obvious point of the excerpt is that states have authority to declare a federal law contrary to the Constitution and refuse to follow it. A similar point was made in the Kentucky and Virginia Resolutions in response to the Alien and Sedition Acts (1798).

45 **B** All of the events took place during the 1930s, and deal with foreign policy, not the Great Depression. All of the events contributed to the outbreak of the Second World War.

46 **J** The South was the only region of the country where women did not get the right to vote until the 19th Amendment was ratified. Women had full suffrage throughout the West before 1920, and enjoyed at least partial suffrage in the Midwest and New England.

47 **B** Under the Constitution, it is the states that set the qualifications for voting. This explains why in some states women had full voting rights long before the 19th Amendment was ratified and could not vote at all in other states. The contribution that women made to the war effort between 1917 and 1918 was a key reason for President Wilson's support for the amendment. Once the 19th Amendment was ratified, it had to be followed throughout the country.

48 **H** The excerpt is from President Roosevelt's famous "Quarantine the Aggressor" speech. If that doesn't help you, the date should. All of the other choices were enacted after 1937—destroyer-naval base deal (1940), Selective Service Act (1940), Lend-Lease Act (1941).

49 **C** You should be able to get the right answer by the process of elimination. The main cotton-producing region of the country remains the deep South from South Carolina to Texas. Corn is grown mainly in the Midwest, most notably Iowa. The major tobacco states are North Carolina and Kentucky.

50 **F** Freedom of speech and freedom of religion are specifically protected in the First Amendment. Trial by jury is provided for in the Constitution as ratified and the Bill of Rights. While there is no mention of a right to privacy, the Supreme Court has found such a right in the Fourth and Ninth Amendments, and has applied it to such controversial areas of the law as abortion and right-to-die cases.

51 **B** In Alabama in the 1950s, African Americas were required to sit in seats reserved for them on buses. In December 1955, Rosa Parks refused to give up her seat to a white passenger and was arrested. Her action led to the Montgomery, Alabama, bus boycott that resulted in the desegregation of public transportation in the city.

52 **G** The election of Abraham Lincoln triggered the secession of South Carolina in December 1860. In early 1861, six states of the Deep South—Alabama, Mississippi, Florida, Georgia, Louisiana, and Texas—followed South Carolina's lead, and the Confederate States of America was established. Virginia did not secede until after the attack on Fort Sumter, and the border states—Delaware, Maryland, Kentucky, and Missouri—remained in the Union. Harriet Beecher Stowe published "Uncle Tom's Cabin" in 1852.

53 **C** The 15th Amendment was clearly intended to ensure African Americans the right to vote, but enforcement was lax in the South after Reconstruction. Throughout the South, state laws requiring literacy tests, payment of a poll tax, and similar devices were used to prevent blacks from voting. The Voting Rights Act corrected this, and made it quite clear that the right to vote applied to all elections.

54 **F** The scandal of the Nixon administration was the break-in at the National Democratic Party headquarters in the Watergate complex in Washington, D.C. Congressional hearings determined that the president had tried to cover-up the administration's involvement in the break-in and gave his approval to other illegal activities. On the basis of the evidence, the House Judiciary Committee recommended that President Nixon be impeached by the full House.

55 **C** A large number of banks failed during the early 1930s. People began to question the entire banking system, and rushed to get their money out of their own banks. No bank has enough cash on hand to pay off all of its depositors. Faced with the possibility of a "run on the bank," many institutions closed their doors. One of the first things that President Franklin Roosevelt did in March 1933 was to declare a national bank holiday, closing all the banks in the country. Only those banks that were financially sound would be allowed to reopen.

Science

1 **D** The distillation of an alcohol-water solution is based on their distinct volatilities. Heating the solution first boils off the alcohol which has a lower boiling point than water. The alcohol vapor is then condensed to liquid.

2 **H** The job, or function, of the lungs in a person is similar to the function of the gills in a fish. Human lungs allow oxygen from the air to enter the bloodstream. Almost all animals require oxygen to live.

3 **C** Speed is defined as distance per unit of time. Using the ruler you can see that the distance from City A to City B is 15 cm. Since 1 cm equals 3 miles, the actual distance traveled from City A to City B was 45 miles. Since the trip goes back to City A, the total actual distance is 90 miles. Now divide 90 miles by 6 hours and you get 15 miles per hour.

4 **H** A virus can infect animals (horse, lobster), plants (pine). A protein is not an organism, only an organic molecule.

5 **A** Fluorine, chlorine, and bromine are non-metals. They are usually found combined with other elements. They are too reactive to occur on their own in nature.

6 **J** Since the gray squirrel and the fox squirrel both come from the genus Sciurus, they would be most closely related.

7 **C** The correct formula for zinc carbonate is $ZnCO_3$.

8 **G** Energy transformations result when a change of form takes place. All forms of energy can be converted into other forms. The battery converts stored (potential) chemical energy to electrical energy.

9 **B** Remember that acceleration is the change of velocity per change in time.

$$\text{acceleration} = \frac{\text{change in velocity}}{\text{change in time}} = \frac{1.3\,\text{m/s} - 1.1\,\text{m/s}}{20\,\text{s}} = \frac{0.2\,\text{m/s}}{20\,\text{s}} = 0.01\,\text{m/s}^2$$

10 **G** Oil acts in much the same way as paint to prevent chemical changes in iron. Wiping tools with an oily rag is a common practice.

11 **C** The wave nature of light allows beams to cross without any scattering, as photons of light do not behave as particles.

12 **F** You should never heat chemicals in any type of closed container. The expanding gas inside will cause the closed container to explode or project the cap or stopper with dangerous force.

13 **C** Because the magnetism in an electromagnet is produced by a powerful electric current, interrupting the current would cause the magnetism to disappear. Choice **B**, sending the electricity through the coil in the other direction, is wrong because you would still have an electromagnet.

14 **G** An inclined plane is a ramp that consists of a sloping surface that is used to raise objects. The efficiency of an inclined plane is given by the formula

$$\text{Efficiency} = \frac{W_{out}}{W_{in}} \times 100\% = \frac{F_{resistance} \times \text{distance} \times \text{resistance}}{F_{effort} \times \text{distance}_{effort}} \times 100\%$$

$$= \frac{600\,\text{Newtons} \times 2\,\text{meters}}{300\,\text{Newtons} \times 5\,\text{meters}} = \frac{1200\,\cancel{Newton \cdot meters}}{1500\,\cancel{Newton \cdot meters}} = 80\%$$

15 **A** The blood, circulatory system, is the body's way of carrying oxygen to its tissues.

16 **H** The maximum potential energy will be at point C. At the peak of the ball's flight, the ball will have zero kinetic energy (the energy of motion) and maximum potential energy. The ball slows as it reaches its peak and then comes to a stop before it starts downward. At this point, the ball is at rest.

17 **A** The key to answering this question is recognizing that a parasite feeds on living tissue. While most fungi are beneficial, some fungi cause disease in humans (athlete's foot; ringworm) and in plants (rust). Disease-causing fungi produce spores at the site of infection. Fungi are also important in fighting disease (penicillin). Only choice **C** is a parasitic relationship.

18 G Since there are a total of 4 hydrogen (H) and 6 oxygen (O) on the left, then there must be 4 hydrogen and 6 oxygen on the right. K_2SO_4 has 4 oxygen, so 2 oxygen and 4 hydrogen must be accounted for. Therefore the coefficient of H_2O is 2.

19 A If you look closely at the diagram, you can see that the closest atoms are sodium (+) and chlorine (–), and that is because unlike charges attract each other. Choice **C** is not correct because the faces are squares.

20 .25 kg The formula including momentum, velocity, and mass is:

$$momentum = mass \times velocity$$

Since you are looking for mass, you could rearrange the formula as follows:

$$\frac{momentum}{velocity} = mass$$

Now plugging in the values gives

$$\frac{10}{40} = mass$$

Since $\frac{10}{40} = .25$, the mass is .25 kg.

21 B By definition, all acids contain hydrogen, and acidity is proportional to the concentration of hydrogen ions. Hydrochloric acid is HCL and sulfuric acid is H_2SO_4.

22 H In the carbon cycle, carbon circulates through animals, plants, soil and the air. Plants absorb carbon dioxide (CO_2) and produce sugar and oxygen in a process called photosynthesis.

23 D All flies reproduce rapidly, but fruit flies have the advantage of having genetic variations that are easy to see, such as eye color and wing type.

24 F Since tap water is composed of water and dissolved minerals (ionic compounds), which make water hard, it can conduct electricity.

25 D The stratigraphic law of superposition states that younger formations are deposited atop older formations. Note that formation C is the oldest in the cross-section.

26 J Rearrange the formula for speed (speed $=\frac{distance}{time}$). To solve for time, the formula becomes time $=\frac{distance}{speed}$. By substituting the values into the formula it becomes $\frac{3630\,meters}{330\,meters/second}$, which equals 11 seconds.

27 D Comparing each series in the table, you can see that alcohols differ from alkanes and alkenes in that they contain oxygen (O), so they contain atoms other than carbon and hydrogen.

28 F A lever is a rigid object that rotates around a fixed point. In the diagram of a seesaw, the fixed point is called the fulcrum. The fulcrum allows the rigid bar to rotate or pivot. A screwdriver is also an example of a lever.

29 C Water pressure increases with depth. The deeper the water, the greater the pressure. In the experiment, the water near the bottom of the bottle has the force of all water above it.

30 J Weak tea is a very clear liquid, so you are able to see the spoon inside the cup. As light rays leave the air and enter the tea, they bend and travel at an angle to their original direction. This change in direction of light (refraction) causes the spoon to seem bent as it enters the tea.

31 A Because you are seeking the largest atoms, you find the weakest bonds. The first sentence tells you that gases have weak bonds. Of the four elements, the one with the lowest boiling point (cesium) is the easiest to change into a gas. So, cesium has the largest atoms, and lithium has the smallest atoms.

32 J pH is a measure of the concentration of hydronium (H_3O^+) ions in a solution. Solutions with a pH lower than 7 are acidic, with 0 being the strongest acid. Solutions with a pH greater than 7 are basic, with 14 being the strongest base. Solutions with a pH of 7 are neutral (pure water). The pH scale is based on powers of 10. A pH of 4 is an acid ten times stronger than a pH of 5; a pH of 3 is one-hundred times stronger than a pH of 5; and a pH of 2 would be 1,000 times stronger. Conversely, a pH of 5 is 1,000 times *weaker* than an acid with a pH of 2.

33 A To answer this question, you must evaluate the relationship between a tumbleweed and its environment. The description tells you that the tumbleweed does not grow in normal, undisturbed communities. Evidently, it is not able to compete successfully with established plants.

34 H Once underground water is poisoned, it is almost impossible to clean up. Because the question mentions the word *unseen*, you should select C; it is the only water source listed that is not easily seen. You could eliminate choice **A** because it is more than 1.00 percent.

35 A Any piece of safety equipment that is shared with another person must be disinfected or sanitized. This must be completed before the goggles are reused. The use of ultraviolet lamps is one of several methods to sanitize goggles.

36 G Conduction is the transfer of energy through matter by direct contact.

37 A All organisms manufacture proteins from amino acids. Plants make all their amino acids from still simpler nutrients, but animals always depend on plants to supply some amino acids they cannot make themselves.

38 G According to the diagram, the only animals that eat snakes are hawks and weasels. You must look at the arrows in the diagram to answer the questions dealing with the network of feeding relationships.

39 D Because weasels eat rabbits, a reduction in the number of weasels would allow an increase in the number of rabbits. Since bobcats eat rabbits, the larger number of rabbits would allow an increase in the number of bobcats. Probably the chicken farmers do not realize that their weasel campaign could lead to more bobcats.

40 G The temperature of the soup remains the same. While the soup is boiling, both liquid and vapor are present in the covered kettle. The temperature of the liquid cannot be higher than its boiling point (212 degrees Fahrenheit), and the temperature of the water vapor cannot be less than the boiling point. Therefore, the soup stays at the boiling point.

41 A Soon after the fire, new trees grow. These young trees now have the opportunity to grow quickly because the old trees do not block the sunlight.

42 G From Table 1, you can determine that the effects caused by heavy trucks come from quakes of about 3.7 magnitude. From Table 2, you can see that a 3.7 quake would be described as slight.

43 C Since chimneys collapse in a destructive quake (one of 6.1–6.5), and since a disastrous quake (one of 7.1–7.3) is stronger than a destructive quake, you could reasonably assume that chimneys would be destroyed in a disastrous quake (among other things that would occur).

44 J The trachea is part of the human respiratory system, being the windpipe between the mouth and the lungs. The basic human circulatory system is heart to artery to capillary to vein to heart. The aorta is the large artery from the left ventricle of the heart.

45 B You should be aware that normal room temperature is about 68°F or 20°C. Therefore, the answer is in the middle of the three viscosity columns in the chart. Mercury has the highest viscosity, 15.47 millipoises.

46 F The best way to solve this problem is to divide the grams of carbohydrate by the total grams of food, so that they can all be compared to each other. Choice **F** is 50% carbohydrate; **G** is 40% carbohydrate; **H** is 20% carbohydrate; and **J** is 20% carbohydrate. Therefore, choice **F** has the highest content of carbohydrate by mass.

47 B The size, or volume, or the tires increases because the friction between the tires and the road causes heat. The increase in temperature increases the volume of the air in the tires, expanding them. Charles's law states that as temperature increases (at a fixed pressure) so does volume. Choice **A** is a correct statement, but it does not answer the question. Gases can be compressed, but the opposite happens in the tire example. Choice **C** is a misstatement.

48 F Because all these animals are very mobile, answer choices **F** and **G** are the only ones possible. The segmented bodies and hard external skeletons are the final clues.

49 C Since green plants make their own food, they need no other organisms to survive. So they begin any food chain.

50 H In 1907 the deer population was approximately 7,000. In 1923 the deer population was approximately 100,000. Subtracting, 100,000 – 7,000 gives 93,000.

51 **B** Power is the rate at which work is done. In other words, power is a measure of the amount of work done in a certain amount of time. To calculate power, divide the work done by the time required to do the work. Power is measured in watts. A watt (W) is one joule per second. A watt is about equal to the power used to raise a glass of water from your knees to your mouth in one second. In this problem:

$$\text{Power} = \frac{\text{Work}}{\text{Time}} = \frac{\text{Force} \times \text{distance}}{\text{Time}} = \frac{25,000 \text{ Newtons} \times 30 \text{ meters}}{60 \text{ seconds}} = 12,500 \text{ watts}$$

52 **G** An organism which lives in or on another organism from which it derives its nourishment is called a parasite. This is an example of parasitism.

53 **D** The dog and tuna are most closely related since the amino sequence of each organism only differs by 4 amino acids.

54 **H** A wave's crest is the top of its "hill." A wave's amplitude is its height, the distance between its resting position and its crest. Wavelength is defined as the distance between two consecutive points on a wave (crest to crest). The pitch of a sound depends on how fast the particles of a medium vibrate. The number of waves produced in a given time is the wave's frequency.

55 **C** Animals that have body temperatures that vary with the environment are defined as cold-blooded animals. Lizards are cold-blooded animals.